Urban Ecosystem

M000317150

Ecological Principles for the Built Environment

FREDERICK R. ADLER

Department of Mathematics and Department of Biology, University of Utah

COLBY J. TANNER

Department of Ecology and Evolution, University of Lausanne

CAMBRIDGE
UNIVERSITY PRESS

CAMBRIDGE UNIVERSITY PRESS
Cambridge, New York, Melbourne, Madrid, Cape Town, Singapore,
São Paulo, Delhi, Mexico City

Cambridge University Press
The Edinburgh Building, Cambridge CB2 8RU, UK

Published in the United States of America by Cambridge University Press, New York

www.cambridge.org
Information on this title: www.cambridge.org/9780521769846

First published 2013

Printed and bound by CPI Group (UK) Ltd, Croydon CR0 4YY

A catalog record for this publication is available from the British Library

Library of Congress Cataloging-in-Publication Data

Adler, Frederick R.
  Urban ecosystems : ecological principles for the built environment / Frederick R. Adler, Colby J. Tanner.
    pages   cm
  Includes bibliographical references and index.
    ISBN 978-0-521-76984-6 (Hardback) – ISBN 978-0-521-74613-7 (Paperback)
1. Urban ecology (Biology)   I. Tanner, Colby J.   II. Title   2. Urban ecology (Sociology).
HT241.A35 2013
307.76–dc23
                                                                                    2012040143

ISBN 978-0-521-76984-6 Hardback
ISBN 978-0-521-74613-7 Paperback

Additional resources for this publication at www.cambridge.org/9780521769846

Contents

Preface

This book describes the challenges and opportunities that urban environments present to the plants and animals that inhabit cities and the ways that those organisms and entire ecosystems respond. The broad outlines of life are always the same: the need to find resources, to avoid being eaten or being killed, and to reproduce successfully. Ecologists have long studied how these factors determine which species live in a particular place and how those species interact with each other and the ecosystem. Only recently, however, has the focus of ecological science turned to life in urban environments.

The science of ecology developed in the late nineteenth century through the integration of three advances: detailed natural history of species and their habits, Darwin's emphasis on species interactions and change over time, and improved understanding of the physiology of plants and animals. The new field struggled to define the very nature of its subject of study, the communities of plants and animals that coexist and interact in one place and time. Was each community a tightly knit whole or merely a loose assemblage? What key factors determine how communities function?

Faced by these fundamental questions, ecologists deferred thinking about the massive disruption that cities bring to natural processes until those processes themselves could be better understood. As that understanding emerged, ecologists began turning their attention to cities. The modern practice of urban ecology grew from several distinct sources. In nineteenth-century Europe, studies of the plants of urban gardens, cemeteries, and highly disturbed building sites established a foundation of natural history information. These studies were among the first to distinguish between introduced and native species, and show how urban climate and urban pollution determine which plant species persist.

Early studies in the United States focused on interactions between humans and nature. Contemporary with early studies on European plants, George Perkins Marsh emphasized the potentially catastrophic effects of humans on the environment. Faced by possible environmental collapse, the term urban ecology became linked with the ecological challenges underlying urban planning. A group of sociologists, often called the Chicago School, applied ecological ideas about communities, competition, and spatial spread to describe how humans and their institutions change over time. In her attack on traditional urban planning, Jane Jacobs stressed the ecological nature of cities, and the danger of ignoring how different elements interact.

The more purely ecological appreciation of urban plant and animal communities and the interplay between ecological thinking and social science have found a potential synthesis in the establishment of two long-term ecological research sites in the cities of Phoenix and Baltimore in the United States. The sites will be monitored for decades to provide baseline data on ecological functioning to parallel studies in non-urban forests, grasslands, and wetlands. In addition to providing fundamental ecological data, these studies have spurred the effort to create a new synthesis that links human and non-human elements into a single framework.

Organization of the book

This book is structured like a play, in five acts, each with several scenes.

- Act 1 introduces the setting, the built environment, and the protagonists, the non-human residents of the urban world.
- Act 2 introduces the basic tension between intended and unintended consequences.
- Act 3 is the rising action, with development of the abiotic factors such as nutrients and weather that create the challenges faced by the protagonists.
- Act 4 is the climax, where we find out which protagonists fare well, which fare badly, and why.
- Act 5 is the resolution that looks at humans as urban organisms and challenges us to think where we go from here.

For some characters, such as the rock pigeon, we could see this as a comedy. All ends well, and the pigeons celebrate a new order. For others, such as the wood thrush, it is a tragedy as their world disappears. For urban humans, it is neither a comedy nor a tragedy, but an epic backyard drama. Nothing is resolved, for the story continues and indeed accelerates, but we hope to emerge wiser and more observant, and better able to see the world and ourselves.

How to use this book

This book is based on a one-semester course at the University of Utah. It is designed either to be read directly or used in the classroom. In the classroom, rather than presenting information in lecture format over a single semester or quarter, we recommend mixing lectures with discussion and choosing to give some topics less detailed classroom coverage. Centering class discussion around short papers based on the articles highlighted at the end of each chapter gives students a chance to focus and share their own ideas. Coupling classroom activities with field trips, based on the availability of local experts and sites, shows that the ecology discussed in this book is everywhere. For example, streams and reservoirs illustrate the transformation of urban water movement, parks or brownfields illuminate the factors that control urban biodiversity and the distribution of invasive species, and the college campus itself provides an overview of urban land types and their management.

Intellectually, the central goal of this book is to provide a framework of fundamental principles for thinking about ecological processes in urban environments. For this reason, we present only statistically significant results, and do not include error bars that of course can be found in the primary references. But more immediately, we seek to make readers aware that urban ecosystems are indeed ecosystems, and that fundamental life processes are happening all around us. For most people, a city consists of buildings, roads, and the humans that use them, ignoring the ways that urban residents interact with ecology. Urban residents, often unwittingly, shape the ecology around them, while that ecology shapes the lives of urban humans, again whether or not they are aware of it.

While working on this book, we returned to Salt Lake City by plane, and looked out the window as the plane flew low over the Salt Lake Valley, over suburbs planted with trees that would not have been there 100 years ago, over the straightened and polluted Jordan River bordered by a thin and threatened strip of green, over warehouses with their abandoned areas overgrown with weeds, and over playing fields planted with non-native grasses that can tolerate constant trampling, before descending into the paved expanse of the airport. These environments, so different from each other and so different from the sagebrush steppe on the surrounding foothills, were packed together in closely abutting contrast. How different this would be from the perspective of a bird or a floating plant seed! Filled though it is with charts and graphs very much of human origin, this book, we hope, is a path to seeing the urban world through different eyes.

1 Urban ecosystems and the science of ecology

Every fall, the weather cools, the days shorten, the soil starts to dry, and leaves drop from deciduous trees in temperate regions. These leaves carpet the ground, changing how nutrients and water infiltrate the soil, determining which plants will grow the following spring, altering the insect community, and changing the very scent of the forest. How long these changes persist depends on the availability of water and warmth, and the properties of the leaves themselves, with some being highly resistant to decomposition and others far less so. Sometimes these changes are beneficial for the tree itself, and sometimes they are not. Trees do not drop their leaves in order to create these changes, but the changes come nonetheless, the final consequences of water moved from deep beneath the ground and sunlight captured and stored over the course of an entire summer.

A tree imports energy, water, and nutrients from a relatively small area around and beneath it to achieve ecological and evolutionary success through survival and reproduction. Weather conditions beyond its control force it to drop some of those hard-won imports, creating a whole set of unintended consequences for the tree itself as well as the surrounding ecosystem (Figure 1.1).

The central themes of this book reflect both the similarities and differences between cities and trees. Like a tree, urban areas change the habitats around them, and import and concentrate resources for a set of intended purposes. The concentration of these resources and the resulting outputs produce a panoply of unintended consequences. Compared with trees, however, urban areas draw a much wider array of resources from a much larger region, have a more pervasive effect on the environment they occupy, and export those effects over a broader area.

In this chapter, we lay out the groundwork for urban ecology. We begin by introducing the concept of the ecosystem engineer, a role played to perfection by urban humans. Next we meet some of the habitats in urban areas and the plants and animals that occupy them. This lays the foundation for reviewing the central questions of the science of ecology itself, how those questions fit within the urban context, and the major ways in which urban ecosystems differ from those with less human influence. Finally, we sketch the goals of the field of urban ecology, and of this book in particular.

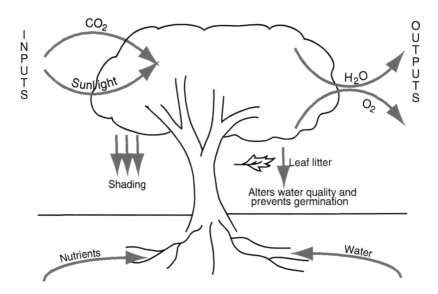

Figure 1.1 Like cities, trees import and export a whole range of materials, often transforming them in the process. These inputs and outputs create a wide array of intended and unintended consequences.

1.1   Engineered ecosystems

All organisms, however small, change their environment by their presence and by their use of resources. Most simply use available resources, with their existence affecting only a few nearby organisms. Early human hunter-gatherers may have shared the environment in this way, although early humans have been implicated in extinctions of some large mammals [18].

Other organisms, in contrast, have such major effects that they are termed *ecosystem engineers* [286] (Figure 1.2).

- Beavers build dams that change the flow of water, changing streams to ponds that flood surrounding forests.
- Woodpeckers drill holes in living or dead trees, making homes for themselves and other birds and animals, and opening up living trees to a range of pests and dead trees to decomposition.
- Trees change the climate and water flow patterns around themselves, and drop leaves that alter the properties of soil and determine which other plants can germinate and grow.
- Ants dig nests that alter the structure of soil and the movement of water within it, trim the vegetation around them, and import food and resources from many meters away. In this way, ants create "cities" with high densities of individuals that provide a revealing comparison with human cities.

Figure 1.2 Three ecosystem engineers: beavers, woodpeckers, and ants.

These animals and plants transform the environment, shifting the balance from one type of community, such as a forest with few aquatic plants, to another, such as a pond with few trees. Low intensity agriculture falls into this category, where only a relatively small proportion of land is used for crop production and the intervening tracts continue to support relatively undisturbed flora and fauna.

Ecosystem transformation can take place to various degrees. Changes can be subtle, such as a hole in a tree, or they can be extreme, such as an entire ecosystem being replaced. A coral reef can turn a large area of shallow open ocean into a richly diverse community. A non-native plant, such as cheatgrass *Bromus tectorum* that now dominates vast stretches of western North America, can replace native flora and fauna with a simplified and less diverse community. But it is modern humans who have mastered the art of ecosystem replacement.

Cities can change a shaded forest into a landscape of exposed rock, or a desert into a shaded forest. These transformed cities harbor an utterly different assemblage of plants and animals from the surrounding region, and have profoundly changed water movement and weather. The concentrated human demand for food requires large areas of high intensity agriculture, creating another set of novel environments that are dominated by single species such as corn, cattle, or soybeans.

Humans can be thought of as the definitive ecosystem engineers, making a whole range of changes simultaneously (damming rivers, building homes, moving resources, altering the climate) and over very large areas. But humans engineer the urban environment not just by modifying the locally available materials and resources, as beavers do by cutting and moving trees, but also by importing huge quantities of distant materials, energy, and nutrients, and exporting the resulting wastes. These unprecedented levels of input and output create, for the plants and animals that persist or flourish in the novel environment, an intensification of life similar to that experienced by the human residents of densely populated cities.

In some ways, however, humans have not so much created novel habitats as recreated or extended habitats favored by our distant ancestors[347]. During human evolution, people left the forests for savannas and sought refuges in cliffs, caves, and rocky outcrops. Early cities, built with natural stone, recreate many of the rocky aspects of these habitats, although new structures of glass and steel do not. The other component of the ancestral human habitat, the savanna of mixed open country and trees, has been mirrored in the mix of lawns, gardens, and trees that make up the suburbs that many people prefer to inhabit[419].

In urban areas, the effects of humans are never absent, almost by definition. Yet those effects vary in strength across the urban landscape, from preserved environments such as parks, transformed environments such as yards and gardens, to replaced environments such as buildings, roads, and landfills. How plants, animals, and other organisms make a living in this combination of environments is the central focus of this book.

1.2   Urban habitats

This book is about the functioning of ecosystems and the lives of plants and animals in the urban environment. But what, in fact, do we mean by "urban"? Many definitions are in use, often based on a specific population density threshold. For example, Japan defines urban areas by a density of at least 40 people per hectare. In comparison, the most densely populated city, Mumbai, India, has nearly 300 people per hectare, with the central zone packing over 1000 people into each hectare. This density exceeds that of a family of four living in a single-story $200\,m^3$ square meter house by a factor of five, even without accounting for the yard, street, or other spaces between homes. The most densely populated US state is New Jersey, with just under five people per hectare. If the

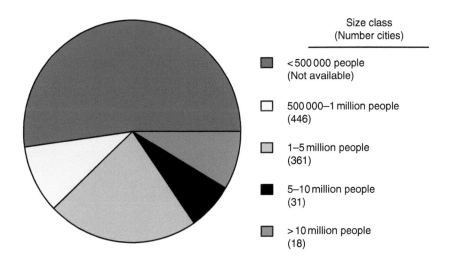

Size class
(Number cities)

■ < 500 000 people
(Not available)

□ 500 000–1 million people
(446)

■ 1–5 million people
(361)

■ 5–10 million people
(31)

■ > 10 million people
(18)

Figure 1.3 Percentage of urban people in cities of different sizes, along with the worldwide total number of such cities (after Gaston, 2010).

whole human population were spread evenly over the Earth's land area, there would be 0.5 people per hectare[612].

Other definitions involve the density of buildings or the distance between them[201]. This book is not tightly tied to any specific value, but focuses on how the changes characteristic of urbanization affect organismal and ecosystem processes. For planning purposes, different definitions can carry very distinct implications and must be considered more carefully[465].

By any definition, urban areas have grown vastly over the last three centuries. The first decade of the twenty-first century marks the first time in history when a majority of people live in cities, up from less than 10% in 1700[201]. This leads to a concentration of the human population, with more than half the population in a small fraction of the Earth's habitable area. In fact, cities take up only 1–3% of the Earth's area (depending on the definition and the method of analysis) with agriculture and grazing taking up roughly 20%[595].

There are now over 400 cities with more than 1 million people, up from a handful before 1800, such as ancient Rome, medieval Baghdad, or industrializing London. The current urban population is distributed among cities of widely different sizes, with the majority in smaller cities and relatively few in the megacities of over 10 million people (Figure 1.3).

All ecosystem engineers modify habitats, and the urban environment includes some of the most modified habitats on Earth, the *built environment*. The urban environment, however, consists of a wide variety of habitats from completely built up to those with few or no buildings or roads. Urban habitats vary in their degree of modification, the type and amount of inputs, including pollutants such as excess nutrients or poisons such as arsenic. Although traditionally thought of decreasing from more to less built as a function of distance from an urban core, urban land use is in fact a complex and

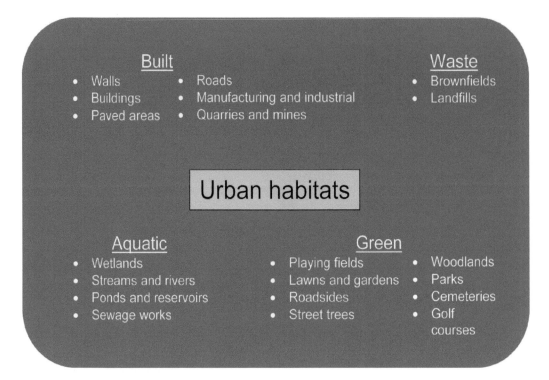

Figure 1.4   The various categories of urban habitat.

idiosyncratic response to historical and geological factors that rarely resembles a neat concentric arrangement[467].

We divide urban habitats into four broad categories (Figure 1.4).

1. **Built habitats** are structured primarily by human construction.
2. **Waste habitats** have been largely replaced with human discards.
3. **Green habitats** are covered primarily by plants.
4. **Aquatic habitats** are covered primarily by water.

Several careful inventories of urban lands show how different land uses are associated with different land types. In Manchester, UK, areas with high, medium, and low human population density differ in the percentage associated with different land cover[134] (Figure 1.5). The built environment is broken into buildings and other *impermeable surfaces*, surfaces that water cannot penetrate, like roads and parking lots. With rare exceptions, even the most heavily populated areas have a substantial proportion of land covered with vegetation, with much of that taking the form of managed grasslands or lawns[32] (Figure 1.6).

Although all ecosystems include a range of habitat types, urban areas are unusual in having profoundly different habitats in close proximity with sharp transitions (Figure 1.7). From the perspective of organisms that can survive only in a few of these

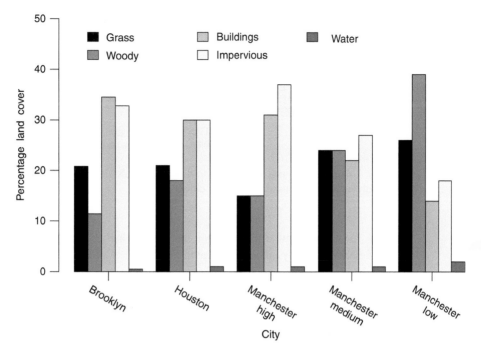

Figure 1.5 Distribution of habitats in two cities in the United States compared with in high, medium, and low density sections of Manchester, UK. High density areas have a preponderance of built habitats while low density areas are primarily green (after Douglas, 2011).

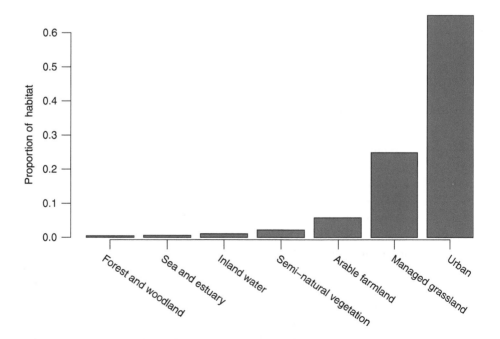

Figure 1.6 Distribution of habitats in London (after City Limits Report, 2002).

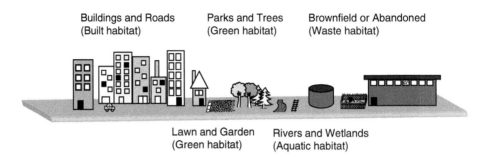

Figure 1.7 Urban areas contain a mix of contrasting and closely abutting habitats ranging from completely built by humans to nearly unmodified.

habitats, the urban environment can look like a set of habitat islands (often referred to as *patches*) separated by inhospitable environments.

Built habitats

Built habitats effectively define urban areas, designed for human use to the nearly complete exclusion of other organisms (Figure 1.8). Nonetheless, these habitats do support life, and the details of materials, architecture, and location determine which organisms can persist.

Walls in some cities cover as much vertical area as the city covers horizontally. Although generally quite inhospitable due to exposure to high levels of light, ultraviolet radiation, temperature and pollutants, and to low water availability, walls still accommodate some species. For example, walls built from porous materials such as limestone can support lichens, mosses, and climbing plants (Figure 1.9) along with a variety of algae and cyanobacteria[482]. Joints and cracks, particularly at the bottom of walls, provide places for water and nutrients to accumulate[607]. The plants that survive in these islands of life can support communities of small insects, spiders, and snails[576].

Buildings include more complex physical structures than just their walls. Window gardens and roof gardens support small communities of flowers and plants (Figure 1.10). The physical structures of buildings provide nesting sites for birds of prey such as falcons that feed on the pigeons and sparrows that inhabit the city center, roof-nesting birds such as gulls, shorebirds, and ravens, and bats and swifts that nest in chimneys and attics. Within buildings, humans share space with a variety of "pests", such as mice, rats, and roaches, in addition to overwintering insects like moths and beetles. Spiders capture insects that enter either accidentally or intentionally to find food, water, or trash.

Paved areas include sidewalks, parking lots, and city squares. Plants that colonize paved areas must overcome the challenges of trampling and compacted soil, but those that succeed can flourish in pavement gaps that accumulate water and nutrients. In the most trampled areas, only low-growing herbaceous plants and grasses tend

Figure 1.8 The built environment of Paris.

Figure 1.9 Aging building walls can provide habitat for hardy plants.

Figure 1.10 Window gardens, like these in Dublin, provide small patches of green on otherwise inhospitable walls.

to survive, and many of them are self-pollinating or wind-dispersed *annual plants* that live a fugitive existence in these short-lived patches. Other areas, particularly close to the bases of walls, are trampled less often, and longer-lived and taller plants can survive.

Roads are distinguished from other paved areas by vehicle traffic. Roads themselves tend to support few if any plants and animals as residents, and can reduce habitat quality for many hundreds of meters through modification of neighboring habitat, noise, and other pollution[145]. Animals that attempt to cross roads may perish in the attempt, and roads thus act as barriers to *dispersal*. Underpasses, sometimes designed specifically for animal passage, and drainage culverts under highways are used by many species (including humans) as a relatively safe way to cross roads.

Waste habitats

The effects of urban economic and business activity spread beyond the residences and workplaces where human activity is concentrated. When buildings or parking lots are abandoned, they remain in the landscape as *brownfields*. Discarded materials are transported and concentrated in landfills.

Brownfields are manufacturing and industrial areas that have been abandoned or are rarely used (Figure 1.11). As in other highly disturbed sites, the first species to arrive are typically wind-dispersed annual plants and hardy grasses, followed by taller perennial plants and, in sufficiently wet climates, by trees. Sites with large quantities of rubble or trash can have poor water retention and soils that are inhospitable to many plants.

Figure 1.11 A brownfield in Edinburgh, UK.

The first insects are typically highly dispersive herbivores and scavenging predators that subsist on fallen insects that cannot survive the harsh conditions. As the plant community changes, however, the animal community, beginning with insects, shifts in response[555].

Landfills, when active, have high degrees of disturbance and toxins, and support only the toughest of plants. However, landfills provide stable, renewable resources for those organisms that can use and defend them, such as scavenging gulls, and the heat produced by decomposition at landfills can lengthen the plant growing season.

Green habitats

Few cities, even in their most densely populated core, consist entirely of built habitats, but include areas primarily covered by plants. In European cities, the percentage of green space ranges from less than 2% to as high as 46%, corresponding to a range of 3 to 300 m^2 per person[201]. In Sheffield, England, the average distance to public green space is 400 m, and 96% of people live within 900 m, or a 15 minute walk[16], with many of course having access to private green areas in their own yards or gardens.

Green habitats vary in size, use, management, and disturbance regime, and break into three categories based on their history and purpose[380].

1. **Remnants** consist of habitat patches that have been left largely undisturbed.
2. **Spontaneous** sites have been recolonized by plants, sometimes on challenging *substrates* like pavement or walls.

Figure 1.12 Cemeteries can provide an oasis of life within older cities (photo courtesy of Kara Houck).

3. **Deliberative** sites are intentionally managed, with cultivation and landscaping that can involve nurturing of desirable species and removal of undesirable ones.

Woodlands in urban areas tend to be small and *fragmented*, broken into isolated patches. Trees are usually short and fill a low percentage of the canopy[385]. Disturbance by humans and pets makes it difficult for small plants to survive and grow in the gaps between trees. Urban forests are often remnants along streams or on steep slopes that are difficult to develop[282]. Small animals, such as rodents, that depend on these habitats may have restricted movement due to fragmentation, and can build up to extremely high local densities. Some patches are too small to support large predators, enhancing the conditions that can allow populations of smaller animals to build up[393].

Parks vary greatly in their ecological characteristics and resulting species' distributions and abundances. More recent parks, and those closer to the city center, are usually managed more heavily through mowing and weed control, and support species that can coexist with humans and grass. With the appropriate climate and management regime, parks harbor high densities of squirrels, and can support a mixture of urban and non-urban bird species.

Cemeteries are much like parks, but in older cities some cemeteries have been relatively undisturbed for long periods of time and can maintain relict populations of native species (Figure 1.12). Gravestones support a wide variety of lichens, and have even been used for scientific study[324].

Golf courses and playing fields also resemble parks, but with contrasting management. In golf courses, trees, shrubs, and water bodies provide aesthetic variety and sporting challenges, and they also provide habitats for plants, birds, small mammals, and

Figure 1.13 Heavily used and developed playing fields may provide little opportunity for species other than grass (photo courtesy of Kara Houck).

insects. Other types of playing fields are frequently less hospitable, consisting mainly of highly trampled grass or bare soil (Figure 1.13).

Lawns and gardens are among the most variable and widespread of urban habitats. Lawns are estimated to cover over 3% of the area of both the United States and England. Grass is now the largest irrigated crop in the United States[382]. Lawns and gardens in less densely populated cities can cover a substantial fraction of urban area, such as nearly 20% in Dayton, Ohio[115]. Front and back gardens are often managed quite differently, with Australians placing wooded and shrub gardens in the front, and vegetable or flower gardens in the back[115]. Although lawns tend to be managed for only a few preferred grass species, many other plants persist, particularly around the boundaries. Gardens can support a wide variety of pollinators and other insects.

Roadsides face an unusually wide range of disturbances, including noise and wind from passing vehicles, pollutants ranging from nitrogen oxides in the air to road salt, metals, and rubber washing off the road surface. These potentially stressful environments can harbor high diversity, due to the concentration of water created by runoff and the availability of the nutrient nitrogen. In some places, rare species that specialize in challenging habitats persist along roads. Butterflies tend to do well along roadsides, as do certain predators such as kestrels, small falcons often seen sitting on telephone wires. Vultures and other scavengers capitalize on concentrations of roadkill, and squirrels use power lines as transportation corridors.

Street trees can be associated with private residences or businesses or be publicly owned by the city or the community[119]. These trees must tolerate a multitude of stresses, including soil loss, poor water retention in shallow soils, pollution, damage by vandals and other human disturbance, and shading by buildings. Many are sick, and have longevity as little as 10–15 years[119]. The medians of roads can be particularly stressful, surrounded as they are by pavement and traffic. Those trees that do survive alter the environment around them in many ways. The plants that grow at the bases of trees can benefit from soil that is more stable and more permeable to water, from reduced air temperatures, and from the nutrients deposited by dogs. Trees shelter nearby buildings and surfaces from sun and wind, potentially improving habitats for humans and other nearby animals.

Aquatic habitats

Human beings like to live near water, and urban residents are no exception. The majority of cities are clustered near coasts or rivers[179], and thus include a variety of *aquatic habitats*, areas covered partly or mainly by water. These habitats may be remnants or modifications of previous water bodies, or may be newly created by humans.

Wetlands, areas where soil is saturated with water, have often been lost in urban areas through development or changes in water flow that lead to drying of the soil. Wetlands are magnets for plants and wildlife, but are also sinks for many urban outputs, including pollutants, nutrients, and particles. The cleansing capacity of wetlands is well established, but long-term inputs of material can lead to their filling and drying.

Streams and rivers in urban areas are often canalized (straightened) to increase the speed of flow and to handle surges of water due to stormwater runoff from the large area of impermeable surfaces that water cannot penetrate (Figure 1.14). These high-velocity floods disturb organisms on the bottom and along the sides, in addition to loading the

Figure 1.14 A straightened, walled urban river with a weir that slows and stabilizes water flow, adds oxygen to the water, and stops fish from swimming upsteam.

water and soil with pollutants, sometimes including untreated sewage. Organisms persisting in urban streams and rivers must be able to tolerate these conditions, and may in extreme cases resemble the species living in sewage works. *Riparian habitats* along the edges of streams and rivers harbor plants, whether grasses, shrubs, or trees, that play an important role in soil stability and functioning, and are often the sole remaining woodlands in urban areas[385]. These habitats can support a high diversity of plants and animals, but face the typical urban stresses from disturbance and pollution.

Canals, although usually straight like canalized urban rivers, are designed to have low flow rates and controlled water levels. These regimes make them susceptible to invasion by aquatic plants. **Ponds and reservoirs** can have a similar array of species as canals. Frequently *eutrophic* (overloaded with nutrients), these areas can support amphibians and wintering ducks. **Sewage works** have extremely high nutrient levels, and support worms and larvae that are food for birds. Nutrient-loving plants, such as nettles, can grow nearby and support communities of insects.

Although the majority of research regarding aquatic habitats and urbanization has focused on the water that enters and leaves a city, coastal habitats that abut cities are also profoundly influenced by urbanization. In fact, coastal aquatic habitat has been found to be sensitive to the same types of factors as urban *terrestrial* habitat, including increased vertical structure and hardening of surfaces[65].

The distribution of habitats

Urban environments thus contain many more habitats than the built environment of buildings and roads. Although human urban residents may not notice this diversity, most non-human residents depend upon it. Urban habitats are not only diverse, but are packed tightly together, with highly contrasting habitats in close proximity. For example, two sides of the same street can be more different than locations in cities on different continents. Because nearby urban habitats interact through exchange of materials, organisms, and nutrients, or through alterations of wind and water movements, all remain dependent upon each other as parts of the same urban ecosystem.

The distribution of habitats depends on the way that cities grow. Historically, most cities spread outward from an original center with gradually decreasing density. Modern technology and transportation has made possible other patterns, where new urbanized centers arise at some distance from the original settlement, and then potentially spread and eventually coalesce[201]. These patterns, along with the current trend toward dispersed lower density housing, sometimes called *exurban* development or urban sprawl, alter the distribution of urban habitat types[179].

Mediterranean cities, which were traditionally more compact, have expanded greatly in area in recent decades, increasing use of land, energy, transportation, and even water because lower density housing has more gardens and swimming pools. In Barcelona, the overall population remained steady between 1981 and 2001, but the urban core lost 400 000 people and the periphery gained 500 000, with both the density of housing and the number of people per household decreasing. Some of these trends are driven less by

Figure 1.15 In urban areas, sharply contrasting habitats can occur right next to each other, and suitable patches of habitat can be isolated by inhospitable intervening regions.

people's preferences than by the economic reality that housing in the city has become unaffordable[131].

Because habitat patches are often small, organisms or ecosystem processes that depend on larger areas can be lost as a region urbanizes (Figure 1.15). The mosaic of habitats in an urban environment is thus conducive to some organisms, but the resulting fragmentation, and the potentially harsh and dangerous barriers between habitat islands, can be deadly to others.

Scientists too can be challenged by the complex mixture of habitats. Studies of urban ecology are particularly sensitive to the *spatial scale*, or size, of the area under study. Studies of small areas might miss the key factors affecting a process, while studies of large areas can be difficult to run and analyze.

1.3   Urban organisms

Parents are sometimes maddened when children, treated with a chance to see exotic and expensive animals in the zoo, spend the entire time chasing pigeons through the crowds of people (Figure 1.16). Sometimes maligned as "a rat with wings," the rock pigeon *Columba livia* is a case study in urban success. Native to cliffs in Europe and North Africa, pigeons have followed humans around the world, nesting on buildings and subsisting on the many foods humans plant and discard.

To many humans, living beings in the city consist of people, with occasional "pests" such as pigeons and rats. Remarkably, however, urban areas harbor representatives of most forms of life. For some groups of species, such as plants and birds, cities

Figure 1.16 The ubiquitous rock pigeon *Columba livia*.

can even have higher *biodiversity*, the variety of species present in the area, than surrounding regions, although most groups of organisms tend to be less diverse in cities[370].

The study of urban biodiversity provides powerful insights into the factors that control where different species live and how common they are in various habitats. The following four aspects of habitat choice, habitat modification, and movement of resource and species play central roles in controlling the diversity of life in the city.

- People tend to settle in desirable locations with available water, tolerable climate, and substantial *topographic* variation.
- Humans fragment urban areas into a tightly packed mosaic of contrasting habitats that can favor diverse organisms.
- Humans input extensive resources in the form of water, nutrients, food, and waste.
- Humans directly import, intentionally or unintentionally, many new species from the surrounding countryside or from other continents.

Within an urban area, several groups of plants and animals show a "hump-shaped" relationship of diversity with the degree of urbanization. The number of species of mammals, birds, bumblebees, ants, and lizards can be highest in suburban areas with intermediate levels of modification[370], where the four factors listed above are most important. In contrast, the highest *biomass* (the total mass of living organisms) sometimes occurs in the most urbanized area (Figure 1.17). This brings us back to the rock pigeon, whose

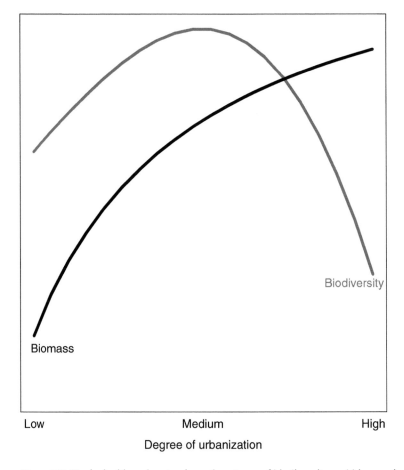

Figure 1.17 Typical, although not universal, patterns of biodiversity and biomass in urban areas, with a peak in biodiversity in regions of moderate development, and a peak of biomass in the city center.

population in an urban area can weigh collectively more than all birds combined in a comparably sized non-urban area.

Studies linking the number of species and human population density have focused on familiar and apparent organisms like birds, mammals, and plants with less attention paid to amphibians, fish, and insects[344] (Figure 1.18). In addition, not all regions on Earth have received equal attention, with a focus on the cities of North America and Europe (Figure 1.19) that lie in the middle latitudes of the northern hemisphere[153] (Figure 1.20).

Classification of urban life

There are several useful ways to classify the organisms that live in urban areas. First, species can be distinguished by where they come from. Those species that were

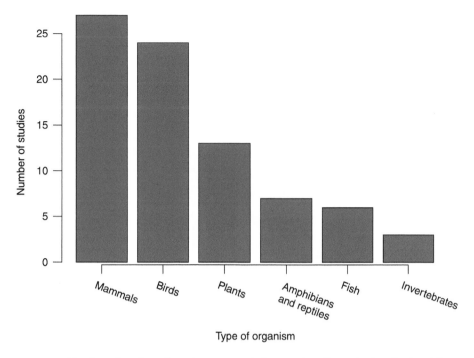

Figure 1.18 Number of studies of how human population density affects biodiversity for different types of organisms (after Luck, 2007[344]).

imported or introduced are called *exotic* or non-native. Second, species can be classified through their ability to survive in different degrees of urbanization. Urban species can be separated into three broad categories[35] (Figure 1.21).

- **Urban exploiters**: These species are successful in urban habitats because they are highly tolerant of pollution, disturbance, and human presence, can consume the by-products of urban life, and are generally good at dispersing. They represent the few species that flourish in the highly built city center, and many are found in cities throughout the world.
- **Urban adapters**: These species are able to persist in urban habitats by having broad diets and the ability to capitalize on newly disturbed habitats, particularly in the absence of their usual predators. They are found in both moderately urbanized and suburban habitats.
- **Urban avoiders**: These species are sensitive to harassment from human presence, disturbance, or other aspects of the urban habitat. They persist only in fragments of less urbanized habitat, such as woodlands or wetlands.

Urban exploiters and adapters are referred to as *synurbanized* or *synanthropic* species. From this perspective, at least throughout most of its range, the pigeon is an exotic urban exploiter.

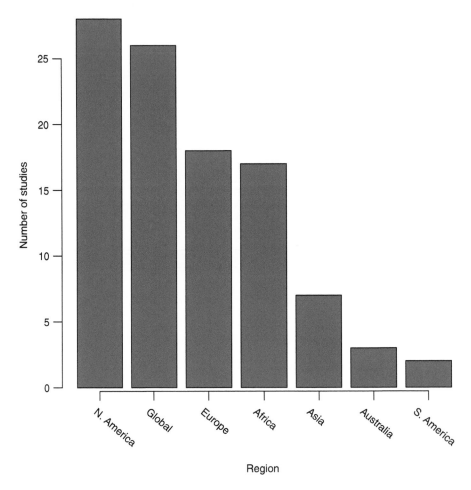

Figure 1.19 Number of studies of how human population density affects biodiversity for different regions (after Luck, 2007[344]). S. America includes both South and Central America.

Characteristics of urban life

Successful urban species tend to have broad diets and broad geographic ranges, and are thus equipped to cope with novelty both in the form of climate and available resources. For example, gulls and raccoons have learned to capitalize on garbage (Figure 1.22). Urban environments also present a wide range of novel stresses, including light and noise, pollution, heat, and human or pet disturbance; many animals simply cannot cope with one or more of these stresses. The animals that do persist in urban habitats can learn to avoid human disturbance through coming out at night, using concealed locations, or developing ways to tolerate stress.

Insects play an important yet underappreciated role in urban ecosystems[367]. Successful urban insects have traits similar to those of urban birds and mammals. Urban bees tend to have broad diets, and survive by visiting a wide variety of flowers. Urban

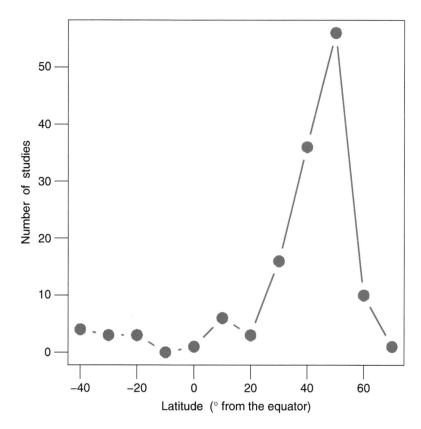

Figure 1.20 Distribution of studies on the ecology and life history of urban populations as a function of latitude (after Evans, 2010[153]).

insects are usually able to move rapidly between sites, and have large geographic ranges. Although the majority of urban insect species live outdoors, prominent urban exploiting pests such as cockroaches thrive in buildings. These insects use human structures for protection, and the leftover materials from human activities for food.

Plants, with their inability to move after germinating from seed, must cope with urban environments in different ways than animals. Many urban plants are able to arrive and germinate quickly in newly disturbed sites via wind-dispersed seeds or seeds that are effectively spread by humans. The ubiquitous dandelion *Taraxacum officinale* has many of these traits, with its wind-powered seeds on parachutes and its ability to pop up seemingly instantaneously both in disturbed sites and lawns. The most successful plants in the urban habitat are able to tolerate high nutrient levels, which are detrimental to more delicate plants such as orchids, and some can even tolerate high levels of toxic pollutants.

Less visible organisms can serve as useful indicators of urban habitat conditions. Lichens, for example, are highly sensitive to pollution, and have lower diversity in most urban areas relative to non-urban habitats. The "canine zone" near the base of

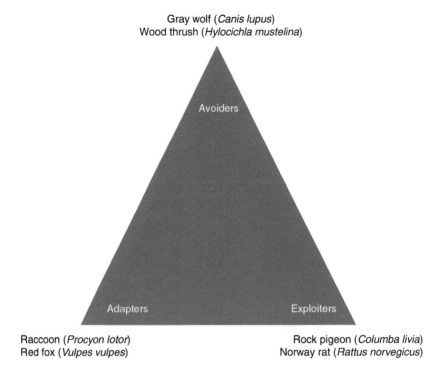

Gray wolf (*Canis lupus*)
Wood thrush (*Hylocichla mustelina*)

Avoiders

Adapters   Exploiters

Raccoon (*Procyon lotor*)   Rock pigeon (*Columba livia*)
Red fox (*Vulpes vulpes*)   Norway rat (*Rattus norvegicus*)

Figure 1.21 Examples of three responses to the urban environment. Most organisms lie somewhere between these extremes (after Blair, 2001).

a tree, which is watered and nourished by dog urine, has been hypothesized to have a very different population of algae than sections of the tree trunk just a few centimeters higher[214]. Like lichens, mosses are also sensitive to pollution and human disturbance. One species of moss *Bryum argenteum*, however, is found throughout the world, but only in urban areas (Figure 1.23).

Some of the most widespread urban organisms, such as rats, mice, and pigeons, have as their ancestral habitats the rocky outcrops that humans first colonized long ago and have replicated, at least in part, in buildings[347]. Like *Bryum argenteum*, the house mouse *Mus musculus* is always found in association with human habitation.

Conclusions

Urban areas are characterized by novel habitats, high levels of inputs and outputs, high levels of disturbance, and the intended and unintended consequences of human actions. Some organisms persist by adapting to these extreme conditions, a few organisms exploit them and become widespread, and many organisms cannot tolerate them and must avoid cities. Urban exploiters are often found in cities throughout the world, and represent species most likely to remain extant for future generations.

Figure 1.22 Urban raccoon raiding a garbage can.

1.4   The science of ecology

Ecology is the study of the relationship between organisms and their environment, focusing on the forces that control the distribution and abundance of species, the ways that those species live, and the characteristics of the environments or ecosystems that they inhabit[74]. We have met the modified habitats and some of the organisms that make up the urban ecosystem, and now introduce the ecological approaches to their study.

The science of ecology can be broken into five broad and overlapping areas:

- Ecosystem ecology describes flows of energy, water, nutrients, and other materials.
- Community ecology describes patterns of biodiversity and species interaction.
- Population ecology describes how the factors important in community ecology control the population dynamics of individual species.

Figure 1.23 The urban specialist moss *Bryum argenteum*, or silvergreen bryum moss.

- Behavioral and physiological ecology describe how organisms respond to the challenges of different environments.
- Evolutionary ecology describes how costs and benefits of different ecological strategies translate into survival and reproduction.

This section introduces the central principles and questions for each area, and highlights key changes in urban ecosystems.

Ecosystem ecology

Ecosystem ecology follows the flows of energy, water, nutrients, and other materials through an ecosystem, seeking to understand how those flows affect and are affected by living organisms.

- **Energy** is the ultimate driver of ecological systems, with availability determined by *primary productivity*, the conversion of sunlight into chemical energy through *photosynthesis*, and by the fate of that stored energy, such as the consumption of photosynthetic sugar by animals. Because these energy-storing molecules can move through water, some ecosystems, such as streams and coral reefs, persist largely through imported energy.
- **Weather and climate** shape the temperature, rainfall, humidity, and wind of a region, setting limits on where many organisms can live. Hot dry deserts have much less living biomass than warm moist areas, and tall trees cannot persist in areas with intense winds. In turn, living organisms can alter the local *microclimate*. Large trees increase humidity, moderate temperatures, and reduce wind.

- **Hydrology** describes the movement and availability of water. Water is essential for plants and animals to survive, and plays a key role in the movement of nutrients. The timing and duration of water flow and availability, whether slow and constant or fast and intermittent, largely determines which organisms can live in a location. Conversely, plants affect the flow of water. A barren hillside has faster water flow, and more erosion, than a forested one.
- **Nutrients**, such as carbon, nitrogen, and phosphorus, are also essential for life. Nutrient availability is determined by rates of input and output, and by the efficiency of recycling. Recycling can occur within a location, such as between living and dead organisms, or between different geographic locations when nutrients are carried by water or wind.

The **principles of ecosystem ecology** center around the following properties of cycles of materials and energy:

1. Availability of essential materials and energy depends on their sources of input, the fates of outputs, and the degree of recycling,
2. Cycles depend on the physical and biological properties of the material,
3. Cycles of different materials and energy interact with each other,
4. Cycles are linked across different locations in space and across time.

Urban ecosystem cycles are profoundly changed. All cities import huge quantities of chemical energy in the form of fossil fuels. Urban residents use this energy to live, and to move water, nutrients, and materials over great distances. Internal combustion engines and paved surfaces alter temperature and humidity, and particulates can seed the clouds and alter rainfall patterns. Chapter 3 investigates in detail how urbanization modifies and amplifies ecosystem processes.

Community ecology

Community ecology studies the patterns of biodiversity and how species survive and interact in a given environment. Species can be classified as producers, consumers, parasites, or decomposers, and different communities can have different balances among these lifestyles. Similarly, different communities could be dominated by different interactions between species, such as competition, predation, infection, or mutualism. The most important natural processes that regulate ecological communities include the following.

- **Disturbance** removes or damages individuals, opening space for other organisms. Disturbance can come from many sources, including wind, flooding, fire, or trampling, with each of these being controlled at least in part by the community itself. For example, dense forests reduce winds, and grasses such as cheatgrass promote fires.
- **Succession** describes how a community recovers from disturbance, and how the species in a recovering community change over time. The course of succession depends on the spatial extent, the magnitude, and the frequency of disturbances.

Areas that are constantly being cleared remain in an *early successional* state, often characterized by fast-growing weeds with small seeds. Areas with more infrequent disturbances can reach a *late successional* state, with slower growing and longer-lived plants and animals.

- **Fragmentation** describes how the suitable environment for a particular species is distributed in space. An orchid might experience a highly fragmented landscape with only a few suitable habitats due to its need for a special soil type. A fast-growing weed might also experience a highly fragmented landscape, but due instead to the unpredictable appearance of the recently disturbed sites it depends on. A bird that can use a wide variety of habitats for survival and reproduction may experience an unfragmented habitat.
- **Biological invasion** describes the arrival of exotic species into an area. All regions are susceptible to invasions to a greater or lesser degree, depending both on the rate at which new species arrive and the probability that those species persist.

The **principles of community ecology** focus on how the species present in an area interact, and the ways that they interact depend on:

1. The type, distribution, and quality of habitat,
2. Changes over time due to disturbance and succession,
3. Ecosystem processes governing availability of energy and nutrients,
4. The processes controlling the arrival and survival of new species.

As the definitive ecosystem engineers, humans alter each of the processes that structure communities (Figure 1.24). Humans alter the magnitude and frequency of disturbance via construction of buildings and roads and by suppression of floods and

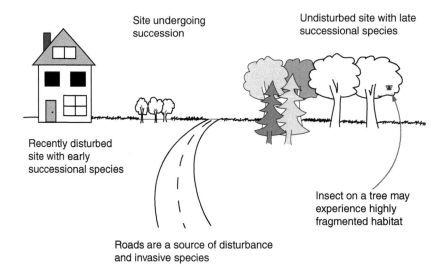

Site undergoing succession

Undisturbed site with late successional species

Recently disturbed site with early successional species

Insect on a tree may experience highly fragmented habitat

Roads are a source of disturbance and invasive species

Figure 1.24 Which species inhabit a particular location depends on both the environment and the way that those species interact.

fires, fragment habitats through such actions as road construction, and transport exotic species intentionally for horticulture and agriculture or unintentionally on ships and airplanes. Urban community ecology focuses on how communities respond to the changes created by human action (Chapter 4), examining in detail the effects on biodiversity (Section 4.1), the types of species that persist (Section 4.2), and their interactions (Section 4.3).

Population ecology

Population ecology tracks the population of a single species, and describes how the number of individuals is controlled by the factors important in community ecology. These population dynamics determine which species go extinct, which can persist, and which are most abundant in a given environment The outcome depends on the fit between the following aspects of a species' *strategy* and its environment.

- **Life history** describes when members of a species reproduce, how many offspring they have, and how long they live. For example, early successional species tend to have early age of first reproduction, high *fecundity*, and a short lifespan. In contrast, late successional species typically have delayed reproduction, few offspring, and longer lifespans.
- **Dispersal** describes how members of a species move between different spatial locations and at what life stage, whether as a seed, a juvenile, or an adult. Dispersal determines how populations occupy suitable habitats and persist in a fragmented landscape.
- **Dormancy** describes the ability of certain life stages such as seeds to survive harsh conditions in a relatively inactive state. For example, desert annual plants persist primarily as an underground *seed bank* that can wait many decades before sufficient rains induce germination.

The **principles of population ecology**, like those of community ecology, describe how species prosper in response to such features of their habitats as spatial arrangement and frequency of disturbance, the availability and distribution of resources in time and space, and how a species interacts with competitors, predators, and diseases.

Humans affect the survival and reproduction of urban organisms directly through hunting or removal programs, and indirectly through habitat modification, fragmentation, and the introduction of competitors, predators, and diseases (Section 4.4). Urban population ecology focuses on how populations respond to these changes. Urban ecosystems can accelerate population responses, with species that use ineffective strategies being driven to local extinction and those with effective strategies rising to high density.

Behavioral and physiological ecology

Behavior describes how an organism reacts to its environment, including tolerance or aggression towards competitors, communication with members of its own species, avoidance of predators, and strategies for resource collection. Physiology describes an organism's size and shape, its ability to cope with various forms of stress, and its reproductive status. Behavioral and physiological ecology study how organisms respond to the following three aspects that characterize all environments.

- **The physical environment** consists of the many *abiotic* factors an organism faces. The substrate upon which organisms live, whether hard and infertile or soft and fertile, determines behavioral and physiological strategies such as plant germination and construction of nests and shelters by animals. **Light** affects the timing of activity, reproduction, migration, and emergence from dormancy. **Noise** can interfere with communication or disrupt sensitive reproductive behaviors. **Temperature** can control the speed of development, the timing of reproduction, and the ability to forage for resources at different times of day. **Disturbance** quickly reshapes the physical environment and can demand rapid behavioral and physiological responses.

- **Resource availability** determines whether an organism must focus on resource collection, or has sufficient energy to pursue other objectives such as reproduction and predator avoidance. In a high resource environment, populations usually grow. Individuals then face increased competitive challenges that favor different types of behavior and physiology than when populations are small. Behavior and physiology must also respond to resource availability in space and time. Dispersal, dormancy, and social behavior are all favored in highly variable environments.

- **The biotic environment** consists of interactions with living things, played out upon the stage set by the physical environment. Within a single species, individuals compete intensely for food, mates, and shelter. Survival requires avoiding being eaten by predators or herbivores or dying of disease. Other organisms can also alter the physical environment, such as compacting soil by trampling, removing soil by digging, or flooding soil by dam-building. **Invasive species**, including competitors, predators, and diseases, can create new challenges even when the physical environment remains largely unchanged.

The **principles of physiological and behavioral ecology** describe how species cope with the physical, resource, and biotic challenges that their environments pose. Some organisms cannot deal with these challenges and fail to persist in that area, while others can adjust their bodies or behaviors to cope with new challenges.

Urban ecosystems transform all three of these aspects of the environment (Figure 1.25). The built environment includes many hard and impermeable substrates. These environments are brighter, louder, and warmer than surrounding habitats, and face a novel disturbance regime. Pollutants can disrupt biochemical pathways. Urban resources, although often different in kind from those in non-urban settings, tend to be highly available on average, predictable in space and time, and distributed in concentrated patches. The urban biotic environment experiences high rates of biological invasion and creates interactions among previously unfamiliar species. The degree of transformation varies greatly both within and among cities, leading to different behavioral and physiological responses. Urban behavioral and physiological ecology studies

Figure 1.25 The diverse and novel habitats in the urban environment of Vancouver, Canada, create stresses from temperature, pollution, invasive species, artifical lighting, and physical disturbance, and elicit a wide range of behavioral and physiological responses.

how organisms either respond or fail to respond to the human-altered environment (Section 4.5). Human residents of urban environments face many of these same challenges, with a wide range of effects on health (Section 5.1).

Evolutionary ecology

To persist, each organism needs to have a strategy to deal with the challenges created by both biotic and abiotic environments. Evolutionary ecology compares the *fitness* consequences (the effects on survival and reproduction, and thus on the growth of a population) of different strategies.

- **Life history theory** predicts which patterns of survival and reproduction will be most successful in different environments, and how these might evolve in response to changing conditions. Patterns of disturbance can play a key role, for example, because organisms in an unstable habitat will be favored to reproduce as early as possible.
- **Foraging theory** asks which behaviors will be most successful in locating and gaining access to resources. Animals must balance the benefits of food collection or mating with the risks of being eaten, and the best choice depends on its environment and its state of health.
- **Dispersal theory** compares approaches to movement. The success of different strategies depends on the degree of environmental fragmentation, which affects both the probability of finding a suitable new site and of successfully crossing inhospitable

intervening terrain to get there. Many animals must decide when to move either within or between habitats, while plants create seeds with properties that determine whether they are likely to disperse long distances.

- **Evolutionary theory** adds the realism of genetic evolution to these strategic considerations, asking how quickly genetic solutions evolve when a species is confronted with new problems. This evolutionary rate depends on the mutation rate, population size, fecundity, the age at which organisms reproduce, and the flow of genes between populations.

The **principles of evolution** describe the conditions under which new traits are likely to evolve. Species must have enough variability for natural selection to work, which requires a sufficiently large population size. A population, particularly one in a novel environment, must also be sufficiently isolated from the rest of its species in order to evolve along a separate path. A novel environment needs to favor new traits, when they arise, strongly enough for natural selection to work.

Evolutionary ecology seeks to make specific predictions about how organisms will respond to human alterations. Will birds give up migration when bird feeders become available in a location that no longer freezes in the winter? Will animals such as fish begin to reproduce at younger ages and smaller sizes in the face of harvesting? Will plants produce seeds that no longer blow in the wind because so many land on parking lots and die? Urban evolutionary ecology focuses on understanding how rapid and how common evolution is in urban habitats and on how evolution differs between urban and non-urban habitats (Section 4.6).

1.5   What makes urban ecosystems different?

Each of the major components of ecology (Section 1.4) can be fundamentally altered in urban ecosystems[101]. The key differences between urban and non-urban systems form the basis for the specific ecological processes discussed in this book.

Urban ecosystems

The novel aspects of urban ecosystems result from the habitat modifications and changes in inputs and outputs driven by the human ability for goal-directed behavior[364] (Figure 1.26). Achieving almost any objective within the built environment requires inputs and outputs of energy and materials. These inputs and outputs have both intended and unintended consequences[479]. Building a road requires energy, labor, and materials, and creates a whole range of disturbances, all for the purpose of facilitating transportation. But that road also creates a whole range of unintended consequences. Flowers that live beside that road receive the water and pollutants that run off from that road not as a design feature, but as an unintended byproduct of the impermeability of pavement. Animals risk danger crossing that road as an unintended consequence of high-speed transport.

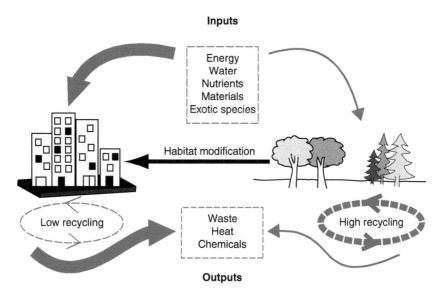

Figure 1.26 The ways in which urban ecosystems differ from those less affected by humans.

Urban systems invariably have extreme inputs of energy, water, nutrients, and materials (Section 2.3). Fossil fuels and transported food concentrate calories to unprecedented levels. Reservoirs and delivery systems bring distant water to urban homes and gardens, urban industry, and even urban agriculture. Fertilizers, packed with nitrogen and phosphorus extracted far away, enhance lawns and gardens. Bricks, cement, metal, wood, paper, and plastic arrive by the ton and are used for building, packaging, and goods.

Movement of materials, construction, and high human population density create levels of disturbance unlike those in other ecosystems in their frequency, magnitude, and type. Building sites are cleared of one community to be replaced by a fully built environment in some cases, or by highly managed grounds in others. Plants near sidewalks face constant trampling and the risk of vandalism. This range of disturbances creates a highly fragmented landscape, where habitat suitable for an organism might be splintered into small and distant patches.

Habitat modification through pavement and construction of buildings makes water more likely to run off rapidly after storms and less likely to soak into the soil. In contrast to streams, much urban water arrives in pipes that are largely, although not completely, inaccessible to plants, animals, and bacteria in the soil.

Basic properties of air flow and weather are also transformed in urban areas. The air is warmed by heat absorbed and produced by buildings, and humidity is shaped by water released by irrigated lawns and combustion.

Urban areas have high levels of both novel and familiar chemicals. Plastics and medications introduce compounds that can have unexpected effects on plants and animals. Combustion of fossil fuels generates large quantities of such pollutants as nitrogen oxides. Sunlight falling on this and other compounds creates other chemical challenges, such as ozone. Even carbon dioxide, the source of carbon molecules for plant photosynthesis, can be elevated to levels double those in nearby non-urban areas.

Urban outputs are large because inputs are large and recycling tends to be low. Urban areas output wastes in the form of sewage and garbage, which, after varying degrees of treatment, return to water bodies and land often far from the city itself. Other pollutants created in urban areas enter the water or air and spread to environments both near and far. Exotic species introduced into urban areas can invade neighboring non-urban ecosystems. Large as these outputs are, they frequently fail to match inputs. An imbalance between inputs and outputs can lead to concentration of particular chemicals or nutrients in urban areas. These materials and concentrated nutrients can be *sequestered* in buildings or soils that have been covered by pavement, and thus effectively removed from their natural cycles.

Urban organisms

The magnitude of inputs and outputs and rapid habitat modification present urban organisms with novel challenges far exceeding those typical of non-urban systems. Those organisms that persist and flourish must either be preadapted to human presence, be able to adjust their behavior or physiology, or evolve sufficiently quickly to reproduce.

In addition to creating new types of habitats in complex spatial patterns, urbanization generates novel patterns of habitat change over time. Economic and social development lead to a process of succession in urban areas quite different from that in undisturbed ecosystems[624]. Older neighborhoods can resemble older forests in having larger plants and lower levels of disturbance, but urban decay can create brownfields or abandoned areas that resemble early successional sites. Other areas undergo constant disturbance or management that maintains a diversity of successional stages[73].

Urban organisms must also cope with altered resource dynamics, with those that succeed best capable of capitalizing on increased inputs. Humans in cities also import other species, both intentionally and unintentionally, at rates exceeding those in ecosystems less extremely altered by humans. Some exotic species, such as the Argentine ant *Linepithema humile*, arrive in new habitats by hitchhiking through the transportation system. Exotic plants arrive intentionally to adorn gardens, homes, and parks, and can potentially escape. As a result, large urban gardens might have the most species of any habitat on Earth, even more than tropical forests[566]. Pets can act as predators, and as sources of waste, disease, and disturbance.

Urban science

The final difference between urban and non-urban ecosystems concerns the science of ecology itself, rather than the ecosystems and organisms it studies. Finding field sites in urban areas can be challenging due to private property or heavy human traffic. Many key processes occur at large spatial scales, accentuating the difficulties of finding appropriate research sites. Large political and economic forces make controlled experiments nearly impossible on a large scale.

The relatively recent rise of the scientific study of urban ecology results from many causes[200]. The interest began with three psychological realizations: the majority of humans now live in cities, humans have come to dominate ecosystem processes throughout the world[595], and cities are indeed ecosystems with their own way of functioning. The appreciation of human economic dependence on ecosystems extends to an acceptance of the effects that habitats, and particularly heavily built urban habitats, have upon human health and well-being. These new attitudes have led many scientists to take on the substantial challenges of this new endeavor, which include not only the logistic difficulties of research, but also the intellectual challenge of working with scientists and social scientists from many different backgrounds.

Conclusions

The differences between urban and non-urban ecosystems, although large, can be thought of as differences in degree rather than in kind. Each of the key ecosystem processes has been studied in more pristine systems, and a body of ecological principles has been developed to predict its consequences. That these principles continue to apply to the modified processes in urban systems provides the working framework for this book[403].

Whether ecological theories extend to make sense of the responses of humans themselves is more debatable. Humans, like any organism, make decisions about where to live, what to eat, and how to respond to stress, but do so with superior tools for cognition, communication, and transportation. This book focuses on the new environments that humans create for other organisms, placing the causes of human decisions and their effects on human society in the background.

1.6 The goals of urban ecology

This book describes the functioning of urban ecosystems, from the movement of materials and nutrients to the interactions and physiology of the organisms that inhabit them. We focus on three themes that link the multitude of processes occurring in urban areas[201].

- Urban areas transform habitats.
- Cities vastly increase inputs and outputs, and decrease recycling, of materials and nutrients.
- Habitat modification, inputs and outputs create intended and unintended consequences for the urban ecosystem and the organisms that inhabit it.

The science of urban ecology is only part of the larger enterprise of understanding and planning cities. These approaches can be distinguished by the contrast between *ecology in cities*, the study of ecological processes and the lives of organisms within cities, and *ecology of cities*, which uses ecological thinking to understand how urban ecology, sociology, and economics interact[444]. Although this book seeks to understand cities as a whole by linking ecosystem, population, and community processes, it introduces only a few of the scientific and policy challenges created by human behavior.

Our working premise is that the principles of the science of ecology can be applied in the urban context. Our central goal is then to introduce those principles and use them to make sense of the urban ecosystem. Indeed, our starting point must be that an urban ecosystem is, in fact, an ecosystem[73]. Just as in any other ecosystem, nutrients move and cycle while species persist, go extinct, interact, and adapt[364]. The key difference is that humans, with our goal-directed behavior and powerful technology, are the primary drivers, rather than abiotic factors such as climate or nutrient availability that typically govern other ecosystems. Just as scientists can study desert ecology without delving deeply into the climatic causes of aridity, this book studies urban ecology without claiming to explain the human behavior that shapes it.

Scientific study of urban areas breaks into two broad approaches. The first capitalizes on the *urban–rural gradient,* the sequence of habitats and urban effects progressing outward from the urban core[365], or more generally the variety of habitats in cities without a clearly defined core[467]. Ideally, observed differences can be attributed to a particular factor that differs between urban and nearby non-urban sites, controlling for geographic differences and broad climate effects[364]. Urbanization is an ongoing uncontrolled experiment, and these sorts of observational studies are often the best tool that ecologists have. The second takes a more traditional approach of designing experiments, such as removal of particular species or addition of resources, to pinpoint causes within complex webs of interaction. These experiments usually cover a much smaller spatial and temporal scale than observational studies.

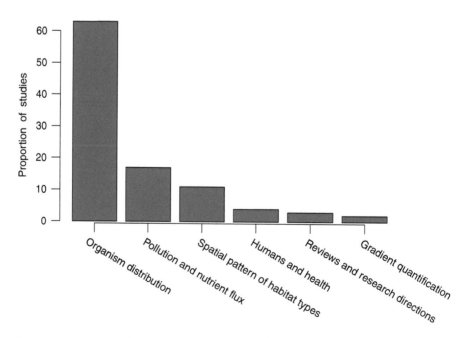

Figure 1.27 Percentage of studies that focus on different topics in urban ecology (after McDonnell and Hahs, 2008).

Using the gradient approach, scientists have addressed a wide range of questions from across the full range of ecological approaches. Our goal is not to present the results of every study, but to extract from them the way that ecological principles play out in the urban environment. These studies have largely focused on the first essential job, that of characterizing the urban environment, but this large body of work has given the first insights into the way that ecological principles work in those environments[364] (Figure 1.27).

In addition to seeing the urban ecosystem from the perspective of an ecological scientist, we also seek to see it from the perspective of an urban organism. For urban plants and animals, the urban ecosystem presents a set of novel challenges in the ancient battle for survival and reproduction. These two perspectives contribute to a broader appreciation of cities as ecosystems and ecological communities, in addition to being places where people live, work, and play.

1.7   Questions and readings

Discussion questions

For Section 1.1
1. How do humans "engineer" an ecosystem, and why?
2. What are the positive and negative effects of human-engineered ecosystems within and beyond the engineered portion of the ecosystem? Do non-human ecosystem engineers have similar positive and negative effects?
3. How are humans similar to other ecosystem engineers, and how are they different?
4. What are the advantages and disadvantages of being an ecosystem engineer?

For Section 1.2
1. What habitats do you see in Figures 1.8–1.14? How would these look to you if you were a bird?
2. List the types of habitats in your area, and discuss the variability that this collection of habitats brings to the local, urban environment.
3. Which habitats are you most familiar with in your area, and why?
4. Compare the habitats in your area with those in the photograph of Paris (Figure 1.8). What is similar and different?
5. Using your list of local habitats, list the familiar plants and animals that make use of each habitat type.
6. How are each of the habitats in your list similar and dissimilar to their counterparts (if they exist) outside of the city?

For Section 1.3
1. What traits allow a species to live in an urban environment? Compare this list of traits with those of humans; why are humans good at living in cities?
2. How would you characterize the personality traits of people who are good at living in cities? Do they resemble those of urban exploiters?

3. Why might biodiversity increase, to a point, with increasing urbanization? What types of species usually account for this biodiversity, and does it matter?

For Section 1.4

1. How does your perspective of a city change when you think about the five approaches to ecology?
2. How might this perspective be affected by the spatial or temporal scale of your focus? For example, does it matter whether you focus on the street where you live rather than the entire city? Why would scale be an important part of urban ecological studies?
3. Think of one common species that lives near you, and describe it in terms of each approach to ecology. Now do the same for a species not found in urban environments. What do the similarities and dissimilarities between these descriptions indicate about urban ecological processes?
4. How do behavioral and physiological responses to urbanization compare with evolutionary responses? Why might this present difficulties for scientists studying how a species responds to increasing urbanization?

For Section 1.5

1. What evidence can you see that urban inputs and outputs are large?
2. Among the animals you see in your city, how prominent are pets? How do they interact with other urban organisms?
3. How and where would you conduct an ecological experiment near your home or classroom? What difficulties would you anticipate?

For Section 1.6

1. Read the essay by Robert Young[624]. Why do you think previous urban ecology research did not become part of "mainstream" ecology?
2. What has changed (e.g., ideals, perspectives, needs, research itself) to bring urban ecology into the realm of mainstream science?
3. What are your own goals and objectives regarding this field of study?

Further Reading

For Section 1.1

- Jones, C., Lawton, J., and Shachak, M. Organisms as ecosystem engineers. *Oikos*, **69** (1994), 373–386.
- Lundholm, J. Urban cliffs. In *The Routledge Handbook of Urban Ecology*, ed. Douglas, I., Goode, D., Houck, M. C., and Wang, R. (New York: Routledge, 2011), pp. 252–263.

For Section 1.2

- Barbosa, O., Tratalos, J. A., Armsworth, P. R., *et al.* Who benefits from access to green space? A case study from Sheffield, UK. *Landscape and Urban Planning*, **83** (2007), 187–195.
- Gilbert, O. L. *The Ecology of Urban Habitats*. (New York: Chapman and Hall, 1989).
- Wheater, C. P. *Urban Habitats*. (New York: Routledge, 1999).

For Section 1.3

- Blair, R. B. Birds and butterflies along urban gradients in two ecoregions of the United States: is urbanization creating a homogeneous fauna? In *Biotic Homogenization,* ed. Lockwood, J. L. and McKinney, M. L. (Dordrecht, the Netherlands: Kluwer Academic, 2001), 33–56.
- McIntyre, N. E. Ecology of urban arthropods: a review and call to action. *Annals of the Entomological Society of America*, **93** (2000), 825–835.
- McKinney, M. L. Urbanization, biodiversity, and conservation. *Bioscience*, **52** (2002), 883–890.

For Section 1.4

- Cain, M. L. Bowman, W. D., and Hacker, S. D. *Ecology*. (Sunderland, MA: Sinauer Associates, 2008).
- Odum, E. P. *Ecology*, 2nd edn. (Austin, TX: Holt, Rinehart, and Winston, 1975).
- Pickett, S. T. A., Cadenasso, M. L., Grove, J. M., *et al.* Urban ecological systems: linking terrestrial ecological, physical, and socioeconomic components of metropolitan areas. *Annual Review of Ecology and Systematics*, **32** (2001), 127–157.

For Section 1.5

- Cadenasso, M. and Pickett, S. Urban principles for ecological landscape design and maintenance: scientific fundamentals. *Cities and the Environment (CATE)*, **1** (2008), Article 4.
- Collins, J. P., Kinzig, A., Grimm, N. B., *et al.* A new urban ecology. *American Scientist*, **88** (2000), 416–425.
- Niemela, J. Is there a need for urban ecology? *Urban Ecosystems*, **3** (1999), 57–65.
- Vitousek, P. M., Mooney, H. A., Lubchenco, J., and Melillio, J. M. Human domination of the earth's ecosystems. *Science*, **277** (1997), 494–499.

For Section 1.6

- McDonnell, M. J. and Pickett, S. T. A. Ecosystem structure and function along urban-rural gradients: an unexploited opportunity for ecology. *Ecology*, **71** (1990), 1232–1237.
- Pickett, S. T. A., Cadenasso, M. L., Grove, J. M., *et al.* Urban ecological systems: linking terrestrial ecological, physical, and socioeconomic components of metropolitan areas. *Annual Review of Ecology and Systematics*, **32** (2001), 127–157.
- Young, R. Interdisciplinary foundations of urban ecology. *Urban Ecosystems*, **12** (2009), 311–331.

Labs

A. Using the 'ruler' and 'add polygon' functions in Google Earth, make $1000\,m^2$ quadrats along urban–rural gradients of the city where you live. Begin in the center of the city, and make a new quadrat every 10 km (you can modify this scale according to the size of your city), moving out from the center to the north, south, east, and west. Once you have made five quadrats in each direction, zoom in on each quadrat separately and estimate the amount of area covered by the various habitat types (built, waste, green, and aquatic). Record these values, and plot how they change along the urban–rural gradient. Does your region have a clear gradient?

B. In the quadrats you built in **A**, using either streets, landmarks, or GPS, develop a sampling regime such as a transect across each quadrat or a number of random samples within each quadrat. Travel to each quadrat and record all of the organisms you encounter. If you don't know the official name, make one up but make sure to either get a good picture or a sample, such as a leaf from a plant or a single insect. Keep track of the approximate number you find of each. Try to categorize them as urban exploiters, adapters, and avoiders. As in **A**, plot the number of each type of organism on an urban–rural gradient. Describe the main problems you encountered.

C. Using a river or stream that passes through your city, sample aquatic invertebrates along an urban–rural gradient. Sample each site by holding small nets downstream as you kick along the river bottom (moving rocks, plants, and digging into the river bottom). Collect the organisms into sampling jars and identify them using a freshwater macroinvertebrate key. Look up the characteristics of each organism, and see how the community changes along the transect. If possible, record the upstream inputs (such as street runoff, point source inputs, farm runoff), as well as stream attributes (such as temperature, water flow, and amount of channeling) at each sampling location. Develop hypotheses about the main factors that control the stream community.

2 Urban accounting: metabolism, energy, and the ecological footprint

Cities play an increasingly important role in society, with over half of the population now living in urban areas for the first time in history. These increasingly large and demanding concentrations of people, as well as their associated artifacts, raise a whole series of questions about the effects of humans on the environment.

1. How do urban areas survive, with their dense populations, high demand for resources, and large outputs of wastes?
2. How can the ecological effects of cities be quantified?
3. How do those effects depend on the properties of the surrounding region?
4. Can the methods used to describe and quantify human effects be applied to other social organisms and ecosystem engineers?

This chapter introduces four approaches to quantifying urban resource use and its environmental consequences.

- **The urban metabolism** tracks the inputs and outputs of a city as if it were a single enormous organism. Just as a bird eats, drinks, and collects materials for its nest, cities receive inputs of food, water, materials, and energy. That same bird excretes wastes and sometimes succeeds in raising offspring. Cities too output a variety of waste products, and export manufactured, cultural, and biological products.
- **The urban energy budget** focuses on a single currency, *energy*, as the driver of urban life. Every aspect of the urban metabolism, whether it be the import of food and materials, construction of housing, or treatment of wastes, requires energy. How and where that energy is used and collected tells much about how a city functions and survives.
- **The ecological footprint** estimates the land (and sometimes ocean) area a city requires to harvest its inputs, treat its outputs, and perform its tasks. The land required for food and energy production, the land required to absorb and treat wastes, and the land on which houses and roads are built, can be summed together into a single number, the ecological footprint. The footprints of cities can be hundreds or even thousands of times larger than their political boundaries.
- **The ecosystem services** approach also quantifies the effects of urbanization in a single currency, but uses money instead of energy or land. The monetary value of a wetland is the cost of the water treatment plants that would be needed to replace it, and the value of a tree is the energy saved by its shade, shelter, and carbon uptake. Although all such accounting is incomplete and can only roughly capture the value

of more intangible factors like biodiversity, the total value of ecosystem services may exceed global economic production[106].

The way that cities are evaluated can depend as much on the way that we think of them as on the way that we account for their use and transformation of resources. There are many metaphors for the city[33], and here we present just five.

- **The city as a superorganism:** Although an ant colony or a beehive is made up of multiple individuals, the entire group acts in some ways like a single composite individual that eats, reproduces, and eventually dies. Within the city, parks can be thought of as the "lungs" and wetlands as the "kidneys." Cities consist not just of people, but of machines, pets, and structures. This conglomeration of energy-demanding and material-demanding entities is the urban superorganism, with its own metabolic processes, products, and effects on the environment.
- **The city as an ecological community:** This metaphor sees the city as less tightly integrated than a superorganism and more as a loosely knit ecological community, one characterized by the organisms that live there each with its own needs. This community has its own patterns of physical spread, succession through various stages of development, and resource recycling.
- **The city as a parasite:** Parasites make a living by taking the resources of their host, and depositing their wastes into the body of that host. Large concentrations of people can be viewed in the same way. Cities demand resources, whether food, water, clean air, or materials, from the surrounding area, and release their wastes into that same area.
- **The city as a cancer:** Somewhat like parasites, cancers take and use the resources of their hosts. But unlike parasites, cancers are not of another species, but are cells of the host itself. In this view, people are part of nature, but a part that has begun playing by its own rules[253]. Cancer has several *hallmarks*, including ignoring the body's growth regulation mechanisms and signals to die, recruiting blood vessels to bring oxygen and nutrients from the rest of the body, and spreading to new organs (metastasis)[242]. Cities have evaded "natural" controls on growth by importing food and energy, and by concentrating the political power needed to increase those imports. Cities create their own "circulatory systems" for water, nutrients, materials, and energy, and can quickly spread by establishing satellite communities with similar growth potential and resource demands.
- **The city as a patient:** Good health depends on both curing and preventing diseases. Just as a physician must decide how to treat and care for a patient in the face of uncertainty about the future and about how the complex human body will respond to different treatments, urban planners must think about how to solve and prevent problems. In the case of urban planning, conflicting goals, such as economic growth and quality of life for people and animals, must be balanced in the face of uncertainty and political pressures.

Obviously, these metaphors carry very different connotations. Few people relish the thought of being small parts of a parasite or cancer, while being part of a superorganism sounds at least somewhat heroic. More importantly, each metaphor focuses attention on different aspects of a city's interaction with its surroundings, either its needs, its wastes, or its products, and provides a framework for thinking about urban processes, problems, and opportunities.

2.1 The urban metabolism

Metabolism describes the processes by which an organism maintains life by obtaining inputs such as food, and transforming those inputs into structures, growth, reproduction, or wastes. Urban ecosystems have metabolic pathways of input, processing and output that can be analyzed much like those of a single organism. In this accounting, cities import food, water, materials, and energy; transform those inputs into new humans, buildings, and products; transport humans, materials, and wastes from place to place; and export a range of biological and non-biological wastes (Figure 2.1).

As societies have become more centralized, the extent of material inputs and outputs has increased greatly. Even without including water, a resident of a modern urban area imports roughly his or her own weight in materials every day. Much of this is stored

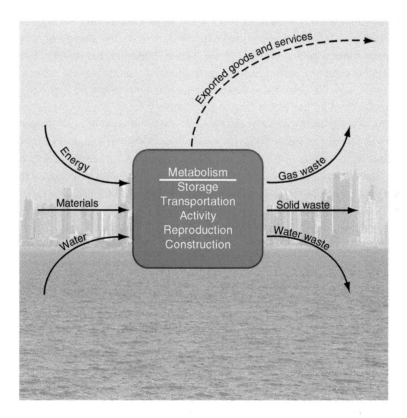

Figure 2.1 Urban inputs, processing, and outputs.

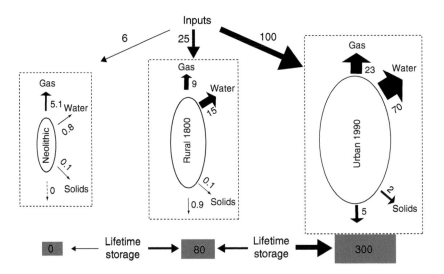

Figure 2.2 Annual imports and exports (in metric tons) of different materials in various societies (after Decker *et al.*, 2000).

energy in fossil fuels, quickly exported as gas after combustion. Urban residents generate their own body weight in solid waste in as little as one week[32]. In a lifetime, the difference between imports and exports ends up as the storage of roughly several thousand times a person's weight in the form of buildings and goods (Figure 2.2). The average resident of London adds 2.1 metric tons of materials to the urban environment each year, with the exact value depending on which materials are included[32].

The needs of an individual human are relatively small. A person eats approximately 250 kg of solid food per year, breathes in 300 kg of oxygen, and drinks 1200 kg of water, and outputs roughly 100 kg of solid waste, 500 kg of liquid waste, and 1000 kg of gaseous waste (about 60% as water vapor with most of the remainder as carbon dioxide). The additional inputs and outputs of a Neolithic individual, before the advent of agriculture, were due to solid fuels, primarily wood, used for heat, cooking, and protection (Figure 2.2). The modern urban environment demands inputs, outputs, and storage vastly exceeding those of its human occupants.

Food and water

Although people in cities consume roughly the same number of calories as those in non-urban areas, or even their Neolithic forebears, urban residents purchase food through stores and restaurants, resulting in a substantial quantity of unsold food being thrown away. The amount of food thrown away by urban residents or stores varies globally. For example, total solid waste in Bangkok is made up of less than 2% food refuse, although residents do discard approximately 20% of their food[159]. In Hong Kong, however, 30% of solid waste is food, and in cities such as Los Angeles and Mexico City, over 40% of

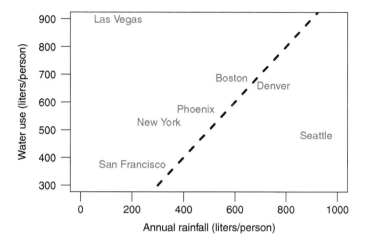

Figure 2.3 Water available from rainfall (L/person/yr falling on the entire metropolitan area) versus annual domestic per capita water use for seven selected cities in the United States (after Simmons *et al.*, 2011). Although Denver has lower precipitation than Boston, its population density is also lower. The dashed line indicates where water use is equal to rainfall.

solid waste is food refuse[121,402]. Each urban resident can import twice as much food as he or she consumes[604].

Urban residents, like most residents of developed countries, use large amounts of water. In the United States, domestic use is approximately 500 L per day, about 150 times that used for personal consumption. This value includes indoor and outdoor use around the home, but not the water required for manufacturing and energy generation, which can be up to five times as much as domestic consumption.

The challenges of collecting and treating rainwater means that essentially all water used is imported into the city or pumped from the ground. If all the rain falling on a city were captured for domestic use, leaving none for natural areas or runoff into streams, most large cities in the United States would have barely enough water to survive and some in drier areas could not survive at all (Figure 2.3).

The majority of domestic water is used outside the home, primarily for irrigating lawns and gardens[531]. Water usage is thus lower in more densely populated areas that have smaller yards (Figure 2.4a). Outdoor water use depends on temperature, increasing in hotter and generally drier areas (Figure 2.4b).

As is typical of urban areas, both reuse and recycling of water are rare. In fact, rainwater is often treated as a nuisance by urban water planners who rely on a water supply from beyond the urban ecosystem. Sewage, even when relatively clean, is directly exported to treatment plants and discharged downstream, although some cities are reusing some water in the form of *graywater* generated from household or other domestic use[539].

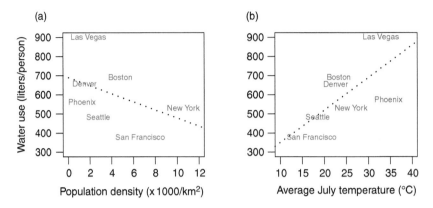

Figure 2.4 (a) Population density (people per square kilometer) versus domestic per capita water use, (b) Mean July temperature (in °C) versus domestic per capita water use. The dotted lines indicate the best fit line to the relationship (after Simmons *et al.*, 2011).

Materials and energy

The concentration of human artifacts in the built environment is perhaps the most striking aspect of a modern urban area. The materials needed to construct buildings and pavement are nearly all imported from outside the area. Humans now move more rock and sediment than all natural processes combined[373]. In a young, growing city, material inputs can exceed economically valuable exports by a factor of ten[61,299]. The remainder is stored within the built environment, or output as waste[121].

As cities grow, materials are imported from greater distances, and require more energy for transportation. Cities can thus violate the typical pattern of growth of an ecosystem, where production and *respiration* come to match when local resources have been depleted and biomass accumulation stops (Figure 2.5). Prior to fossil fuels, pre-modern cities stopped growing when importing resources became too expensive or slow[121].

In contrast, the population of the modern city of Hong Kong increased from just under 4 million to approximately 7 million people between 1971 and 1997, all packed into 120 km^2 of built-up land. During this period, per capita consumption of plastic, iron, and steel more than doubled, while inputs of more traditional materials such as glass and wood decreased (Table 2.1). People now use nearly as much plastic as food[604].

Many of these materials, such as those in packaging, are for daily use. Others are for building and road construction, the primary forms of urban material storage. New house construction consumes 450 kg of material per square meter of floor space[121]. In the United States, a relatively small 150 m^2 house can weigh as much as 60 000 kg, roughly 300 times as much as the family of four living within.

Although materials imported into an urban environment fulfill their intended roles, such as providing shelter, many imports come with unintended consequences as well. For example, inadvertent inputs of lead in water pipes or the heavy metal cadmium in floor liners can create local buildups of dangerous pollutants[61]. There is a rough

Table 2.1 Changes in material use in Hong Kong (after Warren-Rhodes, 2001)

Material	Per capita input in 1971 (kg/year)	Per capita input in 1997 (kg/year)	Change since 1971 (ratio)
Cement	330	510	1.5
Glass	25	19	0.8
Iron/steel	170	380	2.2
Paper	94	140	1.5
Plastics	63	180	2.9
Wood	170	110	0.6

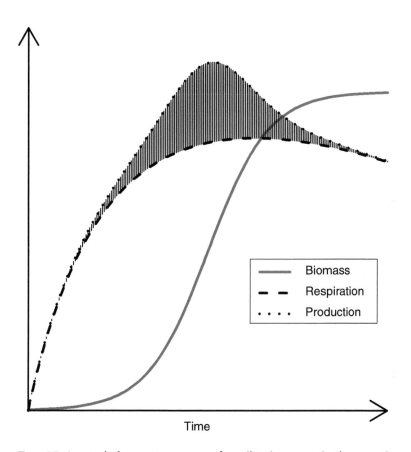

———— Biomass
— — Respiration
· · · · Production

Time

Figure 2.5 As a typical ecosystem recovers from disturbance, production exceeds respiration (the shaded region) leading to growth in biomass, which plateaus when local resources have been fully utilized (after Decker *et al.*, 2000).

negative relationship between the quantity of different materials used and their environmental impact[170]. Those used in large amounts, such as water, sand, and gravel, can be harvested from the environment with little transformation. Those used in small quantities, such as hazardous chemicals and pesticides, are novel and potentially damaging compounds (Figure 2.6).

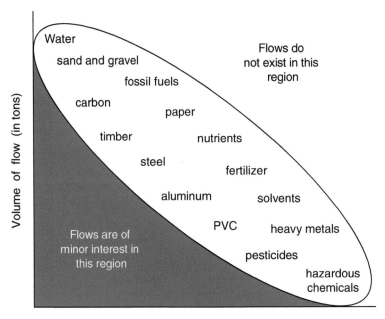

Figure 2.6 Schematic diagram of the environmental impact and quantities used of various material (after Fischer, 1999).

Energy is chief among these inputs (Section 2.2). Even in the Neolithic, the total weight of fuel imports exceeded that of food, and continues to do so even in this era of highly concentrated fossil fuels. As a city grows, the inputs of food, materials, and energy and the outputs of waste must be moved larger distances, increasing the energy needed to sustain the urban metabolism. In addition to moving resources and waste, people also need to move. The energy needs for transportation are now the largest sector of energy consumption in many large cities. In comparison, even athletes use barely half of their energy for movement.

Waste

Due to conservation of matter, all inputs that are not stored within the urban environment must be exported as solids, liquids, or gases. In comparison to other ecosystems, urban areas have substantially less recycling, which acts as a form of temporary storage. Imagine, for example, a city that imports 1 000 000 metric tons of water per day. If that water is only used once, the full 1 000 000 metric tons must be imported and exported each day. However, if that water were used twice, only 500 000 metric tons of new water would need to be imported each day, with the same reduced amount exported (Figure 2.7). Fully one-third of plastics and over one-half of glass, materials often used in packaging, are output as waste. Only a tiny fraction of iron, steel, and wood, materials

Table 2.2 Changes in material outputs in Hong Kong (after Warren-Rhodes, 2001)

Material	Per capita output in 1971 (kg/year)	Per capita output in 1997 (kg/year)	Change since 1971 (ratio)
Food	36	110	3.0
Glass	14	13	0.9
Iron/steel	6	13	2.1
Paper	64	91	1.4
Plastics	17	60	3.5
Wood	59	5	0.1

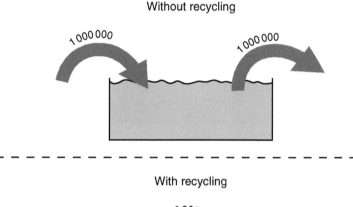

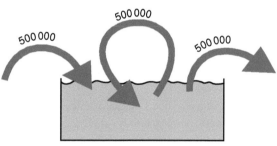

Figure 2.7 The effect of recycling on inputs and outputs of water.

used primarily in construction, are outputs, with the rest being stored in the urban environment (Table 2.2).

In most urban areas, solid waste is sent to landfills. But as landfills reach capacity, solid waste must be shipped further, thus increasing energy consumption and the area of land directly disturbed by a city. The resulting buildup of solid waste can create ecological, social, and economic problems. Recycling can reduce outputs, and cities with recycling do indeed see a reduction in solid waste storage[299]. Accumulation of waste in some large cities has created a new means of existence. In modern megacities, "rag pickers" make a living foraging in dumps and landfills, thus recycling wastes and reducing waste storage[121]. In addition to sites for recycling solid waste, landfills can

Table 2.3 Annual per capita inputs and outputs
of materials in London, in metric tons[32]

Substance	Mass
Energy inputs	1.8*
Material inputs	5.7
Food	0.93
Water inputs	120 000
Residential	60 000
Commercial/industrial	26 000
Leakage	34 000
Solid waste outputs	3.6
Residential	0.47
Commercial/industrial	1.08
Construction/demolition	2.05

*In the equivalent of metric tons of oil.

perform other services. For example, although large amounts of energy are invested in dealing with waste byproducts, landfills can be put to alternative uses such as methane production to restore some of that energy[121].

Conclusions

Like an individual organism, cities receive inputs of materials, water, energy, and food. Cities transform and store some of those inputs, and generate wastes in the process. Although they cover only 1–3% of the Earth's land area and house 50% of the population, cities command roughly 70% of CO_2 production, 60% of residential water usage, and 76% of industrial wood use[373].

The average resident of a city like London in a developed country mobilizes, moves, and transforms vast quantities of materials (Table 2.3). These materials make possible the concentration of people in cities with their flowering of cultural and economic products and opportunities. Researchers are now taking the next steps in understanding how the urban metabolism responds to human factors such as housing pattern, history, and economic development.

2.2   Urban energy budgets

All ecosystems require energy, but urban ecosystems are the most energy-demanding on Earth. Unlike materials, nutrients, and water that can in principle be reused indefinitely, all energy is eventually dissipated as heat. Energy used for locomotion, whether by an animal or a vehicle, cannot be reused or recycled back into a usable form. Energy used for growth or chemical reactions can be stored in chemical bonds, but each time that energy is used, some fraction is lost. Because nothing can move or grow without

Table 2.4 The basic units of energy and power

Symbol	Name	Definition	Conversion
J	joule	basic unit of energy	
kJ	kilojoule		1 kJ = 1000 J
W	watt	basic unit of power	1 W = 1 J/s
kcal	kilocalorie	unit for food energy	1 kcal = 4.185 kJ
kWh	kilowatt hour	alternative unit of energy	1 kWh = 3600 kJ

energy, quantifying energy inputs and usage provides a powerful way to summarize the metabolism of an ecosystem.

With the exception of the relatively few habitats supplied by geothermal heat or chemical energy from rocks, ecosystems receive their energy from the sun. The sun provides a small amount of direct heating for *ectotherms* (cold-blooded animals) and for plants, but most solar energy enters an ecosystem through photosynthesis. Plants and many algae use photosynthesis to transform solar energy, carbon dioxide, and water into sugars that store energy in chemical form. This is the energy available to the consumers that eat the plants, to consumers that eat the consumers, and to humans, in fossilized form as coal, oil, or natural gas. A small amount of energy can be imported into an ecosystem if prey move in, consumers or predators leave temporarily to harvest resources, or when water deposits energy-rich materials such as dead leaves or animals.

To compare different ecosystems, we must distinguish *energy* from *power*. Energy is the ability of a system to do work, such as moving objects or driving chemical reactions. A *joule* is the basic unit of energy, whereas power, often measured in joules per second or *watts*, describes the rate at which energy is used. For convenience, we report power in the familiar units of watts and energy in units of kilowatt hours or kWh (key conversion factors and definitions are given in Table 2.4).

As a basis of comparison, what is the wattage of an average human being who consumes 2000 kcal per day? Kilocalories can be converted into watts as follows.

$$2000\,\text{kcal} = 2000\,\text{kcal} \times 4.185\,\text{kJ/kcal} \approx 8400\,\text{kJ}$$

$$8400\,\text{kJ} = 8400\,\text{kJ} \times 1000\,\text{kJ/J} = 8\,400\,000\,\text{J}$$

$$1\,\text{day} = 60\,\text{s/min} \times 60\,\text{min/hour} \times 24\,\text{hour/day} = 86\,400\,\text{s}$$

$$2000\,\text{kcal/day} = \frac{8\,400\,000\,\text{J}}{86\,400\,\text{s}} \approx 100\,\text{J/s} = 100\,\text{W}.$$

Operating a single human being thus uses a bit less energy than two standard incandescent light bulbs (but about the same as seven compact fluorescent bulbs). During one day, this person's body uses

$$100\,\text{W} \times 24\,\text{hours} = 2.4\,\text{kWh}.$$

Residents of urban environments use vastly more energy than this to import, process, and export materials and wastes.

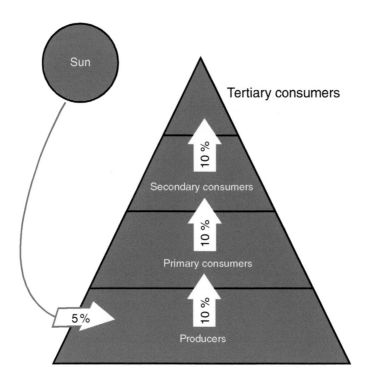

Figure 2.8 A typical ecosystem has less and less energy available as one moves from primary producers (plants) up through consumers (herbivores) and predators.

As a second standard for comparison, we can compute how much energy a typical solar-powered ecosystem uses. The sun provides about 160 W/m² averaged over the entire Earth, although this value is higher in regions closer to the equator and lower in regions close to the poles. Plants convert 5–10% of that energy into chemical bonds via photosynthesis, providing roughly 10–15 W/m² if the entire area were covered with photosynthetically active plants[626]. A consumer, such as a herbivore, can convert at most 10% of that energy into biomass. This low conversion efficiency means that the amount of energy available to organisms decreases as one moves from producers to higher and higher levels of consumers (the *energy pyramid*, Figure 2.8).

Non-urban ecosystems are constrained by other factors that limit photosynthesis, such as water and nutrient availability. Energy budgets range from 0.1 W/m² in deserts and the open ocean to as high as 4.0 W/m² for systems that receive substantial inputs of organic matter such as oyster beds, coral reefs, and some rainforests[409]. In comparison, high density urban ecosystems can use 100 to 300 W/m² (Figure 2.9). Although cities account for only 1–3% of the Earth's area, they have the potential to consume nearly as much energy as all non-urban ecosystems combined[3].

Urban energy use

Because urban energy consumption exceeds photosynthesis, energy must be imported. An urban ecosystem is therefore *heterotrophic*, meaning that it relies on solar energy

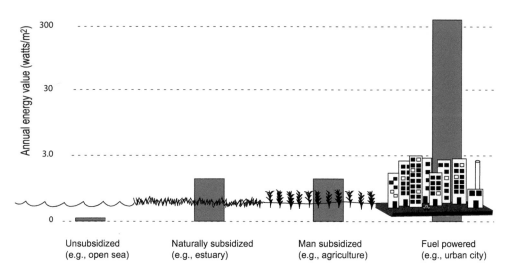

Figure 2.9   Energy used in a modern fuel-powered city can exceed that of a typical ecosystem by a factor of
100 or more (after Odum, 1975).

fixed by plants distant in space or time. In earlier eras, the majority of energy came
from wood or other biomass fuels harvested in or near the urban environment. The
majority of energy has come from fossil fuels since around 1900, and less than 10%
comes from biomass fuels today[536]. Fossil fuels concentrate solar energy that has been
stored for millions of years. With greater access to distant and ancient energy sources,
urban ecosystems can achieve higher population densities that require additional
energy-collecting infrastructure. This feedback creates the extreme energy demands
of modern cities.

Unlike most ecosystems, the urban ecosystem is not constrained by locally available solar energy; when more energy is needed, more fuel is imported. This breaks
the constraint that generates the typical ecosystem pyramid (Figure 2.8), creating an
inverted pyramid that is "top-heavy" with consumers, mainly in the form of human
beings (Figure 2.10). The unimportance of current primary productivity within an
urban environment is underlined by the fact that, with its many built surfaces and
reduced vegetation, the urban environment can have lower primary productivity than
the surrounding area[274].

Most imported energy is directly available only to humans. Non-human urban organisms still depend on primary productivity for much of their energy. The built portions of
the urban environment support essentially no photosynthesis, while remnant patches of
vegetation can be highly productive due to their more consistent supply of resources and
reduced temperature fluctuations[527]. For example, a roughly 2% increase in urban land
cover led to only a 0.35% decrease in primary productivity in the relatively moist and
fertile southeastern United States. Urban animals therefore experience a highly fragmented energy landscape, that intersperses areas of low and high energy availability.

Just as urban ecosystems use up to 100 times as much energy per unit area as the average non-urban ecosystem, the typical resident of an urban environment in a developed

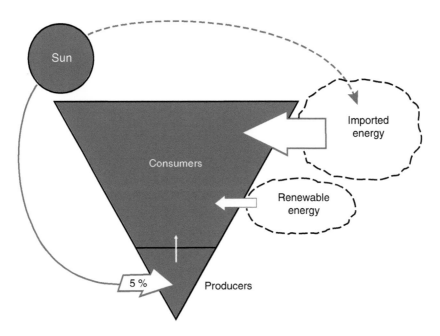

Figure 2.10 In an urban ecosystem, the huge mass of consumers is supported not by local primary production but by imported energy.

country uses 100 times the energy required to sustain a single individual, or approximately 10 000 W. This is 40 times more energy than an individual in a hunter-gatherer society[121]. This additional energy runs the urban metabolism: creating and moving materials, water, food, waste, and energy, and maintaining the built environment. The materials used to create the built environment come with associated energy costs, including production, transportation, and construction. Production of 1 kg of cement, glass, or steel requires 1.63, 7.17, or 11.67 kWh, respectively[589]. It then takes approximately 0.03 kWh to transport 1 kg of these materials for 100 km[589]. Constructing 1 m^2 of a typical building requires approximately 1600 kWh[121], enough energy to run an adult human being for nearly 2 years.

Many factors determine which cities consume the most energy. Cities with more seasonality consume more energy per capita, with hot cities using energy to stay cool and cold cities using energy to stay warm[299]. Population and demographic traits of a city also affect energy use. More densely populated cities require less energy intensive transport, and cities with more automobiles per person use more energy for transportation[299] (Figure 2.11). Although this trend holds between cities within a region, different regions vary in energy use according to many other characteristics. For example, cities with lower per capita income use less energy[2].

Over recent decades, the number of homes in North America has increased faster than the population size, meaning that there are fewer people per household, leading to increased per capita fuel use and land conversion[333]. Increases in efficiency, however, have balanced these changes, producing little change in average per capita residential

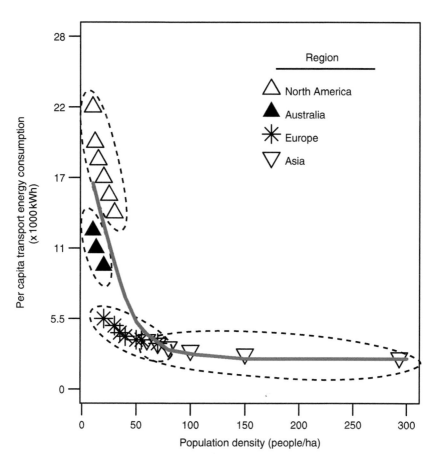

Figure 2.11 Transportation energy use is generally lower in more densely populated cities (after Kennedy *et al.*, 2007).

energy consumption since 1980[260]. Urban sprawl, or dispersed lower density exurban development, increases transportation and per capita carbon emissions[157,221]. However, people living in more densely populated cities partially compensate through increased air travel[260].

A single hamburger from a fast-food restaurant, without including the energy put into machinery, buildings, packaging, waste treatment, human labor, transport from shop to consumer residence, or solar energy to get the whole process started, requires between 2.2 and 5.6 kWh of energy to produce, equivalent to the energy needed to run up to 50 human beings for 1 hour. The large range in this energy estimate arises from differences in transport method, refrigeration requirements, and lettuce growing practices[79].

Apples imported into Great Britain demand similar quantities of energy. Imported apples have been increasingly filling the British market since 1950 (Figure 2.12). These apples may be shipped from relatively nearby France or halfway around the planet from New Zealand. It takes approximately 0.75 kWh to import 1.0 kg of apples to British

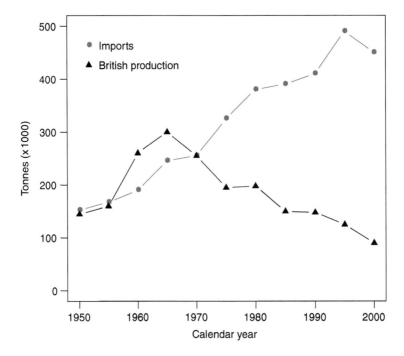

Figure 2.12 British apple production and imports during the second half of the twentieth century (after Jones, 2002).

shops, while the same kilogram of locally produced apples requires approximately 0.025 kWh [285].

As urban residents become more affluent their diets become more energy intensive. For example, in Sweden the energy required to feed one person ranges from 1400 to 5500 kWh annually. Low values result from diets based on locally grown foods consumed in season, and high values reflect a diet rich in meat and imported foods. Local fruits and vegetables require considerably less energy to produce, but do not provide as much energy per kilogram as meat [79].

Conclusions

Urban ecosystems demand huge quantities of energy, far exceeding that available locally. In fact, energy use in the United States exceeds the net primary productivity of the entire country by a factor of two [612]. The fossil fuels needed to run the urban metabolism come primarily from distant sources. The materials that supply the urban infrastructure and the food that feeds urban residents also come from afar, requiring even greater amounts of energy for production, transport, and delivery. The unprecedented concentration of energy-subsidized imports creates an extreme imbalance between consumption and production, comparable only to the most productive oyster beds or coral reefs.

Although accounting for energy provides perhaps the starkest illustration of the intensity of the urban ecosystem, it merely sets the foundation for the wide range of ecological effects of urbanization. Imported energy underlies the transformation of ecosystem processes and ecological communities that form the focus of this book.

2.3 The urban ecological footprint

The urban metabolism describes the full range of inputs and outputs of an urban area, but does not facilitate comparison of different cities or assess the capacity of the local ecosystem to support a city. The *ecological footprint*, the total area of productive land needed to sustain a population, creates a convenient measure to make these comparisons and assessments[599].

Cities, by definition, have a sufficiently high population density over a sufficiently large area to require substantial land modification and extensive infrastructure to import and export goods and wastes[346]. Historically, cities only arose where resources could be efficiently imported to feed and supply the population (thus the famous Roman roads), particularly along rivers or where trade routes met.

The ecological footprint quantifies the amount of land area needed to create and move the inputs of food, water, energy, and materials that an urban area uses, as well as the land needed to treat and transport the outputs of waste and pollution that it produces. As such, the ecological footprint accounts for two of the major themes of urban ecology, habitat modification, and increased inputs and outputs. The ecological footprint can also trace the land used to provide the inputs and to process the outputs, whether that land is in the more traditional "hinterlands" outside the city, or on the opposite side of the globe (the "distant other")[475].

Elements of the footprint

Although there are several approaches to computing the footprint, all begin by categorizing basic human activities and land use types (Table 2.5, Figure 2.13). Activities

Table 2.5 Five activities and six land use types used to calculate the ecological footprint. "High" and "Low" indicate relative level of use by each activity; for example, agricultural land is used primarily for food production and secondarily to produce goods and services (based on Lewan and Simons, 2001)

Land type	Food	Housing	Transportation	Goods	Waste
Agricultural	High			Low	
Pasture	High			High	
Forest		Low		High	
Built-up/degraded		High	High	Low	Low
Energy	Low	Low	High	High	Low
Water	High		Low		Low

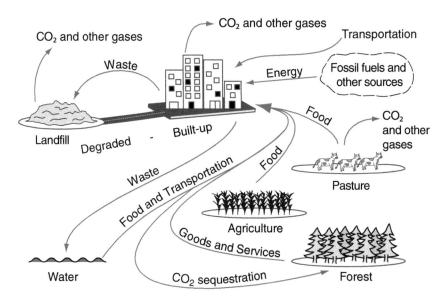

Figure 2.13 The activities and land use types involved in calculating the ecological footprint.

that directly or indirectly use land can be broken into five categories: (1) Food production, (2) housing and other structures, (3) transportation, (4) goods and services, and (5) waste. These activities require six different types of land.

- **Agricultural land** grows crops that provide food for humans and domesticated animals, along with some products used for goods and services, such as building materials.
- **Pasture** raises livestock for meat and dairy production as well as products like wool and leather.
- **Forests** grow wood used for construction, paper, and other goods.
- **Built-up or degraded land** is highly modified and largely unavailable to other organisms. This land is taken up by buildings for housing and production of goods, roads for transportation and delivery of goods and services, or land used for mining and waste disposal.
- **Energy land** can be thought of in two ways. First, it can describe the land needed to absorb the carbon dioxide generated by fossil fuel use. Second, it can describe the land needed to produce sufficient biomass fuels like wood to replace the energy used by fossil fuels.
- **Water** provides food and transportation corridors, and receives waste outputs.

Calculation of the footprint

The quantities summarized by the urban metabolism can be used to compute the ecological footprint. The 7.4 million residents of London have a footprint roughly 300 times the area of Greater London (Table 2.6). The materials used in the largest quantities,

Table 2.6 Main components of the ecological footprint for residents of
London, with their largest elements [32]

Component	Hectares per person	Percentage of total or subtotal
Energy	0.69	10
Gas	0.38	55
Electricity	0.31	45
Materials and waste	3.05	44
Paper and plastic	1.66	54
Food	2.80	40
Meat	0.78	28
Pet food	0.42	15
Milk	0.33	12
Transport	0.34	5
Cars	0.29	84
Water	0.02	0.3
Built land	0.05	0.7
Total	6.95	100

sand, gravel, clay, cement, and other building materials, have a smaller overall footprint than materials used in much smaller quantities, such as paper, plastic, and manufactured goods (Figure 2.6).

The ecological footprint for consumption of wood, paper, energy, and food by the 29 largest cities in the Baltic region is 200 times greater than the area of the cities themselves [174]. Each $1 km^2$ of city requires $18 km^2$ of forests, $50 km^2$ of agricultural land, and $133 km^2$ of marine area due to the high demand for seafood in this area and the low average productivity of marine systems (Figure 2.14).

Wastes, although more difficult to quantify, can create an even larger footprint. The study that analyzed the Baltic region, for example, was limited to the area needed to absorb nitrogen, phosphorus from human waste, and carbon dioxide produced by fossil fuel combustion. The region has approximately enough wetlands to handle the nitrogen ($30–75 km^2$ per km^2 of city), and more than enough agricultural land for the phosphorus (about $11–30 km^2$ per km^2 of city). Sequestration of carbon dioxide, removal from the atmosphere, and storage in living tissue would require all of the existing inland waterways (about $48 km^2$ per km^2 of city) and more than the existing area of forests (from 354 to $874 km^2$ per km^2 of city), even without considering the other wastes created by fossil fuel combustion [588]. The waste assimilation footprint is thus at least twice as large as that for consumption. In combination, these footprints are approximately equal to the area of the entire geographic region encompassing the 29 cities.

Rather than computing the area needed to sequester carbon as the energy land component of the ecological footprint, an alternative method computes the area required to grow the amount of biomass fuels needed to create the energy in the first place. The average primary productivity on Earth is approximately 15 kg of carbon per day per hectare. Each urban resident in the Baltic region produces about 10 kg of carbon dioxide per day. At an average density of 100 people per hectare, the production of carbon

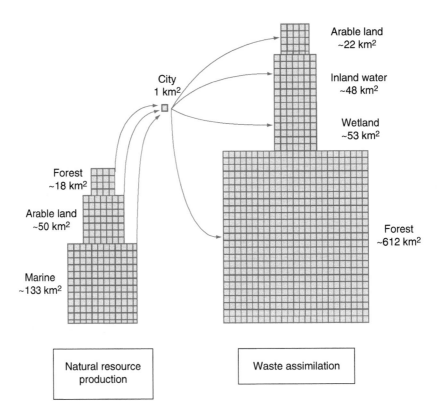

Figure 2.14 The components of the ecological footprint for the Baltic states (after Folke, 1997).

dioxide by humans exceeds the primary productivity by a factor of about 60. The much larger areas found using the carbon sequestration method result in part from the low productivity of coniferous forests in this region. Both calculations assume a young growing forest that adds biomass and absorbs carbon much faster than a mature forest.

Limitations of the footprint

There have been many criticisms of both the method of calculation and the interpretation of ecological footprints. The detailed calculation of a footprint depends on the location, the amounts and types of consumption, and the region of origin of materials and food. Much of this information can be difficult to acquire, creating practical challenges for calculating the footprint. Beyond this challenge, some criticisms raise important questions about urban ecology itself, and we highlight those here.

First, concentrating on the ecological footprints of cities can create a negative view of urban life. Although urban areas can indeed have huge footprints that stretch far beyond their physical boundaries, the footprint per individual in a city is often smaller than that in a non-urban area. The concentration of infrastructure for transportation and delivery of goods and services that characterizes cities can make them substantially more efficient than more diffusely populated non-urban areas. Per capita resource use is in fact often lowest in older cities that might seem to have the most dilapidated infrastructure[295].

Second, it is fundamentally difficult to fully account for the complexity of the urban metabolism by placing all effects in the single currency of land area. For example, some calculations include *biodiversity land*, preserved to maintain native species[88]. But what fraction of land is needed to maintain a suitable number of species, where should that land be, and, perhaps most importantly, how are preservation decisions made? Values such as biodiversity and other aspects of quality of life, such as clean water or pleasant views, are difficult to include in a footprint analysis. Similarly, urban water demand places stresses on the environment that are difficult to include in a footprint[376]. Many forms of waste create accounting difficulties. The study of the Baltic region accounted for nitrogen by the area of wetlands needed for processing, but did not include the effects of nitrogen accumulation within the city or the possible effects of distant pollution such as those created by acid rain. Cities also generate substantial heat, both through combustion and retention of solar energy, leading to alterations in climate that do not take up land area.

Third, accounting for land use by adding up different types of land neglects the fact that land can simultaneously serve different purposes. Agricultural and pasture land, for example, can support substantial biodiversity and absorb carbon or other wastes. In addition, the diverse urban landscape itself supports appreciable, if somewhat unusual, biodiversity.

Fourth, the ecological footprint does not include the many benefits of cities. People move to cities for access to a wide variety of products from around the world. Although producing and transporting these goods does have real ecological costs, there can be equally real economic benefits to the source region, which can translate into ecological benefits if managed appropriately[376]. As any visitor to New York or London knows, urban inhabitants have access to the cultural resources that only cities can offer. In other words, cities may be net consumers of the products of nature, but are net producers of human economic, social, and cultural artifacts[477]. In fact, per capita intellectual productivity is higher in large cities, even as per capita resource use is lower[33].

The ecological footprint alone does not predict ecological consequences. Sometime during the 1980s, the combined ecological footprint of all the people on Earth surpassed the total area of the planet. However, unlike a balloon that pops when its capacity is exceeded, Earth's ecosystems have not collapsed. There are several resolutions of this apparent paradox. Some argue that humans are living in debt, and that the ecological costs of exceeding capacity are beginning to be seen in the form of climate change, accelerated extinctions, and buildup of wastes in regions distant from human occupation. Others argue that the ecological footprint assumes fixed resources by ignoring the human capacity to expand the resource base. Over the last century, the efficiency of energy use has more than doubled[536]. Agricultural production per hectare has increased by as much as six-fold[612], due in part to higher inputs of nutrients and energy. Continuing innovations could effectively expand the size of the planet relative to the human ecological footprint. This book does not claim to resolve these debates, but only to help understand the ecological effects of consumption, waste, and habitat modification.

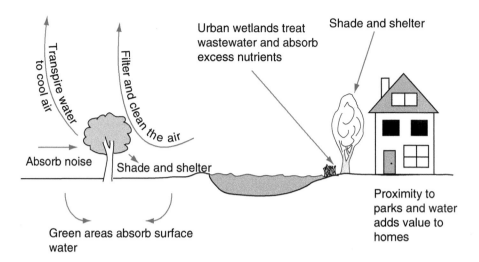

Figure 2.15 Some ecosystem services provided by urban habitats in Stockholm, Sweden (after Bolund and Hunhammar, 1999).

Ecosystem services

The single "currency" most popular among economists is, of course, money. *Ecosystem services*, the economic value generated by elements of the natural environment, break into three broad categories: provisioning of food and water, cultural, and regulatory (such as climate and pollution control).

Stockholm illustrates some of the opportunities and challenges of this approach[41]. Urban habitats such as street trees, lawns, parks, urban forests, wetlands, lakes, and streams provide at least the following six types of ecosystem services (Figure 2.15).

- **Air filtering:** One hectare of mixed forest removes about 15 metric tons of particulates, while spruce forests can remove up to 45 metric tons. Stockholm is a fairly heavily forested city, with up to 10% of the area composed of forest land.
- **Micro-climate regulation:** In this region, a large tree transpires 450 L of water per day, consuming up to 300 kWh of energy in the process and cooling the air. Combined with the summer benefits of shade and the winter benefits of shelter from wind, three trees per building lot may save $50–90 per year. Similarly, lakes and streams absorb energy and cool surrounding areas.
- **Noise reduction:** Noise stress can create psychological stress and may reduce economic productivity[235]. Although lawns, trees, and shrubs are known to absorb noise, the economic benefits have not been quantified. Engineering alternatives, such as reducing noise by building noise walls along highways or equipping buildings with heavily insulated windows, tend to be costly.
- **Rainwater drainage:** Vegetated areas absorb far more water than impermeable surfaces like parking lots, and can reduce the amount of water that runs off into storm sewers and streams by a factor of six. The economic value of the resulting reduction in erosion and flooding is difficult to quantify.

- **Sewage treatment:** Wetlands retain up to 96% of nitrogen and 97% of phosphorus, and can be less costly than building and operating sewage treatment plants.
- **Recreation/culture:** Green habitats reduce stress, encourage exercise, and promote better health (Section 5.1), and people pay a substantial premium to live near parks and water.

In five cities across the United Kingdom, services such as carbon sequestration, reduction in urban water runoff, reduction of maximum temperature, and maintenance of biodiversity were lower in areas with high building density[575]. Less heavily built land provides substantial services, indicating that moderately urbanized areas do double duty as places to live and as part of the functioning ecosystem, which calls into doubt accounting for all built land as part of the ecological footprint. In many ways, urban mixed use areas preserve more ecosystem functioning and services than lands under intensive agricultural cultivation[203].

Placing these ecosystem services into the context of the whole urban ecosystem provides further perspective[433]. The ability of urban trees to absorb carbon dioxide is limited, and is less than 1% of the total generated in Los Angeles. The ability of trees to capture particulates is restricted to their surfaces, which are not substantially more effective than non-living surfaces like walls[433]. The ability of trees to reduce urban ozone by cooling the urban climate might well be offset by their production of volatile organic compounds (Section 3.4). Accounting for services' needs thus should also include *ecosystem disservices* such as emissions, allergies, and the financial and ecological costs of maintenance. Even the well-established cooling effects of trees in dry climates depend on substantial watering, which in turn requires energy and may deplete water from other locations.

Conclusions

The ecological footprint accounts for the many effects a city has on the environment by computing the land area required to sustain a city's existence. Although there are many challenges associated with this calculation, the basic ecological principle that the intense urban metabolism requires a substantial land area is undeniable. The ecological footprint estimates just how large this area is.

This accounting has many parallels with the energy approach (Section 2.2). In the most densely occupied cities, energy use is approximately 100 times that of the surrounding ecosystem. Simply generating that energy accounts for a substantial fraction of the ecological footprint.

Specifying the precise land or water appropriated as part of the footprint can be more difficult. The greenhouse gases associated with automobile use can be generated in distant steel plants and oil refineries, and the ecological costs of eating beef may be realized as land clearing on the other side of a continent[325].

Urban areas command vast amounts of materials and energy, and consequently transform the land that provides them. The urban metabolism, energy accounting, and the ecological footprint all provide useful summaries, but without evaluating the complex ecological effects that urban areas create. Understanding these effects, ranging from nutrient loading, local climate change, altered species interactions, novel animal behaviors, and even evolutionary change, is the main focus of the remainder of this book.

2.4   Comparison with other social organisms

Any large animal that lives in social groups will demand large quantities of materials and food. All ecosystem engineers enhance their impact by using materials to reconstruct their environments[169]. Humans stand out through the complexity of society and the extent of engineering, leading to more extreme and extended demands on the environment. This section compares humans with other animals, focusing in detail on comparing and contrasting ant colonies with human cities.

Even when they are not social, large animals can profoundly alter their environments. Some, such as moose, are sufficiently energy-demanding to consume a substantial fraction of their favorite plants, giving a competitive edge to those plants they like less[269]. The largest living land animal, the elephant, rips up entire trees and shrubs, which can change the frequency of fires, alter the food supply for other organisms, and damage soils and plants in riparian zones sufficiently to change the movement of nutrients[395]. The addition of social behavior, as in the elephant, accentuates and concentrates these effects.

Humans further extend these effects through their high population density. For their typical energy usage, a population of carnivores of approximately the size of human beings would have a density of about 0.001 per hectare, and similar-sized herbivores would be only 10 times as dense[612], or 0.01 people per hectare. These values are hundreds of times below those of cities, and indeed less than the population of humans if spread evenly over the entire land area of the Earth (Section 1.2).

Applying urban accounting to an ant colony

Ants obviously differ profoundly from humans in their size and mental capacity, but they are similar in their extremely social behavior, their nearly worldwide distribution, and their wide range of effects on ecology. On land, ants live everywhere except the poles and a few locations with very limited sunshine[603]. Fossils indicate that the morphology of ants has remained largely unchanged for the last 30 million years. The key innovation that made them into a worldwide success was a broadening of their diet from predation and scavenging to many forms of food-gathering including seed-eating, group hunting, and even versions of farming and ranching. Their flexible and social lifestyle allows the various species of ants to create many of the changes associated with human cities. Indeed, some ant species are most successful in urban environments[378].

Housing

Like humans, ants structurally modify the space they live in. Ant hills are familiar as sites covered with the stones and soil excavated during the building process. Such mounds can cover up to 10% of the surrounding area, and play many of the same roles as human homes, including defense, temperature regulation, and water drainage[146]. Equally impressive are the large cleared areas created by the seed harvester ants in the genus *Pogonomyrmex*, which can cover up to 6 m^2 for a single nest.

Not all ants live in the ground. Tropical ants in the genus *Azteca* have been carefully studied because of their mutualistic relationship with trees in the genus *Cecropia*, from which the ants receive a source of nutrients and a place to live in return for protecting the trees from herbivores. As part of this defense, an *Azteca* colony often clears a large area around its tree, mimicking the characteristically reduced vegetation of the built environment.

Some ants protect their territory against intrusion by other ants, and even place "signs" in the form of chemical markings that in effect say "no trespassing". This can be thought of as a form of private property, albeit not enforced by the police as in humans. These defended regions alter the spatial distribution of ant colonies, creating an even distribution of homes that more resembles a suburban neighborhood than a densely packed city. Other ants produce herbicides, such as formic acid, to remove unwanted plants growing near their home tree, producing a plant monoculture as extreme as some agricultural habitats[182].

Goods

The seed harvester ants, along with other desert ants, not only build large mounds and clear large areas around them, but import gravel, charcoal, and stones to cover their mounds[261]. The purpose of these objects, many of which are dark in color, remains uncertain but has been hypothesized to provide a form of temperature regulation. In addition to importing building materials, many ants also import their food in the form of seeds. The combination of seed imports and soil modification near the nest can lead to a remarkably different flora growing in the vicinity of an ant nest than in the surrounding area.

Transport

Some ants, including seed harvesters and leaf-cutter ants in the genera *Atta* and *Acromyrmex*, build systems of trails (Figure 2.16). These areas cleared of vegetation can extend for tens or even hundreds of meters, and thus tens of thousands of times the length of an individual ant. This trail system can cover a full hectare, making it comparable in area to the ecological footprint of a person[262]. Other ant species make extensive tunnel systems that require moving huge quantities of soil[146].

Food

Like human cities, most ant colonies exhibit *central place foraging*, meaning that individuals live at a central location and concentrate food from a wide area. The need to do so favors the development of innovative food-gathering strategies. Some ants, like the trail-building leaf-cutters, are farmers that use the leaves they collect to grow a co-evolved fungus that serves as their food (Figure 2.16). These ants can collect over 15% of new leaf production in tropical forests[261]. They constantly maintain their fungus

Figure 2.16 The farmer and ecosystem engineer *Atta* or leaf-cutter ant.

Figure 2.17 Ants tending aphids for honeydew.

gardens to remove any unwanted "weeds," and even use their own feces as fertilizer. Other ants maintain food stores above ground by "ranching" aphids and other related species of sap-feeding Hemiptera. Ants clean these insects and protect them from predators in return for access to the carbohydrate-rich honeydew that they excrete (Figure 2.17).

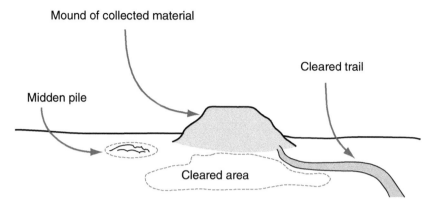

Figure 2.18 A nest mound and environs for *Pogonomyrmex*, the seed-harvester ant.

Waste

As with humans, the concentration of individuals and resources at a central location leads to a build up of waste. The seed-harvester ants have a well-defined midden (Figure 2.18), or solid waste trash heap, which has little live vegetation but can provide resources for future plant generations[222].

The leaf-cutter ants have a complex system of waste removal from their fungal gardens. Most species sequester potentially infected material in special chambers within the nest that can hold as much as 500 kg of waste. Some species remove the waste to an external dump. Dump workers are carefully segregated from other workers, suffer high mortality, and are selected from the oldest workers. These ants show a strong aversion to their own waste, which can be used as a deterrent to keep other ants from attacking a garden[262].

Water

The movement of water is altered by bare areas around nests and by the movement of soil within nests. Many ants are intolerant of flooding and create modifications, particularly of the nest structure, to quickly disperse water and reduce this danger.

Ecological effects of ants

The changes that an ant colony creates could, in principle, be combined into a single number like the ecological footprint or a detailed analysis of energy flow. Rather than attempting that calculation, we instead highlight a few ecological effects created by these insect societies.

Soil

As primarily soil-dwelling organisms, ants have a substantial effect on soil structure and fertility. In fact, ants turn more soil than earthworms, creating the air pockets needed for plant roots to grow[603]. A colony of several million leaf-cutter ants can excavate as much as 8 m^3 of soil weighing many tons.

Habitat modification

Cleared areas around ant colonies share similarities with the urban built environment. The lack of plants leads to the buildup of nutrients. The edges of cleared areas may, like roadsides, experience increased fertility, sometimes enough to compensate for the missing biomass within the cleared areas[352]. In other spots, particularly in the tropics, ants trim plant roots near the nest, leading to nutrient buildup and eventual leaching into deeper soil.

Biodiversity effects

Throughout the world, several ant species have become highly invasive. The Argentine ant *Linepithema humile*, a small ant native to South America, has invaded many continents. In some parts of North America, these invasive ants eliminate almost all native species of ant[264]. In Australia, the big-headed ant *Pheidole megacephala* reduces populations of many insects, but, rather like humans, increases local cockroach populations[258]. In addition to their effects on other insects, some ants promote the establishment of invasive plant species, usually accidentally, by moving their seeds into new habitats. Like humans planting gardens, the seeds moved by ants can modify the local plant species to match those that they prefer.

Invasive species can have traits unknown to ants in their introduced ranges. For example, big-headed ants have such severe effects on native ants and other insects in part because they live at extremely high densities, exceeding the biomass of the native ants they displace by as much as a factor of ten. This high density is made possible due to their ranching of aphids, and perhaps even more so by changes in their social structure. Several of the "tramp" ants that have invaded many continents, including the Argentine ant and the big-headed ant, may be *unicolonial*. In these species, ants from distant nests show little hostility when they meet. Removing intraspecific competition may increase the efficiency with which these ants can collect resources and improve their ability to aggressively displace native species.

Conclusions

The ecological effects of ecosystem engineers depend on six main factors[286] (Table 2.7). Human cities concentrate large numbers of individuals, each with a metabolism that greatly exceeds his or her individual biological needs for food, water, and materials. Cities persist for long periods of time, changing the physical structure of the land

Table 2.7 The six factors determining the ecological effects of ecosystem engineers (after Jones, 2004)

1. Life-time per capita resource use,
2. Number and type of resource flows modified,
3. Population density,
4. Spatial distribution of population, whether clustered or more evenly dispersed,
5. Duration of occupation of site,
6. Durability of constructs.

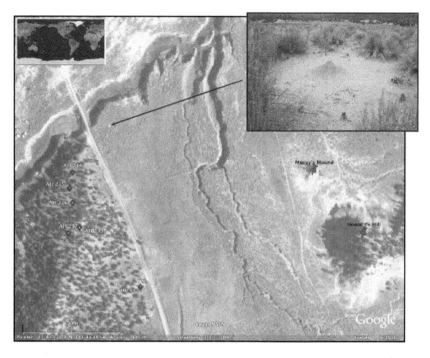

Figure 2.19 The cleared areas around colonies of the ecosystem engineer *Pogonomyrmex* or seed-harvester ant are visible from space (photo courtesy of Dennis Bramble).

and water with long-lived structures like buildings, roads, and canals. The most organized of the ant societies are similar, creating long-lived societies with individual ants living at extremely high densities and altering a wide range of ecosystem processes. Some colonies of the seed harvester ant *Pogonomyrmex* are visible from satellite, and persist for as much as 50 years (Figure 2.19). These persisting structures, for both humans and ants, satisfy goals thought of as intentional in humans and as the result of evolution in ants: defense, reproduction, and efficiency. The unintended effects, however, can extend far beyond these goals and often beyond the boundaries of the city or colony. Indeed, one might say that ants, like humans, "act locally and affect globally."

As with the ecological footprint, accounting for these effects must acknowledge that ants do not "remove" land, even that land they clear of plants. Life of many sorts continues below ground, and the nutrients and water from that area can benefit nearby plants. Eventually, ant colonies die and the ecosystem regrows, although the effects may persist for decades. The changes that ants make to an area are complex; they benefit some plants or insects while they harm others. A high density of ants can lead to a more variable landscape and either higher or lower biodiversity, just as in human cities.

For all of their similarities, the scope, permanence and global reach of humans far exceeds that of ants. Humans perpetuate and accentuate their effects through a unique ability to accumulate knowledge and technology. The great innovations, fire, language, and agriculture, which are all quite recent from an evolutionary perspective, provide the foundation upon which human civilization developed, and upon which current urban ecosystems continue to grow[476].

2.5   Questions and readings

Discussion questions

For Chapter 2

1. Which metaphor best fits the city you live in? Would it be the same for other cities you have visited? Why?

2. Do the answers to Question 1 change the way that you would conduct an urban ecology study, from the hypothesis, to methods, to conclusions?

3. List five specific aspects of the city you live in that associate it with each of the metaphors in this section. Some items in your list can be used more than once, but try to come up with as many as you can.

4. Some have proposed the additional metaphor of a city as a crime scene. How does this compare with the other metaphors? What types of questions does it promote?

5. Is there some other metaphor you would propose for a city? Is the exercise of creating metaphors useful or is it a distraction from the real questions?

For Section 2.1

1. Why has centralization led to more imports, exports, and storage of energy and materials than in pre-urban societies? What effects does this import/export process have on urban inhabitants?

2. Why do you think recycling of materials and water is reduced in urban areas? What effects does this have outside the city?

3. How are cities able to maintain almost indeterminate growth? What do you think are the ecological effects, both in and outside the city, of this relatively recent phenomenon?

4. How would you design a study to test your hypotheses regarding Question 3?

For Section 2.2

1. How are cities able to achieve such high densities of people?

2. What factors contribute to urban ecosystems being so energy demanding? Which of these factors is most prominent in your location?

3. How does this energy input affect the local ecology (physically and biologically) of your area?

4. What are the possible implications for your local ecology were new energy sources (renewable or non-renewable) to become available?

For Section 2.3

1. How does your ecological footprint relate to and/or affect your local ecology? Does this change if you include ecosystem services in your area?

2. What are some of the difficulties with using ecological footprints to compare different cities? How would you correct for these problems?

3. Read the paper by Pataki *et al.* (2011) and outline the ecosystem services and disservices associated with trees in your neighborhood.

For Section 2.4

1. From an engineered-ecosystem perspective, how are human cities and ant colonies similar, and how are they different? What factors promote similarities between them, and what factors constrain each from becoming more like the other?

2. How do these two engineered ecosystems differ in their effects on both local and global ecological processes?

3. Although ants and humans both engineer their surroundings to fit their needs, some ant species are more adept than others at living in human cities. Why do you think that is?

4. Does the reduced conflict between nests in unicolonial ants in any way parallel the reduced violence in many modern human societies?

5. Which of the six factors in Table 2.7 most clearly differentiate humans from ants? How about humans from elephants?

Exercises

For Section 2.1

1. Figure 2.7 shows that water imports are reduced by 50% when 50% of water is recycled.

   (a) Is it true that water use is reduced by 75% when 75% of water is recycled?
   (b) Redraw the figure using this percentage.
   (c) Work out the values for input, output, and recycling when a fraction p of water is recycled.
   (d) How many times on average is water reused in each case? What problems might this create?

2. Reuse reduces inputs and outputs. Does using materials for a longer time have the same effect?

   (a) Suppose a campus requires 100 buildings, each of which weighs 1000 tons. If these buildings were built over a period of 20 years, how much material would be imported each year for new construction?
   (b) If each building lasts 20 years, how much material would be imported during each of the 20 years after completion of construction? Why would this amount remain the same thereafter?

(c) Now suppose each building lasts 40 years. How much material would be imported during each of the 40 years after completion of construction? What is the average amount?

(d) Work out the imports during and after the period of construction if buildings last only 10 years. What is the average amount?

(e) Is the average amount of material imported inversely proportional to how long the buildings last? In what ways is this similar to or different from the results on recycling?

3. Figure 2.5 shows the typical pattern of biomass growth in an ecosystem. We can work out some numbers to see what underlies this process. Suppose that biomass starts out at 100 (in arbitrary units that you can think of as kg). Each year, production is 20% of biomass, respiration is 5% of biomass, and 90% of existing biomass survives.

(a) Total biomass in the next year is surviving biomass plus production minus respiration. How much biomass is there after one year?

(b) Continue with these rules for 10 years and graph the results (they should not follow the pattern in the figure).

(c) This simple model leaves out one key factor, the depletion of local resources. One way to include this is to reduce production as biomass gets large. Suppose that production is $20(1 - 0.001B)\%$ where B represents current biomass. What is production in the first year? How much difference does resource depletion make?

(d) How much biomass is there after one year if we include the effects of resource depletion?

(e) Continue with these rules for 10 years and graph the results. Do they now follow the pattern in the figure?

(f) Think of two additional ways that resource depletion or other forms of competition could affect the terms in this model.

For Section 2.2

1. The average energy density of some common fuels is given in the following table.

Fuel	Energy density in kJ/kg
Wood	0.02
Charcoal	0.03
Coal	0.03
Crude oil	0.04
Gasoline	0.045
Methane	0.055

(a) How much of each of these fuels would you need to burn to run your own body?

(b) How much would it take to run the urban metabolism of a typical person?

(c) Table 2.3 lists a person as importing the equivalent of 1.8 tons of energy in the equivalent of fuel oil. Do your numbers come out close to this value?

(d) Convert the amount of gasoline into liters using the density of 0.75 kg/L. How does this compare to the amount of gasoline used for transportation?

2. We have seen that production of 1.0 kg of cement requires 1.63 kWh, 1.0 kg of glass requires 7.17 kWh, and 1.0 kg of steel requires 11.67 kWh. Furthermore, it takes 0.03 kWh to transport 1.0 kg of materials a distance of 100 km.

(a) Suppose a 1000 ton building is made of 30% steel, 60% cement, and 10% glass. How much energy is embodied in the materials?

(b) Suppose the steel is shipped 1000 km, the cement 200 km, and the glass 300 km. How much energy is taken by shipping and how does this compare with the overall energy?

(c) A building weighs roughly 300 kg/m^2. Do your figures come close to the estimate of 1600 kWh/m^2 in the text?

(d) If you wanted to reduce the energy used to build, what would you change first?

For Section 2.3

1. We can use the energy density of wood (0.02 kJ/kg) from Exercise 2.2.1 to estimate the energy land component of the ecological footprint.

(a) How much wood would be required to run a small city of 100,000 people each of whom uses 100 times more energy than required for their own metabolism?

(b) Suppose that forests receive 160 W/m^2 of energy and convert 10% of that to wood. How much area would be required for this city?

(c) How would you combine this calculation with the effects of respiration? Why might an older forest, or a slow-growing tree, lead to a larger estimate of energy land?

(d) How could you include the energy costs of transport into this calculation?

2. Humans live at extremely high population density compared with other organisms. For herbivores, the population density D in numbers of mammals per km^2 is approximately

$$D = 50 \, W^{-0.75}$$

where W is an individual's mass in grams [114].

(a) Find the expected population density of a mouse with a mass of 20 g. How many mice would you find in a typical urban yard of 0.05 hectares?

(b) Find the expected population density of humans, say with a mass of 50 kg. How many people would survive in Hong Kong (area of 120 km^2) according to this rule?

(c) As we've seen, there are actually 7 million people in Hong Kong. How large a mammal could persist at this density without resource inputs?

For Section 2.4

1. Consider the seed-harvester ant *Pogonomyrmex*.

    (a) Describe in detail how you would compute the ecological footprint of a colony. What information would you need for each of the components?

    (b) Read the paper by Mackay on the energy budget of these ants[351]. What information is included in this paper and what is missing?

Further Reading

For Chapter 2

- Bettencourt, L., Lobo, J., Helbing, D., Kühnert, C. and West, G. B. Growth, innovation, scaling, and the pace of life in cities. *Proceedings of the National Academy of Sciences*, **104** (2007), 7301–7306.
- Carlsson-Kanyama, A., Ekström, M. P. and Shanahan H. Food and life cycle energy inputs: consequences of diet and ways to increase efficiency. *Ecological Economics*, **44** (2003), 293–307.

For Section 2.1

- Decker, E. H., Elliott, S., Smith, F. A., Blake, D. R., and Rowland, F. S. Energy and material flow through the urban ecosystem. *Annual Reviews in Energy and the Environment*, **25** (2000), 685–740.
- Kennedy, C., Cuddihy, J., and Engel-Yan, J. The changing metabolism of cities. *Journal of Industrial Ecology*, **11** (2007), 43–59.
- Ngo, N. and Pataki, D. The energy and mass balance of Los Angeles County. *Urban Ecosystems*, **11** (2008), 121–139.

For Section 2.2

- Collins, J. P., Kinzig, A., Grimm, N. B., *et al.* A new urban ecology. *American Scientist*, **88** (2000), 416–425.
- Jones, A. An environmental assessment of food supply chains: a case study on dessert apples. *Environmental Management*, **30** (2002), 560–576.

For Section 2.3

- Bolund, P. and Hunhammar, S. Ecosystem services in urban areas. *Ecological Economics*, **29** (1999), 293–301.
- Folke, C., Jansson, A., Larsson, J., and Costanza, R. Ecosystem appropriation by cities. *Ambio*, **26** (1997), 167–172.
- McManus, P. and Haughton, G. Planning with ecological footprints: a sympathetic critique of theory and practice. *Environment and Urbanization*, **18** (2006), 113–127.
- Pataki, D., Carreiro, M., Cherrier, J., *et al.* Coupling biogeochemical cycles in urban environments: ecosystem services, green solutions, and misconceptions. *Frontiers in Ecology and the Environment*, **9** (2011), 27–36.
- Wackernagel, M. and Rees, W. *Our Ecological Footprint: Reducing Human Impact on the Earth*. (Gabriola Island, Canada: New Society Publishers, 1996).

For Section 2.4

- Hölldobler, B. and Wilson, E. O. *The Superorganism: The Beauty, Elegance, and Strangeness of Insect Societies.* (New York: W. W. Norton & Co., 2008).
- Naiman, R. Animal influences on ecosystem dynamics. *BioScience*, **38** (1988), 750–752.
- Ward, P. Ants. *Current Biology*, **16** (2006), 152–155.

Labs

A. Go online, and use at least two different sites to compute your personal ecological footprint. How do the estimates compare? Were there any factors with surprisingly large or surprisingly small effects? What are some of the weaknesses of each? What would you include to improve the analysis?

B. Over the course of 1 week, keep a record of how much water you use per day, and scale this value up to how much water you use annually. Find how much water is available as rainfall where you live (in liters per person), and compare with the values in Figure 2.3. If you use more water than is available from rainfall, determine the source of this excess water. How much of your water use comes directly or indirectly from rainfall that falls close to where you live?

C. Over the course of 1 week, calculate the amount of energy you use per day (in W), including as many energy-using processes as you can (e.g., lights and heating/air conditioning, transportation, food consumption, and work/recreation). Is your value close to the figures given in the text? Use this value to estimate how much energy per square meter is consumed in the city where you live. How does this compare to the $160 \, \text{W/m}^2$ provided by the sun?

3 Urban ecosystem processes

The urban metabolism and the urban energy budget quantify one of our themes, the increased inputs and outputs characteristic of urban areas. The ecological footprint broadly quantifies another theme, the extent of habitat modification in the built environment. These analyses establish the background for detailed examination of our third theme, the intended and unintended consequences of human action for the functioning of the urban ecosystem. This chapter focuses on ecosystem ecology, tracing how urbanization alters the movement and use of materials and energy.

The following principles (Figure 3.1), expanding on those in Section 1.4, organize our discussion of three key forms of material and energy that characterize an urban ecosystem: temperature, water, and nutrients.

1. Ecosystem processes depend on cycles, how materials and energy move between locations and transform into different states.
2. The basic physical properties of a material or form of energy determine how it is stored, recycled, and transformed.
3. The basic biological properties of a material or form of energy determine the role of living organisms in its storage, transformation, and loss.
4. The habitat, including both its physical structure and the organisms that live there, shapes ecosystem cycles.
5. Different ecosystem cycles interact with each other, often in unexpected ways.
6. Processes occurring at one point in space or time are linked with those operating at other locations or times.

Most human alterations amplify ecosystem processes, increasing the magnitude and rate of nutrient, material, and water movement. These alterations are done for many reasons, such as obtaining water or food, transportation, housing, aesthetics, and recreation. These intended consequences rarely, if ever, occur without unintended consequences that then interact with the complex cycles governing ecosystems, creating unpredictable responses.

Although this chapter treats climate and the water and nutrient cycles in separate sections, these cycles are tightly linked (Figure 3.2). For example, rain removes nitrogen compounds from the atmosphere, deposits them in the soil, and washes them downstream. Pavement creates impermeable surfaces that change how water moves and concentrate nutrients. Nitrogen in the atmosphere can be exported downwind or deposited

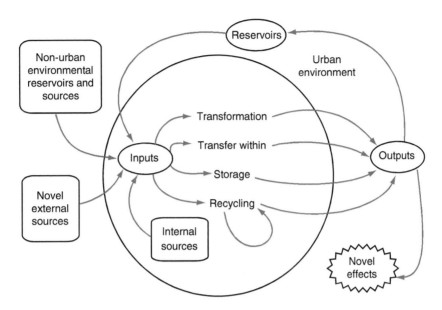

Figure 3.1   Ecosystem principles in the urban environment.

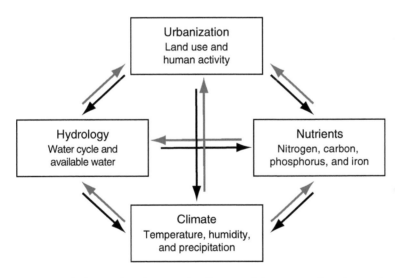

Figure 3.2   The interactions between the climate and the water and nutrient cycles.

locally and fertilize soils. These fertilized soils can in turn alter the microbial communities responsible for nitrogen cycling in the first place.

Many of the effects of urban ecosystems occur well outside the urban boundaries themselves, as emphasized in ecological footprint analysis. Agriculture dominates the ecosystems that feed cities, while water and wastes exported by design or by accident influence downwind and downstream rural and wilderness areas. Much research has focused on these upstream and downstream effects. While outlining that work, this book focuses on changes within the urban area itself.

3.1   Urban climate

The physical structure of the urban landscape decreases the fraction of area with vegetation and increases the fraction built with hard surfaces impermeable to water. Building and maintaining structures requires substantial energy inputs, mostly in the form of fossil fuels. Together, these factors alter the way that heat energy flows into, through, and out of an urban region, which can modify both urban weather and climate.

Climate is the set of meteorological patterns or conditions that characterize a region. Climate plays an important role in determining which species inhabit an area, as well as how they make their living there. *Weather*, in contrast, describes the day-to-day, small-scale changes in conditions. All cities change both climate and weather relative to their surroundings, but due to differences in size, structure, and location, cities differ from one another in their effects. Indeed, there can be substantial variation within cities themselves. The built environment involves abrupt landscape changes, leading, for example, to substantial differences in temperatures between nearby areas. These combined localized effects scale up to include the entire city, creating the overall effects on the urban ecosystem.

Principles affecting temperature

Temperature and rainfall are the two key aspects of a region's climate. This section focuses on temperature, but introduces some of its many links with rainfall before the more detailed coverage of the water cycle in Section 3.2.

Temperature measures the heat energy contained within an area. Heat is the ultimate byproduct of almost all energy use, created as an intended consequence of biological metabolism and combustion for heating, and an unintended consequence of friction in mechanical processes and combustion for locomotion and manufacture. The properties and use of heat determine how urbanization affects temperature.

1. Heat occurs in multiple forms, as photons (radiation) or stored in solids, liquids, or gases. Heat is released from chemical bonds by combustion or respiration.
2. Heat is stored in solids for a period of hours or days before being conducted into the atmosphere where it is dissipated through movement, or *convection*.
3. Conversion of water from solid to liquid or from liquid to gas requires a substantial amount of heat energy, creating a key link between temperature and water.
4. Almost all heat on Earth derives, either directly or indirectly, from the sun. The amount of solar energy arriving and remaining at a surface depends on three things:
   • The angle of the sun, as determined by the latitude, the season, and the slope of the surface.

- The clarity of the intervening atmosphere, as determined by the extent of cloud cover, water vapor, and pollution.
- The properties of the surface that it strikes, particularly its ability to reflect or store heat.

This section begins by quantifying the changes in energy flow that characterize urban areas, and how urban materials and the urban metabolism drive these changes. The resulting *urban heat island*, typified by warmer temperatures within a city relative to the surrounding area, occurs in almost all cities. This section concludes by outlining the effects of the urban heat island on local weather, ecology, and human health and well-being.

The surface energy budget

Just as energy drives the urban metabolism, energy drives the climate. The urban environment changes the inputs and outputs of energy, summarized in the *surface energy budget* (Figure 3.3). The surface has three sources of energy input:

1. **Solar input** (QI): Energy coming from the sun as high energy (or *short-wave*) radiation.
2. **Incoming infrared radiation** (QL_{in}): Energy reflected back from the atmosphere as low energy (or *long-wave*) radiation.
3. **Anthropogenic heat input** (QF): Energy released from the processes and activities of inhabitants, primarily combustion of fuels.

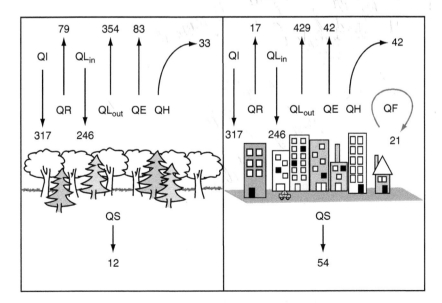

Figure 3.3 Typical non-urban and urban surface energy budgets in W/m^2 (after Shepherd, 2005).

Table 3.1 Typical elements of the surface energy budget (all values W/m^2 averaged over a typical day, after Shepherd, 2005).

Input or output	Symbol	Non-urban value	Urban value
Inputs			
Solar input	QI	317	317
Infrared input	QL$_{in}$	246	246
Anthropogenic heat	QF	0	21
Outputs			
Reflected	QR	79	17
Infrared output	QL$_{out}$	354	429
Latent heat loss	QE	83	42
Sensible heat loss	QH	33	42
Storage	QS	12	54

Energy is lost from the surface of a region in four ways:

1. **Reflected radiation** (QR): Radiation reflected directly back into the atmosphere or outer space.
2. **Outgoing infrared radiation** (QL$_{out}$): Heat radiated by warm objects as low-energy long-wave radiation.
3. **Latent heat loss** (QE): Heat lost through *evaporation* of water, including *transpiration* by plants.
4. **Sensible heat transfer** (QH): Heat lost through direct transfer (convection) via movement of air or water.

If heat inputs at the surface exceed outputs, the surface warms by storing heat (QS) in buildings, the ground, or the atmosphere.

The balance between inputs, outputs, and storage can be written as the equation

$$QI + QL_{in} + QF = QR + QL_{out} + QE + QH + QS.$$

That is, the heat entering the surface equals the heat leaving the surface plus the heat stored within the surface. This budget provides a useful way to compare different habitats.

Typical urban and non-urban surface energy budgets differ substantially in several important ways[519] (Figure 3.3, Table 3.1).

- More anthropogenic heat (QF) is produced in urban areas.
- Less heat is reflected (QR) from urban areas.
- Less latent heat (QE) is lost from urban areas.
- More long-wave radiation (QH$_{out}$) is lost from urban areas.
- Slightly more sensible heat (QH) is lost from urban areas.
- More heat is stored (QS) in urban areas.

We now examine how habitat modification, inputs, and outputs produce these changes, and how they combine in most cases to a distinctive pattern of higher temperatures[446].

Impermeable surfaces and the effects of water

The impermeable surfaces that characterize the built environment alter the behavior of both water and radiation. In one of the most important interactions between ecosystem cycles, water plays a major role in shaping climate because the heat required to evaporate water is enormous[612]. It takes as much energy to evaporate 1.0 cm of rain as to heat a 1.5 m thick slab of concrete by 10°C, or the entire 10.0 km column of atmosphere above that slab by 2°C. The urban temperature is thus strongly influenced by whether water that falls on the city evaporates there or elsewhere. Because a large fraction of rain runs off from impermeable surfaces and leaves the city, it takes its cooling potential with it[9].

Plants play a key role in shaping where water changes from liquid to gas form. In heavily vegetated areas, much of the water that falls is used by plants and lost to the atmosphere by *transpiration*, the transport of water from roots to its leaves and eventually into the atmosphere as water vapor. Only a small fraction of this water is used for photosynthesis, with over 90% evaporating into the atmosphere through small pores on leaves, called *stomata*, that must open to take in carbon dioxide.

On a hot dry day a large tree may use as much as 1000 L of water. Evaporation of this water requires 625 kWh, which exceeds even the energy use of an urban resident. This energy, the latent heat loss in the surface energy budget (Table 3.1), comes from the surrounding atmosphere, thus reducing the temperature of the surrounding area via evaporative cooling.

In urban areas, the latent heat loss within the urban area itself can be only half that of the non-urban area (Table 3.1), due to the combined reduction of evaporation and transpiration, or *evapotranspiration*. However, cities in arid areas with their large inputs of water and associated vegetation can have higher evapotranspiration levels than nearby non-urban areas, creating a temporary "oasis effect"[127].

The structure of the built environment

The impermeable surfaces that replace vegetation alter the movement of light rays as much as that of water. Buildings dominate the urban center, with walls that can have as much vertical as horizontal area (Section 1.2). These vertical surfaces receive sunlight at different times of day, such as early in the morning or late in the afternoon, and at different angles from the somewhat more regular *topography* of non-urban areas[245]. Urban areas thus absorb *insolation*, or solar radiation, for a longer period each day than non-urban areas. Incoming solar radiation that is reflected can bounce between buildings until it is eventually stored as heat in materials[573].

The urban surface topography consists of the following elements (Figure 3.4).

- The **urban canyon** is the deep chasm between tall buildings that can channel wind or concentrate and trap heat.
- The **urban canopy** is composed of the tall buildings.
- The **urban canopy layer** is the air within the urban canopy in the area below the tops of buildings and the trees.
- The **urban boundary layer** is the air directly above the urban canopy.

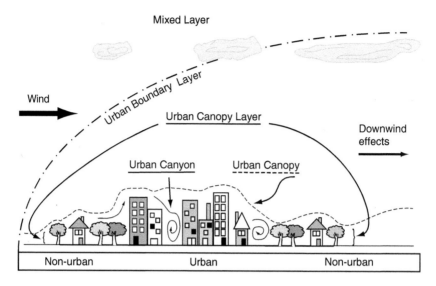

Figure 3.4 The rough urban surface.

The urban boundary layer, urban canopy layer, and urban canyon interact with one another much like different layers in non-urban ecosystems. Trapped heat energy rapidly warms the canyon, but gradually dissipates in the urban canopy, delaying the heating of the urban boundary layer. The slow process of heat transfer can maintain very different temperatures in close proximity[412]; two sides of one building can be different enough to host two different plant communities.

Urban vertical structures, usually made of concrete, steel, and glass, also absorb outgoing long-wave radiation from the surface. The energy absorbed by buildings in the morning and throughout the day re-radiates at night only to be trapped once again[228]. This slows the release of heat into the urban boundary layer and urban canyon (QL_{out})[410].

The urban center thus loses little latent heat due to the lack of plants and surface water (low QE), absorbs more solar radiation during the day, and reabsorbs more long-wave radiation at night (high QL_{in}), resulting in increased temperature. How much of that heat energy is exported as sensible heat (QH), primarily through convection of air, depends on the wind speed. Although the urban canyon can have extreme wind speeds, the average wind velocity tends to be reduced in urban areas due to the obstruction of larger scale air flows by buildings[483]. Although urban wind velocity averages lower during major weather events, it is higher during relatively calm periods[322]. This lower average wind speed reduces the average horizontal heat transfer, again trapping heat in the urban environment[322].

Materials

Like a real canyon, the urban canyon consists mainly of stone and other hard materials. The specific characteristics of these materials play as large a role in urban heat movement as their physical shape. Urban stone is mostly concrete, which has a relatively high *albedo*, meaning that most radiation is reflected and only a small amount is absorbed. Concrete structures have albedo values of roughly 0.8, and thus reflect 80% of incoming radiation, often to another building. Steel and glass have even higher albedo. In comparison, most plants have an albedo of 0.20 to 0.25 [263].

In contrast to the high albedo of concrete and glass that comprise the vertical surface of the urban canyon, the surrounding horizontal surfaces, primarily roofs and roads, consist mainly of dark materials like asphalt with very low albedos. For example, newly laid asphalt has an albedo of approximately 0.05 and absorbs 95% of the heat energy that strikes it. The radiation reflected among vertical surfaces of buildings with high albedo can eventually strike a horizontal surface with low albedo, where it is absorbed and stored.

Cement buildings and other urban surfaces have a large *heat capacity*, meaning that they can store large amounts of heat energy. Unlike water, these structures also have a large *thermal conductivity* and can quickly absorb large amounts of thermal energy. For example, 4 hours of full sun can increase asphalt or roof temperatures by 30°C, but increase the temperature of water in a lake by only 3.5°C [511].

As a consequence of repeated reflection and eventual absorption of heat energy, the central business district of a city can absorb six times as much energy as a non-urban area [564]. At the high end, Mexico City absorbs 60% of all incoming heat radiation during the winter [413]. Suburbs with more dispersed housing and more vegetation such as lawns and gardens absorb only 1.5–2 times more energy than the surrounding non-urban area.

Anthropogenic heat

Although habitat modification and reduced evapotranspiration play the largest role in modifying the urban climate, inputs of energy for human use can also significantly change the surface energy balance, particularly in the winter. Anthropogenic heat flux is primarily waste energy from human technology. Human energy production in non-urban areas averages $0.025\,\text{W/m}^2$, almost 10 000 times less than solar energy inputs, but jumps to $7-14\,\text{W/m}^2$ in suburbs, and $20-70\,\text{W/m}^2$ in urban areas although values of $200-400\,\text{W/m}^2$ are not uncommon [109].

In winter, human energy production can rival or even exceed heat from solar radiation [6]. By one estimate, Tokyo generates up to $1590\,\text{W/m}^2$, far more than the available solar radiation during winter [271] and exceeding the typical annual average for large cities (Figure 2.9). Other estimates for Tokyo are much lower, emphasizing the challenge of measuring this quantity [6]. In mid- and high-latitude areas, the winter increase in human energy production occurs at precisely the same time as decreased solar input, promoting increased urban winter temperatures, particularly during cold spells and at night.

Alteration of atmosphere

In addition to waste heat, the combustion of fossil fuels and solid biofuels generates *aerosols*, small particles in the atmosphere. This pollution can reduce solar energy input (QI) by reflecting some solar radiation back into the stratosphere [122]. This reflectance is often concentrated near the wavelengths used by plants, so that primary production is

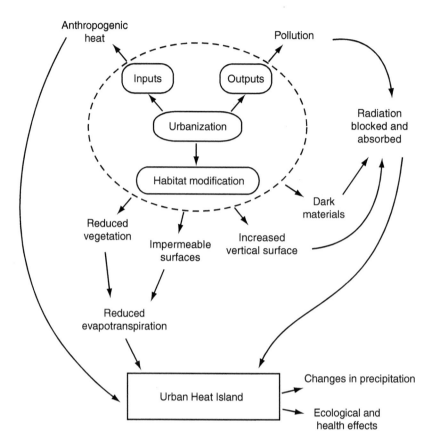

Figure 3.5 The chains of cause and effect leading from urban habitat modification, inputs, and outputs to the unintended urban heat island.

reduced, potentially reducing plant transpiration and its associated cooling. Conversely, aerosols trap and re-reflect outgoing long-wave radiation, holding heat in the urban area. The balance between these two effects depends on the particular city, but usually comes out on the side of increased heat storage.

The urban heat island

Human changes to the urban habitat, along with energy inputs and atmospheric outputs, interact with the physical properties of heat to create the *urban heat island*. Five major changes underlie this unintended consequence of urbanization (Figure 3.5).

- The replacement of vegetation with concrete and asphalt in the urban core leads to decreased evapotranspiration of water.
- Vertical surfaces collect incoming solar radiation for long periods throughout the day and trap outgoing radiation at night.
- Dark building materials trap and store incoming radiation.

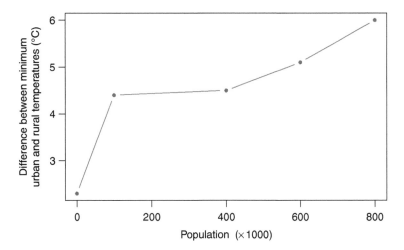

Figure 3.6 The strength of the urban heat island in Phoenix as a function of population size over recent decades (after Brazel *et al.*, 2000).

- Anthropogenic heat production can match or exceed solar energy input, particularly in the winter.
- The more polluted urban atmosphere can absorb and reflect more heat.

The urban heat island is defined as the difference in temperature between urban and non-urban sites that can be attributed to effects of the built environment, thus correcting for differences in topography that might have existed before humans arrived[357,411]. The strength of the urban heat island depends on the size, properties, and location of a city, in addition to the time of day, the time of year, and the weather conditions.

Cities with the defining characteristics of urbanization, larger population size, higher population density, and more extensive building and pavement tend to have a more pronounced urban heat islands[54,319] (Figure 3.6). For this reason, the magnitude of the heat island grows over time in growing cities. The strength of the heat island in Baltimore increased almost exponentially over its last half century of rapid urbanization[289] (Figure 3.7a), and the temperature in the Phoenix area has increased consistently during its recent rapid expansion[551] (Figure 3.7b).

Several of the key aspects of urbanization that accentuate the urban heat island can be summarized by the *sky view factor*[410], the proportion of the sky visible from a location. Places deep in the urban canyon see only a tiny fraction of the sky, and are indeed associated with the greatest temperature increase in the canopy layer (Figure 3.8).

The surrounding climate also affects the timing and extent of the heat island effect. Phoenix, which is located in an extremely dry, or *xeric*, region, can be cooler than surrounding non-urban sites during the day due to increased evapotranspiration. The extensive use of imported water, primarily outside the home, creates an "oasis effect," with green lawns and gardens providing the vegetative cooling often associated with less urbanized sites[127]. Not all of Phoenix, however, is cooler than the surrounding desert during the day. Sky Harbor Airport does not have extensive landscaping or water

(a)

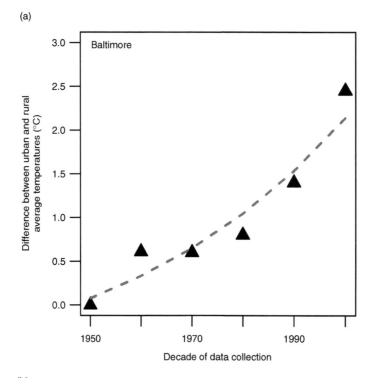

(b)

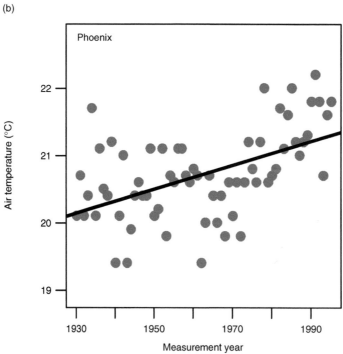

Figure 3.7 (a) Average urban heat island in Baltimore, Maryland (after Kalnay and Cai, 2003). (b) Urban temperature increase in Phoenix, Arizona (after Stefanov *et al.*, 2004).

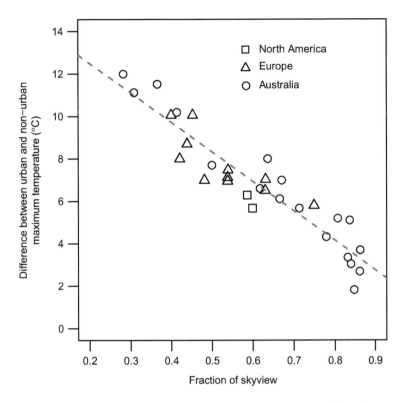

Figure 3.8 Relationship between skyview factor and the urban heat island in 31 urban centers in three continents (after Oke, 1982).

imports and reports a mean daytime temperature 3.1°C warmer and a nighttime temperature fully 5°C warmer than nearby non-urban areas[13].

In comparison, Baltimore has a wetter, or *mesic*, climate. The effects of watering and evapotranspiration are less important, leading to a more typical pattern. The urban heat island is strongest at night due to the absorption and slow release of daytime solar energy, and in winter due to artificial heat production[100] (Figure 3.9). Minimum temperatures are thus more affected than maximum ones, which can have important effects on the ecology of urban organisms. Due to their higher coverage by vegetation, parks usually have a reduced heat island effect, primarily during the day. Nonetheless, Central Park in the heart of New York City has warmed as much as other sites in the city[191].

In tropical cities, the climate is dominated by wet and dry seasons rather than winter and summer. The largest urban heat island effect typically occurs during the dry season[495]. In the wet season, the higher vegetation cover in non-urban areas provides little evaporative cooling because humidity is high.

The effects of water and weather on the urban heat island are quite different in cities that are close to large water bodies such as the ocean. These water bodies moderate temperature fluctuations and reduce the urban heat island in three ways[54].

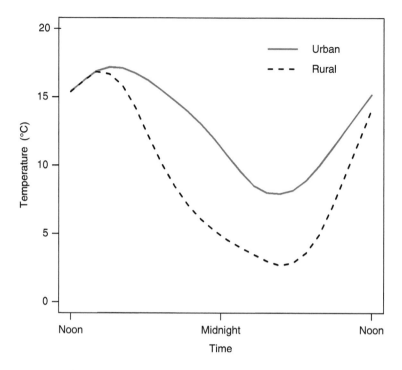

Figure 3.9 The urban heat island on a typical winter day in Baltimore (after Collier, 2006).

- Water, with its high heat capacity, absorbs a large amount of heat.
- Increased humidity decreases the importance of non-urban evapotranspiration.
- *Synoptic* (large-scale) weather events play a larger role in mixing air from the urban boundary layer with the upper, well-mixed layer.

Despite the dependence on surrounding habitats and climate, urban heat islands have been measured in almost every climate region (Figure 3.10), including

- Equatorial tropical wet (Singapore and Kuala Lumpur),
- Tropical highland (Mexico City),
- Subtropical (Johannesburg, South Africa),
- High latitude (Göteborg, Sweden),
- Mediterranean (Athens, Greece),
- Arid desert (Erzurum, Turkey).

Although the heat island can extend as much as 10 km from the city itself[412], it is generated by small-scale processes such as the heating of dark surfaces and evapotranspiration from vegetation. In Phoenix, patches of vegetation of only 6.1 m by 11 m made nearby shrubs 3°C cooler than gravel, concrete, or asphalt, with the highest difference during the hot summer months and little effect in the winter[391].

The urban center is thus generally warmer than more heavily vegetated nearby rural or recreation areas[247]. Areas with less vegetation show the largest urban heat island

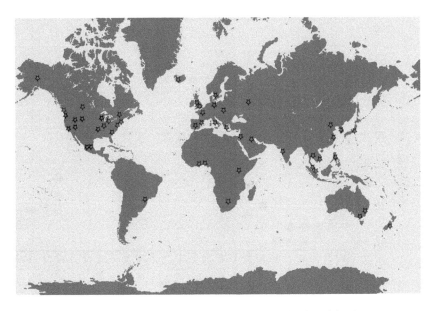

Figure 3.10 A few of the cities that have a demonstrated urban heat island.

effect[612], which can correlate with average income or other socioeconomic variables within a city[70]. Areas where residents have low incomes tend to be the warmest due to reduced watering and vegetative cover[551]. In Phoenix, every $10 000 increase in median income is associated with 0.28°C decrease in summer morning temperature, due to the effects of increased vegetation[279].

There is an ongoing debate regarding the role of the urban heat island itself with the overall pattern of warming across the planet, although no debate about the role of urban greenhouse gas emissions. A warming trend at a particular location might be due to increasing urbanization at that site rather than a global trend[54]. Studies that have accounted for the local effects of urbanization have also found increasing surface temperatures, indicating that the effects are not entirely local. Global trends aside, one thing is certain; where land is converted from non-urban to urban, surface temperatures increase.

Humidity

The *humidity* is the amount of water contained in air, and is often measured as the *relative humidity*, or fraction of the maximum amount of water that air of a given temperature could possibly hold. Because warm air can hold more water vapor than cold air, the relative humidity depends on both the water content and the temperature of the air. This value provides a useful measure of the apparent temperature, or how hot it feels. High relative humidity feels hotter because there is less evaporation, and sweating provides little cooling. In areas with high relative humidity, trees can open their stomata to take in carbon dioxide without losing substantial amounts of water through

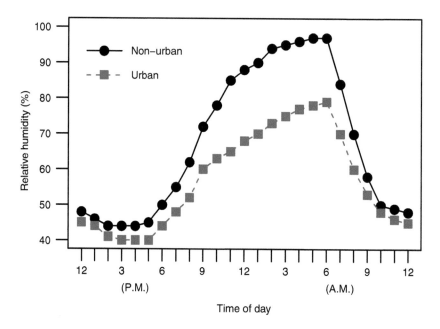

Figure 3.11 Typical daily pattern of urban relative humidity (after Fortuniak *et al.*, 2006).

evapotranspiration, thus reducing their need for water, but also reducing the amount of cooling through latent heat loss.

Urban humidity results from interactions between weather conditions, the availability of water, and the temperature. Reduced evapotranspiration usually leads to reduced absolute humidity for urban areas[66]. Because air temperatures in cities are warmer than surrounding areas, the air in cities could potentially hold more water, leading to a reduction in relative humidity. However, in arid regions such as Arizona and Turkey, the increased water used to irrigate urban plants, in addition to water vapor produced through combustion, can increase absolute humidity[54].

Urban humidity changes over the course of a day. The urban heat island maintains warmer nighttime temperatures. This can keep the city above the dew point, the temperature at which water precipitates out of the air. The cooler surrounding region, however, may drop below the dew point, and have water precipitate from the air to the grass and trees. As a consequence, the city starts the day with more water vapor in the air than the non-urban area. During the day, the temperature difference between the urban and surrounding areas diminishes. The lack of plants in the city can then lead to reduced evapotranspiration and drier air during the urban afternoon[55,177] (Figure 3.11).

Consequences of the urban heat island

Although it is a relatively simple change in the regional climate, the urban heat island leads to significant changes in many other aspects of the climate and ecology of a city.

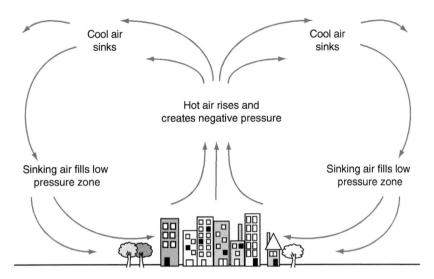

Figure 3.12 The urban dust dome.

Effects on air circulation

Warm air rises. In the absence of synoptic weather conditions, the warmer air created by the urban heat island does just that. Rising warm air expands and cools, which reduces local air pressure at the surface and sucks air from the urban periphery into the resulting low-pressure zone. The rising and cooling urban air descends and fills in the low pressure areas created in the urban periphery. This cycle of rising, replacing, and descending creates a *circulation cell* that can trap urban air and accumulate pollution, an effect called the *urban dust dome*[210] (Figure 3.12).

When warm moist air rises and cools its ability to hold water decreases, leading to condensation and formation of clouds. These clouds can initiate urban-induced convective thunderstorms or precipitation, particularly when synoptic conditions do not disperse them (Figure 3.13). The strength of the urban heat island correlates with the amount of induced precipitation[521]. However, the precipitation induced in urban areas will fall outside of the city when storms are pushed downwind by synoptic events (urban rainfall is discussed in detail in Section 3.2).

Effects on ecology

Many organisms are limited by temperature, especially by extreme maximum and minimum values. Temperature creates both heat stress and cold stress. Although animals, including humans, suffer from heat stress, higher temperatures have the greatest effects on plants. To conserve water, plants reduce photosynthesis when stressed by heat. This reduction affects the local environment. Trees over asphalt, which can be 20°C hotter than turf, have much warmer leaves (probably due to increased long-wave radiation) even when air temperatures are relatively similar. These hotter trees do not lose much more water because they respond by closing their stomata, leading to less evaporative

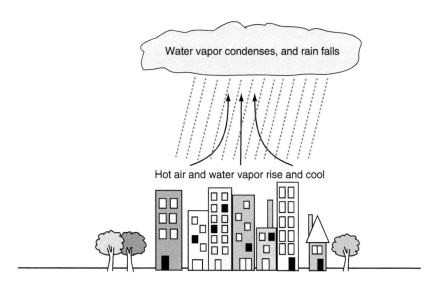

Figure 3.13 The changes in urban circulation patterns created by the urban heat island, and their effects on precipitation.

cooling, drier air, and potentially even more stomatal closure[303]. This creates one of several *positive feedbacks* that can amplify increased temperature.

The less extreme low temperatures associated with the urban heat island determine which plants and animals can persist in the urban environment, and the timing of key behaviors. More species of plants can persist in climates with less extreme low temperatures, with many colonizing cities well outside their normal range (Section 4.2). Warmer winter and springtime temperatures induce changes in the migratory and reproductive behaviors of urban birds (Section 4.5). Urban plants have longer growing seasons[625], and urban birds have longer breeding seasons[87] than their non-urban counterparts. Insects and other arthropods are also sensitive to low temperatures, and are generally unable to move and feed effectively outside the temperature range from 15–38°C[497]. Their active seasons can increase by as much as a full month in urban areas due to earlier spring warming and later autumn cooling, potentially increasing insect damage (Section 4.3).

Effects on humans

The urban climate changes temperature, humidity, and rainfall (Table 3.2). All urban residents experience higher highs, higher lows, relatively drier air, and more rainfall. Like plants and animals, people can respond by changing behavior, but can also use the power of ecosystem engineering to locally modify their environment. To ameliorate the effects on themselves and on their lawns or gardens, people use more water when temperatures increase. High evening temperatures encourage the use of air conditioning for a longer fraction of the day and often well into the night[522]. This creates another positive feedback; more energy use leads to increased human energy production and more heat input into an already hot system[515].

Table 3.2 Summary of differences in climate between urban and rural sites in Erzurum, Turkey (after Bulut, 2008).

Element	Mean difference	Maximum difference	Minimum difference
Temperature (°C)	1.7	3.4	0.7
Minimum temperature (°C)	0.9	2.6	0.0
Maximum temperature (°C)	3.4	9.4	2.1
Relative humidity (%)	−2.5	−8.0	−1.6
Rainfall (mm)	4.8	31.3	0.3

Heat has substantial effects on human health (discussed more fully in Section 5.1). More people die from heat waves than floods, tornados, or hurricanes[46]. The discomfort of the extended periods of high temperatures, exacerbated by urban pollution, creates intense stress on city-dwellers. This stress finds outlet in health and social problems, including even an increase in violent crime[13].

Conclusions

Like the Earth, cities have become warmer over the last 80 years[551]. Indeed, some see the changes in cities as windows into the future of global change[89]. The factors that shape the local urban climate are different from those that alter the global climate. Land-use changes, particularly the increase in the built environment and the decrease in vegetation, create the strongest effects near a city. Increased energy use, and the resulting pollution and waste heat, are usually secondary in importance, although they can be the primary effects during winter. At the global scale, the release of greenhouse gases, especially carbon dioxide, play the leading role in climate change. Although many of these gases are generated in urban areas, their climatological effects are rapidly distributed around the globe, and are in fact largest in the least populated areas such as the Arctic.

It is an old saying that people talk a lot about the weather but never do anything about it. However, if enough people get together, they build cities, which do change the weather whether or not this is the intention. The urban heat island is a nearly universal phenomenon in cities around the world and is among the most prominent unintended consequences of urbanization. The built environment was not intended to do more than create a safe and efficient environment for human residents, but has interacted with sunlight and the cycles of heat and water to warm large areas and change local weather patterns. The heat island in turn alters the way that species interact, behave, and evolve[215] (Chapter 4), along with the lives of the humans who unwittingly initiated the process.

3.2 The urban water cycle

The built environment alters climate partly by directly changing the inputs and outputs of energy, primarily radiation from the sun, and partly by reducing evaporation and transpiration. These are just two of the ways that urban environments alter ecosystem cycles. Urban water demand and impermeable surfaces radically alter the flow of water, increasing inputs and outputs and reducing recycling and local storage. The urban heat island can increase precipitation both in and around the urban environment. Given the essential role of water, particularly for the plants that form the base of the ecological energy pyramid, these changes in water supply propagate through the entire urban ecosystem.

Principles of the water cycle

In one form or another, water is constantly on the move. *Hydrology* is the study of the movement and distribution of water, whether underground, on the surface, or in the atmosphere. The inputs, outputs, and movement of water are described by the *water cycle*. The diverse and unusual properties of water determine the role of the effects of urbanization on the water cycle.

1. Little water is created or destroyed, although plants use some in photosynthesis to create sugars. Respiration and combustion reverse this reaction and generate relatively small amounts of water.
2. Water is stored in a variety of reservoirs: in solid form as ice, in liquid form in fresh water, salt water, or underground aquifers, and in gaseous form as water vapor throughout the atmosphere and as concentrated in clouds.
3. Water is necessary for all life and is required in large quantities for plant growth.
4. The flow of water depends on the slope and properties of surfaces. Flowing water can enter above-ground water bodies such as the ocean, *infiltrate* the surface to be stored in soil or aquifers or be used by plants, or evaporate into the atmosphere.
5. Water can dissolve a wide array of chemicals and nutrients, and carry these and larger items over long distances.
6. Conversion of water from liquid to gaseous form requires substantial energy that creates significant local cooling (Section 3.1).

In contrast with heat energy, water is rarely created, can be stored for long periods of time, is recycled many times, and moves over long distances. These differences, along with its vital role in maintaining all life, means that urbanization affects water very differently from energy.

Water plays a major role in shaping ecosystems, such as the contrast between deserts and rainforests. The availability of water largely determines which plants and animals can inhabit an area, which in turn shapes how water is recycled or exported. Moving water also transports nutrients and pollutants both in and out of ecosystems. Water availability thus has far-reaching effects not only on the local ecology, but also the ecology of places downstream or downwind.

The water cycle and the effects of urbanization

Like the surface energy budget, the water cycle can be summarized as a balance between inputs, outputs, and storage (Figure 3.14). Unlike energy, however, water can be reused

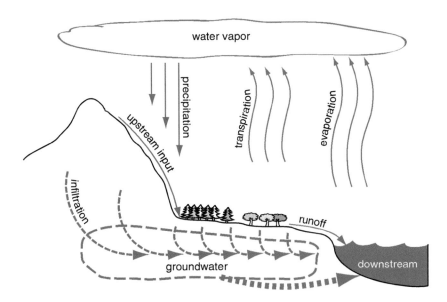

Figure 3.14 The non-urban water cycle.

or recycled many times in a given area. The balance of inputs and outputs of liquid water obeys the equation[229].

$$P + I_a + I_u = E + T + R + G + W + \Delta S.$$

In this equation,

- P represents precipitation,
- I_a represents anthropogenic inputs,
- I_u represents inputs from upstream ecosystems,
- E represents evaporation,
- T represents transpiration,
- R represents runoff to downstream ecosystems,
- G represents infiltration or groundwater recharge,
- W represents wastewater discharge,
- ΔS represents change in water storage.

   Three main factors contribute to the changes in the urban water cycle[229] (Table 3.3, Figure 3.15).

1. The replacement of vegetation with impermeable surfaces increases runoff, speeds the movement of water, and reduces infiltration, evaporation, and transpiration.
2. Channeling of streams and rivers, often for flood control, also accelerates water flow through and out of the city.
3. High urban water use for manufacturing, domestic needs, and irrigation alters the extent, timing, and location of inputs and generates increased outputs.

Table 3.3 Elements of the water budget and the effects of urbanization

Input or output	Symbol	Effects of urbanization
Inputs		
Precipitation	P	Can be increased or decreased
Anthropogenic input	I_a	Often large
Input from upstream	I_u	Usually reduced
Outputs		
Evaporation	E	Reduced due to rapid runoff
Transpiration	T	Reduced due to decreased vegetation
Runoff downstream	R	Increased by impermeable surfaces
Groundwater recharge	G	Decreased due to reduced infiltration
Wastewater discharge	W	Can match or exceed precipitation input

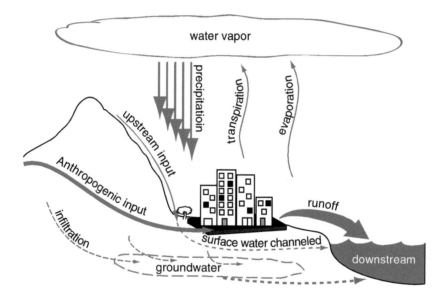

Figure 3.15 The urban water cycle.

Human control buffers the urban water cycle from the effects of large differences in inputs, primarily those due to precipitation. In the relatively small and young city of Curtin, Canberra, a wet year can receive almost four times as much precipitation as a dry year, generating an excess of stormwater leaving the city. Human wastewater, however, remains nearly constant from year to year, and levels of evapotranspiration are buffered by replacement of precipitation with piped-in water[384] (Figure 3.16).

Impermeable surfaces

The most prominent effects of the built environment result from the increase in the area covered by impermeable surfaces that water cannot penetrate[528] (Figure 3.17). These surfaces typically replace vegetation, thus reducing transpiration (T), infiltration, and recharge of groundwater (G). Instead, water from precipitation runs off rapidly into

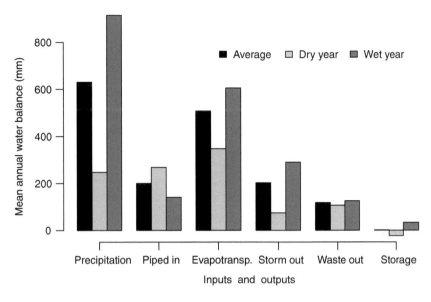

Figure 3.16 Inputs and outputs of water (in how many millimeters of water would cover the area) in the city of Curtin, Canberra in wet, dry, and average years (after Mitchell, 2003).

Figure 3.17 Impermeable surfaces and limited vegetation in the urban center of Dublin.

streams and storm sewers (R). The more rapid movement of surface water also reduces evaporation (E), as less water pools or remains in soil near the surface[10].

Rapid runoff can create more frequent and intense peak flows, and increased erosion downstream[135]. Impermeable surfaces accumulate contaminants during dry periods, including oil, detergents, nutrients, pesticides, and trash[528]. Runoff from these surfaces,

Table 3.4 Percentage of impermeable surface in selected cities
and regions

Region	Percent impermeable
New York City[605]	95%
Downtown Indianapolis[605]	75%
Urban counties of southern Minnesota[22]	36%
State of Minnesota[22]	1.9%
Contiguous United States[148]	1.4%

Table 3.5 Estimated percentage of water
infiltrating different land use types (after
Pauleit and Duhme, 2000)

Land	Infiltration percent
Built	5
Asphalt	5
Pavement	20
Bare soil	50
Coarse railway gravel	60
Woody vegetation	25
Meadow and pasture	35
Arable land	40

particularly at the beginning of a rainstorm, can be highly polluted. As we have seen, dark impermeable surfaces store substantial amounts of heat, and water that runs off can be significantly warmed[135].

Even a small percentage of impermeable surface cover profoundly alters the water cycle. When 10% of the land area is impermeable, downstream channel shapes change, water temperature rises, and pollution levels increase[528]. Although the planet as a whole lies well below this threshold, some urban areas are almost entirely impermeable (Table 3.4). The 1.4% of the contiguous United States covered by impermeable surfaces in the year 2000 roughly matches the area of the state of Ohio ($112\,610\,km^2$) and exceeds the total area of herbaceous wetlands in the country ($98\,460\,km^2$)[148].

Not all human modified surfaces are equally impermeable. Different land use types have quite different levels of infiltration (Table 3.5). For the city of Munich, the average percentage of water infiltrating the surface is 23%, about the same as for woodlands, although woodlands differ in having much more evapotranspiration and less runoff[437]. In this city, up to 75% of rain runs off in multistory housing blocks, and only 25% in low density housing.

Water movement and flood control

Urban areas accelerate the movement of water. Impermeable surfaces not only increase the fraction of precipitation that runs off, but also increase the velocity of that runoff. In addition, water that enters and passes through urban areas is often accelerated by design[135]. Because urban areas are intolerant of flooding, urban streams and rivers are

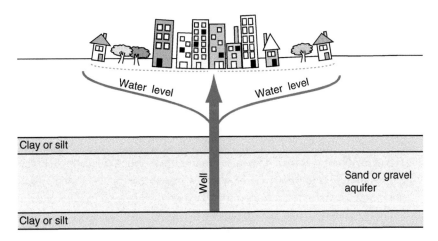

Figure 3.18 Land subsidence due to groundwater extraction.

often channeled so that water moves through quickly without spreading over the surrounding land. Many streams are relegated to underground pipes, sometimes joining
stormwater drainage systems that pipe water underground and out of the city as rapidly
as possible. Flooding in non-urban habitats can create large areas of temporary standing water which would be intolerable in the built environment. Flood control minimizes
these areas, but does sometimes replace them with *retention ponds* (Section 5.2) or other
methods for temporarily storing peak flows[236].

Water use

Residents of cities use large amounts of water, as much as 500 L per person per day[299].
Whether this usage exceeds local precipitation, as in Las Vegas or Los Angeles, or
is less than local precipitation as in New York City (Figure 2.3), it has major effects
on the ecosystem. Urban water generally follows a linear path from input to use to
output with essentially no recycling. Intensely urbanized cities like Tokyo can discharge
as wastewater almost 100% of inputs, although cities with substantial irrigation can
discharge as little as 40%[299,402]. The average city in the United States discharges 80%
of inputs as wastewater[299].

Even in areas with sufficient precipitation, water use comes primarily either from
groundwater or more distant sources. Overexploitation of groundwater from *aquifers*,
water stored in underground substrate, can lower the local *water table*. For example,
in Beijing, the water table dropped 45 m between 1950 and 1990[299]. The removal of
groundwater can lead to *land subsidence*, the lowering of the land surface (Figure 3.18).
In Mexico City, land levels have subsided by up to 7.5 m due to groundwater depletion[420]. Shallow groundwater in or near urban centers can be polluted by runoff from
impermeable surfaces, requiring people to dig deeper or transport water from more distant alternative sources. In coastal cities, groundwater pumping can lead to saltwater
intrusion into aquifers, again making water unfit for consumption[299].

In areas without sufficient groundwater, water must be imported. Only 34% of Los Angeles' water consumption is supplied by local groundwater extraction, with the remainder piped in from the Colorado River, the Sacramento–San Joaquin River delta, and runoff from the Sierra Nevada mountains[402]. This importation of water can drain external ecosystems like Owens Lake and Mono Lake, the latter of which is over 500 km away from the city itself.

Ironically, urban areas often divert water from nearby agricultural land, and thus reduce their own local food supply. This food shortage must be replaced by imports. The agricultural practices needed to produce these crops can be highly water intensive. For example, up to 1000 tons of water are used to produce a single ton of grain[452], stretching the urban water footprint far beyond the city's boundaries and the boundaries of the agricultural lands that support it.

Within the urban area itself, leakage from piped water supplies can partially refill areas of land subsidence, potentially destabilizing nearby structures. Up to 50% of piped water leaks in some large older cities[121], which can be a significant source of water for urban plants.

The boundaries between terrestrial and aquatic ecosystems are among the most sensitive habitats in urban areas. Urban wetlands have been largely lost to draining and construction, although some urban areas are now reversing this trend[300]. Urban riparian zones, the vegetated areas along the sides of streams and rivers, suffer from the acceleration of water flow through channelization. Less water infiltrates the banks of channelized streams, leading to a *hydrologic drought*[230]. Although water may be rushing by, it is not available to plants. This effective drought can induce a shift from wetland to upland plant species, a loss of rare species, and changes in ecosystem functioning. Riparian zones and wetlands serve as pollutant buffers, especially of nitrate, one of the most common groundwater pollutants in the United States (discussed in detail in Section 3.3).

Connections between the water cycle and weather

Urban habitat modification changes both temperature and water movement, and thus can have complex and conflicting effects on precipitation[519]. As we have seen, the urban heat island tends to increase precipitation. Warm air at the urban center rises, cools, and forms precipitation (Figure 3.13), as observed in temperate cities such as St. Louis and New York, and in desert cities such as Phoenix[47].

The amount and timing of locally generated precipitation depends on the interaction between the water and energy budgets of an urban area. Lower evapotranspiration in urban cores due to the lack of vegetation and rapid surface-water runoff reduces the moisture available to fall as precipitation. In dry climates, urban irrigation and water use during periods of low precipitation and high heat enhance generation of urban summer thunderstorms[490].

This locally generated weather interacts with large scale synoptic patterns, modulated by the vertical structure of the city and the strength of the urban heat island[520] (Figure 3.19).

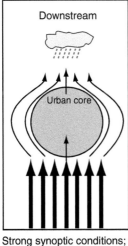
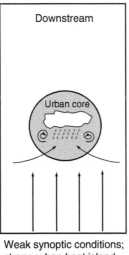
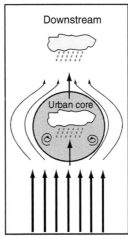

Figure 3.19 The interaction between large-scale weather patterns and the urban heat island, and its effect on precipitation.

- With a large synoptic event and a weak urban heat island, storms diverge around the city, the *building-barrier effect*, leading to decreased precipitation in the city and increased precipitation downwind.
- With a weak synoptic event and a strong urban heat island, the city has low pressure due to rising air, and storms converge into the city, increasing precipitation.
- With a moderate synoptic event and a moderate urban heat island, the convergence zone may be created within the city but then be carried downwind, moving some precipitation out of the city.

Fossil fuel combustion adds particulates and aerosols to the atmosphere, which can interact with local topography to create complex effects on precipitation. Particulates from urban industry and transportation can act as nuclei that seed urban rainstorms[89]. However, sufficient anthropogenic aerosols can have the opposite effect. With too many nuclei, cloud water vapor can be distributed among droplets that remain too small to fall as rain[491]. In a dry area with substantial aerosols such as Los Angeles, rainfall can be delayed by these small droplets. When rain finally falls, it may have bypassed nearby downwind upslopes and fall on more distant downslopes. This can lead to an overall decrease in precipitation within the basin of the city[216].

In extreme cases, aerosols can block incoming solar radiation. This decreases surface solar heating, reduces the convection generated by the urban heat island, and decreases the associated rainfall[468].

The combination of the urban heat island, moisture input, surface roughness, and urban aerosols leads to more precipitation and lightning around Atlanta, Georgia, although the relative importance of these different factors remains uncertain[490]. The number of lightning flashes in and downwind of urban areas is typically higher, although

Figure 3.20 A Roman aqueduct near Montpelier, France.

it is unknown whether this effect results primarily from more storms or from more intense storms[549]. In contrast, the large desert city of Cairo has lower rainfall than the surrounding non-urban area throughout the year, perhaps due to the substantially drier air in the city[483] or urban aerosols[521].

Just as the built environment breaks the urban environment into physical scales determined by humans, such as city blocks, the cycles of urban life can create urban weather patterns with temporal scales determined by humans[98]. In areas with large numbers of commuters, auto emissions can drive a strong weekly pollution cycle, with low air pollution levels early in the week (Sunday through Tuesday) and high pollution levels later in week (Thursday through Friday). Although the mechanisms are not fully understood, these aerosols may be involved in the "weekend effect" on temperature, with higher daytime temperatures on weekdays than on weekends[176]. These aerosols may also induce a 7-day precipitation cycle[28] with most rain on Saturdays when pollution peaks and the least rain on Mondays when air pollution is lowest. These effects are far from universal, however, with many studies finding no significant weekly trend[512].

Conclusions

In Neolithic times, water fell from the skies or arrived in streams, outside the control of the people who used it. Such sources of input were highly variable and highly unpredictable. Large concentrations of people in cities could not tolerate this unpredictability. To maintain a consistent supply of clean water, the natural water cycle had to be supplemented if not completely replaced. Early Roman cities built aqueducts to solve this problem (Figure 3.20). Contemporary cities follow the same design, but on an even

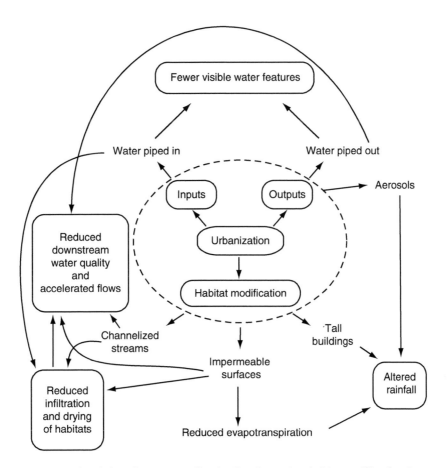

Figure 3.21 The chains of cause and effect leading from urban habitat modification, inputs, and outputs to changes in the urban water cycle.

grander scale. Water is now piped in and out of cities, while rainfall and streams are rushed out of the urban landscape into pipes and downstream.

Along with these intentional changes, the unintentional effects created by the built environment and impermeable surfaces in particular alter the flow of water and the timing and location of precipitation (Figure 3.21). The urban heat island generates its own weather in the form of convective thunderstorms. Pollution can seed the clouds, while tall buildings can interrupt prevailing weather patterns.

As with the climate, the urban environment has very different effects on the water cycle at the local and global scales. Locally, urban areas have low levels of water recycling. Globally, all water is eventually recycled, although it can be effectively unavailable for thousands of years when stored in the ice caps, oceans, or deep underground. Only a tiny fraction of water on Earth is available as fresh water. Humans use more than half of this[595], with much targeted to the agriculture that supports large cities. As with the ecological footprint, changes in the water cycle produce huge effects within the urban area that ripple outward, often unpredictably, beyond the urban boundary.

3.3   Urban nutrient dynamics

Living organisms, principally plants, play major roles in urban climate and urban water cycles through their ability to transpire large quantities of water. The cycles of nutrients are controlled even more strongly by living organisms. In urban areas, where the human industrial metabolism dominates the inputs and outputs of nutrients, nutrient cycles result from the interplay of pre-existing flows, inputs by humans, and the way that urban organisms use, transform, and embody these elements.

Nutrients are the elements and molecules necessary to sustain life. Nonetheless, every nutrient has a reservoir outside living organisms. Obviously this is true of water, which persists in liquid, solid, and gaseous forms. Nitrogen and carbon, the two elements in addition to hydrogen and oxygen most abundant in the human body, have large atmospheric reservoirs, with nitrogen primarily in the form of N_2 and carbon primarily in the form of carbon dioxide, CO_2. Carbon also has enormous stores in rocks, water, and living and dead organisms. Most other important nutrients, such as phosphorus, sulfur, and iron, are primarily stored in rocks and sediments.

When nutrients cycle through an ecosystem, moving among living organisms and reservoirs, they undergo chemical transformations (Figure 3.22). *Biogeochemical cycles* describe how an element shifts back and forth among different states, such as liquid, solid and gas, and different chemical compounds. Each element is useful to living things in only certain compounds, and which compound is useful depends on the organism.

Understanding nutrients is facilitated by the *Redfield ratio*, originally developed for marine phytoplankton[473]. This ratio relates the abundance of three key nutrients: carbon, nitrogen, and phosphorus as 106:16:1. Each molecule of phosphorus is matched by about 16 molecules of nitrogen, and 106 molecules of carbon (Figure 3.23). Although

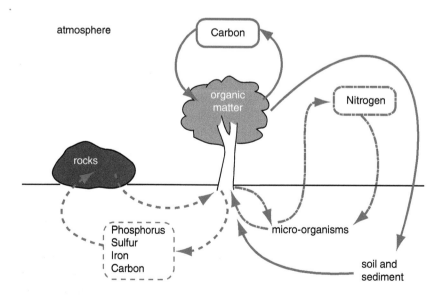

Figure 3.22 Cycles and reservoirs of five biologically important nutrients.

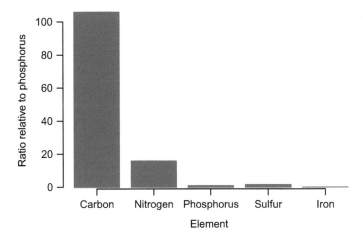

Figure 3.23 The Redfield ratio.

developed for organisms in the ocean, these values also provide a useful baseline for the plants that form the base of the terrestrial food chain. If one element falls below this ratio, it becomes the *limiting nutrient*, while if one greatly exceeds this ratio it can become a toxin or pollutant.

The nitrogen cycle most clearly illustrates the interactions between humans, other organisms, and the physical environment and is the most dramatically modified in the urban setting. The carbon cycle involves a simpler but still dramatic set of responses to urbanization. For many other nutrients, exemplified by sulfur, phosphorus, and iron, urban environments are more a site of increased inputs than a place where cycles are profoundly changed. In each of these cases, we examine the nutrient cycle in areas undisturbed by humans, sketch the global effects of humans, and look in detail at how the cycle is modified within the urban area itself.

The nitrogen cycle

Nitrogen is an unusual nutrient. It is extremely abundant but difficult to transform into biologically usable forms. Although it makes up 78% of the atmosphere, over 99% of atmospheric nitrogen exists in the form of nitrogen gas, N_2. N_2 is chemically inert because the two nitrogen atoms are linked by a highly stable triple bond that makes it unavailable for all but the most energy-demanding chemical reactions. Because nitrogen atoms are necessary chemical building blocks of nucleic acids and proteins, which are themselves the building blocks of life, atmospheric N_2 must be liberated for chemical availability through some process that can break that triple bond. Once that bond is broken, nitrogen cycles through a series of chemical forms in soil, water, organisms, and the atmosphere before eventually returning to the atmosphere as N_2 (Table 3.6).

Table 3.6 Important compounds in the nitrogen cycle

Name	Formula	Source and comment
Nitrogen gas	N_2	Atmosphere, denitrification
		Nearly chemically inert
Ammonia	NH_3	Bacteria, fertilizer
		Usually a gas, converted to ammonium
Ammonium	NH_4^+	Reactions involving ammonia
		Biologically available to bacteria
Nitric oxide	NO	Combustion, denitrification
		A nitrogen oxide, source of smog and ozone
Nitrous oxide	N_2O	Combustion, denitrification
		Source of smog and ozone, potent greenhouse gas
Nitrogen dioxide	NO_2	Combustion
		A nitrogen oxide, source of smog and ozone
Nitrate	NO_3^-	Bacterial nitrification, rain
		Biologically available to plants, negatively charged, soluble in water
Nitrite	NO_2^-	Like nitrate
		Rapidly interconverts to nitrate, together called nitrate
Nitric acid	HNO_3	Reactions of nitrogen oxides
		Component of acid rain and acid deposition

The non-urban cycle

The first step in the nitrogen cycle is *nitrogen fixation*, the conversion of atmospheric N_2 into reactive and potentially usable forms. In the absence of human effects, most nitrogen fixation is done by *nitrogen-fixing bacteria*. Although some of these bacteria live free in the soil, the majority are involved in mutualisms with plants that exchange sugars in return for nitrogen. One of the most important mutualisms is that between bacteria in the genus *Rhizobium* and legumes, plants in the pea family Fabeaceae, that includes roughly 20 000 species such as alfalfa, clover, and beans. These bacteria fix approximately 115–130 Tg (one *teragram*, Tg, equals 10^{12} g or 10^9 kg, and is equal to one megaton) of nitrogen per year (Figure 3.24). A smaller amount, approximately 10% as much or 10 Tg of nitrogen per year, is created by lightning, which has sufficient energy to directly fix N_2. Other events involving intense heat, such as forest fires and volcanos, contribute smaller amounts. Even larger amounts might be fixed in the oceans, although this has yet to be accurately quantified[77].

Nitrogen fixed by bacteria creates ammonia, NH_3, which can be converted to the ion ammonium NH_4^+ that can be used directly by plants, bacteria, or other organisms living in the soil. Nitrogen fixed by lightning creates nitrogen oxides, which dissolve in rainwater to eventually fall as nitrate, NO_3^-, which is also directly available to plants[195]. Animals receive all of their nitrogen either through consumption of plants or each other.

Eventually, all plants die or are eaten by herbivores. The excreted wastes from herbivores, along with the tissue from dead plants and animals, contains nitrogen in a variety of organic molecules. Bacteria, once again, return this nitrogen to biologically available ammonium through the process of *mineralization*. This cycle of mineralization,

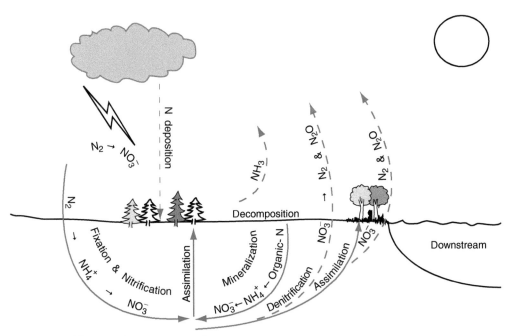

Figure 3.24   The non-urban nitrogen cycle.

uptake, and death can maintain usable nitrogen in an ecosystem for long periods of time[494].

When not taken up by plants, ammonium can be used by some bacteria as an energy source. Via reactions that require oxygen, they convert ammonia or ammonium into nitrite, NO_2^-, or nitrate, NO_3^-, a process called *nitrification*. Because these nitrite and nitrate ions convert readily into one another, they are often referred to collectively as *nitrate*. Both can be taken up directly by plants. These negatively charged compounds are highly mobile in the soil because soil itself is usually negatively charged, making nitrates more likely to reach flowing water or groundwater[53].

Nitrate can leave the biological cycle through *denitrification*. This chemical reaction occurs primarily in *anaerobic* conditions, the absence of oxygen, where nitrate is used as a substitute for oxygen during respiration[308]. In this process, most of the nitrate returns to the atmosphere as N_2. Globally, the amount of nitrogen lost from ecosystems by denitrification roughly balances the amount fixed, with a large majority of global denitrification occurring in lakes, rivers, estuaries, and shallow portions of the ocean[514].

Because it is necessary for all life, yet is directly available to only a few organisms, usable nitrogen is the limiting nutrient in many terrestrial ecosystems[594]. Aquatic ecosystems tend to have much more available nitrogen due to runoff of nitrate, and are often limited instead by phosphorus[74]. On land, the availability of nitrogen affects fundamental aspects of ecology, including community composition, species distributions, and interactions. For example, the species of plants that colonize areas with low nitrogen tend to associate with nitrogen-fixing bacteria[594].

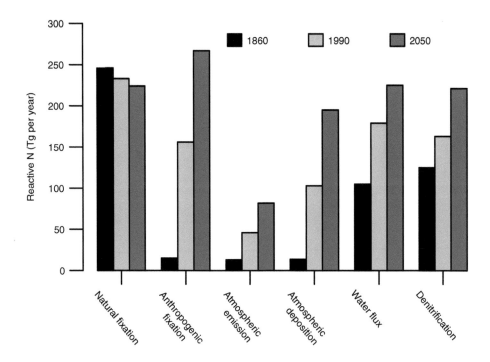

Figure 3.25 The global nitrogen budget and the effects of humans (after Vitousek *et al.*, 1997).

In non-urban ecosystems, nitrogen is typically recycled many times. Nitrogen is lost in two primary ways: when nitrate enters groundwater or runoff, and when denitrification returns nitrogen to the atmosphere. High levels of recycling reduce the amount that needs to be added to maintain a particular level.

Human effects on the nitrogen cycle

If the total terrestrially fixed nitrogen from natural sources (about 150 Tg) was spread evenly over the land area of the entire Earth (15×10^9 ha), it would provide about 10 kg of nitrogen per hectare per year[595]. Divided instead among the approximately 7.0×10^9 humans alive in 2012, this natural production would supply about 20 kg of nitrogen per person per year. Given that the average nitrogen content of protein is about 16% and the average person consumes about 24 kg of protein, the average per capita direct consumption of nitrogen is roughly 4 kg per year. Thus, natural nitrogen fixation could supply about five times as much protein as all humans require to survive.

Humans have greatly accelerated every component of the global nitrogen cycle by expanding and imitating the role of nitrogen-fixing bacteria and increasing nitrogen fixation by heat and combustion (Figure 3.25). Anthropogenic sources today fix more nitrogen than terrestrial bacteria and lightning combined[593].

Humans imitate nitrogen-fixing bacteria through production of fertilizer. The Haber–Bosch process uses large amounts of energy and methane to change atmospheric

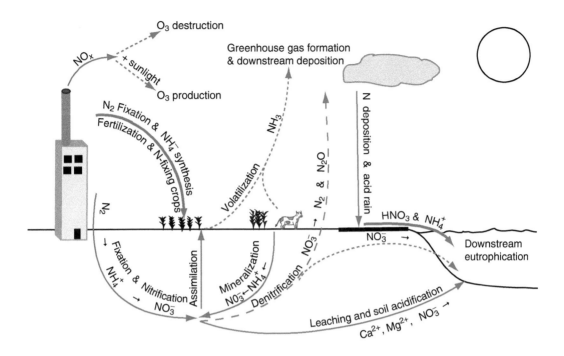

Figure 3.26 The urban nitrogen cycle.

nitrogen into ammonia. Humans use this and related processes to fix 80–100 Tg of nitrogen per year, an amount comparable to the total production by nitrogen-fixing bacteria[593]. This process alone commands roughly 2% of the world's annual energy use and 5% of the world's natural gas use[538]. Thanks to fertilizer input, agricultural production over the last century has increased about six-fold, approximately matching the increase in nitrogen inputs[612]. Planting of nitrogen-fixing agricultural crops, primarily legumes such as alfalfa grown as animal fodder, has increased the numbers of nitrogen-fixing bacteria themselves, effectively fixing an additional 40 Tg of nitrogen per year[595].

Human fossil fuel combustion mimics the effects of lightning and forest fires. Burning of fossil fuels also releases stored nitrogen, much as it releases stored carbon. These effects combine to add over 20 Tg of nitrogen per year to the atmosphere[593].

Of these sources, only combustion occurs primarily in urban areas. However, the concentrated demand for food in urban areas requires highly productive agriculture that can use as much as 300 kg of nitrogen per hectare per year and creates high nutrient, low diversity ecosystems[361].

The urban nitrogen cycle

Increased inputs and outputs and decreased recycling characterize the urban nitrogen cycle (Figure 3.26). Within the urban environment, nitrogen is imported, produced,

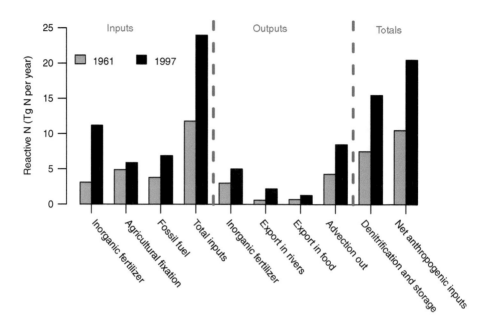

Figure 3.27   The chief inputs, production, and outputs of nitrogen from urban environments (after Howarth *et al.*, 2002).

and exported, with a large amount remaining as a stored surplus within the ecosystem itself[268] (Figure 3.27).

Urban nitrogen imports come in three main types: food, pet waste (itself a consequence of pet food importation), and fertilizer. At a density of 100 people per hectare, imported food supplies approximately 4 kg of nitrogen consumed per person per year, which would contribute 400 kg of nitrogen per hectare and swamp the average rate of natural nitrogen fixation. When combined with imported food that is thrown away, cities would be effectively poisoned by nitrogen without efficient export. The vast majority of nitrogen-rich human and food waste is exported from cities, but the same is typically not true of pet waste. Pet excrement is a significant source of surface nitrogen, adding up to 15 kg per hectare per year[14]. Pets are not the only other recipients of imported food. For example, in Mexico City, rodent excrement is also a major source of ammonia pollution[121].

Plants too require nitrogen, and humans input substantial quantities of fertilizer for lawns and gardens. Although the amounts have been little studied and surely vary widely from city to city and person to person, residents of Baltimore in 1982, for example, applied an average of 99 kg of nitrogen per hectare per year[321]. This quantity depends on the landscaping preferences of the residents, in addition to such factors as the age of the home (new homes typically receive more fertilizer). Even without fertilizer, urban plants receive higher nitrogen inputs. Although neither was directly fertilized, an urban arboretum experienced inputs of both ammonium and nitrate four to five times higher than a rural forest[563].

Urban nitrogen production comes primarily from fossil fuel combustion, with the resulting release of nitric oxide (NO) and nitrogen dioxide (NO_2), referred to collectively as nitrogen oxides or NO_x. Unlike fertilizer production and use for agriculture that occurs in areas of low population, the release through industry and transportation occurs within or near the urban ecosystem itself. In most cities, about half of urban NO_x production is from cars, with the rest primarily from industry. In Manchester, England, for example, vehicles add 40 000 metric tons of NO_x to the urban system each year[471].

Urban nitrogen exports come from human waste, nitrate exports in water, and atmospheric nitrogen exported via wind. The nitrogen concentration in water, where many of these pollutants dissolve, is positively correlated with population density within a watershed[593]. Urban centers typically have poor nitrogen retention, primarily due to changes in the water cycle resulting from impermeable surfaces (Section 3.2). In contrast, vegetation and soil in suburban watersheds retain nitrogen fairly effectively[233]. The fate of nitrogen used to fertilize urban lawns depends on lawn care practices, with urban lawn trimmings having the potential to retain or export over 100 kg annually per hectare[296]. As a result, nitrate concentrations in streams are highest in agricultural areas, moderate in urban areas, and lowest in forests[292].

Changes in the water cycle can also lead to a reduction in denitrification[230], which only occurs in the anaerobic conditions characteristic of saturated soils below the water table. Urban riparian streams have lower average flows at higher velocity, leading to lowered water tables, reduced infiltration into nearby soils, and hydrologic drought. This can leave soils in urban riparian areas "high and dry," and the bacteria unable to denitrify.

Urban nitrogen levels increase when inputs exceed outputs. Nitrogen accumulates in the city in several forms in soil organic matter and groundwater[14]. Like agricultural systems, urban areas can be effectively saturated and no longer nitrogen limited. When nitrogen is not limiting, it is taken up less quickly by plants or bacteria and builds up in soils. This excess nitrogen leaves the system either through the atmosphere as volatile ammonia or in water as negatively charged nitrate[231]. This dissolved nitrate can travel long distances in urban, suburban, and agricultural land before being removed by plants, again due to the high nitrate concentrations that exceed demand[240]. Urban forests that have four to five times as much nitrogen input show an even more extreme increase in the amount of nitrogen leaching out[563].

Wetlands serve as "kidneys" that retain and remove nitrogen and other nutrients, and this retention of nitrogen is often counted as an ecosystem service (Section 2.3). Wetlands are particularly effective as a buffer that can assimilate excess nitrate before it reaches lakes or oceans[231]. Urbanization tends to eliminate or degrade wetlands, resulting in decreased capacity to store nitrogen or remove it via denitrification[232]. Drying of wetlands quickly stops denitrification, triples nitrate release, and decreases N_2O production by 95%[183]. When functioning, both urban and non-urban wetlands denitrify roughly 10% of nitrates, mostly to N_2 rather than N_2O[246].

In the absence of wetlands, lawns can replace at least the storage function and act as net nitrogen sinks. Nitrogen retention levels in urban lawns and soils can be similar to those in urban forests[464].

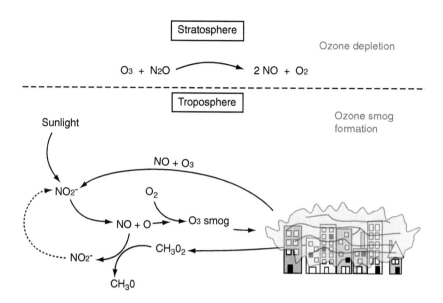

Figure 3.28 Some of the key reactions of nitrogen in the atmosphere.

Wetlands do not simply remove nitrogen from circulation. Nitrogen-saturated wetlands also convert nitrate to atmospheric nitrogen oxides, a form of atmospheric pollution[398]. In nitrogen-enriched wetlands, denitrification can produce and release smelly dimethyl sulfide $(CH_3)_2S$. As in nitrogen-rich urban areas themselves, wetlands can release volatile ammonia into the atmosphere, where it is transported and deposited as dust far downwind[183,398]. Similarly, water-soluble nitrogen compounds such as ammonium and nitrate can be released and transported far downstream. Thus wetlands may not provide a complete answer to urban nitrogen loading, as they can transfer the problem downstream or downwind.

Urban nitrogen effects include those on local and downstream biological communities and atmospheric conditions. The shift from nitrogen limitation to nitrogen saturation can have large-scale effects on communities. Initially, excess nitrogen enhances plant productivity. However, nitrogen-sensitive species such as mosses and ferns decline when nitrogen deposition exceeds about 25 kg per hectare per year[447], values vastly exceeded in both urban and agricultural areas.

Export of urban nitrogen downstream can lead to *eutrophication* of water bodies. After an initial period of fertilization and producer biomass accumulation, there can be a massive die-off of producers that leads to *hypoxic*, low oxygen, conditions caused by their decomposition. Nitrogen-associated eutrophication is particularly common in and near marine ecosystems and estuaries because freshwater lakes and rivers are usually phosphorus limited and thus less affected by increased nitrogen[508]. The dead zone, a hypoxic region in the Gulf of Mexico at the Mississippi River Delta where little life can be supported, results from high fertilizer inputs from urban and agricultural sources upstream[463].

The increased productivity facilitated by fertilization can transfer significant quantities of the greenhouse gas carbon dioxide from the atmosphere into living plants. However, this effect might be more than balanced by the increased production of nitrous oxide from denitrification in nitrogen-rich environments[294]. Nitrous oxide is a powerful greenhouse gas, more than 200 times as effective per molecule as carbon dioxide, that absorbs long-wave radiation outside the spectrum absorbed by most other greenhouse gases[320]. Only water vapor, carbon dioxide, and methane absorb more total radiation. Nitrous oxide remains in the atmosphere for over 100 years, meaning that high concentrations would take a long time to decline even if direct and indirect human production were to diminish[175].

Nitrogen compounds, particularly the nitrogen oxides, initiate complex reactions in the atmosphere (Figure 3.28). Nitric oxide, NO, is highly reactive in the *troposphere* (the lower atmosphere), where it contributes to photochemical ozone (smog) formation through a series of reactions involving sunlight[612].

Ozone formation can be delayed because nitrogen oxides released in an urban area may not react with sunlight until they have drifted downwind, often leading to higher ozone levels in downwind non-urban areas than in the original urban source. Ozone exposure prevents normal stomatal control in plants, interfering with gas exchange and water balance, and reducing photosynthesis and biomass production[225]. Because high ozone levels extend into heavily vegetated habitats outside the urban area, nitrogen pollution leads indirectly to reduced plant growth downwind[224] that can alter the carbon cycle by substantially reducing primary productivity[165].

Nitrogen oxides also react to form nitric acid, HNO_3, a principal component of acid rain and acid deposition[140]. Acid deposition usually occurs far from the source of production. Prevailing winds concentrate outputs from multiple urban centers, industrial plants, and power plants in the northeastern United States and northern Europe. Acidification of soil and water can lead to loss of sensitive species through several routes. Some are killed directly by the low pH[454], while others are harmed by leaching of important nutrients such as calcium and magnesium, or by the increased availability of toxic metals such as aluminum[330,571].

Nitrogen also poses direct and indirect health risks to humans (Section 5.1). Nitrate levels in drinking water are rising, and can interfere with basic physiological processes and cause adverse health effects, particularly in infants. The fine particulates created by nitrogen oxides have been associated with asthma and other lung diseases. Ozone in the troposphere can inhibit lung function and trigger acute discomfort and even death in urban inhabitants[27].

The complex chemistry and biology of the nitrogen cycle make it a source of a wide range of unintended consequences. Nitrogen inputs for the nutrition of humans, pets, and cultivated plants, coupled with releases from fossil fuels, saturate the urban ecosystem. Interactions with atmospheric cycles export some of the excess long distances as ammonia or acid rain. Changes in the urban water cycles can exacerbate nitrogen buildup by reducing denitrification, the process that returns nitrogen to its non-reactive form, and simultaneously promote rapid export of nitrate downstream to pollute distant water bodies (Figure 3.29).

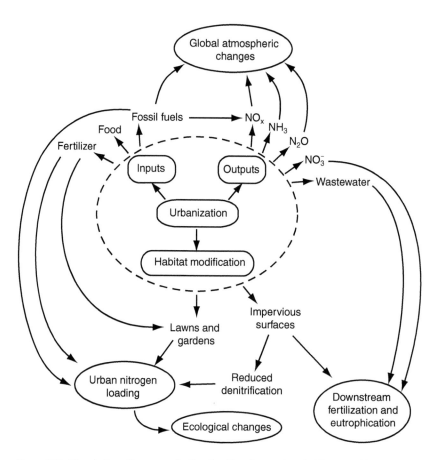

Figure 3.29 The chains of cause and effect leading from urban habitat modification, inputs, and outputs to changes in the urban nitrogen cycle.

The carbon cycle

Nitrogen is essential to life as the elemental building block of protein. Carbon is so closely associated with the whole range of molecules that make up living organisms that the presence of carbon defines an *organic molecule.*

As with nitrogen, the dynamics of carbon are largely governed by life. Earth's atmosphere had significantly more carbon dioxide in its early development. Through a combination of physical and biological processes, this level dropped to its current low value of less than 0.04% of the atmosphere. Key among these processes was the evolution of photosynthesis, when cyanobacteria began using carbon dioxide and emitting oxygen.

In its simplest terms, the carbon cycle begins when carbon dioxide from the atmosphere is fixed by plants, algae, and cyanobacteria through photosynthesis. This reaction uses solar energy to combine carbon dioxide and water to create sugars that store chemical energy. These chemical stores of carbohydrate molecules provide the energy that

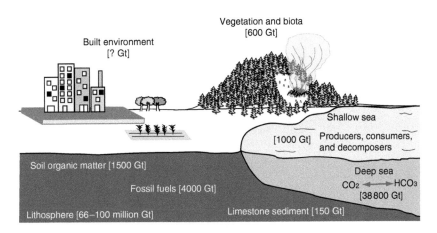

Figure 3.30 The major reservoirs of carbon on Earth. The total carbon stored in the physical structures of the built environment remains uncertain, but has been estimated at about 1.0 Gt for the United States alone[95].

flows through the food chain. Indeed, the fossil fuels upon which modern urban societies depend are stored carbohydrates from the distant past.

The non-urban carbon cycle

The vast majority of carbon on Earth is stored in rocks, many of which are deep underground. Changes in the slow exchange between these stores and the available carbon in the atmosphere and the oceans, through volcanic activity and movement of the tectonic plates, have driven the enormous changes in atmospheric carbon over periods of hundreds of millions or billions of years. Over the shorter time that humans have existed on Earth, exchange with these stores has been relatively constant, and faster biological cycles have been dominant.

The major accessible carbon stores are in the land, water, air, and living beings[451] (Figure 3.30). Atmospheric carbon is almost entirely in the form of carbon dioxide, with trace amounts of methane. Living organisms and soils contain more carbon than the atmosphere, with the amount in living marine organisms being much less due to their rapid turnover and generally small bodies. Ocean water holds far more carbon than marine organisms, in the forms of dissolved carbon dioxide, carbonic acid, and bicarbonate.

Carbon fluxes describe the movement of carbon among these stores (Figure 3.31). Carbon stores and fluxes are often measured in *gigatons* (10^9 metric tons, or 10^{12} kg). One gigaton is 1000 Tg, the units used to measure global nitrogen fluxes, meaning that carbon fluxes are much larger than nitrogen fluxes. The atmosphere and ocean exchange roughly 90 Gt of carbon each year, as carbon dioxide dissolves in the ocean or is released back into the atmosphere. Plants soak up about 111 Gt of carbon each year, almost all

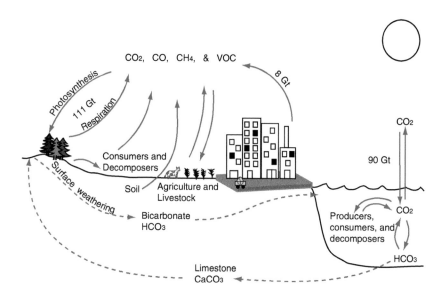

Figure 3.31 The carbon cycle.

of which returns via respiration by plants or soils. Humans add over 8.0 Gt per year to the atmosphere, or more than 1 metric ton per person per year.

Human effects at the global scale

Since the beginning of the industrial revolution, humans have been mobilizing carbon in fossilized plants and animals through combustion of fuels such as coal, oil, and natural gas. Atmospheric carbon dioxide levels have increased from 280 parts per million in 1800 to 315 parts per million in 1957 and over 390 parts per million at present[562] (Figure 3.32). This long-term trend contains an annual fluctuation, where carbon dioxide levels drop during the northern hemisphere summer due to the storage of carbohydrates in growing plants. The northern hemisphere dominates this global cycle because it has well over half the Earth's land area and a majority of plants.

Of the approximately 8.0 Gt of carbon humans add to the atmosphere per year, the majority, about 6.4 Gt, is from fossil fuel combustion and cement production. The remaining 1.6 Gt derives from land conversion, the removal of living plants via burning, and their replacement with grasslands or urban areas. These releases are partially balanced by absorption into the oceans, growing plants, and an unknown carbon sink, leading to an atmospheric increase of about 3.2 Gt per year[504]. Although the human inputs are dwarfed by the natural cycles, this steady human input has been sufficient to generate a long-term trend.

Urbanization acts as a primary driver of the global carbon cycle. In North America, approximately 40% of total fossil fuel emissions are from the transportation and residential sectors[237]. Agriculture, particularly the intensive agriculture needed to generate food for urban populations, converts large amounts of land and uses large amounts of energy. Cement production for building releases substantial carbon from the processing

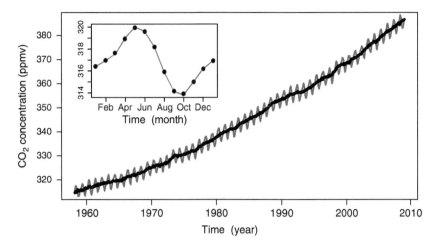

Figure 3.32 The increase of atmospheric carbon dioxide in parts per million (after Tans, 2009).

of calcium carbonate rich limestone, and accounts for 4–5% of anthropogenic atmospheric carbon, or 0.3 Gt per year[618].

Methane is the only other significant form of carbon in the atmosphere, with levels hundreds of times lower than those of carbon dioxide. Methane is produced by anaerobic fermentation, and thus comes primarily from low oxygen environments, with wetlands generating over 80% of the natural total. However, Earth's methane concentration has more than doubled from 700 parts per billion in the preindustrial era to 1750 parts per billion in 2000. Roughly half of total methane emissions are associated with humans, coming primarily from fuel combustion, landfills, gut-fermenting livestock, and rice paddies[48,180].

The urban carbon cycle

Due to fossil fuel combustion, urban centers have elevated carbon dioxide concentrations, often 50% higher than surrounding non-urban areas[309]. The level varies over the course of the year, and indeed over the course of a single day. Urban carbon dioxide levels usually peak in the morning, after vegetation has respired and released carbon dioxide during the night, and while cars release carbon dioxide during the morning commute. Levels are usually lower in the afternoon between the morning and afternoon commutes when plants consume carbon dioxide via photosynthesis (Figure 3.33). These patterns are strongest in areas with high traffic density and during the growing season in places with abundant urban vegetation[227].

Urban carbon dioxide production exceeds non-urban production by the greatest amount during winter, when respiration from plants and soil is low and fuel use for heating is high. In Los Angeles, as much as 60% of urban carbon dioxide can come from natural gas heating in winter and a much smaller percentage from plant and soil respiration. In the spring and early fall, this relationship reverses. Gasoline combustion contributes a relatively steady 15–30% of carbon dioxide throughout the year[432].

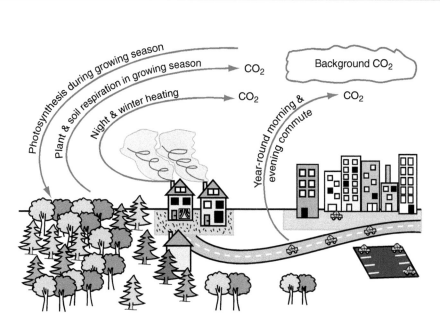

Figure 3.33 The carbon cycle in urban areas.

These factors can combine to produce an impressive *urban CO$_2$ dome* over a city, much like the urban dust dome (Figure 3.12). In the Phoenix area, carbon dioxide levels in the central city regularly reach over 600 parts per million on weekdays, with much lower levels in nearby non-urban areas[272] (Figure 3.34). The size and strength of this dome depends on the spatial structure of a city. For example, low density housing spreads urban-associated carbon dioxide emissions over a larger area.

Carbon monoxide, which can be deadly to humans in high concentrations[619], comes almost entirely from combustion and shows a much stronger urban–rural gradient than carbon dioxide. Levels can be over 100 times higher in an urban area than in nearby non-urban areas. Cars produce over 90% of urban carbon monoxide, thus making concentrations in enclosed locations such as tunnels extremely high, often over 200 parts per million and well above the level where humans experience short-term symptoms[471]. Carbon monoxide is not harmful to plants, which can oxidize it into carbon dioxide.

Carbon dioxide levels in the atmosphere today, even with the increase due to humans, are much lower than when plants first evolved on land, and are among the lowest during the past 500 million years[496]. Plants today are therefore comparatively carbon dioxide limited, and can grow more quickly within the urban CO$_2$ dome and can absorb a small amount of the excess carbon. In the United States, urban trees store 0.7 Gt of carbon, and soak up an additional 0.02 Gt per year.

Carbon storage by trees requires, of course, that trees can survive in the urban environment, which requires in turn the persistence and health of the soils in which they grow. As we will see, urban soils are often highly modified and stressed (Section 3.4). Nonetheless, urban soils globally store about 2.0 Gt of carbon, more than twice the amount in urban trees although only a small percentage of the total found in soils

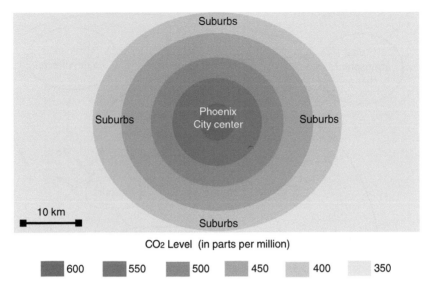

CO2 Level (in parts per million)

| 600 | 550 | 500 | 450 | 400 | 350 |

Figure 3.34 The carbon dome over Phoenix (after Idso *et al.*, 2001).

worldwide[21]. Urban areas can store as much carbon as a tropical forest, with most in soil and vegetation, lower amounts in water and buildings, and rather little in the actual people[95]. Estimates of urban carbon storage differ by as much as a factor of five depending on the particular definition of urban[465].

Urban development initially leads to loss of carbon from soils, but subsequent reduced biological activity coupled with continued carbon inputs eventually increases soil carbon. Turfgrass can sequester substantial quantities of carbon, as much as 1000 kg per hectare per year for up to 30 years after establishment, an amount comparable to that in land set aside for conservation reserves[462]. In the relatively dry climate of Denver, soil carbon in turfgrass can reach levels higher than those of the surrounding shortgrass prairie after about 40 years[458].

Although somewhat less complex than the nitrogen cycle, carbon inputs and habitat changes create unintended consequences for plants, the atmosphere, and urban humans (Figure 3.35). The atmosphere transports these effects around the globe, creating climatic changes that are becoming increasingly evident.

Other nutrients

Among the many other elements necessary for life, we consider just three: sulfur, phosphorus, and iron. In the Redfield ratio, sulfur and phosphorus are about a factor of ten less abundant than nitrogen in living beings (Figure 3.23). Iron does not follow such tight ratios, but is essential both for photosynthesis in plants and oxygen transport in animals[208]. In contrast with carbon and nitrogen, living organisms and the atmosphere play a relatively small role in the dynamics of these other nutrients, and their cycles are less strongly affected by urbanization.

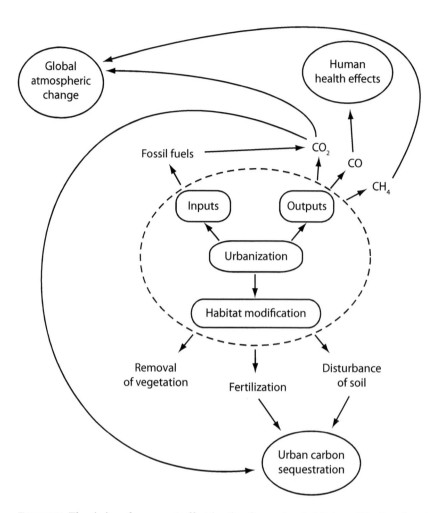

Figure 3.35 The chains of cause and effect leading from urban habitat modification, inputs, and outputs to changes in the urban carbon cycle.

The sulfur cycle

Sulfur is an essential element in all cells, being required in some of the amino acids that build proteins, and in many enzymes. Like nitrogen, sulfur cannot be extracted from the environment by animals, and thus cycles through plants[298]. Unlike nitrogen, however, the major reservoir of unreactive sulfur is in solid mineral form in sedimentary rocks that can be made reactive when dissolved in water.

Because all plants contain sulfur, fossil fuel combustion releases the sulfur stored by ancient plants into the atmosphere. About 75 Tg per year of sulfur are mobilized through fossil-fuel combustion. Human activity mobilizes an additional 75 Tg per year through ore refining, dust from farming, ranching, increased dry lake sediment exposure, and dimethyl sulfide released from nitrogen-loaded wetlands[194]. In combination, these processes vastly exceed the natural rates of sulfur mobilization. Although many of these processes occur outside the urban boundary, combustion increases sulfur levels in urban soils[532], and generates sulfur dioxide that is a significant urban and downwind pollutant.

The phosphorus cycle

Phosphorus, as a component of DNA, RNA, and ATP, is essential for all life, particularly in animals that use it to build bones and teeth. Although it makes up only a small fraction of the mass of most plants, phosphorus, along with nitrogen and potassium, is used in fertilizers. Phosphorus is quite scarce in the Earth's crust, and acts as the limiting resource in many ecosystems, such as the oceans[579]. Over short periods of time, the phosphorus cycle acts like a one-way flow: weathering from rocks, rapid cycling through living organisms, and eventual loss to sedimentation[76].

Humans mobilize large quantities of phosphorus through mining and extraction from phosphorus-containing rock with sulfuric acid. This phosphorus is used mostly as fertilizer and less so in carbonated drinks and animal feed[57]. Fertilization both increases human food production and increases the phosphorus content of crops. Humans have approximately tripled global phosphorus mobilization, leading to phosphorus saturated ecosystems[537].

As with sulfur, these processes occur primarily outside the urban boundary, but urban areas can act to concentrate phosphorus[171]. Urban soils have significantly elevated phosphorus levels[445]. Of the phosphorus imported into the Twin Cities in Minnesota, over 33% derives from chemicals such as detergents, about 28% from consumed food, 12.5% from wasted food, and 13.5% from pet food[12]. These inputs are only partially balanced by outputs, primarily in wastewater, with about 65% stored as sludge, landfills, septic systems, and the ecosystem itself. About 3.7 kg/person of phosphorus enter the city of Gavle, Sweden, each year, with only about 30% being exported. The rest remains in the urban area, primarily in the form of sewage sludge in landfills, which can slowly leach into the surrounding environment[121]. Thus the city can act as both a sink and a source, concentrating and slowly releasing materials.

Very little urban phosphorus is deliberately exported, such as only 4% from the Twin Cities, even though it could potentially provide enough fertilizer for 50% of the city's food needs[12]. Instead, phosphorus either remains in area or moves downstream. In the absence of appropriate treatment, urban sewage containing concentrated human waste and phosphate detergents can lead to eutrophication downstream. Recent laws have limited phosphates in cleansers and improved sewage treatment, substantially reducing urban outputs over the last several decades[12].

The iron cycle

Iron is the only metal we include in our brief inventory of nutrients. It is the most abundant heavy metal in the human body, and has long been central to industry and building. Urban areas import huge quantities of iron and export at least some of the excess[392]. The durability and value of metals means that iron is stored and recycled more efficiently than the other nutrients we have considered.

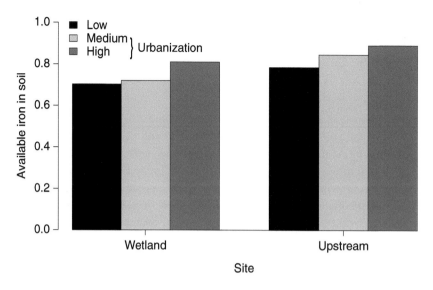

Figure 3.36 The fraction of biologically available iron in soil as a function of urbanization (after Hogan and Walbridge, 2007).

Because of the large amount of impermeable surface, urban wetlands receive more iron deposition than non-urban wetlands (Figure 3.36). Furthermore, construction and erosion common to cities lead to the iron being deposited in urban wetlands in a highly crystalline form, which alters downstream absorption of other nutrients such as phosphorus[259].

The elements that make up the human body

The urban environment depends on the same nutrients and elements as an animal. Combustion releases the stored elements from ancient plants, including most of the elements in the human body in addition to the carbon, nitrogen, and sulfur we have already considered (Table 3.7). It is remarkable that almost all of the essential elements are more concentrated in the urban environment.

Conclusions

The urban metabolism alters the basic cycles of nearly every element that is essential for life through a combination of increased inputs, altered natural processes, accumulation, or storage within the urban system, and increased outputs. The uses and sources break into four main categories.

1. Fertilizer for urban plants (nitrogen, phosphorus, sulfur, potassium, and many others).
2. Building materials (iron, calcium, and carbon).
3. Industrial materials (zinc and other heavy metals).
4. Byproducts of combustion (carbon, nitrogen, sulfur).

Table 3.7 The 15 most common elements in the human body, the mass in a typical 70 kg person, and key changes in the urban system [150].

- **Oxygen** (43 kg) Primarily in water molecules, abundant in the atmosphere, reactive and converted to atmospheric pollutants including ozone and nitrogen compounds.
- **Carbon** (16 kg) Enriched in urban areas.
- **Hydrogen** (7 kg) Primarily in water molecules, component of many atmospheric pollutants.
- **Nitrogen** (1.8 kg) Enriched in urban areas.
- **Calcium** (1.0 kg) Concentrated in urban systems due to presence in cement and other building materials, a component of many fertilizers, elevated in urban soils [445].
- **Phosphorus** (780 g) A component of many fertilizers, enriched in urban areas.
- **Potassium** (140 g) A component of many fertilizers, elevated in urban soils [445].
- **Sulfur** (140 g) Released by combustion and a component of many fertilizers.
- **Sodium** (100 g) Elevated in urban areas primarily due to the use of road salt.
- **Chlorine** (95 g) The other element component of salt, similar to sodium in both the body and the urban environment. Also a component of many fertilizers.
- **Magnesium** (19 g) A component of many fertilizers, elevated in urban soils [445].
- **Iron** (4.2 g) A component of many fertilizers and building materials.
- **Fluorine** (2.6 g) Present in chlorofluorocarbon and other industrial processes, elevated near some sources and probably in urban areas due to combustion [187].
- **Zinc** (2.3 g) A component of many fertilizers, accumulating due to imports of about 5.0 kg/person each year, only a fraction of which is discarded or recycled [547].
- **Silicon** (1.0 g) Often bound to metals, including lead, exported from agricultural soils in foods [586], not known to accumulate in urban areas.

The physical and biological properties of each nutrient determine both its range of human uses and the effects of the urban metabolism. Individual decisions and lifestyles create wide variation in the amount of nutrients that different households consume, particularly for transportation [171] (Figure 3.37).

From the perspective of nutrients, a city is like a large organism such as an elephant. Both have huge resource demands and rely on their environments and their own ability to transform chemicals in order to obtain essential nutrients. Those that survive are thriving concentrations of reactive nutrients. The elephant ultimately relies on plants to provide usable carbon, bacteria and plants to provide usable nitrogen, and physical processes to provide usable phosphorus, sulfur, and iron.

Humans have taken matters into their own hands. Fertilizer and irrigation enhance carbon fixation by plants, ancient carbon stores provide enormous supplies of energy, chemical technology fixes previously unusable nitrogen from the atmosphere, and mining harvests geological stores of phosphorus and iron. This intentional nutrient collection can be overshadowed by associated unintentional nutrient releases. Fossil fuel combustion releases carbon compounds and reactive forms of nitrogen and sulfur. Changes in land use and the water cycle modify the biological and physical processes that naturally regulate nutrient cycles, often further increasing availability of reactive forms. Together these intentional and unintentional processes create the urban concentration of reactive nutrients.

How long these processes can take to alter biological communities is illustrated by the Park Grass experiment, which began in 1856 and compares plant communities at

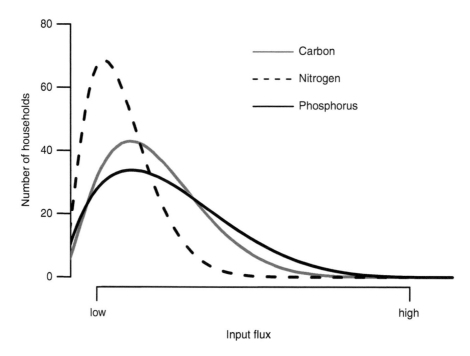

Figure 3.37 Distribution of household inputs of carbon, nitrogen, and phosphorus in the Minneapolis-Saint Paul region of Minnesota (after Fissore *et al.*, 2011).

different levels of fertilization[530]. Although plant communities diverged in as little as 20 years, it took about 50 years for them to settle down to a relatively constant state. Halting fertilization did not quickly return the plots to the characteristics of unfertilized plots because the fertilized plots had reduced pH (became more acidic), which rebounded only slowly. Low pH eliminates earthworms and reduces microbial activity, leading to a buildup of undecomposed matter, high soil carbon, and reduced root penetration, which in turn leads to increased drought sensitivity. The complex and slowly developing results of this controlled experiment give some indication of the delayed and unpredictable effects of urban nutrient concentration.

We know that nutrient concentrations can transform the ecology of plants, animals, and bacteria within the city, overflow to similarly modify downstream ecosystems, and indeed spread around the increasingly nutrient-rich globe. Living things today find themselves awash in nutrients. How some flourish in these resource-rich conditions while others decline is a focus of Chapter 4.

3.4   Urban ecological amplification and its consequences

For the organisms that inhabit them, urban ecosystems operate faster, with more inputs, outputs, and novel challenges. The concentration of materials and nutrients, higher temperatures, and the accelerated pace of cycling can be described as amplification.

Amplified cycles spill over the urban boundaries, and transform environments both in and near urban areas.

As the ultimate ecosystem engineers, humans have always transformed their environment. Hunter-gatherers, who live at low population density, change fire regimes and local flora and fauna. Agriculture, by modifying the land more completely and accentuating resource and labor inputs, allows people to live at higher population density and create built environments.

Built environments enable yet higher population density and increase the demand for inputs of resources and outputs of waste. Cities concentrate consumption, transformation, and production of goods and waste, creating the intense pace that characterizes urban life. Although urban areas take up only 1–3% of the Earth's land surface, they directly or indirectly generate the majority of global greenhouse gas emissions and of residential water and wood demand (Section 2.1).

This energy-intensive amplification of ecosystem processes creates the changes in climate, the water cycle, and nutrients studied in this chapter. The urban heat island accelerates life for plants and animals. Land transformation intensifies disturbance. Increased impermeable surface area generates accelerated and highly variable water flow. Fossil fuel combustion loads the ecosystem with chemicals and nutrients.

Amplification characterizes the links among the urban cycles of water, weather, and nutrients, and ultimately of urban life itself. This section considers three such links. First, increased material and chemical movement generates *pollution*, either in the form of excessive nutrients or novel compounds. Second, urban soils, the often neglected "downstream in the city" serve as a sink for nutrients and pollutants and a buffer for the outputs of amplified ecosystem processes. Third, the transport of goods over long distances creates chains of intended and unintended consequences, where amplification at one spot and for one purpose affects distant locations and apparently unrelated processes.

Urban pollution

Pollution is an inevitable consequences of amplified processes. The effects of pollution depend on many factors: its nature, concentration, source, movement, and eventual fate. Most urban pollution arises from the same processes that increase nutrient levels:

- Fossil fuel combustion,
- Inputs of food, fertilizer, and materials,
- Outputs of household and manufacturing waste,
- Accumulation and export of compounds on impermeable surfaces.

These diverse processes generate a diverse array of pollutants (Table 3.8), each with its distinctive characteristics and effects.

Although many cities still house industries that generate *point-source pollution*, where outputs emerge from effluent pipes or smokestacks (Figure 3.38), urban areas are characterized by *non-point source pollution* with sources spread over large areas. Automobiles are a key non-point source, by expelling the products of combustion into

Table 3.8 Common urban pollutants, their sources, and their fates

Name	Formula or acronym	Source and fate
Carbon dioxide	CO_2	Fossil fuels Distributed worldwide
Carbon monoxide	CO	Fossil fuels Urban atmosphere and downwind
Volatile organic compounds	VOC	Trees, fuels, solvents, refrigerants Distributed widely in atmosphere
Methane	CH_4	Fuels, livestock, landfills Distributed widely in atmosphere
Ammonia	NH_3	Bacteria, fertilizer Reacts with water to make acid rain
Ammonium	NH_4^+	Bacteria, fertilizer, excrement Downstream water bodies
Nitric and nitrous oxide	NO, N_2O	Combustion, denitrification Urban atmosphere and downwind
Nitrate	NO_3^- or NO_2^-	Nitrification, rain Downstream water bodies
Nitric acid	HNO_3	Nitrogen oxides Downstream water bodies
Ozone	O_3	Nitrogen oxides, heat, and sunlight Urban atmosphere and downwind
Sulfur dioxide	SO_2	Fossil fuels, volcanoes Precursor to acid rain and particulates
Particulates	$PM_{2.5}, PM_{10}$	Combustion, disturbance Urban atmosphere and downwind

the air[20] and through the oil, road salt, worn tires, and atmospheric pollutants that accumulate on roads and run off during rain into urban water[505]. Other impermeable urban surfaces accumulate pet and pest waste that can also end up in the water. When accelerated runoff from impermeable surfaces overloads the storm-sewage system capacity, untreated sanitation sewage can enter downstream waters, a problem more common in older cities where storm and sanitary sewers are not separated[168,600].

The use of de-icing salts provides a case study in unintended consequences. The United States uses about 10 million metric tons of salt per year, or 30 kg/person. This salt does not just disappear, but can move through soil to groundwater, run off from the surface into surface waters, enter the atmosphere as dust or droplets, or enter the soil and be taken up by plants[111].

Urban waters show an increasing salinity as a function of the percentage of impermeable surfaces, with many exceeding the 250 mg/L recommended for freshwater life[293]. In winter, salt concentrations can rise to 5.0 g/L, which is 25% as salty as seawater[293]. Urban stream salinity, although highest in the winter, stays high all year, and exceeds that of streams draining forests and agricultural areas by roughly 100 times[293]. Because salt breaks into its component ions, it generates a chain of chemical effects that include acidification and release of heavy metals in soil[358], and physical effects on the mixing of deep and shallow layers of water[466]. The chemical effects translate into biological

Figure 3.38 Urban industry can release point-source pollution as in this photo of Dublin.

effects by interfering with denitrifying bacteria, promoting growth of some algae, and altering communities by promoting invasion by salt-tolerant species[293]. Salt is both widespread and persistent, and remains to change ecosystems not only over the course of a single year, but for decades[293].

In the atmosphere, fossil fuel combustion for transportation releases compounds we have studied, such as carbon monoxide and carbon dioxide, nitrogen oxides, and sulfur dioxide. Particulates, or small particles, also play key roles in the urban atmosphere, and are classified by size into the fine fraction (less than 2.5 µm, or $PM_{2.5}$) and the coarse fraction (less than 10 µm, or PM_{10}). The smaller particles, which are largely anthropogenic in origin, present the most severe health dangers because they can penetrate deeply into the lungs and have longer atmospheric residence times[25]. The largest particles, or dust, are lifted from the ground into the atmosphere by wind. Although some dust is natural, human disturbance can vastly increase quantities. In California, where the ocean generates the majority of coarse particulates in non-urban areas, urban particulates derive primarily from transportation-related sources[93] (Figure 3.39).

Depending primarily on their size and half-life in the atmosphere, pollutants generated in the urban environment may remain concentrated there, spread to nearby downwind locations, or spread around the entire globe[317]. Particulates and dust remain mainly in the urban core, with PM_{10} concentrations in Mexico City up to 10 times greater than in non-urban areas[121], and urban carbon monoxide levels also much greater than the non-urban background. In contrast, urban carbon dioxide and methane levels are rarely more than twice those in surrounding non-urban regions[342,592]. The less mobile pollutants, such as carbon monoxide and nitrous oxides, have daily peaks during rush hour[317].

The 2008 Olympics in Beijing provided a natural experiment regarding the sources and timing of urban air pollution. The Chinese government shut down many polluting industries, reduced powerplant operations by 70%, and banned driving by the approximately 50% of cars that failed to meet emissions standards. In consequence, NO_2 levels

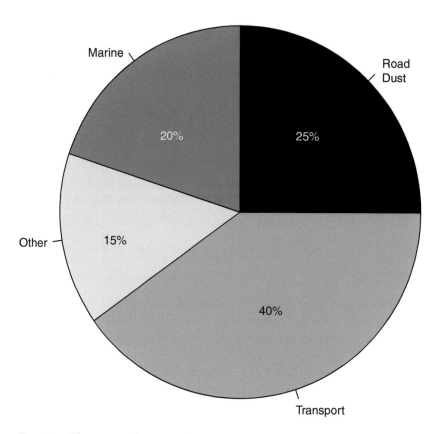

Figure 3.39 The sources of PM_{10} particulates in Santa Barbara, California (after Chow *et al.*, 1996).

decreased by 43% in the city, and carbon monoxide and sulfur dioxide levels decreased by about 12% in surrounding areas[613].

The production of ozone results from a complex set of reactions involving volatile organic compounds (often called VOCs), nitrogen oxides, and sunlight. In relatively wet urban areas, trees generate the majority of volatile organic compounds, often in the form of the potent ozone-producer isoprene C_5H_8, although human production from fuels and solvents is substantial[612]. Humans generate the majority of nitrogen oxides, although some occur naturally in nitrogen-enriched ecosystems. These sources create complex patterns of ozone production. Ozone levels are highest in the spring and summer due to the role of sunlight, and often later in the work week after pollutants have built up[612]. The time taken for ozone to be produced means that downwind ozone levels can exceed those in the urban source[224].

When not dispersed by wind, urban atmospheric pollutants can adhere to surfaces, often to be eventually washed off by rain. Urban forests and vegetation sequester some atmospheric pollutants[25], although the estimated effects on air quality improvement remain low[406] (Figure 3.40). The large vertical and horizontal surface area of cities acts as an "urban scrubber" that removes particulates from the air as effectively as trees[341].

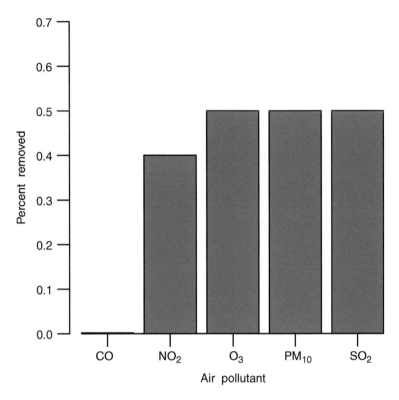

Figure 3.40 Estimated fraction of different pollutants removed from the atmosphere by urban trees (after Nowak *et al.*, 2006). The percentage removed is well below 1% for each pollutant.

This brief section only sketches some of the sources, movement, and effects of urban pollutants. The ways that habitat modification, inputs, and outputs interact with ecosystem and ecological processes ranging from air and water movement to plant growth determine how pollutants affect the urban ecosystem, surrounding regions, and the rest of the planet.

Soils

Urban pollutants in the atmosphere or water are either quickly or slowly exported and usually diluted. Those that enter the soil can instead be concentrated. Urban soils are at the receiving end not only of chemical pollutants but also many other forms of urban amplification: disturbance and alterations of surfaces, changes in water movement, and material, chemical, and nutrient inputs[439]. Like a photograph, soils retain an image of the urban ecosystem around them. Although the image can be freshest immediately after development or major disturbance, soils evolve in novel ways thereafter, rarely returning to their pre-urban state[444].

Soil consists of a mix of mineral and organic matter capable at least in principle of supporting plants[142]. Urban soils range from completely novel types to more or

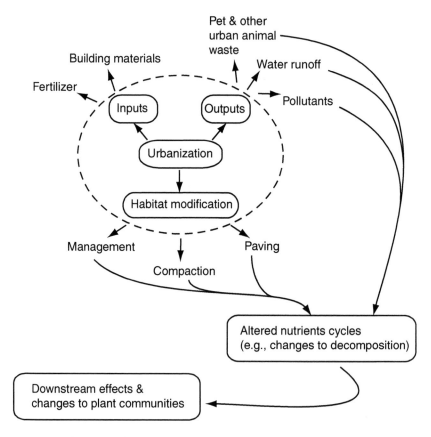

Figure 3.41 The chains of cause and effect leading from urban habitat modification, inputs, and outputs to changes in the urban soils.

less unmodified versions of non-urban soils. Because soil does not move as readily as air or water, many aspects of local conditions make urban soils extremely variable in space[439]. The most extreme urban soils are *made land*, the composite debris from building material and soil deposited during construction[444]. Most urban soils, however, combine existing soil material with anthropogenic materials from landfills, construction, or other human activities[142]. Some of these soils have been buried beneath impermeable surfaces, and cut off from inputs of light, water, and nutrients. Exposed soil frequently experiences *compaction* by heavy machinery or trampling that reduces the amount of air space, the ability to transport water, and suitability for plant growth[358].

Given the importance of soils in ecosystem functioning, the consequences of amplification are far-reaching (Figure 3.41). Most nutrient recycling takes place in soils, which provide the platform for plant uptake to recycle nutrients through the ecosystem[439]. Soils control the flow and storage of water, and intercept and potentially store pollutants such as heavy metals and pesticides[444] which can end up in plants[532]. Lowering the water table may create a hydrologic drought, oxygenating the soil, and short-circuiting the nitrogen cycle.

Table 3.9 Examples of local factors that affect soils.

- Soil resources
  1. Water
  2. Nitrogen and other fertilizers
  3. Leaf litter and detritus
- Abiotic conditions
  1. Temperature
  2. Metals and other pollutants
  3. Soil acidity or pH
- Disturbance
  1. Mowing
  2. Pesticides
  3. Compaction

Compaction diminishes percolation of surface water into the groundwater, and can create a water-repellent surface layer, similar to an impermeable surface[358], both of which reduce removal of soluble chemicals and promote higher soil chemical content[455]. Urban soils have higher concentrations of heavy metals, nitrogen, phosphorus, organic matter, salts, and acids than their non-urban counterparts[455]. Soil disturbance can effectively invert soils, burying decomposers that typically live on the surface and exposing subsoil organisms[339] (Table 3.9).

Given its position downstream from urban processes, urban soil chemistry experiences complex and often contradictory forces. Some factors increase the pH of urban soils, thus making them more basic: mineral rich irrigation water and weathering of rubble add positively charged calcium ions, and road salt adds positively charged sodium ions[358]. This higher pH occurs primarily in built areas designed for commerce, transportation, and industry[457]. Conversely, nutrients and acid rain can decrease the pH of urban soils and make them more acidic. High inputs of sodium can displace the key nutrients calcium and magnesium, build up a positive charge that disperses organic and inorganic particles, decrease permeability to water, and increase runoff and erosion[466].

The resulting stress on soil decomposers and primary producers affects the quality and quantity of soil organic matter[456]. In general, urban soil has a higher carbon to nitrogen ratio, making these soils of lower quality for plant growth[366]. Earthworms are more abundant at the urban end of a gradient from New York City to western Connecticut, where both nitrogen mineralization and nitrification are also higher[552]. Many of the earthworms at the urban end are non-native (Section 1.3), an example of the interplay between ecosystem change and species identity that forms the focus of Chapter 4.

The change in soil nutrient ratios can also initiate a chain of ecological changes in plants. An increased carbon to nitrogen ratio favors plants that use the more ancient C_3 version of photosynthesis over those using the more recently evolved C_4 photosynthesis, which is used by many crop plants and weeds, including maize *Zea mays* and crabgrass *Digitaria*[500]. C_3 grasses tend to be higher in protein than C_4 grasses[15], and thus favor many herbivores[49]. These two forms of photosynthesis also respond differently to the

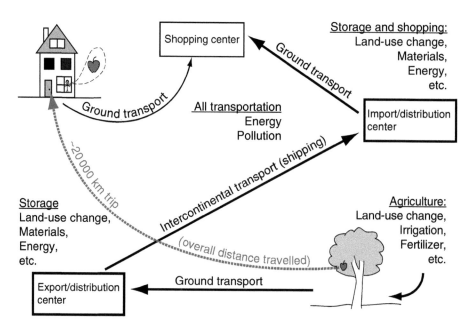

Figure 3.42 Some of the consequences of wanting an apple.

urban heat island and CO_2 dome. The C_4 form of photosynthesis functions best in hot and dry conditions, and might be favored in hot urban areas. Increased carbon dioxide benefits all plants, but benefits C_3 plants more because they must cease photosynthesis in dry conditions to avoid excessive water loss. High levels of CO_2 reduce the protein content of C_3 plants, but have little effect on C_4 plants [15].

The C_4 pathway has evolved many times, but probably emerged first about 30 million years ago [421]. The spread of C_4 plants to about 5% of all land plants has been a slow but steady response to underlying climate and ecological change. These changes might be accelerated to occur over a period of decades in urban areas.

Consequences of ecological amplification

Every action urban residents take, whether individually or collectively, enters into a long chain of unintended consequences. For example, urban consumers have become accustomed to a variety of food options beyond what the local environment could provide. In 1976, a typical Swedish shop would have approximately 2700 food items available to customers. In 1997 however, similar shops in Sweden contained approximately 4200 food items from around the world [79].

If Charles Darwin had wanted an apple for his 28th birthday in February 1837, he would probably have had to wait until autumn. Today, when a London resident wants an apple in February, she can hop in her car and drive to the store to buy one. What makes this simple act possible, and its consequences, stretch around the world [285] (Figure 3.42).

- Her car burns fossil fuels, releasing carbon dioxide and other pollutants that contribute to local pollution and worldwide climate change, nutrient loading, and affect human, animal, and plant health.
- The road absorbs and stores energy from the sun contributing to the urban heat island, and forms an impermeable surface from which water, now warmed and possibly polluted, quickly runs off during storms.
- The supermarket uses large amounts of energy to store food, requires a large parking lot that creates many of the effects of the road, and discards large amounts of food and packaging in landfills.
- The apple may come all the way from New Zealand, where the orchard requires fertilization and irrigation. Trucks carry it on roads to huge ships that bring it to the large port of Exeter in England, manufactured from materials ranging from wood to metals. Trains pick it up and carry it on metal tracks to a warehouse near London, where it can be transferred to a lorry and carried to the shop.
- The ship, the train, or the lorries may carry unwanted hitchhikers in the form of invasive species or pests.

Conclusions

It might seem that ecological processes have come to a halt in cities. The built environment is often designed precisely to keep nature at bay. Roads and buildings remove plants, bury the soil, and endanger animals. But the city, by definition, buzzes with the life of its dense human population. People have the same need for food, water, and safety as other animals, and the urban lifestyle amplifies those basic needs far beyond those of animals of similar size. Satisfying those needs requires the whole apparatus behind the urban metabolism, and makes the urban ecosystem the most energy and material intensive on Earth. Although mobilized for human beings, these materials, nutrients, and water overflow into the ecosystem of the city itself and the surrounding region.

The interactions among land use, water, weather, and nutrient changes can be difficult to predict. The increased availability of nitrogen and atmospheric CO_2 in cities increases the growth of plants and their ability to sequester carbon, while impermeable surfaces reduce that capability[577]. How this balance is resolved, just as in other complex aspects of urban soil and plant ecology, depends on the prior history of the site, local conditions, the duration of change, and many factors we are only beginning to understand.

The study of urban ecosystems extends our analysis of the urban metabolism by including the long chains of ecosystem effects initiated by inputs, outputs, and transformations. This chapter has presented how these chains change and link urban ecosystem processes ranging from water flow and climate to nutrient dynamics. The next chapter considers in detail how urban ecological amplification affects the many organisms that make their living in the city.

3.5   Questions and readings

Discussion questions

For Section 3.1

1. What is the relationship among cities being heavily engineered ecosystems, the urban metabolism, and urban effects on climate?

2. Would you include changes in climate in your ecological footprint? If yes, how? If no, why not?

3. Is there an urban heat island where you live? How would you find out?

4. How should the answer to Question 3 affect the ecology of your surroundings? Do you notice any of these effects?

5. Which parts of your region would you expect to have the greatest and least urban heat island, and what factors are they correlated with?

For Section 3.2

1. Why is water moved out of the city so quickly? How does this affect physical and ecological factors within the city? And downstream of the city?

2. What are streams like before entering and after leaving a city? Does this change have anything to do with how excess stormwater is dealt with?

3. How would you incorporate the changes of Question 2 into an ecological footprint measure?

4. What is the relationship between a city's metabolism and its effects on the water cycle?

5. The connections between climate and the water cycle depend on location. What are some of these connections in the area where you live? How do these connections affect the ecology within your city?

For Section 3.3

1. What parts of the nutrient cycle pathways are the most modified in urban ecosystems? How are these changes similar or different for the different nutrients? Why?

2. How do changes in the water cycle and climate interact with urban nutrient dynamics?

3. What are the effects of these interactions within and downstream from the urban ecosystem?

4. What do you think is the limiting nutrient for plants in your community? What could you do to increase primary productivity in your area, and what other effects might that have?

5. How have changes to nutrient cycles in urban areas affected the ecology of plants and animals near you?

6. Why are urban areas rarely considered as being "downstream" from other areas?

7. What factors contribute to the shape of the distribution of resource consumption in Figure 3.37, with its long tail of households with high use? Why do you think the distribution for nitrogen is less spread out than those for carbon and phosphorus?

For Section 3.4

1. Why does urbanization amplify so many processes? Does such amplification lead to more or less energy, nutrient, and material usage per capita? Why does this differ among cities, and how does your city compare with others in your country or region?

2. Which processes are most amplified where you live? How do these amplifications affect local ecosystem services?

3. In what ways does amplification link the consequences of urbanization studied in Chapters 2 and 3?

4. For one pollutant, trace the chain of cause and effect created by habitat and ecosystem modification from its input and to its eventual fate and effects.

5. What are some of the obvious, as well as less noticeable, ecological effects of amplification in your city? How would you include these effects in your ecological footprint?

Exercises

For Section 3.1

1. Heat capacity is measured in units of J/g/°C, or the energy required to raise 1 g of a substance by one degree.

Substance	Heat capacity	Density
Air	1.01	0.0013 g/cm^3
Concrete	0.88	2.4 g/cm^3
Water	4.18	1.0 g/cm^3

It takes 2260 J to evaporate 1.0 g of water.

   (a) How much energy would it take to evaporate $1.0\,m^2$ of water 1.5 cm deep?
   (b) How much could this energy heat the water if it didn't boil?
   (c) How much could this energy heat a 1.5 m thick slab of concrete with the same area? Does this match the value in the text?
   (d) How much could this energy heat a 10.0 km column of air? Does this match the value in the text?

2. Solar energy is typically around 160 W/m^2, but with a maximum of 1000 W/m^2 when the sun is directly overhead on a clear day.

   (a) At this maximum rate, how much energy strikes $1.0\,m^2$ of concrete during 1 hour?
   (b) The albedo of concrete is 0.8. How much energy is absorbed?
   (c) Using the information in Exercise 1, how much will this heat the concrete?

(d) The albedo of water is typically quite low, around 0.1. How much energy would 1.0 m^2 of water absorb and how much would the sun heat it?

3. Relative humidity is defined as

$$\text{relative humidity} = 100\frac{e_w}{e_{max}}$$

where e_w is the pressure of water vapor in the atmosphere and e_{max} is the maximum water vapor pressure at a given temperature. At standard atmospheric pressure,

$$e_{max} = 6.138e^{\frac{17.502T}{240.97+T}}$$

where T is the temperature in °C.

(a) Suppose the temperature is 20°C. Find e_{max}.
(b) Suppose the relative humidity at this temperature is 50%. What is e_w?
(c) How much lower would the relative humidity be if e_w remained the same but the temperature increased by 5°C due to the urban heat island?
(d) Redo this calculation but with a very hot temperature of 40°C. Is the effect of the urban heat island on relative humidity larger or smaller at high temperature?

For Section 3.2

1. Consider the infiltration percentages given in Table 3.5.

(a) What is the average fraction of water that infiltrates in an area that is evenly divided between woody vegetation and meadow?
(b) What is the average fraction of water that infiltrates in a more industrial area that is evenly divided among pavement, bare soil, and railway gravel?
(c) What is the average fraction of water that infiltrates in a heavily built area that is evenly divided among pavement, buildings, and lawns?
(d) Apply these percentages as best you can to the data on Manchester shown in Figure 1.5. How different do you think infiltration is in the low, medium and high density areas? What other information would you like to have?

2. The data from Curtin, Canberra, shown in Figure 3.16, in millimeters of water that would cover the area, are given in the following table.

Input or output	Average year	Dry year	Wet year
Precipitation	630	247	914
Piped in	200	268	141
Evapotranspiration	508	347	605
Stormwater output	203	74	290
Wastewater output	118	107	126
Storage	1	−23	33

(a) Check that inputs, outputs, and storage balance in the three types of year.
(b) What would happen to storage in the long run if the three types of year were equally common?

(c) The total area studied is $27.0\,\text{km}^2$. What is the total amount of wastewater output in liters? If the population is 20 000 people, how much is this per person?

3. A typical sand or gravel aquifer is about 20% water by volume.

(a) Suppose that removal of this water leads to compression of the aquifer, and that this leads to land subsidence of $7.5\,\text{m}$ as in Mexico City. How deep was this aquifer? How much water was extracted per m^2?

(b) How much infiltration would have been needed to maintain this aquifer if the water were extracted over 50 years?

(c) How much rainfall would have been needed if the aquifer lay below a meadow? How about if it lay below a built environment?

For Section 3.3

1. We can estimate the amount of nitrogen deposited by dogs. An average dog produces about $500.0\,\text{g}$ of feces per day. Suppose that feces is about $2.0\,\text{g}$ of nitrogen per $100.0\,\text{g}$. There are roughly 80 million dogs in the United States, or 1 for every 4 people.

(a) Suppose an area has a population density of 50 people per hectare. How much total dog feces would be produced?

(b) How much nitrogen would this add per hectare in a year?

(c) How much would this be reduced if 70% of people cleaned up after their dog?

(d) What information would you need to extend this calculation to include dog urine?

2. A human requires about 2000 kcal per day. Suppose that all of that energy comes from pure sugar, which contains $4.0\,\text{kcal/g}$.

(a) How many grams of sugar would a person need in a day? Approximately how much would they consume in a year?

(b) Glucose has the chemical formula $C_6H_{12}O_6$. If a molecule of glucose is broken down into pure CO_2 and water, how many molecules of each would it make?

(c) Carbon has a molecular weight of 12, hydrogen of 1, and oxygen of 16. What fraction of the mass of sugar molecule would be released as CO_2?

(d) With this diet of pure sugar, how much CO_2 would a person release in a year?

(e) In Section 2.3, we saw that an urban resident of the Baltic region produces about $10\,\text{kg}$ of carbon dioxide per day. How does this compare with the amount their body produces just from living?

For Section 3.4

1. The Leaf Area Index gives the surface area of leaves relative to the ground area, and ranges as high as 10 in dense forests.

(a) Suppose an urban forest is 10% as dense as it could be (and thus covers 10% of an urban area). What is the leaf area index? How much leaf area is there in a hectare?

(b) Suppose that 40% of the area is covered by rectangular buildings that are 5.0 times as tall as the area they cover. What is the total area of walls and roofs?

(c) Find the area of the four types of surfaces: ground, roofs, walls, and trees. Which of them would collect the most pollutants? What assumptions did you have to make?

2. We have looked at some of the effects of transporting apples from New Zealand to England. This exercise quantifies the carbon footprint of pineapples grown in Ghana and consumed in Europe (data from "Summary of Studies on Environmental Performance of Fresh Pineapple Produced in Ghana for Export to Europe" by West Africa Fair Fruit). The overall footprint is 0.954 g of CO_2 per 1.0 g of fruit purchased.

(a) If 50% of the mass of the fruit is consumed, how much carbon is released per gram eaten?

(b) Pineapple is roughly one-eighth sugar with most of the rest being water (there are small amounts of fiber and protein). How many kcal would a person get per gram of pineapple eaten (using the figure of 4.0 kcal/g for sugar)?

(c) Using the results from Exercise 2, how much CO_2 is released by a person who eats 1.0 kg of pineapple? How does this compare with the CO_2 used to produce and ship it?

(d) Of the carbon footprint, about 27% is associated with growing, 15% with packaging, and the remainder with transport. Compare these values with the amount of carbon produced (and thus energy used) by the person who eats the pineapple.

Further Reading

For Section 3.1

- Brazel, A., Selover, N., Vose, R., and Heisler, G. The tale of two climates – Baltimore and Phoenix urban LTER sites. *Climate Research*, **15** (2000), 123–135.
- Changnon, S. Inadvertent weather modification in urban areas: lessons for global climate change. *Bulletin of the American Meteorological Society*, **73** (1992), 619–627.
- Collier, C. The impact of urban areas on weather. *Quarterly Journal of the Royal Meteorological Society*, **132** (2006), 1–25.
- Oke, T. R. The energetic basis of the urban heat island. *Quarterly Journal of the Royal Meteorological Society*, **108** (1982), 1–24.
- Shepherd, J. A review of current investigations of urban-induced rainfall and recommendations for the future. *Earth Interactions*, **9** (2005), 1–27.
- Wilson, W. *Constructed Climates: A Primer on Urban Environments*. (Chicago,IL: University of Chicago Press, 2011).

For Section 3.2

- Elvidge, C., Milesi, C., Dietz, J., *et al.* U.S. constructed area approaches size of Ohio. *EOS*, **85** (2004), 233–240.

- Givati, A. and Rosenfeld, D. Quantifying precipitation suppression due to air pollution. *Journal of Applied Meteorology*, **43** (2004), 1038–1056.
- Kennedy, C., Cuddihy, J., and Engel-Yan, J. The changing metabolism of cities. *Journal of Industrial Ecology*, **11** (2007), 43–59.
- Pauleit, S. and Duhme, F. Assessing the environmental performance of land cover types for urban planning. *Landscape and Urban Planning*, **52** (2000), 1–20.
- Shepherd, J. M., Stallins, J. A., Jin, M. L., and Mote, T. L. Urban effects on precipitation and associated convective processes. In *The Routledge Handbook of Urban Ecology*, ed. Douglas, I., Goode, D., Houck, M. C., and Wang, R. (New York: Routledge, 2011), pp. 132–147.
- Shuster, W., Bonta, J., Thurston, H., *et al.* Impacts of impervious surface on watershed hydrology: a review. *Urban Water Journal*, **2** (2005), 263–275.

For Section 3.3

- Groffman, P. M., Bain, D. J., Band, L. E., *et al.* Down by the riverside: urban riparian ecology. *Frontiers in Ecology and the Environment*, **1** (2003), 315–321.
- Groffman, P. M., Law, N. L., Belt, K. T., *et al.* Nitrogen fluxes and retention in urban watershed ecosystems. *Ecosystems*, **7** (2004), 393–403.
- Kaye, J. P., McCulley, R. L., and Burke, I. C. Carbon fluxes, nitrogen cycling, and soil microbial communities in adjacent urban, native and agricultural ecosystems. *Global Change Biology*, **11** (2005), 575–587.
- Matson, P., Parton, W., Power, A., and Swift, M. Agricultural intensification and ecosystem properties. *Science*, **277** (1997), 504.
- Nowak, D. and Crane, D. Carbon storage and sequestration by urban trees in the USA. *Environmental Pollution*, **116** (2002), 381–389.
- Pataki, D., Bowling, D., and Ehleringer, J. Seasonal cycle of carbon dioxide and its isotopic composition in an urban atmosphere: anthropogenic and biogenic effects. *Journal of Geophysical Research*, **108** (2003), 4735.
- Silvertown, J., Poulton, P., Johnston, E., *et al.* The Park Grass Experiment 1856–2006: its contribution to ecology. *Journal of Ecology*, **94** (2006), 801–814.
- Vitousek, P. M., Aber, J. D., Howarth, R. W., *et al.* Human alteration of the global nitrogen cycle: sources and consequences. *Ecological Applications*, **7** (1997), 737–750.

For Section 3.4

- Grimm, N. B., Faeth, S. H., Golubiewski, N. E., *et al.* Global change and the ecology of cities. *Science*, **319** (2008), 756–761.
- Jones, A. An environmental assessment of food supply chains: a case study on dessert apples. *Environmental Management*, **30** (2002), 560–576.
- Nowak, D., Crane, D., and Stevens, J. Air pollution removal by urban trees and shrubs in the United States. *Urban Forestry & Urban Greening*, **4** (2006), 115–123.

- Pavao-Zuckerman, M. A. and Byrne, L. B. Scratching the surface and digging deeper: exploring ecological theories in urban soils. *Urban Ecosystems*, **12** (2009), 9–20.
- Pouyat, R. V., Russell-Anelli, I. D., Neerchal, J., *et al.* Soil chemical and physical properties that differentiate urban land-use and cover types. *Soil Science Society of America Journal*, **71** (2007), 1010–1019.
- Ramakrishna, D. M. and Viraraghavan, T. Environmental impact of chemical deicers: a review. *Water, Air, & Soil Pollution*, **166** (2005), 49–63.

Labs

A. Find several built-up sites in the city where you live or a nearby city, several sites in a park within the city, and several non-urban sites outside the city. At each site, record the amount of vegetation, surface water, and percent of skyview, along with the temperature, humidity, and CO_2 levels several times each day for at least 3 days (this would be best done by splitting up into groups and assigning each person a time and location to monitor). Plot and compare the mean temperature, humidity level, and CO_2 value at each time to compare the three sites. Does the skyview factor play a major role in the local temperature as predicted?

B. Use a light meter to estimate the albedo of the different types of surfaces in these sites, making sure to include built and green environments, along with water if possible. The values can be calibrated by comparing with a piece of white paper (with an albedo of nearly 1.0) and a piece of black paper (with an albedo of nearly 0.0). Using the quadrats developed in the Lab questions from Chapter 1, use Google Earth to estimate the percentage of impermeable surface within each quadrat. Do you have enough information to estimate how the albedo changes along the urban–rural gradient?

C. Collect soil from several sampling sites within each quadrat above, and using a field test kit, measure the amount of nitrogen (and percent of N as nitrate), carbon, and phosphorus, as well as pH for each sample. Plot the average values for each site, including a measure of variance, along the urban–rural gradient. You can also test for other pollutants and contaminants (such as arsenic or lead), depending on the test kit. Ideally, one of your sites should be a brownfield. Can you identify the different soil types you find? How do they differ in nutrients and pollutants? Are particular plants and insects associated with different soil types?

D. Compare the relative concentration of nutrients in different fertilizers. Could you find any that use NH_4^+ instead of NO_3^-? What recommendations do the manufacturers give for the quantity to use and when to apply it? Is there any evidence that some fertilizers work better than others?

E. Identify a point pollution source in your city or a nearby city. Can you find information on emissions? How do the emissions compare with those generated by automobile transportation?

4   The ecology of urban organisms

The biological and physical properties of urban areas shape the number, type, and behavior of people who live or work there. Factors such as water, open space, and pollution determine who can and will live in particular locations. The spatial pattern of urbanization controls such behaviors as the fraction of trips made on foot or by car. These choices then feed back to reshape the ecosystem itself.

All organisms share this reciprocal relationship with the environment, simultaneously shaping it and being shaped by it. The fundamental ecosystem cycles that affect climate, water, and nutrients arise from an interplay between human forces and organismal uses. This chapter studies how urban habitat modification, inputs and outputs, and ecosystem processes control the identities, abundances, traits, interactions, and evolution of urban plants, animals, and microbes.

From a broad community ecology perspective, urban regions, with their diverse habitat types and large resource inputs, can have surprisingly high levels of biodiversity for some groups of organisms (Section 4.1). In part, urban biodiversity results from the many non-native species that arrive and thrive in urban areas (Section 4.2). Because of these non-native species, the biological composition of two cities from different parts of the world can be more similar to each other than to either of their respective surrounding areas. Interactions between species can take on novel forms as they are shaped by altered resource availability, changed predation risk (Section 4.3), and emerging diseases (Section 4.4).

Surviving in the emerging urban environment also requires the appropriate traits. Some organisms, such as birds that nest on cliffs, have some key traits in advance. Others adjust to cope with new stresses (Section 4.5). As cities become more widespread and predictable features of the environment, consistent pressures shape the evolutionary ecology of urban residents, making urban areas into foci of rapid evolution (Section 4.6).

Whether intentionally planted and carefully watered or persisting as persecuted weeds, urban plants collect energy and nutrients, and produce chemical energy from carbon dioxide. Whether fed at feeders or despised as consumers of garbage and carrion, birds use their behavioral flexibility and mobility to capitalize on the opportunities created by urban environments. This chapter investigates the lives of both successful and unsuccessful urban organisms to identify the factors that determine which species can survive, how they survive, and what their lives are like in the built heart of the human-dominated world.

4.1   Urban biodiversity

The urban environment experiences changes in climate, nutrient loads, pollution, and disturbance that combine to create both opportunities and challenges for the species that live there. These opportunities and challenges determine both how many individuals live there, the *abundance* or *population density*, and how many species *coexist*, the *biodiversity*. Some groups of species in urbanized areas are characterized by the *density–diversity paradox*[524], in that they unusually harbor high population densities but only a few species. In large part, the high abundance of these few species results from their ability to capitalize on novel habitats and increased resources in cities.

Biodiversity can be measured in several ways. *Species richness* refers to the number of species present in a given area, without taking into account their relative abundances. Other indices give less weight to rare species, and can better represent the diversity an observer would experience. For example, imagine seeing 100 birds of five species. If there were 96 pigeons and one individual of each of the other four species, the area is strongly dominated by a single species and the diversity experienced is low. If instead each of the five species were represented by 20 individuals, the diversity experienced would be much higher.

One of the most surprising patterns in urban biodiversity is the positive correlation between human population density and species richness for some groups of organisms,

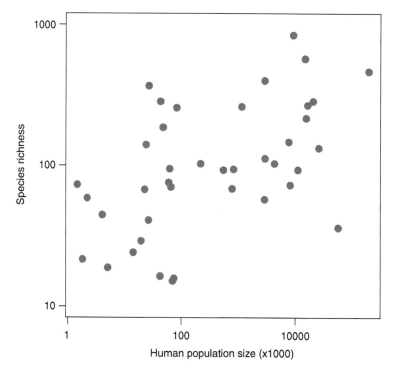

Figure 4.1 A typical relationship of human population size and species richness, here based on birds in the geopolitical units of Europe and adjacent areas (after Gaston and Evans, 2004).

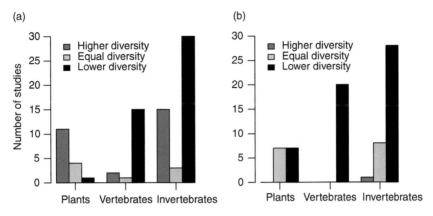

Figure 4.2 Fraction of studies showing higher, lower, or equal species richness in (a) moderately urbanized sites compared with slightly urbanized sites, or (b) highly urbanized sites compared with moderately urbanized sites (after McKinney, 2008).

particularly plants and birds[199,202,438] (Figure 4.1). This positive correlation could result from three causes. First, people may choose to settle in locations with diverse populations of plants and animals. Second, plants and animals may preferentially settle or be introduced near people. Third, both people and other organisms may choose or successfully settle in regions that have similar appealing characteristics, either in their availability of energy or nutrients, their diversity of habitats, or their proximity to water[313]. As we will see, all three of these causes play a role in urban areas. This higher species richness in areas densely populated with humans can persist even though extinction rates are also higher in areas with high human population density[568].

Several factors complicate this pattern. First, some groups of species follow the opposite pattern, showing lower species richness in densely populated areas. Positive correlations are most evident for birds and plants, weaker for mammals, and frequently reversed for reptiles[345]. Second, these patterns are strongest in studies that compare relatively large areas that contain a diversity of habitats[345]. Those that focus on the most heavily built areas of the urban core almost invariably find lower species richness[160]. In over 100 studies of urban biodiversity comparing areas of high, low, and intermediate urbanization, plant species richness is usually highest in areas with intermediate urbanization, while vertebrate species richness is consistently lower in areas with higher urbanization[372] (Figure 4.2). A few studies of plants and invertebrates, however, did find the highest species richness in the most urbanized sites.

A final complication arises from the relative novelty of urban environments. The species composition of most urban ecosystems has not reached an *equilibrium*. Some species might not yet have located and colonized urban areas, a process that can take decades even for mobile and intelligent animals such as birds[156] (Section 4.5). Conversely, habitat modification may restrict some species to small pockets of the urban environment, pockets insufficient to maintain those species over the long term. *Extinction debt* describes this temporary imbalance, when the current number of species exceeds those destined to persist when the environment reaches equilibrium[238]. Older cities typically have higher extinction rates than newer ones, suggesting that new cities

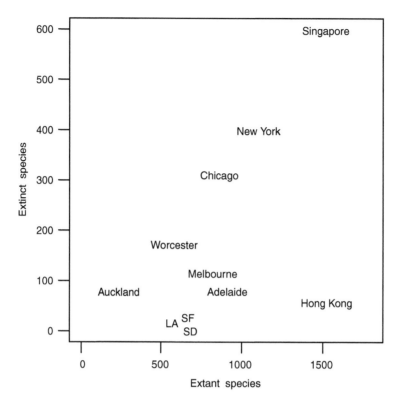

Figure 4.3 Number of extant and extinct native plant species in 11 cities from around the world, where LA is Los Angeles, SF is San Francisco and SD is San Diego (after Duncan *et al.*, 2011).

might simply not have had the time to drive sensitive species to extinction. Observed extinction rates in 11 cities founded after 1600 are quite variable, with less than 2% lost in Los Angeles, San Diego, and San Francisco and over 20% in Singapore and Worcester, Massachusetts[141] (Figure 4.3).

Some urban species are doomed to eventual extinction. Other urban populations might persist as *sinks*, populations that cannot reproduce sufficiently to maintain themselves, but which survive by receiving immigrants from other sites, called *sources*, where the species does reproduce successfully (Figure 4.4). In the worst case, urban areas could be *ecological traps*, sites that have appealing characteristics, such as high availability of low quality resources, but are in fact unsuitable for successful survival and reproduction[509].

Measures of biodiversity depend on the effort scientists spend searching for species, the distribution and diversity of habitats, and the size of the area searched. Spending more time or having superior expertise or equipment will uncover more species, particularly those that are rare. The effect of the size of the area studied is particularly important in the urban environment. The *grain* of a landscape describes the way that habitat types are distributed within it. A *coarse-grained* landscape is made up largely of a single habitat type, while a *fine-grained* landscape contains many different habitats. As we have seen (Section 1.2), urban areas are typically fine-grained.

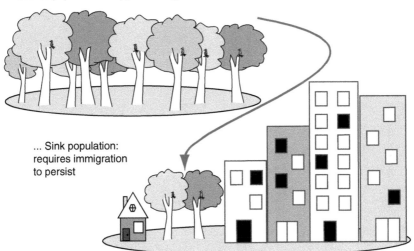

Source population: supplies immigrants to...

... Sink population:
requires immigration
to persist

Figure 4.4 A population made up of sources and sinks.

The *species area curve* provides one way to summarize this effect. Imagine sampling species from successively larger areas. If the region consists of a single homogeneous habitat, the number of species recorded approaches some asymptotic level, the total species richness of that habitat. In a coarse-grained landscape, increasing the area studied produces a relatively small increase in the number of species found because few new habitats are included. In a fine-grained landscape with a diversity of interspersed and contrasting habitats, increasing the area studied should reveal many more species because more and more habitat types are included. *Species accumulation curves*, much like species area curves, show how many new species are found as more and more sites are surveyed (Figure 4.5).

Even very similar habitats will have some different species due to chance, historical effects, or small variations within that habitat. A continually increasing species area curve can occur if patches of similar habitat are isolated from each other and have different species simply because individuals cannot move easily between patches. This sort of habitat fragmentation characterizes many urban areas, and might contribute to biodiversity.

The species that succeed in urban environments share particular characteristics that we investigate in detail in Section 4.5. Because more related species tend to have similar traits, the higher species diversity in some urban areas may come from relatively few closely related groups of species. Having species that come from many groups is called *phylogenetic diversity*[162]. For example, the plant species characteristic of urban areas in Germany do not show substantially higher phylogenetic diversity than their rural counterparts even though species richness is higher[305].

The principles of urban biodiversity describe how species respond to four major factors:

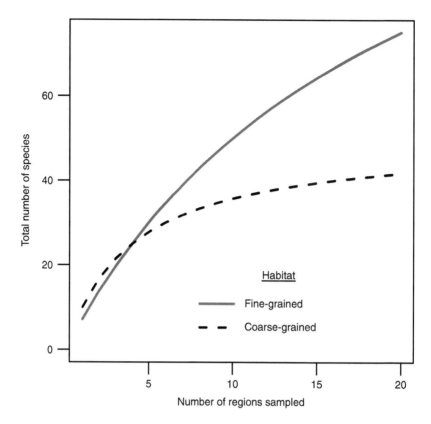

Figure 4.5 Idealized species accumulation curves, one from a fine-grained environment where continued sampling identifies more and more species, and another from a coarse-grained area that saturates after relatively few areas have been sampled.

1. **Habitat**: Size, diversity, spatial distribution, and quality.
2. **Temporal processes**: Addition or loss of species or habitats over time.
3. **Ecosystem processes**: Resource availability, disturbance, and stress.
4. **Ecological interactions**: Competition, predation, mutualism, and disease.

In this section, we address in detail the first three, saving the complexity of urban ecological interactions for a separate and full discussion (Section 4.3). We can think of the urban environment as setting up a series of filters, characteristics of the habitat and environment including the effects of human preference, that some species can tolerate and others cannot[610]. Urban biodiversity results from the interplay of intentional and unintentional species colonizations and the operation of these filters on new and existing species.

Patterns and principles of biodiversity

Ecologists have identified many general patterns of species richness that establish the principles needed to understand urban communities.

Table 4.1 The central principles of biodiversity

Biodiversity highest when large	Biodiversity highest when small	Biodiversity highest at intermediate level
Habitat patch size	Habitat patch isolation	Productivity
Habitat patch age	Temporal variability	Disturbance
Habitat diversity	Stress	Successional stage

- Species richness is higher in the tropics than the poles. A small tropical region, barely larger than a city block, can have more native species of plants than an entire country with a cooler seasonal climate.
- Species richness is higher in mountainous areas. Although mountains tend to be cooler, they also have more topographic variation, creating a broader range of habitats that supports more species.
- Larger areas have more species. Even if the habitat is relatively homogeneous, large areas have room for different histories that allow more species to accumulate or evolve.
- Older areas have higher species richness. New environments may not have had time for species to either arrive or evolve.
- Islands and peninsulas have lower species richness, and the effect is stronger for smaller islands and for islands that are farther from continents.
- Stress, in the form of extreme temperatures, low levels of moisture, or high concentrations of chemicals, tends to reduce species richness because fewer organisms can tolerate such conditions.
- High variability over time reduces species richness because fewer species can cope with a wide variety of conditions. Seasonality provides one example, although it is unusual in being sufficiently predictable for some organisms to evolve responses like dormancy or migration.

From these general patterns and many specific studies, ecologists have developed a series of principles underlying species richness (Table 4.1).

Principles based on habitat

The first set of principles center around the role of habitats, particularly the size and location of suitable sites. The *theory of island biogeography* summarizes the important factors in terms of the inputs and outputs of species. The number of species in any habitat is a balance between colonization and extinction. A small island will have fewer colonizations because it is harder to find and suffers more extinctions because populations are smaller and dispersing individuals are more likely to get lost[160]. Lower colonization and higher extinction leads small islands to harbor fewer species than large islands. An island that is distant from any continent will have fewer colonists that bring new species, and thus fewer species than an island near a continent (Figure 4.6).

In this theory, an island need not be a conventional piece of land in the midst of water, but can be any patch of suitable habitat in a sea of unsuitable habitat. A tree can be an island for an insect, or a park can be an island for a bird. Because different types of

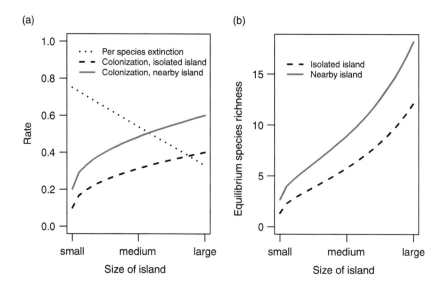

Figure 4.6 The elements of the theory of island biogeography. (a) Species already present on larger islands have a lower extinction rate due to their larger population size. Furthermore, colonists are more likely to arrive because large islands are easier to find, an effect accentuated for islands closer to a mainland or continent. (b) The equilibrium number of species is the ratio of the colonization rate to the extinction rate, producing the maximum number of species on large islands that are close to the mainland.

habitat island, such as forests, wetlands, and grasslands, support different species, an environment composed of a mixture of these habitats will tend to have higher biodiversity. The boundaries or edges between habitat types have features that combine those of both habitats. This can have contradictory effects: promoting high local diversity by supporting specialists on both habitats, promoting low diversity by stressing habitat specialists, or harboring a new set of edge specialists[40].

Principles based on temporal processes

The processes of colonization and extinction also control changes in species richness as a habitat ages. When a new environment appears, either through geological, climatological, or human forces, it takes time for species to arrive and become established before the equilibrium predicted by island biogeography is reached. For example, it can take a long time for the full complement of insects to locate and colonize an isolated tree in a city. Conversely, as we have seen, extinction debt describes the potentially slow loss of species from unsuitable habitats.

The effects of habitat age are closely related to the process of *ecological succession*. After an extreme habitat modification, through a natural process such as flooding or through extensive human disturbance, a relatively small number of early successional species, good colonists capable of thriving in relatively barren areas, arrive. As time passes, more species accumulate as they colonize the new location, and as the environment becomes less stressful due to the effects of existing species. Long after disturbance, late successional species that are superior competitors can come to dominate, potentially reducing the species richness.

Principles based on ecosystem processes

Another class of principles describes how species richness depends not on the location, size, or age of habitat fragments, but on ecosystem processes within them. Environments with moderate climate and highly available nutrients and water are generally the most favorable for life. The primary productivity, the rate at which carbon is fixed from the atmosphere by photosynthesis, provides a useful summary of how favorable a region is. The *intermediate productivity relationship* hypothesizes that species richness is maximized at intermediate levels of productivity. In habitats with extremely low productivity, plants and the animals that eat them have low biomass and population size. These habitats will therefore have a low number of species. Habitats with extremely high productivity, on the other hand, will have high biomass and population sizes. Under these conditions, one species may be better adapted than the rest and come to dominate. Thus, highly productive habitats may also have low biodiversity. Habitats with intermediate productivity can support enough individuals for many species to coexist, but without being dominated by a few.

The related *intermediate disturbance hypothesis* makes a similar prediction. Disturbance resets an environment by clearing out some or all of the existing organisms. Frequent disturbances lead to a stressful and variable environment that only a few organisms can tolerate. Like environments with high productivity, environments that are rarely disturbed can come to be dominated by a single species. Environments that are intermittently disturbed can have the highest biodiversity.

High levels of disturbance and low levels of nutrients are both examples of stressful conditions. Although stressful is a relative description of an environment (a penguin's view of "cold" is different from that of a desert tortoise), general trends emerge from many studies of plants and animals, primarily in temperate areas. Animal species richness is correlated most strongly with warm temperatures, while plant species richness is most correlated with the availability of water[248]. High stress from the perspective of a particular group of organisms tends to lead to lower species richness.

Principles based on ecological interactions

The final class of principles affecting biodiversity depends on the role of interactions between species described by community and population ecology. Species richness generally trickles up from one trophic level to the next. A location with more species of plants, for example, will tend to have more species of herbivores that eat those plants.

Furthermore, the simplest forms of the theory of island biogeography treat all species as equivalent. The principle of *competitive exclusion* argues that two species cannot coexist indefinitely if they use exactly the same set of resources[326]. Species that are found together must differ in some way (sometimes called a "niche"), such as eating different foods, foraging, or reproducing in different sites or at different times, or having different parasites or predators. Locations with relatively few different ways to make a living should thus harbor fewer species. However, with two very similar species, the superior one will displace the other only slowly, allowing a long period of coexistence.

Competition is not the only interaction that shapes ecological communities. Some species of plants, like those associated with nitrogen-fixing bacteria or those with deep roots that alter water availability and soil stability, can act as *keystone species* that shape the composition of an entire community[90]. Ecosystem engineers, such as beavers, create whole new habitats that can enhance the biodiversity of a region. An effective predator can suppress a dominant prey species and open up room for higher diversity. Diseases or herbivores can play similar roles by weakening the most common competitors. Parasites can also accelerate extinction of species in small habitat islands[160]. Animals involved in mutualisms, such as seed dispersers and pollinators, can be essential for the survival of their plant hosts, and their extinction could lead to a cascade of species loss and replacement.

Urban biodiversity

How do these principles of biodiversity function in urban environments? Do highly urbanized areas lie outside the realm where these ideas apply? Do they apply for only some groups of urban organisms and not others? To organize our analysis, recall that urban organisms can be placed in three broad categories (Section 1.3).

- *Urban avoiders* do poorly around humans and the built environment.
- *Urban adapters* tolerate humans without depending on them.
- *Urban exploiters* are found primarily in highly modified areas.

The species in each category respond differently to urban changes in habitat, temporal processes, ecosystem processes, and species interactions, and thus have distinct patterns of urban biodiversity.

Effects of urban habitats
Habitat diversity

One principle of biodiversity states that regions with a wider array of habitats, such as mountains, tend to have higher biodiversity even in the face of stress. People preferentially settle in places with variable topography or near water[313], upon which they superimpose an urban habitat mosaic of highly contrasting environments (Section 1.2). These fine-grained areas will tend to have higher species richness. A mixed habitat golf course near Stanford had more species, more individuals, and more biomass of birds than a nearby preserve (Figure 4.7)[34].

Frequently, the greatest diversity of urban habitats occurs between the densely built core and the less modified fringe. Bird species richness in Seattle peaks at intermediate levels of forest cover[359]. In the United Kingdom, urban adapters are most abundant and diverse at intermediate levels of housing density. Urban avoiders that cannot tolerate even moderate urbanization, including some birds and many lizards, amphibians, and butterflies[345], become less abundant and diverse with increasing housing density[574].

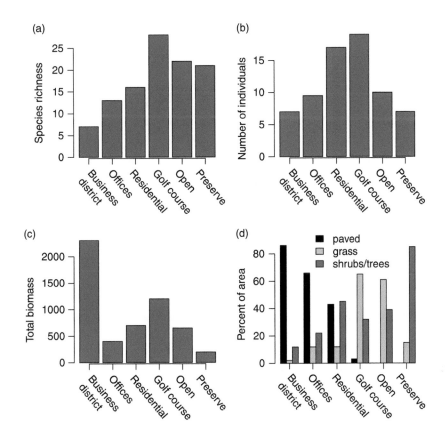

Figure 4.7 Pattern of (a) bird species richness, (b) bird abundance, and (c) bird biomass in six habitats in and around Stanford, along with (d) the composition of the habitat. Paved areas include both buildings and roads, while grass includes both lawns and less managed grasslands (after Blair, 1996).

For the highly sensitive amphibians, species richness declines with as little as 8% urbanization[480].

The most extreme urban exploiters, on the other hand, such as the rock pigeon and carrion crow *Corvus corone*, peak in density precisely where housing density is highest. As an example of the density–diversity paradox, bird biomass in and around Stanford is vastly higher in the business district due largely to the rock pigeon, which can effectively capitalize on human habitats and imports of food (Figure 4.7c).

Habitat size

The theory of island biogeography predicts that large habitat islands will harbor higher species richness. Urban and rural parks tend to follow this central prediction. For a wide range of organisms, including butterflies, snails, birds, lichens, mosses, and vascular plants, large parks have a higher species richness in accord with theory[304]. Area, however, does not provide the whole story. Butterflies, birds, and lichens in urban parks have lower diversity than in non-urban parks of the same size (Figure 4.8). This difference

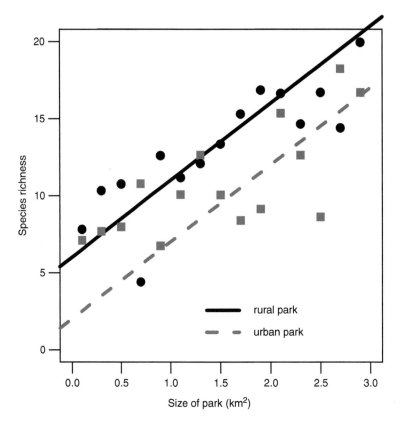

Figure 4.8 Pattern of species richness for butterflies, birds, and lichens in urban and rural parks (after Knapp, Kühn, Mosbrugger, and Klotz, 2008).

could result from lower habitat quality or higher isolation of urban parks that leads to increased extinction or decreased colonization.

Habitat isolation

The theory of island biogeography also predicts that more isolated habitat islands will have lower species richness. Spatial isolation, however, is not the same for all species. Some *matrix-sensitive* urban adapters are restricted to habitat patches such as parks because of their inability to tolerate or unwillingness to traverse intervening highly urbanized areas. *Corridors* can connect patches of habitat with a matrix suitable for dispersal or even successful reproduction by such species. Wooded streets can connect parks and other green spaces. In Madrid, for example, 14 of the 24 bird species found in parks were found on wooded streets, with the most species on those streets with parks at both ends, fewer pedestrians, and more large trees[166]. More heavily wooded streets in the young growing city of Vitória, Brazil harbored more species of bat, although again fewer than in parks themselves[418].

Amphibians require wetlands and the ability to move between them. In urban areas, these habitats are often reduced in size, and the more permanent of them frequently harbor predatory fish and disturbance from humans and lighting. Movement between sites, a necessity for some salamanders, is difficult without appropriate corridors, because roads and steep banks create dangerous or impassable barriers[241], and cats can be a significant source of mortality[617].

Urban adapters, and almost all urban exploiters, can tolerate the full range of urban habitats and experience a much less fragmented world. Indeed, from the perspective of an urban exploiter, the worldwide network of cities is a set of islands surrounded by a sea of inhospitable non-urban habitat. In Argentina, even relatively small cities with 35 000 people have species of birds similar to those in larger cities[197]. Plant species that prefer heavily modified habitats such as walls, pavement, and sidewalks experience the intervening green spaces as inhospitable and new urban habitats as islands that resemble their native habitats of cliffs and talus slopes[349].

Isolated remnants of chaparral, a sensitive shrubland habitat concentrated in the highly populated portions of California, have lost several species of specialized birds to local extinctions. As predicted, extinctions occur more often in small patches and in patches that have been isolated for a longer period of time[545]. The most vulnerable birds are those already rare in undisturbed habitat, and thus with smaller population sizes and fewer colonists. Because many birds of the chaparral are highly matrix-sensitive and unwilling to fly even relatively short distances over urbanized habitat, proximity to other patches has little effect on the probability of extinction. In and around Denver, black-tailed prairie dogs, *Cynomys ludovicianus*, were more able to colonize remnant grassland patches near existing colonies, while more isolated colonies were more likely to go extinct[353]. To compound the challenges of surviving in this fragmented landscape, fully 117 of the 384 habitat fragments were eliminated between 2002 and 2007 alone.

Proximity to other patches often plays only a small role for insects. Carabid beetles and butterflies in Birmingham, UK, readily cross inhospitable terrain to reach isolated habitat islands, with habitat quality rather than isolation playing the largest role in determining species presence and abundance[8]. Even in the heart of New York City, rather small urban gardens harbor 54 species of bees, which is 13% of the entire recorded bee fauna found in New York State[362]. The nearby suburban area of Westchester, with its larger gardens, more diverse plants, and more hospitable intermediate habitat, has roughly twice as many species[167].

Habitat edges

Species distributions also vary within urban habitat patches, with the most sensitive urban avoiders likely to be found deep within large patches far from highly disturbed edges. In woodland patches near Barcelona, Spain, synanthropic species grow near the edges of small forest patches, while shrubland and grassland species, effectively the urban avoiders, are instead most common in the largest patches[234] (Figure 4.9). The surrounding habitat also plays a role, both as a source of possible colonists, and through its unsuitability for potential colonists. Synanthropic species prove particularly rare in large forest patches that are surrounded by crops, with species richness peaking instead in small patches because, for them, the surrounding urban area is part of the habitat.

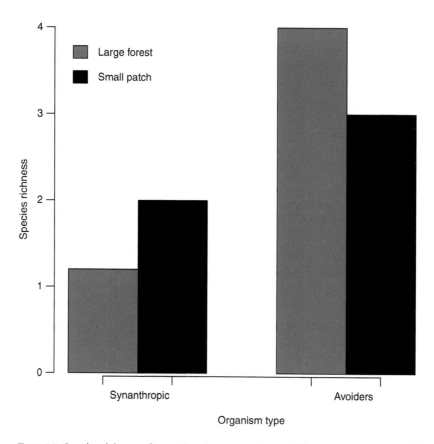

Figure 4.9 Species richness of synanthropic versus urban avoiding plant species in small and large forest fragments near Barcelona (after Guirado *et al.*, 2006).

Human habitat management

Urban humans invest a large amount of time, energy, and nutrients into shaping habitats, and particularly the plant composition of gardens, lawns, parks, and landscaping tucked in among built structures[160]. The choice of plants depends on individual preferences, community regulations, socio-economic factors, and availability. Through directed planting, weeding, and nutrient inputs, humans control the abundance and diversity of some urban plants, while remaining at the mercy of the natural processes of immigration, competition, succession, and extinction in the face of weeds and other "volunteers." We might expect, then, to see unusual patterns of species richness in these highly managed habitats.

A survey of four different habitats in England did indeed uncover some surprising patterns[567]. Lawns have a large number of species, a total of 159, most of which the owners would probably consider to be weeds. The species accumulation curve for lawns falls between two types of relatively undisturbed grassland, a low diversity grassland with harsh acidic soil and a high diversity grassland with less acidic soil (Figure 4.10). Flower and vegetable gardens have species accumulation curves that rise steeply and

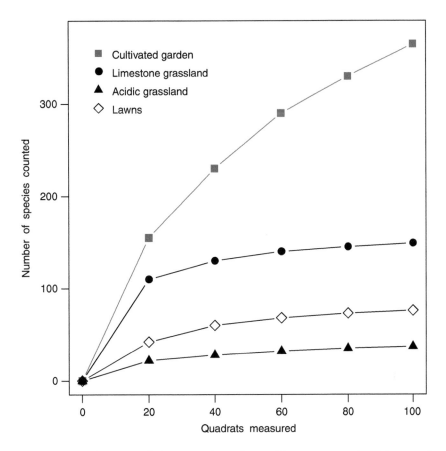

Figure 4.10 Species accumulation curves in gardens and lawns compared with two grasslands in and around Sheffield, England (after Thompson *et al.*, 2004).

seemingly indefinitely. Gardens are designed to contain a pleasing mix of species in a single plot, and tend to differ from each other when people seek exotic plants that their neighbors do not have[218].

Effects of temporal processes
Habitat age
In undisturbed ecosystems, diversity typically increases with time since major disturbance. In urban areas, older neighborhoods have more time for successional processes and the accumulation of species. The strength of this trend, however, depends on human preferences. In parts of the desert city of Phoenix, for example, diversity is substantially lower in older neighborhoods because residents of newer neighborhoods have planted native vegetation which can support up to 10 times more plant species than a more traditional lawn[267].

For patches created by isolation, the biodiversity typically decreases with time since isolation because extinctions outpace colonizations through a process of repaying the extinction debt[39]. In fragments of the California chaparral surrounded by urbanization,

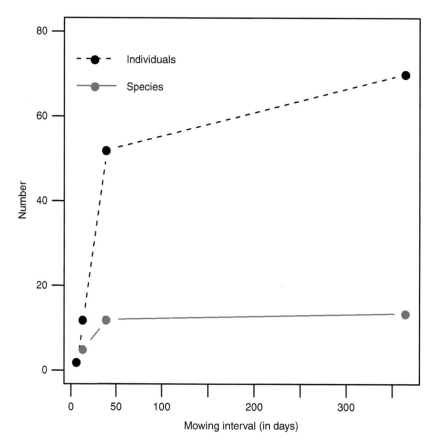

Figure 4.11 Effects of time between mowing on species richness and abundance of hemipteran insects in urban grasslands (after Helden and Leather, 2004).

almost all groups of arthropods followed the predicted pattern of lower diversity in smaller and older fragments, although predators that consume a wide diet increased in diversity with fragment age[40], due perhaps to increased populations of invasive species including the Argentine ant.

Succession

In the urban environment, succession is often controlled by humans. Some sections of a park might be maintained as a grassland with taller plants actively excluded, while other regions might be allowed to grow into forests. Intensively managed parks in Israel showed the lowest levels of bird species richness, particularly for urban adapters[529]. Parks and native streetscapes in Australia have higher species richness and abundance than recently developed streetscapes with non-native plants[608]. Frequency of mowing is the best predictor of both the species richness and abundance of hemipteran insects in urban grasslands in Bracknell, England[250] (Figure 4.11).

Zoning and management can promote significantly higher bird and plant species richness in parks and neighborhoods located in high income areas[302] (Figure 4.12).

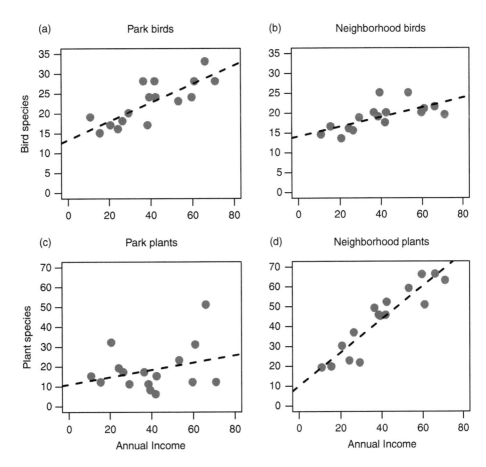

Figure 4.12 Species richness of birds and plants in Phoenix as a function of income, in thousands of U.S. dollars (after Kinzig *et al.*, 2005).

In contrast, bird species richness in Chicago is higher in newer neighborhoods with lower incomes, perhaps due to the presence of more undeveloped patches[340].

Whether urban species richness is maximized at an intermediate successional stage can be difficult to determine because urban succession does not follow the classic ecological progression. Brownfields most closely follow ecological theory, showing increasing species richness as larger woody plants fill in after the early invasion of weeds, and a subsequent decrease in species richness when competitive dominants take over[8].

Effects of ecosystem processes

Productivity

In non-urban habitats, the intermediate productivity hypothesis predicts maximal biodiversity at moderate levels of productivity, and maximal biomass at the highest levels of productivity. High inputs of energy, nutrients, and water make urban areas into loci of high productivity. Spider distributions in the urban setting of Phoenix support this

(a)   (b)

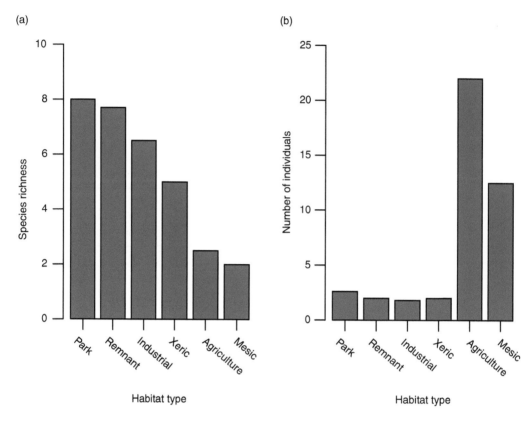

Figure 4.13   Pattern of spider (a) species richness and (b) number of individuals in six habitats in and around Phoenix (after Shochat *et al.*, 2004). The mesic and xeric sites refer to residential yards with large percentages of grass and native plants respectively, while remnant sites are small patches of desert within the city.

hypothesis, with the lowest species richness and the highest numbers of spiders in sites with the highest productivity[526] (Figure 4.13). Insects in the family Odonata (dragonflies) in Pietermaritzburg, South Africa, have intermediate diversity in cities, but generally high abundance[502]. Bird feeders in yards can have a similar effect, enhancing biomass without substantially increasing species richness[86].

Disturbance

The challenge of distinguishing disturbance from the many correlated changes in the urban environment makes it difficult to evaluate the predictions of the intermediate disturbance hypothesis in cities. Furthermore, urban areas also experience many types of disturbance. Some are detrimental to almost all species and lead to reduced species richness. Trampling usually reduces plants species richness[273]. Human presence creates disturbances that interfere with bird feeding and breeding, and may be second only to habitat destruction in excluding some species from urban habitats[510]. Road crossings

Figure 4.14 Monk parakeets in Mallorca, Spain.

create an array of physical disturbances that significantly reduce biodiversity in streams[4] and among birds[323].

Stress

Stressful environments generally have fewer species. But are urban environments necessarily stressful? The urban heat island ameliorates temperature variation and opens up opportunities for species that could not otherwise persist. The urban environment has been described as a *pseudo-tropical bubble*, with cities in cold climates supporting populations of tropical trees and birds[527]. In the most urbanized sections of Montpelier, France, bird species that persist are able to remain all year. In areas with lower building density, birds migrate and the species present change between winter and spring[85]. Populations of the monk parakeet *Myiopsitta monachus* native to sub-tropical Argentina, persist and even thrive in urban areas ranging from Chicago to Amsterdam and Paris (Figure 4.14). The urban heat island can also facilitate larger populations of rapidly breeding arthropods[367].

Effects of ecological interactions

Unraveling the role of species interactions in urban biodiversity can be even more challenging than establishing the role of habitat modification or ecosystem processes. The complex ways that urbanization affects competition, predation, and disease will be discussed in Sections 4.3 and 4.4. Nonetheless, several basic interactions shape urban biodiversity. In general, arthropod species richness is positively correlated with plant species richness, as many arthropods require specific host plants for at least part of their life cycle. In this way, biodiversity trickles up from one group of organisms to another that consumes them. However, this relationship is not strictly proportional, with the number of herbivore species generally increasing less quickly than the number of plant species[470].

In contrast, changes in the abundance of particular predators can shape the diversity of their prey. Exclusion of large predators, such as the coyote *Canis latrans*, can allow an increase in the populations of smaller predators such as cats and opposums, and result in a decrease in the diversity of birds[108].

The combined effects of all processes

Thanks to availability of historical lists of plant species, it is sometimes possible to identify the causes leading to the loss or gain of particular species and the overall effect on biodiversity. The whole range of urban disturbances, particularly more intensive recreational use and increased fire, play a role in explaining the loss of 155 species of plants over the course of the last century in an urban park near Boston[138]. The increased number of trails has fragmented the habitat within the park, opened gaps in the forest that channel invasive plant species, stressed urban-avoiding birds, and changed the microclimate by allowing more air flow and drying the soil. Increased development around the park has converted the park into a habitat island, with the resulting reduction in colonization by matrix-sensitive species. Each of these factors acts against urban avoiders such as forest birds and plants of wet areas, and favors exotic species already adapted to these conditions. Indeed, 64 new plant species have appeared in the park, many of them not native to the region (Section 4.2).

Paved area has increased vastly over the past century and is among the chief causes of plant species loss found over the last century in the Belgian town of Turnhout[583] (Figure 4.15). Of 455 species recorded in 1880, 121 had disappeared by 1979. In Halle, Germany, where plants have been studied since 1687, species that prefer moist soils and low nutrients have decreased, while those that capitalize on human dispersal and warm climates have increased, leading to a species turnover of 22% over 320 years[306].

Conclusions

For some groups of species, urban areas are inhospitable zones of low diversity. Yet for others, particularly plants and birds, urban areas can be hotspots of biodiversity. Humans choose many of the same favorable habitats that harbor diverse species of plants and animals, and often enhance habitat diversity, further promoting species richness[574]. These chosen habitats can include or abut the last populations of species with small ranges, creating a conservation challenge, but also a conservation opportunity[345]. The frequent coincidence of high human population density and high diversity also creates an education opportunity, making urban residents aware of the species, habitats, and ecosystems around them[558].

As a single species, humans are only a small part of urban biodiversity, but in line with the density–diversity paradox they greatly outweigh other organisms. In the heavily urbanized continent of Europe, there are about three breeding birds per person, and 4.0 g of bird per 1.0 kg of human, meaning that people weigh about 250 times more than all of the wild birds[202]. In the United Kingdom, birds outnumber people by only a factor of

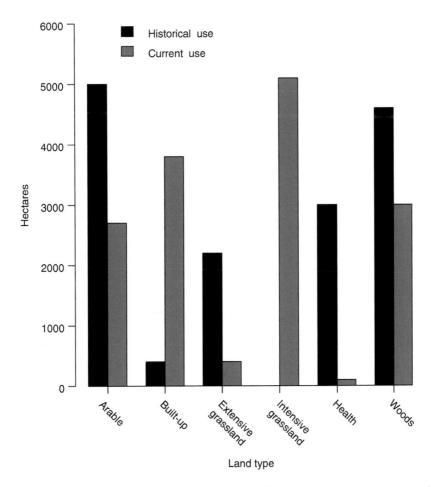

Figure 4.15 Changes in habitat in the Belgian town of Turnhout over the past 100 years (after van der Veken *et al.*, 2004). Extensive grasslands are largely unmanaged, while intensive grasslands consist mainly of highly managed lawns.

two, and are easily outweighed by domestic birds such as chickens (Figure 4.16). The city of Sheffield has only slightly more than one bird per person during both breeding and winter season, with almost two-thirds of these coming from just five species[189].

Human habitat changes of course create negative effects on many species. The most highly modified sites, such as the urban core, are sites of low species diversity, and even favorable mixed habitats like gardens and parks exclude species that are most sensitive to human presence and disturbance. Because of the fragmentation of land into habitat islands, urbanization favors those species that can successfully navigate inhospitable intervening urban terrain.

Within urban habitats, human effects such as disturbance, fertilization, management, and pollution create challenges that some species can overcome while others cannot. As always, these effects are a combination of intended and unintended consequences. The urban heat island allows tropical species to persist well outside of their historic ranges,

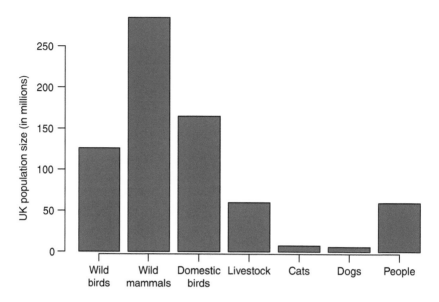

Figure 4.16 Numbers of different organisms in the United Kingdom (after Gaston and Evans, 2004).

a pleasant fact for some urban residents, but hardly the intended result of altering the urban surface energy balance. Less desirable insects, such as aphids, mites, and scales do relatively well in cities, while butterflies tend to be scarce[470].

When given the choice, people seek environments with a mixture of habitats, including buildings, parks, and yards that favor urban adapters, and indeed work to make those habitats appealing to attractive species like flowering plants, songbirds, and butterflies. People with high income have the resources to choose and create preferred environments. In some cases, level of education can be a better predictor of neighborhood biodiversity than income[345].

Gardeners pick and choose plants from the worldwide catalog of biodiversity, intentionally creating mixtures of species never seen before. Human management, both in yards and parks, focuses on plants, with a goal of halting ecological succession and maintaining a preferred set of species in the face of constant pressure from so-called weeds[160]. The rest of the community, such as the insect herbivores, is generally left to assemble itself, meaning that conscious decisions about plants create a variety of unintentional consequences for the diversity of insects and the birds that consume them[561].

Although humans do intentionally introduce and remove species from the urban environment, most changes to urban communities result indirectly and unintentionally from ecological processes shaped by local environmental factors, such as plant diversity and abundance (Figure 4.17). This "template" directs urban ecological and evolutionary processes, and the resulting biodiversity of herbivores and their predators.

What is urban biodiversity worth? Should it be subtracted from the urban ecological footprint? To the functioning of the larger ecosystem, the role of species diversity remains largely unknown. In simplified experimental plots, higher plant species richness

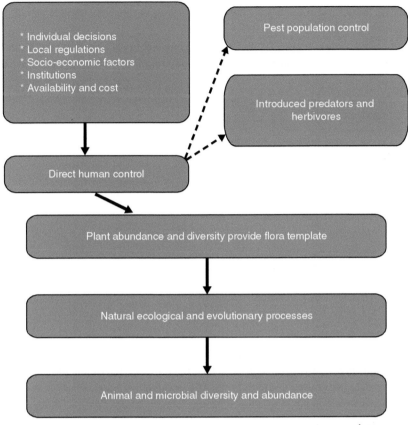

Figure 4.17 Factors affecting urban biodiversity (after Faeth *et al.*, 2011).

can enhance productivity and resilience against challenges like invasive species[394], although the generality of these effects remains only partially understood. The urban system, with its high inputs of nutrients and exotic plants, can provide key insights into the causes and ecological consequences of biodiversity.

4.2 Invasive species and biotic homogenization

For some groups of species, urban areas have high biodiversity, sometimes exceeding that of surrounding regions. In addition to the habitat and ecosystem factors we have considered, this higher diversity results from the establishment of new species that originate from other parts of the continent or from the other side of the globe.

We have seen how species can be classified based on their ability to tolerate or flourish in urban habitats, with urban exploiters sometimes coming to depend on urbanization. Due to the human transportation network, urban exploiters have many opportunities to disperse among the cities of the world. These widespread species can contribute to the increasing similarity of the species living in cities around the world, called *biotic homogenization*.

This section begins by examining the principles of invasive species that determine which species are most likely to become invasive and what makes habitats susceptible to invasion. We then examine the patterns and consequences of invasions in urban areas, and conclude by evaluating whether introduced species have indeed led to urban biotic homogenization.

Principles of biological invasions

Becoming an invasive species involves three steps:

- Arrival or introduction,
- Naturalization and successful reproduction,
- Spread into new areas and invasion.

In accord with these steps, three broad principles govern both how many and which invasive species will colonize an area.

Arrival
Sites exposed to more potential colonists will have more invasive species. These colonists may arrive under their own power, in which case the rate at which they arrive depends on their own dispersal ability and on the size and isolation of the site, as in the theory of island biogeography. In other cases, colonists arrive as unintentional hitchhikers on cars, boats, or boots, with some species proving especially suited to these means of transport[609]. Finally, colonists may be introduced intentionally. Many plant species arrive as horticultural varieties, including fruits, vegetables, flowers, and ornamental plants[270].

Survival
Those species already adapted to the characteristic challenges of urban environments are the most likely to persist. These adaptations include ability to capitalize on urban habitats and resource inputs, and to tolerate disturbance and pollution.

Escape
Plant and animal colonists can escape competitors, predators, parasites, and diseases which controlled their population in their original habitat. This release can allow an increase in population and spread from the site of introduction. The concept of *biotic resistance* predicts that habitats with more species already present will be less likely to provide this sort of escape, and thus better able to resist invasion by new species.

Upon arriving and surviving in a new region or continent, species are classified as *naturalized*. Those that spread far from their site of introduction and have major impacts on the ecosystem or community are called *invasive species*.

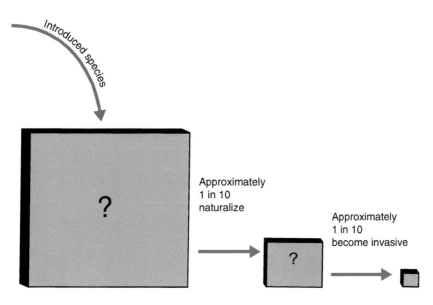

Figure 4.18 The rule of 10 for invasive species (after Williamson, 1999).

Non-native species can be classified based on where they originated. Species that come from the same continent are called *extralimital natives*, while those from other continents are called *exotics*[543]. For birds and some plants, extralimital natives arrive without direct human assistance and find the habitat suitable. For example, many northern hemisphere bird species have expanded their ranges far to the north due to the availability of bird feeders and warmer urban winter temperatures[542]. Many plants, on the other hand, have become extralimital natives via deliberate introduction into gardens and parks.

The *rule of 10* provides a useful rule of thumb for describing the steps of arrival and survival. Only about 1 in 10 introduced species succeeds in naturalizing, and only about 1 in 10 species that is successfully naturalized becomes invasive[611] (Figure 4.18). The European starling *Sturnus vulgaris*, now among the most widespread of invasive species and urban exploiters, was introduced unsuccessfully in North America at least three times. It then took approximately 10 years for the 160 birds that had been released in Central Park in 1890 and 1891 to become naturalized in the New York City area. After that, it spread rapidly across the continent[105]. Ironically, European starlings are now declining in many European cities[189] (Section 4.5).

These rules do not mean that every species has a 1 in 1000 chance of becoming invasive. Many invasive species are closely related to some native species, perhaps as members of the same genus, and thus have many of the adaptations they need to survive in the introduced range. Invasive species also tend to be habitat generalists with broad ranges, often with a weedy lifestyle featuring highly dispersive seeds or offspring, and an early successional preference for disturbed sites.

Historically, more European species have invaded North America and Australia than the reverse. This may be due in part to the prevailing direction of human migration

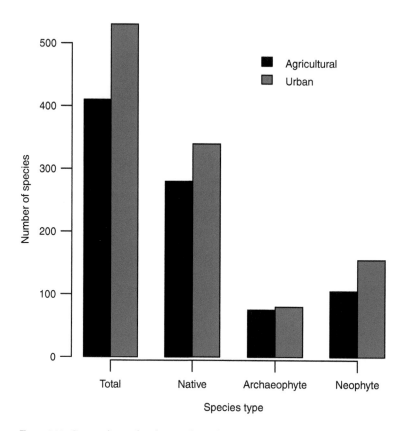

Figure 4.19 Comparison of native, archaeophyte, and neophyte plant species in Europe (after Wania *et al.*, 2006).

and commerce, but is probably due more to the longer history of dense human habitation and plant cultivation in Europe and the resulting higher number of human-adapted species[544].

Invasive species in urban habitats

Urban areas provide two key advantages to invasive species. First, far more species are initially introduced both intentionally in gardens and as pets, and unintentionally through transportation. Second, human disturbance opens up multiple new opportunities for species, particularly early successional species.

Arrival into urban habitats

Among plants, particularly in Europe, exotic species can be classified based on when they first arrived. Plants that were introduced before 1500 are called *archaeophytes*, while those introduced after that are known as *neophytes*[314]. Archaeophytes play a larger role in agricultural landscapes, with neophytes typically more common in urban habitats[602] (Figure 4.19). Due to their close connection with the less urbanized ancient

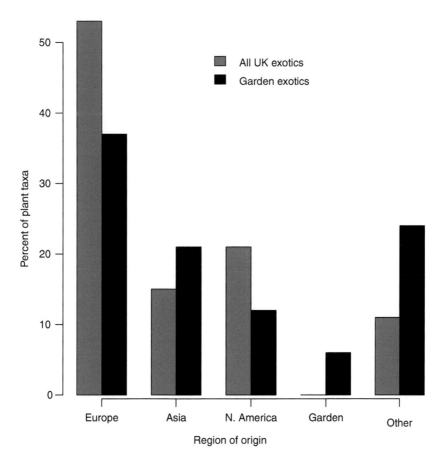

Figure 4.20 Sources of exotic plants in the United Kingdom (after Thompson, 2003). Garden refers to plants developed under cultivation.

landscape, archaeophytes are in decline in many European cities, and in some ways share commonalities with native species[461], while neophytes prosper in urban settings.

Gardens contain extremely unusual combinations of plants (Figure 4.10). Their steadily rising species accumulation curve results from the predominately exotic origins of species. A survey of five cities in the United Kingdom identified 1051 species in gardens, of which only 301 were British natives[338]. Furthermore, the sources of garden plants in the United Kingdom differ substantially from those of exotic plants in less highly managed habitats such as fields, forests, and parks. Garden plants come more from Asia and other distant locales such as South America, South Africa, and New Zealand[566] (Figure 4.20). These intentionally introduced exotic species can usually become established only through much care and effort by gardeners. In fact, 68% of alien plants naturalized in Europe were introduced intentionally, and all but 11 of those escaped from cultivation[318].

The scale of the human transportation system creates unprecedented opportunities for plant and animal movement, and its development led to a sharp increase in the rate of

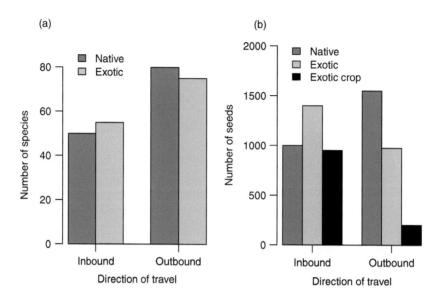

Figure 4.21 Seeds trapped from inbound and outbound lanes of two tunnels in Berlin. (a) Number of species of seed, comparing native and non-native species, and (b) number of individual seeds, where exotic seeds includes plants of both crop and non-crop origin (after von der Lippe and Kowarik, 2008).

plant species introductions in Europe around 1800[318]. The explosion of transportation continues today through shipping and commuting. Seed traps placed in tunnels in Berlin collected large numbers of seeds deposited by passing vehicles. Outbound lanes showed the highest species diversity, with suburban tunnels having substantially more seeds overall. Among the plant seeds found in these tunnels, native seeds and exotic non-crop seeds appear most in the outbound lanes, and exotic crop seeds are found in inbound lanes, suggesting that human activities in cities can both import and export new and potentially invasive species[596] (Figure 4.21).

Distribution of urban exotic species

The urban core tends to have low species richness (Figure 4.2). These few species are disproportionately of exotic origin[34,370]. Exotic plants in Berlin made up fully 54% of the species in the urban core, diminishing to 25% in the suburbs and 6% in a nearby preserve[310] (Figure 4.22). In and around the city of Hesse, Germany, neophytes dominate urbanized habitats, while archaeophytes dominate rural sites[62]. In fish, natives dominate in watersheds with greater forest cover and lower density urban development, while exotics dominate in developed watersheds[513].

Habitat fragments generally lose most groups of native species with time since isolation, but can replace them with relatively few invasive species. In remnants of the California chaparral, the non-native oriental cockroach *Blatta orientalis*, European earwig *Forficula auricularia*, and the Argentine ant *Linepithema humie* are now common[40]. Only the last of these concentrates populations along habitat edges, likely due to water subsidies.

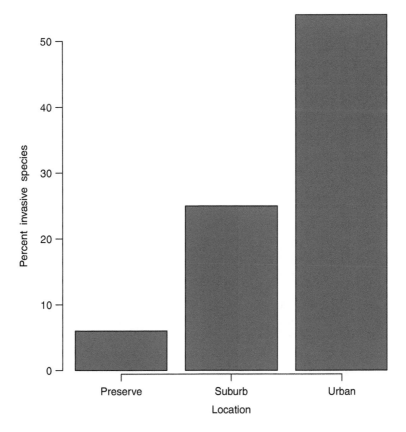

Figure 4.22 Percentage of invasive species in Berlin (after Kowarik, 1995).

Not all species follow these patterns. Neither riparian plants[417] nor plants of forested wetlands[144] are disproportionately exotic in urban areas. The sites preferred by these species may differ from more typically urbanized sites in being less disturbed and fragmented and thus less conducive to invasive species.

Urban centers combine extremes of disturbance and habitat change with the maximum movement of people, goods, and potential colonists. Over the past century, New York City has lost 578 natives (43% of the original plants found there) and gained in their place 411 exotics[371]. The urban park near Boston discussed in Section 4.1 lost 133 native and 22 exotic species over the course of a century of human influence, and replaced them with 28 new native and 36 new exotic species[138] (Figure 4.23).

As the smallest continent, Australia is the most like an island and should be most sensitive to invasives. Consistent with this prediction, between 1836 and 2002 the city of Adelaide lost 89 native plant species and added 613 exotic plant species[559] (Figure 4.24). Birds and mammals had much less extreme levels of replacement, and the sensitive reptile and amphibian groups gained only two and zero introduced species, respectively.

Road medians in the middle of a large city must be one of the most challenging environments for both plants and animals. Nonetheless, 6619 ants of 13 species were

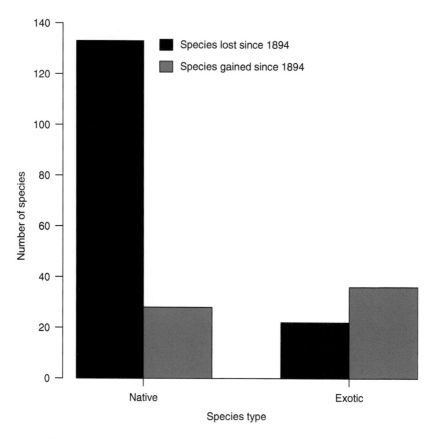

Figure 4.23 Changes in non-native species over 100 years in an urban park (after Drayton and Primack, 1996).

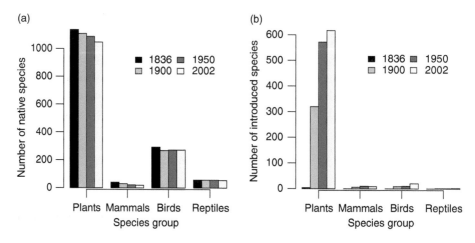

Figure 4.24 Changes in native and introduced species in Adelaide from 1860 to 2002 (after Tait *et al.*, 2006).

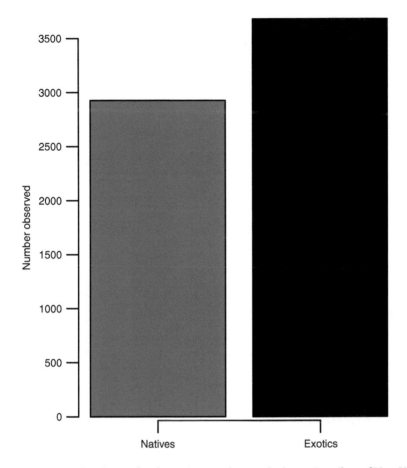

Figure 4.25 Abundance of native and non-native ants in the road medians of New York City (after Pećarević *et al.*, 2010).

collected in the medians of New York City. The non-native pavement ant *Tetramorium caespitum* was most abundant, found in almost all medians, and, in accord with its name, in higher numbers in medians with the fewest trees[441] (Figure 4.25).

Exotic species usually account for the density–diversity paradox (Section 4.1) where urban centers with low species richness have high abundance and biomass[86], such as spiders (Figure 4.13), birds (Figure 4.7), and dragonflies[502]. In each case, non-native species account for the bulk of the biomass. In another example, the extremely high biomass of carabid beetles in urban sites is due almost entirely to exotic species[404] (Figure 4.26).

Effects of urban exotic species

Exotic species can challenge native species as novel competitors, predators, or pathogens[86]. We study these interactions in more detail in Section 4.3, but introduce several striking examples here. Extreme competition occurs with the Argentine ant, an invasive South American ant now found in warm urban and agricultural areas throughout

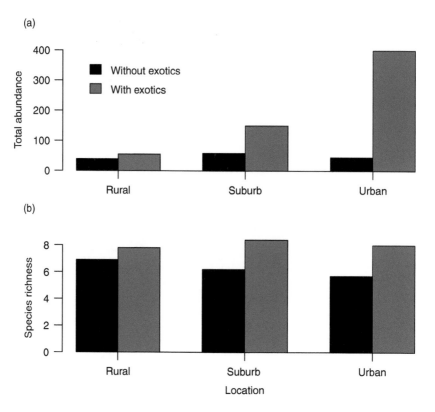

Figure 4.26 (a) Abundance and (b) species richness of carabid beetles in Canada with and without exotic species included (after Niemela *et al.*, 2002).

the world. Through a flexible social structure that involves multiple queens, these ants can rapidly relocate nests in the face of disturbance. They can reach high population densities and can quickly locate food and force other ants away. In urbanized areas of southern California, Argentine ants essentially eliminate all native ant species, including ones with substantially larger workers. As part of the cascade of effects, specialized ant predators, such as the horned lizard, can be lost when their preferred large-bodied prey vanish[265]. Argentine ants are present in 23 out of 24 parks in the moister climate of San Francisco. However, they are found only on the boundaries in many parks, associate preferentially with non-native trees, and avoid extremely wet places, thus leaving room to coexist with some native ant species[96].

In general, however, native species are not completely eliminated by invasive species, but are instead restricted to smaller numbers or fewer habitats. The red imported fire ant *Solenopsis invicta* is a generalist ant that has invaded habitats throughout the warmer regions of the United States, Australia, and parts of Asia. In addition to being a dangerous nuisance, these ants have displaced many native ants, including their congener *Solenopsis geminata*. Disturbed agricultural habitats around the city of Austin, Texas, have been overrun by the red imported fire ant. But within the city limits, older neighborhoods with a high level of plant cover are still dominated by the native ants. Apparently,

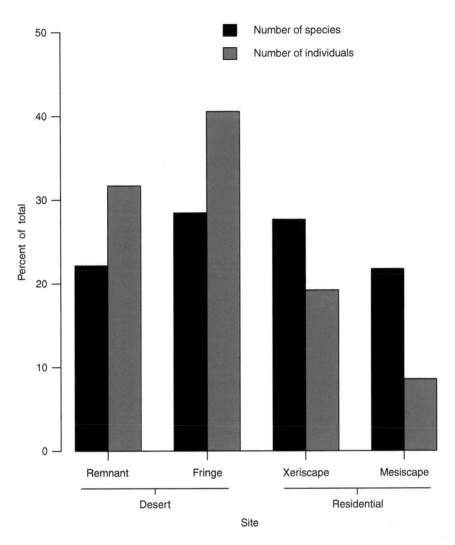

Figure 4.27 Bee abundance in desert and yard habitats in and around Phoenix, Arizona. Remnant sites are parks within the urban area and fringe sites are parks at the edge of the urbanized region (after McIntyre and Hostetler, 2001).

these neighborhoods have a sufficiently low level of disturbance to maintain native populations[448].

The human preference for exotic plants includes many with showy flowers or foliage. To survive, flower-feeding native insects must be able to switch to these potentially attractive novel food sources. In Davis, California, many native butterfly species in urban areas have indeed switched to using alien host plants, often exclusively[517]. In other cases native pollinators that specialize on native plants are replaced by non-natives. In the Phoenix area, bee numbers are lower in turfgrass yards that are managed in ways most unlike the desert habitat that surrounds the city[369] (Figure 4.27). In suburban sites in southeastern Pennsylvania, sites dominated by native plant species have four times as many lepidopteran (butterfly and moth) individuals and three times as many species, which filters up to support a higher abundance of insectivorous birds[67].

Attractive non-native plants can act as ecological traps. The invasive Dutchman's pipe *Aristolochia elegans* dominates extensive portions of urban green space in Australia and serves as the oviposition site for the Richmond birdwing butterfly *Ornithoptera richmondia*[503]. Unfortunately for the growing butterfly larvae, Dutchman's pipe is toxic and cannot support growth or survival.

Urban biotic homogenization

Humans are perhaps the greatest habitat generalists in the world, living in tropics, deserts, high mountains, and the Arctic. As the ultimate ecosystem engineers, humans use technology to make those habitats livable, effectively homogenizing them into something more similar to the environment in which they evolved, the cliffs and caves of the African savanna[348]. This process of homogenization finds its fullest expression in cities, where buildings control the climate people experience for up to 90% of the day, and the built environment is designed for efficient transportation and industry.

Interspersed within the built environment, vegetation is managed for convenience and aesthetics. To provide shade and an attractive environment, trees are planted in plains and deserts where no trees previously existed and cut in areas that were originally forested. Water is rushed out of the urban area when in excess and pumped in when scarce. Water use is higher in locations with limited water availability, as needed to create an environment with lawns and trees that mimics moister regions[371]. The urban heat island moderates cold nights and winters in areas with temperature extremes.

In concert, these factors make the built urban core and the surrounding residential areas across the globe remarkably similar, and certainly more similar than these locations were before human modification. The species that inhabit them, therefore, should also be similar. When successful species are transported between continents, the resulting species compositions of far-away cities may overlap substantially. This similarity of species, potentially across vast distances, is biotic homogenization.

We introduce two closely related ways to quantify biotic homogenization[414]. Suppose species are surveyed in two cities, with a species present in both, b species unique to one city and c species unique to the other (Figure 4.28). *Simpson's similarity index* is computed as

$$S = \frac{a}{a + \min(b, c)}$$

where $\min(b, c)$ represents the minimum of b and c. A large value of the Simpson's similarity index, close to 1, means that almost all of the species that appear in one city are also present in the other. A small value, close to 0, means that essentially all of the species in each city are unique to that city. The *Jaccard index* is defined in terms of the same measurements a, b and c as

$$J = \frac{a}{a + b + c}.$$

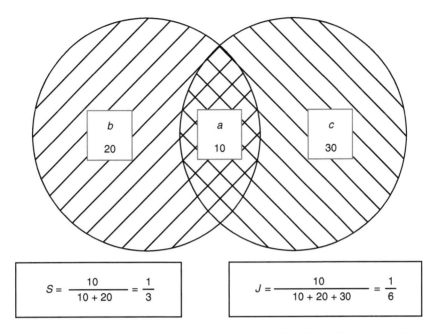

$$S = \frac{10}{10 + 20} = \frac{1}{3}$$

$$J = \frac{10}{10 + 20 + 30} = \frac{1}{6}$$

Figure 4.28 Comparison of the Simpson (S) and Jaccard (J) indices of homogenization.

This index achieves a value of 1 only when all species are present in both habitats, and is again 0 when each city's species are unique.

In all habitats, species tend to be more alike in nearby than in distant sites. Comparisons of the degree of homogenization in urban and non-urban sites must thus correct for distance, often by graphing homogenization as a function of distance between sites with similar habitats. After making this correction, urban habitats do indeed share more species of plants. Although sharing drops off with distance, urban areas that are 2000 km apart can be as similar as adjacent parks[371] (Figure 4.29).

The differing responses of urban exploiters, urban adapters, and urban avoiders help to clarify this general pattern. Urban exploiters tend to be found everywhere, including highly disturbed sites with the lowest diversity. The urban core of virtually every city includes the rock pigeon, European starling, and house sparrow *Passer domesticus*, often with relatively few other species of bird. Suburbs include a much higher diversity, but only of species that are effective urban adapters, often including extralimital natives that capitalize on the urban heat island or urban resource inputs[35]. Urbanization extirpates many urban avoiders that persist only in reserves. For bird species in France, urbanized areas are more homogenized, due to colonization by generalist species and extinction of specialist species[125].

New Zealand provides a case study in some of the challenges and opportunities that biological homogenization creates. The island has 2500 native plants of which 80% are *endemic*, swamped by 25 000 introduced species of which 10% are naturalized[380]. The goals of management in urban sites could range from tolerating homogenization, battling to remove non-native species and spread natives[554], or accepting some benign

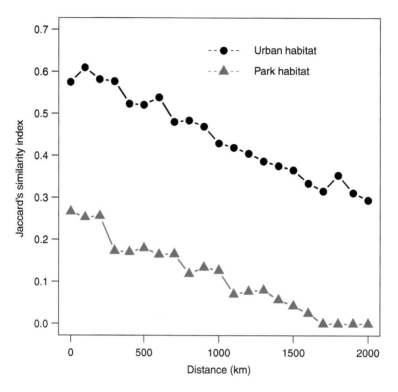

Figure 4.29 Decay of similarity with distance in urban and park habitats (after McKinney, 2006).

or beneficial non-natives as "honorary natives." This last strategy has the potential to maintain the unique character of different regions without pursuing the quixotic goal of returning small patches of habitat to a pre-human state[380].

Conclusions

Urban species reflect a wide range of intended and unintended consequences of human choices. Gardens are intentionally stocked with desirable plants, roadsides with pleasing trees, and bird feeders with songbird-attracting food. That some favored plants and birds are not native to the area, and that some indeed can become invasive, has only recently become a major concern in cities. The majority of species changes, however, result from the unintended consequences of urbanization, including disturbance, habitat fragmentation, nutrient and water inputs, the urban heat island, and long-distance transport.

All urban areas, whether completely or partially built, have been modified for the needs of humans, needs that are similar throughout the world. This homogenization of habitat leads to the homogenization of species. In moderately disturbed areas, such as suburbs, urban adapters such as early successional plants and generalist birds act as regional homogenizers, making species composition within cities more similar than in preserves. In the urban core, a relatively small number of highly synanthropic urban exploiters usually dominate both in species richness and abundance. When moved around the world either intentionally or unintentionally, these species act as global homogenizers. These highly abundant invasive species homogenize not only the species composition but also, through their effects on resources and other organisms, the functioning of the entire ecosystem. This extension of biotic homogenization is called *functional homogenization*[374].

As a consequence, people who live in cities often do not see their own native flora and fauna, much of which persists only in habitat fragments and managed refuges. The same set of urban exploiters are instead perceived globally as "wildlife." In the new urban environment, humans effectively engineer the flora and fauna that surround them. The assemblage of species in a city, with its effects on both ecosystem and human well-being, is as much a part of the ecological footprint as the number of acres of land required to feed its human residents.

4.3   Species interactions in urban environments

How urban species interact with their environment shapes the number and type of species in an urban area. Community ecology and population ecology broaden the focus to include how these persisting species interact with each other. Just as urbanization alters the identities of persisting species, it alters the way that these species interact.

Ecologists traditionally classify interactions based on which organisms benefit from an interaction and which are harmed by it.

- When organisms have negative effects on each other, the interaction is described as *competition*. This interaction can take on two major types: *exploitation competition* for resources, and *interference competition* via direct antagonistic interactions such as fighting or poisoning the environment.
- Several terms describe cases where one organism harms another to its own benefit. *Predation* occurs when one organism eats an animal, *herbivory* when an animal eats a plant, and *parasitism* when a smaller organism takes resources from a larger one. Predators, herbivores, and parasites are referred to as *natural enemies*.
- When organisms have positive impacts on each other, the interaction is a *mutualism*. Important mutualisms include pollination, seed dispersal, protection, and resource collection.
- When one organism capitalizes on another that is already dead, the resources are recycled. *Detritivores* and *decomposers*, respectively, eat and digest dead organic matter.

This section begins with a brief overview of the ecological theory of species interactions and then highlights the key effects of urban areas. We examine the effects of habitat, resources, and exotic species, and conclude with examples of how different types of interactions affect each other. Although the interaction between infectious diseases and their host is just one form of species interaction, we treat it separately because of its medical importance and special characteristics (Section 4.4).

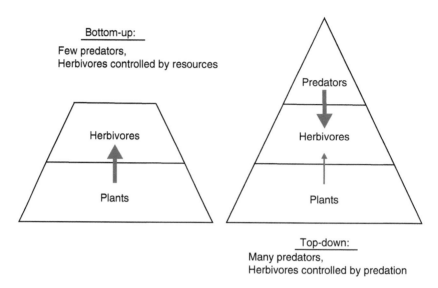

Figure 4.30 Bottom-up versus top-down control of a population.

Ecological principles of species interactions

At its simplest, ecology is the study of the distribution and abundance of organisms. Why do some organisms persist while others go extinct? For those that do persist, what keeps their populations from growing without bound?

Ultimately, population size is determined by the ability of organisms to survive and reproduce. Survival depends on acquiring enough resources and avoiding natural enemies such as predators and diseases. Reproduction too depends on resources, but also on the conditions that facilitate producing offspring, including sites to reproduce and the ability to find partners, which for plants can involve the presence of mutualists like bees.

Population regulation describes the factors that keep a population from growing indefinitely. All regulation requires that members of a species reproduce less on average when that species is common, ultimately due to either depletion of available resources or an increase in natural enemies. Based on the view that food chains represent energy and resources moving up from resources through producers and consumers (Figure 2.8), limitation by resources is called *bottom-up control* while limitation by natural enemies is called *top-down control* (Figure 4.30).

An idealized community includes resources, producers like plants that use nutrients to input energy into the system, the consumers that compete for that energy, and the predators or herbivores that exploit the consumers (Figure 4.31). The *trophic structure* describes how resources, energy, and biomass are distributed and move through an ecosystem.

As an example of bottom-up control, a plant could be limited by nitrogen availability. If many nitrogen-demanding plants of one species grow in a region, they will deplete this resource and be unable to survive or reproduce. This limits their population size,

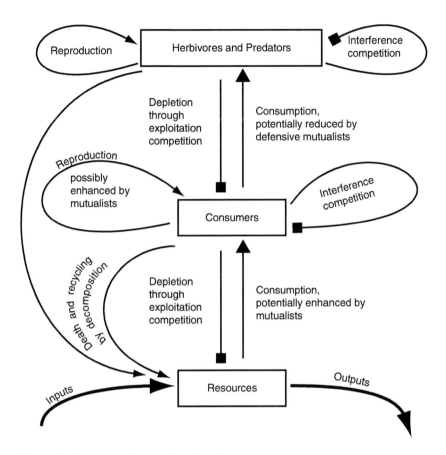

Figure 4.31 Overview of interactions in ecology.

and generates a population of individuals that, although possibly numerous, have only enough resources to replace themselves.

Alternatively, these plants could be limited by herbivores, such as caterpillars, as a form of top-down control. If these plants became common, the population of butterflies that produce those caterpillars that consume them would eventually increase. The plants might have more than enough resources, but be prevented from increasing their population by the caterpillars. Top-down and bottom-up control is a matter of perspective. In this scenario, the caterpillars experience bottom-up control from the plants.

Top-down and bottom-up control are related to limiting nutrients (Section 3.3). In a simplified agricultural setting, plant growth is not limited by the total of all nutrients, but only by the single nutrient that is most rare. In ecology, limiting factors can take on many other forms, including predation, herbivory, disease, or even lack of available pollinators or other mutualists. To unravel these possibilities, experiments can modify a single factor, such as the amount of nitrogen. In a bottom-up system, increasing the availability of a limiting resource should lead to an increase in the growth of plants. In a top-down system, however, increasing resources has no effect on the plant population, but instead leads to an increased population of herbivores. Likewise, removing herbivores from a system under bottom-up control might have little effect on the plant population.

Recent ecological experiments and theory have emphasized how different forms of population regulation interact. Suppose that plants use nitrogen not only to grow, but also to make chemical compounds that defend against herbivores. A reduction in available nitrogen due to competition might make surviving plants less able to defend themselves, leading to an increase in herbivory. Adding nitrogen might increase the plant population, thus appearing as a form of bottom-up control, although population growth really results from a decrease in herbivory. Removing herbivores would also increase the plant population, showing that these plants are controlled by a combination of bottom-up and top-down forces.

The simple contrast between bottom-up and top-down control is further complicated by many other factors.

- Many species use the same resources, and many herbivores or predators may feed upon them. Differences among these species, such as in dispersal or tolerance of disturbance, shape how their interactions are altered by the urban environment.
- The cycle does not end with herbivory or predation, but depends on the rate and efficiency with which resources are recycled. Resources in dead organisms along with the resources excreted during their lives, can be recycled back into or lost from the system. Recycling rates are controlled by the movement of resources through the water or air and by the abundance and identity of detritivores and decomposers. The reduced recycling characteristic of urban ecosystems changes resource availability and the quality of the soil, affecting plants and ultimately the animals that rely on them.
- Mutualisms, such as that of plants with nitrogen-fixing bacteria (Section 3.3) or with their pollinators, can control species abundance and persistence.
- Ecological communities do not exist in isolation. Communities with large inputs and outputs of resources and species will have relatively weak chains of interaction.
- The successional stage, determined by the time since a major disturbance, alters the pool of species present in a community. Many urban environments resemble early successional habitats that emerge after a major disturbance. Such habitats place a premium upon rapid arrival and growth, making bottom-up and top-down forces less important. As the community fills up with more slowly arriving late successional species, competition and predation become more important.

Two broad concepts organize thinking about urban ecosystems. The first is *complexity*, which describes not only the number of species present (Section 4.1) but how tightly the web of ecological interactions links them. A brownfield might be simple in being occupied by only a few species of invasive weeds and few herbivores that experience little competition because constant human disturbance keeps populations small. A tropical forest might be complex with its hundreds of coexisting plant species with their specialized mutualists and herbivores.

The second concept is that all ecosystems change over time. In some, the species and their interactions change relatively little. In others, new species arrive all the time, creating new interactions. These systems are called *non-equilibrium communities*, in a perpetual state of re-assembly by species that can tolerate an unpredictable assortment of competitors or consumers.

Urban species interactions

Because of their rapid changes, intense inputs, and high degree of disturbance, urban ecosystems are likely to be simplified non-equilibrial communities, with many species persisting only in habitat fragment sinks. Species-rich though they can be, the novel set of species and environments may well reduce the complexity of their ecological structure. The reduction of temporal variation in climate and resource availability, however, may have the opposite effect by creating more stable habitats. Urban ecosystems can be evaluated as a balance between these competing effects. This section explores how habitat modification, inputs of resources, and exotic species affect species interactions and the structure of urban ecological communities.

Effects of urban habitat modification
Habitat fragmentation
Urban habitats are fragmented into small, often isolated, patches of many different types. Only some species can succeed in this environment (Section 4.1), and this filtering of species can have profound effects on species interactions. One of the most important filters results from species size and its correlation with trophic level.

Charles Elton, one of the founders of modern ecological theory, observed that "one hill cannot shelter two tigers"[147]. Large top predators require large areas of habitat and low levels of disturbance, and often cannot survive in urban ecosystems. In the California scrub, the mountain lion *Puma concolor* and bobcat *Lynx rufus* need fragments of at least $1.0 \, km^2$, while the coyote *Canis latrans* requires only $0.1 \, km^2$ fragments. These large predators also prefer patches of scrub that connect to or are close to other such patches[107]. Raccoons, skunks, and other smaller *mesopredators* show little response to patch size and isolation, and can be released from control by large predators that are sensitive to habitat structure. In patches without coyotes, mesopredators such as grey fox *Urocyon cinereoargenteus* and opossum *Didelphis virginiana* become more common[108]. The domestic cat *Felis cattus*, in contrast, is found preferentially in small patches that are surrounded by the houses that provide them with food and shelter. Partly due to cats, bird abundance and species richness is higher in patches with even a few coyotes present. Coyotes eliminate or scare away smaller mesopredators including foxes, raccoons, opossums, skunks, and cats. Many cat owners in fact keep their cats indoors when coyotes are present, which reduces the predation pressure of cats on nearby birds.

The effects of patch size and habitat quality can create surprising effects. In the California scrub, bird nest survival is higher in small fragments than in large fragments, and on the edge relative to the interior, the opposite of what might be predicted[435]. These effects are concentrated among ground-nesting birds and strongly correlate with the abundance of snakes (Figure 4.32). Plot edges are subsidized with water from the

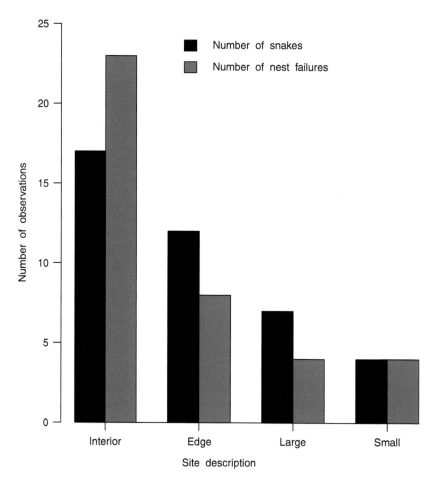

Figure 4.32 Effect of patch size and position on snake abundance and ground-nesting bird nest failure (after Patten and Bolger, 2003).

surrounding urban habitat, and predators from these habitats may reduce the numbers of snakes and indirectly protect the birds.

The effects of urbanization on avian predators such as hawks are complex. Large hawks that depend on large habitat areas and large mammals for food tend to do poorly. However, reduced human hunting pressure and abundant food for consumers of birds, such as Cooper's hawk *Accipiter cooperii* and consumers of small rodents such as the red-tailed hawk *Buteo jamaicensis*, promotes relatively large populations[86].

Bird nests are also attacked by *brood parasites*, birds that lay their eggs in other species' nests, which often respond to urban changes such as habitat fragmentation rather differently from the birds that they parasitize. In North America, the brown-headed cowbird *Molothrus ater* is the most abundant such parasite. This bird of the grasslands of central North America has expanded its range into the fragmented woodlands humans have created throughout the continent. Near Columbia, Missouri, the probability of brood parasitism by the brown-headed cowbird is greater in urban than in

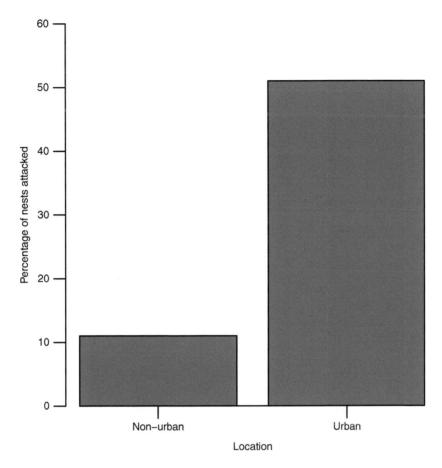

Figure 4.33 Median percentage of nests attacked by brown-headed cowbird brood parasites in urban and non-urban sites (after Burhans and Thompson, 2006).

non-urban sites, even though the nest predation rate does not differ[68] (Figure 4.33). In contrast, nests of the yellow-breasted chat *Icteria virens* suffer more parasitism in large habitat patches and more predation in small ones[69].

Disparities in coping with habitat fragmentation also apply to insects at different trophic levels. *Parasitoids*, insect parasites that lay their eggs in the living bodies of other insects, are important in controlling the populations of many herbivores. These typically small insects can be slow to find isolated patches, such as groups of trees in mall parking lots, leaving those trees open to damaging herbivory[139]. Potted *Artemisia vulgaris* plants in areas near Hamburg, Germany, with a large percentage of paved area showed an overall decrease in the number of arthropod species present, with the decrease being largest among predators and parasitoids[123]. The percentage of herbivores parasitized was lower in more paved sites (Figure 4.34).

In Sydney, Australia, leaves of the native smooth-barked apple *Angophora costata* suffered the highest damage in small remnant patches, apparently due to lower attack rates by the herbivore's enemies at these sites[94] (Figure 4.35).

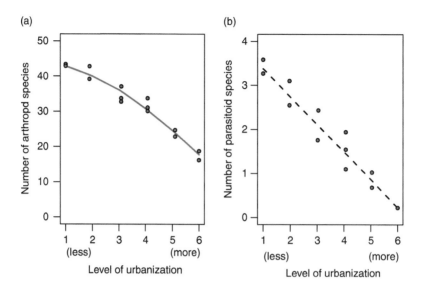

Figure 4.34 Number of species of (a) all arthropods and (b) parasitoids of the tephritid fly *Oxyna parietina* on potted *Artemesia vulgaris* as a function of the level of urbanization (after Denys and Schmidt, 1998).

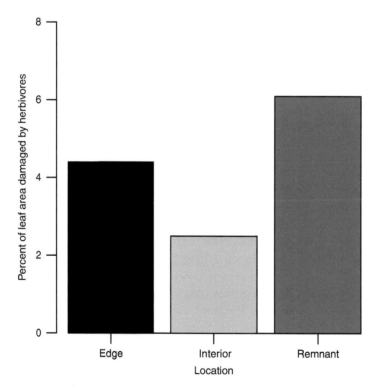

Figure 4.35 Levels of herbivore damage on trees in forest edge, interior, and small remnants near Sydney, Australia (after Christie and Hochuli, 2005).

Habitat quality

Like habitat fragmentation, habitat quality can alter species interactions by favoring some species over others or by inducing changes in behavior. Along a range of habitats in and around Washington DC, nestling survival in a variety of songbirds was higher in sites with more impermeable surface and lower in those with more canopy cover[498]. This high success in lower quality habitat results apparently from the lower number of mammalian predators such as mice, squirrels, and larger mesopredators in the urban sites and their incomplete replacement by nest-predating corvids (crows and jays). Reduced predation might also be due to a change in predator behavior from attacking nests to using anthropogenic food sources. In non-urban environments, nest survival is lower when nest predators such as squirrels, raptors, corvids, and mesopredators are common. This expected correlation breaks down in urban environments, even though urban development surrounding a forest can lead to higher populations of nest predators, likely as a result of predators choosing instead to use the human-supplied resources available in urbanized sites[487].

For many species, small habitat fragments are also of low quality. The armored scale insect *Pseudaulacaspis pentagona* infests some of the isolated mulberry trees in roadsides and parking lots, although infested trees often have close neighbors with no scales[243]. Trees in forested woodlots, in contrast, all have low scale densities. Urban infestations result from the combination of a lack of natural enemies and water stress that weakens the trees. The main factor affecting the abundance of the horse chestnut scale *Pulvinaria regalis* on three tree species in Oxford, UK is impermeability of the substrate, with a secondary factor of proximity to buildings[548].

Decomposition involves complex interactions between soils, abiotic factors, and the resident organisms. Near New York City, leaves decompose more quickly in urban than in non-urban sites, even though urban soil has a lower abundance of key decomposers like litter fungi and microinvertebrates. This increased decomposition rate may result from urban soils having high earthworm abundance and warm temperatures, an example of unexpected effects of urban ecological amplification[552]. When planted in a common environment, urban-derived deciduous leaves decomposed more slowly than non-urban derived ones. Although the soil itself has higher decomposition potential, urban leaves proved, like so many things urban, tougher than non-urban leaves[456]. Much remains to be learned about the ways that habitat quality changes interactions between detritivores and plants. Even after controlling for species, leaf litter decay near Asheville, North Carolina, showed the opposite pattern, with slower decay in urban soils[440].

The importance of predation in a particular habitat depends on the species of both predators and prey present. We have seen how habitat fragment size filters predator species. Habitat quality also acts as a filter that determines which prey species can persist. Urban sites that face high predation pressure, perhaps from cats, could be occupied only by prey that are better able to avoid predation. The overall rate of predation in this habitat might be the same or even lower than in habitats where vulnerable species persist. Near Oxford, Ohio, nest predation tends to be lower in the more urban sites where exotic urban exploiters, which can be more resistant to predation, dominate the population[211] (Figure 4.36). In Missouri, more nest predators and parasites are found in

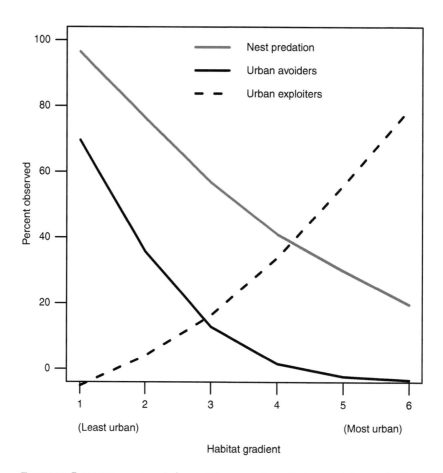

Figure 4.36 Percentage nest predation and the percentage of urban exploiters and urban avoiders among birds in six habitats near Oxford, Ohio (after Gering and Blair, 1999).

"cluster development" sites where the sensitive native birds are absent, meaning again that high predator abundance might not correlate with predation rates[405]. In another example of different responses to habitat quality by predators and prey, both cowbird predation and nest predation were lower in noisy sites near gas wells in New Mexico, apparently due to noise avoidance by nest-predating Western scrub jays *Aphelocoma californica*[178].

Just as predators can respond differently to habitat quality than their prey, competitors of different sizes can be affected differently by urban habitat filters. A remarkable contrast between urban birds common in the northern and southern hemispheres might result from these differences. Urban birds in the northern hemisphere tend to be relatively small bodied exploitation competitors while those in the southern hemisphere are instead medium bodied interference competitors[198]. In Australia, the invasion of aggressive noisy miners *Manorina melanocephala* into areas of moderate disturbance at the edges of urban ecosystems has led to the exclusion of small-bodied local birds from forest edges even when adequate habitat remains[84]. Similarly, populations of a medium-sized omnivorous bird, the pied currawong *Strepera graculina*, are higher in Australian urban areas, leading to increased predation on nests of the willie wagtail *Rhipidura leucophrys*[428].

When habitat filters exclude a predator or a competitor, other species can benefit. Mutualisms, in contrast, depend on the presence of all interacting species and might be expected to require undisturbed habitats to persist. Like predators and parasitoids, some pollinators are highly sensitive to habitat patch size, which can lead to a breakdown of the plant–pollinator mutualism. Small urban patches receive fewer pollinator visits than larger green areas, meaning that plants in these patches can have lower reproduction and reduced genetic exchange[252]. For mobile pollinators, however, the surrounding matrix is not completely deadly. Bees in grassland fragments within suburban development along the Colorado Front Range have a greater density of species per unit area[256]. These suburban patches might combine enough habitat for nesting with supplemented food in the form of flowers in gardens in the surrounding developed areas.

The Western jewel butterfly *Hypochrysops halyaetus* benefits from highly disturbed urban habitat because of a mutualism. The ant *Crematogaster perthensis* guards butterfly larvae in much the same way that ants guard and tend aphids. Both the ants and butterflies thrive in recently disturbed areas because the preferred host plant *Jacksonia sternbergiana* is an early successional species[137].

Effects of urban resource inputs

Resource inputs control the identity, abundance, and spatial distribution of urban species. For example, feeders concentrate small birds, which are potential prey for hawks and cats. One might imagine that these concentrations of well-fed and potentially distracted victims would be particularly vulnerable to predation. However, predation is usually reduced near feeders, perhaps due to dilution (a large number of birds means that each individual is less likely to be captured), or to the increased vigilance of "many eyes" (more birds are present to spot the predator and warn others)[484].

When predator abundance is reduced by urban habitat changes, urban prey must be limited by some other factor, typically resources[525]. In urban environments, many resources are plentiful, either as human refuse or through intentional feeding. Resources also tend to be available relatively consistently throughout the year and in predictable clumps. Urban-adapted species capitalize on this consistent, concentrated, and abundant resource base to build up large population densities, particularly near resource clumps. These are precisely the conditions where competition, both within and between species, should be most intense, and where successful individuals and species must be the most effective competitors[527].

Urban bird species typically do forage more efficiently than their non-urban counterparts, eating both more food and staying longer at patches in the face of possible predation (discussed in more detail as a change in behavior in Section 4.5). Although food may be delivered at higher rates in urban sites, the combination of high foraging efficiency and high forager density will quickly deplete those resources, leading to low food availability per forager. The species that succeed best in these conditions are often non-natives. In Tucson, Arizona, the extralimital native Inca dove *Scardafella inca*, originally a Mexican species, reaches high densities in the city and adeptly capital-izes on seeds both at feeders and in lawns[149]. Native species, with adaptations focused on coping with predation and climate, might be excluded by these highly competitive urban specialists[525].

Urban plants suffer a range of challenges related to resource availability. Low water availability and proximity to impermeable surfaces can stress trees and make them more susceptible to attack[470]. The urban heat island, in addition to stressing trees, can accel-erate the growth of insect herbivores and allow them to escape from predators[470]. Urban resource inputs that improve plant performance can also increase susceptibility to her-bivore attack. The cypress bark moth *Laspeyresia cupressana* is an innocuous herbivore in its native coastal habitat in California, where it feeds on Monterey cypress. In urban areas, however, these trees have thinner bark due to the faster growth made possible by watering and fertilization, and become susceptible to extensive moth damage[139].

Effects of exotic species

Exotic species can enter a community as highly effective competitors, predators, or ecosystem engineers. As competitors, ants often have strong community-level effects, able to almost completely displace native species. In California, the Argentine ant (Sec-tion 4.2) essentially eliminates native ants through its combined ability to locate food (exploitation competition) and to dominate food after discovery (interference competi-tion)[265]. Similarly, the big-headed ant *Pheidole megacephala* (Section 2.4), displaces native ant communities in Australia because its colonies can grow to extremely high densities and outcompete native species for resources[258]. The abundance of native ants in Perth suburban gardens is strongly negatively correlated with the presence of these two species of exotic ant[254]. These invasive ants also prefer non-native garden veg-etation, creating a cascading effect from the garden plants chosen by humans to ant community composition.

Non-native plants also fail to support as many specialist insects, and thus fewer insec-tivorous birds[561]. Although generalist insects make up some of the difference, they do not fully compensate, leading to vastly lower insect biomass and less food for insectiv-orous birds[67].

Some of the most complex effects of exotic species occur below ground. To garner nitrogen and phosphorus from the soil, many plants depend on *mycorrhizal fungi* that attach to their roots and harvest nutrients in exchange for sugars from the plant. These fungi interact differently with different plant species, and can be sensitive to invasive plants. The widespread invasive plant garlic mustard *Alliaria petiolata*, for example, reduces the populations of some of these mutualistic fungi[615]. This reduction can filter back to the plant community, potentially reducing native pine seedling regeneration.

The decay of leaves depends on both the plant species and the properties of the soil. The leaves of the invasive tree of heaven *Ailanthus altissima* decay faster than those of native species[557]. As these trees take over urban riparian areas, the consequences for nutrient cycling and germination remain to be seen.

Soil processes can filter through the ecosystem, and create an "invasional meltdown." In the state of Illinois, the invasive shrub European buckthorn *Rhamnus cathartica*

Figure 4.37 Young cat with a captured bird.

produces litter with high nitrogen that promotes invasion by non-native Eurasian earthworms[251]. These detritivores chew quickly through the nutrient-rich litter, and potentially promote further buckthorn invasion by creating clear patches of soil for subsequent germination. The presence of native oaks, with their characteristically lower quality litter, slow this decay and potentially interrupt this process.

Cats and their effects on birds

The effects of cats on bird populations remains among the most controversial topics in urban ecology (Figure 4.37). Cats are mesopredators, but unusual in their habitat preferences and hunting behavior. Unlike wild predators, domestic cats are not limited by their prey. Instead cats subsist, like humans, on food from distant sources, and are largely regulated, like garden plants, by human preference and taste. In fact, cats can outnumber wild birds in urban areas, a situation unheard of in non-urban ecosystems where prey must outnumber their predators.

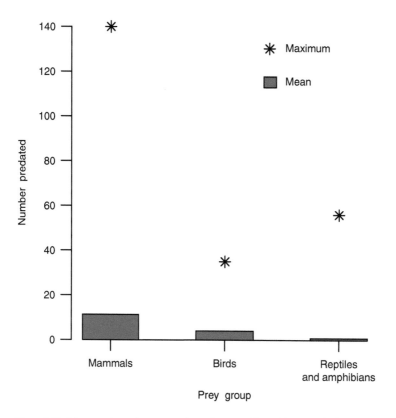

Figure 4.38 Mean and maximum number of prey collected by cats during a 5 month period (after Woods *et al.*, 2003).

Cat densities in England are extremely high, up to 1000 per km², at least 100 times higher than the density of wild cats with similar body size[533] and 20–40 times greater than comparably sized wild predators such as stoats, weasels, and foxes[617]. In the United States, the 60 million pet and 10–60 million feral cats[278] have been estimated to kill 1 billion birds per year, and twice as many mammals[118], in addition to frogs and insects. In England, cats brought home approximately three prey per month, including members of 44 bird species, but with a wide range of other prey and a tendency of a few younger and thinner cats to catch far more than the average[617] (Figure 4.38).

Although a majority of urban cats spend some time outside and kill at least some birds[108], their role in limiting urban bird populations remains uncertain. A large correlational analysis identified little evidence of cat predation reducing bird densities in Britain[533]. In Australia, cats might in fact indirectly protect the nests of small birds by intimidating large avian nest predators that are common there[355]. In the city Dunedin, New Zealand, where cats kill enough birds of some species to make the urban environment into a population sink, nighttime predation on rats might remove another avian predator and partially compensate for this negative effect[584].

Prey choice provides another explanation for the mixed effects of cats. Because they do not depend on hunting to survive, domestic cats tend to hunt only the slowest and

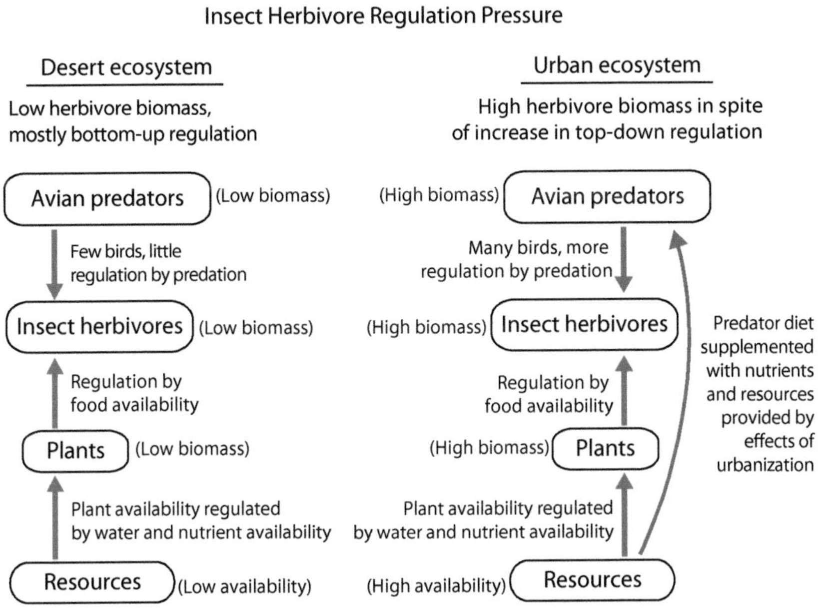

Insect Herbivore Regulation Pressure

Desert ecosystem	Urban ecosystem

Low herbivore biomass,
mostly bottom-up regulation

High herbivore biomass in spite
of increase in top-down regulation

Avian predators (Low biomass)   (High biomass) Avian predators

Few birds, little
regulation by predation

Many birds, more
regulation by predation

Insect herbivores (Low biomass)   (High biomass) Insect herbivores

Predator diet
supplemented
with nutrients
and resources
provided by
effects of
urbanization

Regulation by
food availability

Regulation by
food availability

Plants (Low biomass)   (High biomass) Plants

Plant availability regulated
by water and nutrient availability

Plant availability regulated
by water and nutrient availability

Resources (Low availability)   (High availability) Resources

Figure 4.39 Comparison of the relative strengths of regulation in a community of consumers and resources in Phoenix, Arizona (after Faeth *et al.*, 2005).

most vulnerable birds. In urban areas, the shift from wild predators to cats focuses predation on fledglings rather than adults[161]. Cats would have little effect on bird populations if their predation was only of the "doomed surplus" that would have died anyway from lack of resources[24].

In the United Kingdom, populations of the most extreme urban exploiters, the European starling and the house sparrow, have declined by as much as 60% in the last 30 years. Cat predation has been hypothesized as the cause. Recent evidence implies that increasing populations of sparrowhawks *Accipiter nisus*, which have colonized urban areas only since 1980, might instead be responsible[26]. In fact, house sparrows provide 73% of the prey for sparrowhawks in Berlin, although the sparrow population there has remained relatively stable[312]. This relatively recent colonization by a predator reflects the non-equilibrial nature of urban communities that results from the rapidity of habitat change and the many decades or even centuries it takes for animals to colonize new habitats[156] (Section 4.5).

Interactions among levels

How do all of these changes affect the way that energy and nutrients flow through the urban ecosystem? Comparison of Phoenix with the nearby Sonoran Desert provides perhaps the best studied contrast between urban and non-urban ecosystems[161] (Figure 4.39). In the desert, resources, particularly water, are scarce, leading to relatively low productivity of plants. The insects that eat these plants are regulated by bottom-up effects, and thus the birds that eat the insects will also be rare if they too are regulated from the bottom up.

Urban ecosystems, in contrast, have highly subsidized resources that are stable both in time and space. Plants and herbivorous arthropods convert these resources into offspring, which in turn can become a large and stable resource for birds. This food source, on top of direct supplements from bird feeders and gardens, allows birds to reach high densities, dominated by those competitive species best at monopolizing resources. This leads to a combination of top-down and bottom-up control for urban insect herbivores[527]. In addition, birds themselves are partially released from predation, making them more limited by resources, including any herbivorous insects they eat. Experimentally excluding birds from plots in urban areas leads to large increases in insect abundance, but bird exclusion has little effect in the desert. In contrast, adding water leads to increased plant growth in the desert but not in this urban area.

Remnant patches of desert within the urban matrix are generally more similar to urban than desert sites, perhaps due to resources that leak over from neighboring sites into the urban desert remnants. The effects of increased resource availability are superimposed upon those created by changes in habitat structure. Patches may be too small or too isolated to support arthropod predators or parasitoids, leaving the field open for highly mobile generalist urban birds[212]. This change in predation provides another way in which remnant or reconstructed patches within the urban matrix may look undisturbed, but behave more like urban habitat.

Conclusions

The heavy hand of humanity notwithstanding, urban ecosystems are still ecosystems. Nutrients cycle. Species persist and interact via the full range of competition, predation, herbivory, and mutualism. But in the face of rapid habitat changes, high resource inputs, and constant disturbance, interactions in urban ecosystems are altered, and often simplified and out of equilibrium.

Simplification both shrinks and loosens the web of ecological interactions. The loss of large top predators reduces the length of food chains. This reduction, combined with greater inputs of resources, accentuates the importance of competition in many urban systems. Furthermore, although urban biodiversity can be high across an entire city, particular sites are often dominated by one or a few species of superior, and often exotic, competitors. New predators, such as cats and brood parasites, interact with existing predators and habitat types to create a new structure that is arguably as complex as the one it displaced.

No ecosystem is truly at equilibrium, but it is fair to say that urban systems are in a more rapid state of flux than most. Habitats, resources, and species change quickly and unpredictably, leading to similarly quick and unpredictable changes in interactions. The resulting urban communities can seem more like an assemblage of unrelated parts than a finely tuned set of interacting species and flows. Whether these assemblages will find some novel equilibrium may take centuries to play out.

More studies of more cities will undoubtedly reveal exceptions to these generalizations. No set of "laws" completely explains or predicts the functioning of undisturbed ecosystems, and urban ecosystems can be even more unpredictable and idiosyncratic. Nonetheless, the principles of ecological interaction, such as the interplay between bottom-up and top-down effects, identify the key elements ecologists must attend to. In urban ecology, as in all fields of science, identifying when and where generalizations do not apply refines the science and challenges it to achieve further sophistication and understanding.

4.4   Urban infectious diseases

Although no more than another group of species, infectious diseases are sufficiently important and special to be considered separately by ecologists, in part because many diseases also infect humans. Like predators and herbivores, infectious diseases harm one organism, the *host*, and benefit another, the *pathogen*. Pathogens can be viruses, bacteria, fungi, parasitic worms, or even *prions*, incorrectly folded proteins. As parasites that live within the body, pathogens are tightly tied to their hosts, and typically connected to the ecosystem only indirectly through its effect on their hosts.

Infectious disease *transmission* between host individuals or species links what happens within one host to other hosts, whether of the same or different species. In urban settings, transmission between wild animals and humans or between wild animals and pets can be a significant public health concern.

The factors that control predation and herbivory, such as urban biodiversity, host population density, and environmental stress, also play key roles in the dynamics of infectious disease. Like other interactions, urban disease dynamics are driven by urban habitat and climate modification, and by inputs of resources and species.

Principles of infectious disease

The ecological effects of infectious disease depend on the properties of the pathogen, the host, and the environment they inhabit. The principles of infectious disease describe how these properties affect pathogen *persistence*, its ability to survive in a given habitat or region, and *prevalence*, the fraction of individuals a pathogen infects. Prevalence interacts with *virulence*, the negative effects of the pathogen on infected hosts, to determine whether an infectious disease reduces its host's population size.

Disease dynamics can be broadly divided into *epidemic* and *endemic*. Epidemic diseases, such as the bubonic plague in humans, sweep through and potentially devastate a population. Endemic diseases remain present over long periods of time, often at low levels, such as the common cold. These dynamics and their effects on host populations depend on the range of hosts a pathogen infects, how it is transmitted, and by its effects on hosts.

Disease host range describes the set of species a pathogen infects. It can include only one or a few species, or a large number of species. *Spillover* hosts are infected but not infectious, and thus unable to transmit the infection. When the focus is on human, pet, or domestic livestock, the wild hosts, whether native or non-native, are referred to as a *reservoir*.

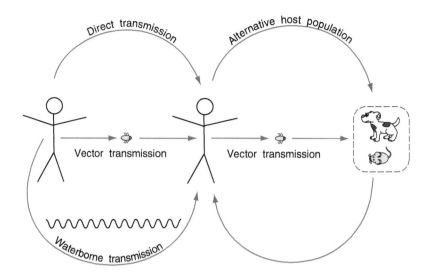

Figure 4.40 Modes of disease transmission between hosts. As examples, HIV and influenza are directly transmitted, Lyme disease involves an alternative host population (rodents) and a vector (ticks), and cholera is transmitted through water.

Mode of transmission describes how a pathogen spreads between individuals (Figure 4.40). *Direct transmission* occurs via contact, including sexual contact, fighting, predation, or parent–offspring interaction. *Indirect transmission* occurs via the water, soil, or an animal *vector* such as the mosquito. For pathogens transmitted by a vector, high biodiversity of potential biting targets might mean that few bites, and even fewer consecutive bites, occur on the host species. The *dilution effect* describes situations where the presence of diverse targets for a vector reduces the prevalence or persistence of a pathogen.

Virulence describes the fitness effects of a pathogen on its hosts. Some pathogens, such as the infamous Ebola virus, kill most of the individuals they infect, while others, such as the common cold, create only temporary inconvenience. Damage to hosts can range from mortality or sterilization to indirect costs mediated through ecological interactions, such as reducing the ability of infected individuals to compete for resources or avoid predation.

Susceptibility describes the ease with which different hosts become infected. Different species, and different individuals within species, can have large differences in susceptibility due to age, nutrition, or general health.

This section examines how these factors interact with the key aspects of the urban environment to control disease persistence and prevalence, and its effects on host populations.

Urban infectious disease dynamics

Urban habitat modification, increased resource inputs, and invasive species alter species interactions ranging from competition to mutualism (Section 4.3) and the interaction

Table 4.2 Some wildlife diseases in urban populations

Name	Description	Host(s)	Human risk
Canine parvovirus	Virus	Dogs and foxes	None
Feline calicivirus	Virus	Cats and bobcats	None
Rabies	Virus	Bats	Fatal if not treated
West Nile virus	Virus	Birds	Fever, rarely neuroinvasive
Mycoplasma gallisepticum	Bacterium	Birds	None
Borrelia burgdorferi	Bacterium	Small mammals	Lyme disease
Trichomonas gallinae	Protozoan	Doves and other birds	None
Toxoplasma gondii	Protozoan	Cats and other mammals	Toxoplasmosis
Echinococcus multilocularis	Tapeworm	Dogs and foxes	Alveolar echinococosis
Baylisascaris procyonis	Roundworm	Mammals	Rare but deadly encephalitis
Sarcoptes scabiei	Mite	Wild and domestic dogs	Rare cases of itching
Chronic Wasting Disease	Prion	Deer and elk	None

between infectious diseases and their hosts is no exception. Urban habitat fragmentation can isolate pathogens in one or a few sites, while transport of species or materials can move pathogens between sites. Clumped food resources in urban environments can increase the population density and aggressive interactions of urban exploiters, facilitating pathogen transmission. Increased movement of water can increase indirect transmission in urban areas. Stresses, such as pollution, can increase susceptibility. Exotic species can carry exotic pathogens, and exotic vectors can increase indirect transmission.

Only a few studies have demonstrated differences between urban and non-urban pathogen prevalence, and even fewer have isolated the causal factors. This section examines the almost entirely unintentional effects of urbanization on infectious disease.

Effects of urban habitat modification

West Nile virus is an emerging infectious disease that infects a wide range of songbirds, and is transmitted by mosquitos (Table 4.2 lists the pathogens discussed in this section). Mosquito abundance can be increased by the presence of breeding sites as well as the urban heat island. In Bakersfield, California, large numbers of abandoned swimming pools, a consequence of the economic downturn, nearly tripled West Nile virus abundance[478]. This reflects a complex chain from economics to habitat to wildlife disease, with potentially important health effects on humans. In sites near Atlanta, Georgia, antibody prevalence in adult birds against West Nile virus was positively correlated with the degree of urbanization[52] (Figure 4.41). However, antibody prevalence measures the number of birds that have had the infection and survived, making it impossible to distinguish whether the pathogen is indeed more common in urban areas, or whether urban birds are in better condition, perhaps due to increased access to food, and are therefore more likely to survive infection.

Chronic Wasting Disease is a prion of deer, with a hotspot in rapidly urbanizing areas of northeastern Colorado and southeastern Wyoming in the western United States[163]. Urban development, particularly in the winter range of the deer, has increased deer

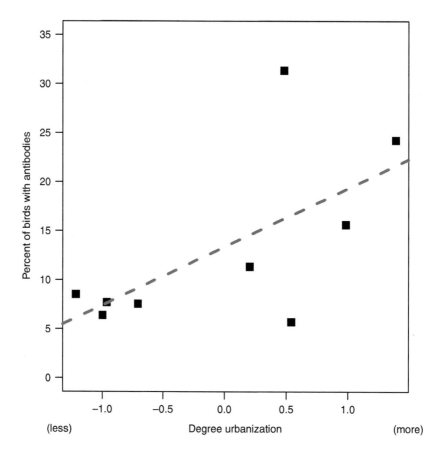

Figure 4.41 Percent of birds testing positive for West Nile virus antibodies as a function of the degree of urbanization (after Bradley *et al.*, 2008).

density because decreased availability of suitable habitat concentrates deer in fewer sites. Decreased hunting and predation further increase deer density while extending deer lifespans. As this infection is inevitably fatal, longer lifespan gives deer more time to be infected, while high density provides more opportunities to transmit the infection. Deer are indeed roughly twice as likely to be infected in the urbanized areas. This effect is stronger in males than in females, perhaps because the removal of hunting pressure has a greater effect on male survivorship.

Lyme disease, caused by the bacterium *Borrelia burgdorferi*, infects many rodents and other species of mammal including humans. Ticks transmit the infection from host to host. The white-footed mouse *Peromyscus leucopus* is highly effective in carrying and transmitting the infection. This mouse is relatively common in suburbs of the eastern United States. Other rodents cannot tolerate these modified habitats creating areas of lower rodent biodiversity. When suburban ticks acquire *Borrelia* they are more likely to bite white-footed mice. As an example of the dilution effect, areas such as suburbs with lower rodent diversity can have higher Lyme disease prevalence[335]. Furthermore, the humans concentrated in these same areas face a higher risk of contracting this disease[51].

Effects of urban resource inputs

For urban exploiters, urban areas offer abundant, concentrated, and dependable sources of food. The resulting concentrated populations of hosts could interact more, both within and between species, resulting in increased pathogen transmission. Bird feeders concentrate many types of birds in a small area. These concentrations of birds may not increase the predation rate on individual birds because more birds can dilute the predation risk or detect predators in time to escape and warn others (Section 4.3). Neither of these factors affect pathogens, which can simultaneously infect many individuals in a group and cannot be seen and avoided. Increased transmission of *Mycoplasma gallisepticum*, a highly contagious conjunctivitis in a variety of bird species, occurs at bird feeders and has contributed to the rapid spread of the infection across North America[484].

In the early 1990s, Bristol, UK, hosted a large, healthy, and rapidly growing urban red fox population that fed on wild birds, rodents, and food supplements from humans. Sarcoptic mange, which is caused by the mite *Sarcoptes scabiei*, arrived in Bristol in 1993. The disease reduces female fecundity and male fertility, and showed a classic epidemic spread, increasing in prevalence from 55% in fall 1993 to 100% in the fall and winter

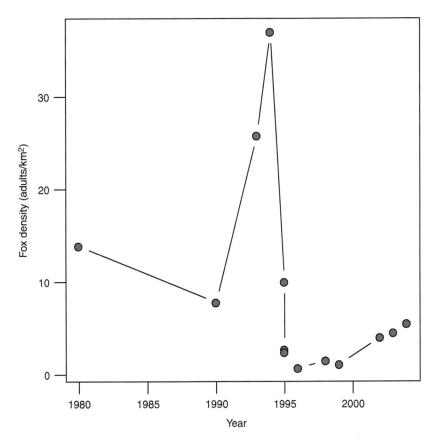

Figure 4.42 The decline of Bristol's urban red fox population after the arrival of sarcoptic mange (after Soulsbury *et al.*, 2007).

of 1995, followed by a reduction to 15–30% in 1996. Domestic dogs track this trend with an approximately 1 month delay, indicating transmission from red foxes to dogs. The population of red foxes crashed and has recovered only slowly[546] (Figure 4.42). In addition to changing the population density, the disease altered the causes of death. Before the mange outbreak, 62% of red fox deaths were caused by cars, about the same as the percentage caused by mange during the outbreak.

Raccoons *Procyon lotor* carry a roundworm, *Baylisascaris procyonis*, that can dangerously infect humans. This roundworm has only slightly higher prevalence in urban than non-urban sites, even though raccoon densities are far higher in urban areas[423] (Figure 4.43). Experimentally increased food availability at a non-urban site led to higher raccoon density, more clumping, and much higher pathogen prevalence as expected[220] (Figure 4.44). However, the life cycle of this roundworm includes small vertebrates such as rodents. Raccoons depend on these prey in non-urban areas, but switch to highly available human discards in urban areas, interrupting the transmission cycle of the roundworm. The two conflicting effects of resources, in combination with the host range of the pathogen, result in only a small increase in prevalence due to higher density.

Effects of exotic species

All cities harbor at least one exotic species, human beings (except in the region of Africa where humans evolved), in addition to many other urban-exploiting species of plants and animals (Section 4.2). These include intentionally introduced and desirable pets, particularly dogs and cats, in addition to undesirable species such as rats and, of course, non-native diseases such as West Nile virus in the United States.

Relatively few studies have compared urban and non-urban prevalences for wildlife infectious diseases. In Golden Gate Park in San Francisco, wild gray foxes interact with pet dogs (as in the spread of sarcoptic mange) and wild bobcats interact with domestic cats, with possible disease transmission in each case. Among the many pathogens compared, canine parvovirus was more common in the urban area, while feline calicivirus was less common (Figure 4.45). The prevalence of several other pathogens, including the protozoan *Toxoplasma gondii*, were unchanged[481]. Assessing the degree of contact and transmission between wildlife and pets remains difficult.

A comparison of wild and feral animals in two small parks in Mexico City found uniformly high levels of canine parvovirus, apparently because of its ability to persist in feces. Both *Toxoplasma* and rabies antibodies, however, were more common in feral cats and dogs than in wild animals[556] (Figure 4.46). In the United States, feral cats are now the primary carriers of rabies[118].

As with many ecological interactions, changing the dynamics of one pathogen can create surprising unintended consequences. Rabies is among the most deadly infectious diseases known, infecting and killing many wild animals and pets, and creating a well-known risk to humans. In continental Europe, successful rabies control released foxes from a significant form of mortality, and facilitated their movement into urban areas where they quickly became a successful urban adapter. Foxes also share a variety of infectious diseases with domesticated dogs. The small tapeworm *Echinococcus*

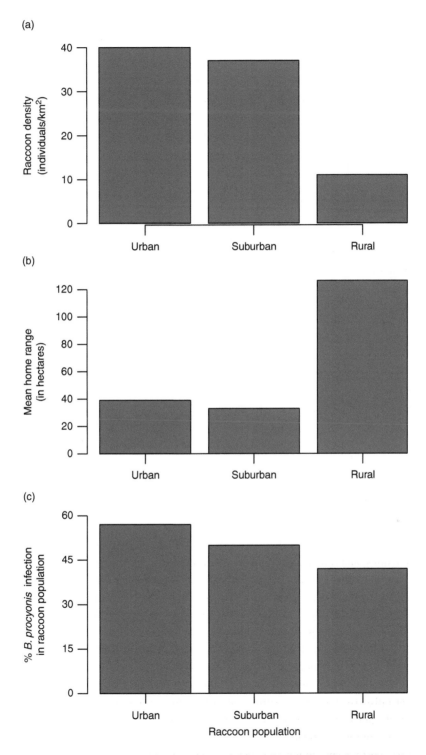

Figure 4.43 Effects of habitat on raccoon populations (a) density, (b) size of home range, and (c) percent infected with *Baylisascaris procyonis* (after Page *et al.*, 2008).

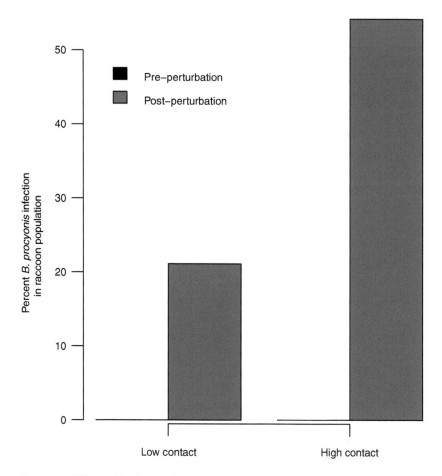

Figure 4.44 Effects of feeding on the percentage of raccoons infected with *Baylisascaris procyonis* (after Gompper and Wright, 2005). There was no infection in either group before the feeding treatment.

multilocularis alternates between infecting carnivores, primarily canids such as foxes and dogs, and rodents. The worms infect roughly 50% of foxes, and are concentrated in a few individuals, with 72% of worms found in only 8% of hosts. These highly infected foxes deposit worm eggs in their feces, a source of perennial curiosity for urban dogs[124]. When infected, dogs can transmit the infection to humans. Although urban dogs have about a 10% chance of being infected during their lifetime, quite a bit lower than the 50% for non-urban dogs, the continued spread of foxes, if not interrupted by mange or another disease, may eventually reverse this trend.

Infection with the protozoan *Toxoplasma gondii* causes 20% of human deaths attributed to food-borne illness, and can cause miscarriages. Although able to infect many species of mammal during its asexual phase, the parasite requires cats, whether wild or domestic, to complete the sexual phase of its life cycle. About 20% of domestic cats are infected, although a much smaller percentage, perhaps 2%, shed the oocytes or eggs at any one time. With 60% of California's human population living near the coast,

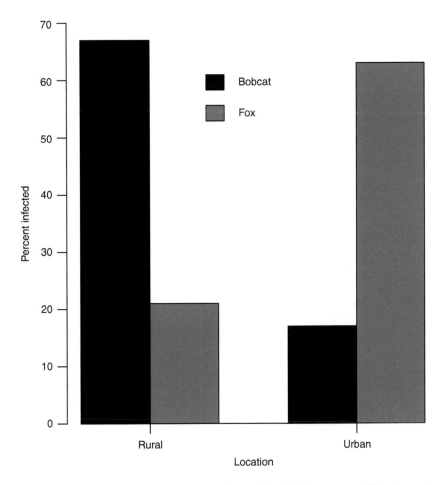

Figure 4.45 Percent of foxes and bobcats testing positive for diseases carried by domestic pets (after Riley *et al.*, 2004).

many cat droppings, either deposited directly outdoors or spread through flushable kitty litter, reach the ocean near river mouths. The sea otters that inhabit this area are highly susceptible to the asexual phase of the infection, with approximately 70% of the southern population infected[281]. The parasite causes about 16% of otter deaths directly, and infected otters are 3.7 times more likely to be eaten by sharks[102]. This parasite can modify the behavior of infected rodents, making them less fearful of cats and thus more likely to enter a host suitable for the sexual cycle. The same sort of behavioral change might also cause higher mortality in otters.

Cooper's hawk, which preys primarily on birds, generally does well in urban areas (Section 4.3). Urban Cooper's hawks feed nestlings twice as much food as non-urban hawks, but still have poor fledging success in the Phoenix area[151]. Fully 51% of urban nestlings died, compared with only about 5% of non-urban nestlings. Of these, 80% of urban nestlings died of trichomoniasis, caused by the parasitic protozoan *Trichomonas gallinae*[37]. Doves that carry this protozoan, such as the extralimital native Inca dove

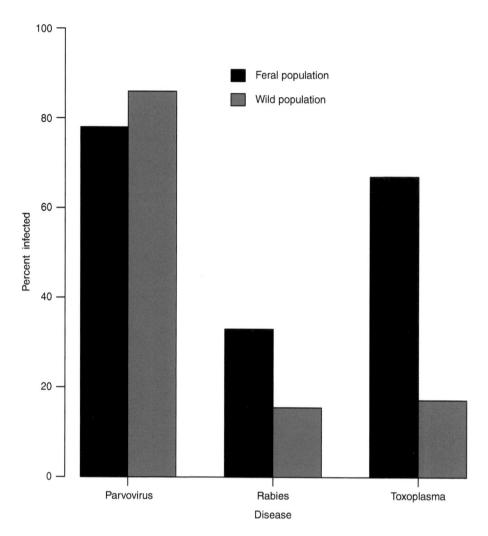

Figure 4.46 Percent of wild and feral animals testing positive for various diseases (after Suzan and Ceballos, 2004).

(Section 4.3), flourish in the urban environment and form a stable but effectively poisoned food supply. In more northern areas that have lower populations of doves, urban and non-urban hawk survival is similar[492]. The abundance of an urban-adapted extralimital native, the Inca dove, interacts with an infectious disease to make Phoenix into an ecological trap for Cooper's hawks.

Conclusions

Pathogens cannot persist without hosts to infect and without a way to be transmitted between hosts. Urbanization can change the identity of hosts, their density, and the

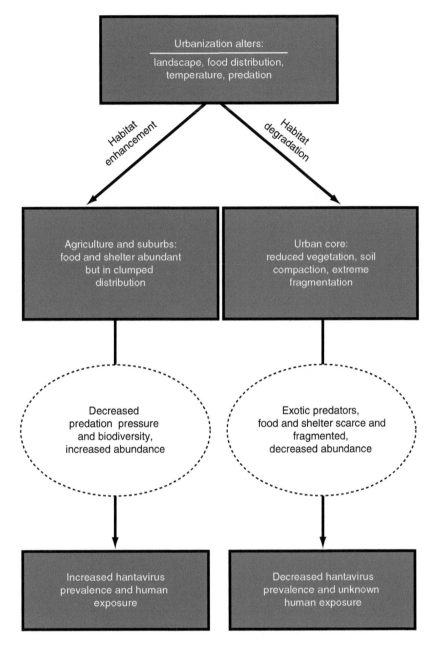

Figure 4.47 Factors affecting hantavirus prevalence (after Dearing and Dizney, 2010).

way in which they interact. Whether pathogens persist or indeed flourish in urban areas depends on how they cope with these changes. Pathogens that can infect multiple host species have multiple ways to exploit urban environments.

The potentially conflicting effects of urban changes are illustrated by hantaviruses (Figure 4.47). Members of this genus of viruses typically infect small mammals, particularly rodents, whose populations are controlled by food availability, harsh winter conditions, and predation[120]. Cities that provide dependable and clumped food, increased winter minimum temperatures, and a decrease in predation pressure, offer a common gathering place for some carriers of hantaviruses. Urban exploiting rats, such as *Rattus norvegicus* and *Rattus rattus* that carry Seoul hantavirus, can board ships that carry them from port city to port city. In contrast, the bank vole *Myodes glareolus* that carries Puumala virus does poorly in areas without forests.

How these differences in prevalence translate into human cases depends on contact between humans and rodents. Residents of heavily urbanized city centers may seek to avoid contact with the rodents that may carry hantavirus. As cities expand into the surrounding countryside, human contact with generalist rodent species well adapted to intermediate levels of disturbance can become common, increasing the risk of exposure. Urbanization shapes human exposure to hantavirus through chains of effects starting with habitat, moving through resource and ecological effects on rodents of multiple species, and ending with changes in human behavior. Urban ecologists are only in the early stages of understanding the many links in these chains.

The story of Dutch elm disease *Ceratocystis ulmi* in North America also combines many themes of urban ecology. First detected in the Netherlands, this fungus was accidentally introduced into Cleveland, Ohio, in 1930. The American elm *Ulmus americana* proved particularly susceptible to this exotic species[213]. The disease spread rapidly, aided by the popular practice of planting monocultures of these elegant trees along urban streets at sufficiently high density for the fungus to be transmitted directly between their roots. Two species of beetle, one native and one exotic, spread the fungus between more distant trees. By 1970, American elms were essentially gone from North American cities, destroyed as an unintended consequence of urban planning and the long-distance movement of species. Some American elms do survive, such as those in Central Park in New York City, thanks to their isolation from surrounding forests.

Infectious diseases connect wild animals, pets, and humans. Through complex routes, pets can create novel risks for wild animals, while wild animals can create risks for pets and their owners. The interaction between foxes, dogs, and *Echinococcus multilocularis* has been described as a form of "wilderness in the city"[124]. People may be surprised and somewhat pleased to find wild animals, such as foxes, successfully and quietly inhabiting cities, bringing with them a taste of wilderness. They may perhaps be less pleased when foxes use human waste products and pets as sources of food. But urban residents can hardly be surprised when the hint of wilderness wild animals bring carries with it infectious diseases that are just as much a part of life as hunting and finding mates.

4.5   Traits of urban organisms

Some species persist in urban habitats while others do not. The success or failure of a particular species depends on its *phenotype*, its set of traits, that determines how it interacts with its environment, including members of its own and other species. The

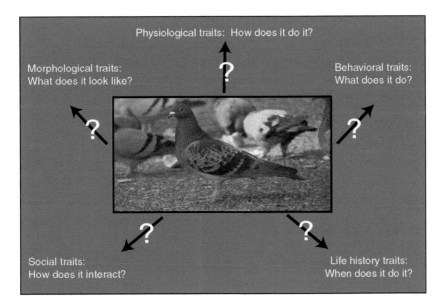

Figure 4.48 The five categories of traits and the key questions they address.

phenotype itself emerges from the interaction of genes with the environment, and thus the traits found in the urban areas are shaped in part by responses to the environment that organisms experience.

We can break traits into five broad and sometimes overlapping categories (Figure 4.48).

1. **Morphological traits** characterize the physical structure of organisms, such as size and shape.
2. **Physiological traits** characterize the functioning of organisms, such as their ability to use resources or tolerate environmental stresses.
3. **Behavioral traits** comprise how an organism responds to its environment, such as aggression and choice of food.
4. **Life history traits** summarize the schedule of reproduction and survival, including the timing of reproduction, fecundity, and lifespan.
5. **Social traits** describe the way that organisms, usually members of the same species, interact with each other.

Changes in urban habitats, resource and nutrient flows, and the whole range of unintended consequences of urbanization create the environment that shapes these traits in urban organisms.

The principles of interaction between traits and environment

The traits of organisms that we see in any particular environment are determined by three major processes.

Sorting

Environments sort species into those that can and cannot persist (Section 4.1). In the context of a novel environment, like the urban environment, successful organisms are sometimes said to be *preadapted* because they have appropriate traits from prior adaptation to other environments.

Phenotypic change

All organisms can adjust their traits during their lifetimes, with some species and types of traits being more flexible than others. The morphological changes that are particularly characteristic of plants are often called *phenotypic plasticity*. Behavioral, life history, and social adjustments occur almost instantaneously in some circumstances, or take a substantial fraction of the life of the individual in others. Learning is a special class of behavioral adjustment based on feedback from experience or observations of others. Like other behavioral changes, learning can be quick or slow, in some cases requiring multiple generations for innovations to crystallize and spread.

The fitness effects of trait changes fall into three class: (1) **adaptive** changes improve survival or reproduction, (2) **maladaptive** changes decrease performance, sometimes enough to make an environment into an ecological trap, and (3) **unavoidable** changes, such as those that result from exposure to pollution or too little food.

Evolution

Species or populations can evolve, showing changes in their genetic composition that can improve the fit between individual organisms and the environment (Section 4.6).

Understanding how the traits of organisms align with different aspects of the environment depends on the following principles:

1. Traits of different types interact; for example, a change in morphology, such as increased size, can lead to a change in behavior,
2. Traits respond to the environment at different speeds, with behavioral changes typically being fastest and evolutionary changes slowest,
3. Trait responses can be adaptive, maladaptive, or unavoidable,
4. Some traits feed back and change the environment itself, such as water use by plants or fires generated by cheatgrass. These feedbacks can make the environment either more or less suitable for the species that generated them,
5. Traits can vary significantly within species, such as body size or behavior, creating the potential for sorting of individuals into different habitats. Many traits change during the lifetime of a single individual,
6. In determining which traits succeed, environmental variability in either time or space can be crucial. For example, an environment that alternates between extreme wet and dry conditions favors different plant water-use strategies from one with more constant moisture even if the averages are the same.

The variability of conditions in space and time plays a key role in determining whether organisms are *specialists* or *generalists*. Specialists use a small set of habitats or a small set of resource types, while generalists can capitalize on many different circumstances. A species can be a generalist in three ways.

1. **Tolerance:** Individuals use the same traits to survive and reproduce in many conditions.
2. **Adjustment:** Individuals adjust to respond appropriately to the environment.
3. **Intraspecific variation:** Individuals of the species could succeed in different environments, making the species more generalist than any specific individual.

Traits associated with urban environments

Urban environments feature accelerated and transformed ecosystem processes, irregular and patchy disturbance dynamics, and novel and closely abutting habitats (Section 3.4). As such, they typically favor generalists over specialists[217]. Bird species found in urban areas have broader elevational and latitudinal ranges than those absent from urban areas, even within the same genus[43] (Figure 4.49). Generalist carabid beetles dominate urban communities at the expense of specialists[275,404], particularly at the edges of fragments[205]. These results do not show which of the three mechanisms of specialization creates the pattern. As we will see, some evidence indicates that urban organisms are more flexible and even intelligent than non-urban organisms, pointing toward the ability of individuals to adjust as key.

Being a generalist does not delineate the specific traits responsible for survival in the urban environment. Urban plants and animals face a whole range of stresses and challenges not present in ecosystems undisturbed by humans[226]. Like those that shape urban biodiversity and species interactions, these challenges divide into the four broad categories of habitat modification, resource inputs, ecosystem processes, and ecological interactions.

Effects of urban habitats
Habitat fragmentation
Urban habitat fragmentation can have conflicting effects on the morphologies and behaviors associated with dispersal between fragments. With sufficient human-induced disturbance, only highly mobile species can locate habitable sites. However, an inhospitable intervening matrix can make dispersal dangerous[92] or even impossible[393].

The urban environment also alters how organisms disperse. Urban plants are less likely to disperse their seeds by wind, and more likely to use animals or humans[307]. Weak urban winds (Section 3.1) might not be sufficiently consistent to move seeds to appropriate habitats, while urban birds, pets, and people are both available and efficient dispersers. Seeds that disperse through transport of soil, such as on motor vehicle tires (Figure 4.21), often come from weedy plants that produce many small seeds.

Many plants must disperse pollen in addition to seeds, and enlist the wind, animals, or other more exotic mechanisms to assist them. Although urban winds are not highly effective in moving large seeds, they can be more dependable than waiting for depleted

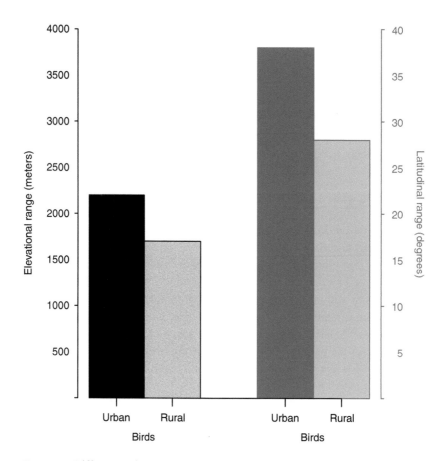

Figure 4.49 Different environmental toleranaces of urban birds (after Bonier *et al.*, 2007).

populations of urban insect pollinators[307]. *Perennial plants* reproduce through vegetative spread, an alternative life history trait that avoids the challenges of seed and
pollen movement in the fragmented urban environment[29]. Some perennials capitalize
on human behaviors to move as whole plants, such as resprouting of discarded garden
plants[257].

The dangers of urban movement can be accentuated for species that use specialized
habitats, such as aquatic habitats, and would be expected to favor traits that reduce
dispersal in urbanized areas where those habitats are isolated and potentially hidden.
However in Australia, the eastern long-necked turtle *Chelodina longicollis* disperses
greater distances in suburbs than in nature reserves[474]. Suburbs import water, creating
more consistent water levels. Furthermore, suburban design often includes culverts for
water drainage that unintentionally facilitate turtle movement, making suburban turtle
habitat more connected than in nature reserves (Figure 4.50). As another side effect of
urbanization, non-urban turtles *estivate*, a form of dormancy that allows for escape from
unfavorable conditions, while those in suburbs, faced by a lack of suitable estivation
sites and provided with more predictable water levels, do not.

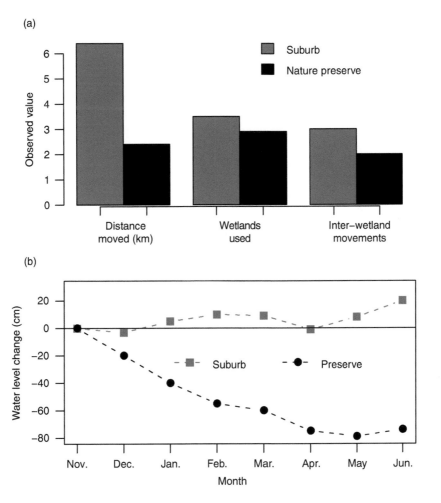

Figure 4.50 (a) Increased dispersal of suburban male eastern long-necked turtles due to (b) more consistent water levels (after Rees *et al.*, 2009).

The built environment

The urban physical environment includes new structures that can serve as residences for animals in addition to people. Birds that use buildings or cavities rather than trees or the ground breed most successfully in urban areas[291]. Along with their ability to capitalize on human food sources, rock pigeons nest on buildings that resemble their ancestral cliffs, while house sparrows nest under eaves or in other sheltered sites near homes. Urban habitats also have reduced density of forests. Although having a nest far above the ground increases nest survival, urban birds on average nest closer to the ground than non-urban birds, because of a lack of preferred sites higher in trees[472]. Nesting on the ground itself, however, is rare in urban areas[149].

On the urbanized campus of the University of California at San Diego, a population of dark-eyed juncos *Junco hyemalis* has left its typical habitat in mountains for a highly modified environment. As many as 13% of these birds have taken to nesting on plants above the ground, a change from their ground-nesting behavior in their native forest habitat[622]. On campus, 77% of off-ground nests succeeded in fledging at least one chick, substantially higher than the 48% success rate of on-ground nests, a difference due almost entirely to reduced predation.

For the odorous house ant *Tapinoma sessile*, urban habitats provide new and larger nest sites. In forested habitats near Lafayette, Indiana, these ants inhabit nuts, and colonies have fewer than 100 workers and a single queen[64]. In the cities of Lafayette and West Lafayette, buildings, mulch, and piles of debris provide sites for nesting that allow these ants to completely change their social structure. Colonies average more than 50 000 workers with over 2000 queens, a transformation which has occurred independently in many cities[378]. Ecologically, instead of being a relatively minor member of the ant community, urban *Tapinoma* colonies act like an invasive species and eliminate all but two other ant species. These two species turn out, predictably enough, to be the two most abundant ants in the road medians of New York City[441], the non-native pavement ant *Tetramorium caespitum* and the native *Lasius neoniger*. In this case, a behavioral change induced by habitat modification leads to a social and ecological transformation.

Effects of inputs and outputs
Resource inputs
Inputs of organic matter and food into urban ecosystems, mostly for human consumption, lead directly or indirectly to major changes in the type, abundance, and spatial distribution of food available to urban animals:

- Trash, birdseed, and roadkill become more abundant.
- Food sources are more constant and predictable over time.
- Food sources are more concentrated in space.

Figure 4.51 Both birds and mammals can capitalize on discarded human food.

Figure 4.52 Animals can be fearless of humans in their search for food.

Urban exploiters and adapters can capitalize on these foods (Figure 4.51). For example, urban birds with an omnivorous diet that includes seeds often replace those specializing on invertebrates like insects[291]. Provisioning with bird seeds plays a key role in this change, with people in the United States distributing as much as 450 million kilograms of bird seed per year[415].

The rock hyrax, or dassie, *Procavia capensis* has adjusted its diet to include trash at the edge of carparks, in addition to grass and leaves. Urban dassies have also lost top-down population pressure by the removal of their natural predators (Section 4.3), and have become bold enough to approach humans in search of food handouts (Figure 4.52).

The physiological and behavioral traits that allow urban organisms to capitalize on food inputs do provide fitness benefits at least for birds. Blue tits *Cyanistes caeruleus* have earlier egg-laying dates and an increase in chicks fledged per nest when fed[485] (Figure 4.53). Experimentally feeding willow tits *Parus montanus* in western Sweden led to increased population size through increased survival and/or immigration. As an example of an interaction between bottom-up and top-down control, well-fed tits experience reduced predation by pygmy owls because they can afford more careful anti-predator behavior[277]. After withdrawing food, the high density populations crashed and the survivors had lower reproductive success during the following summer. If these effects hold throughout urban areas, bird populations could respond quickly to the presence or absence of human bird feeding in cities. In Australia, people often feed larger and more aggressive urban birds such as the carnivorous Australian magpie *Gymnorhina tibicen* (Section 4.3). Fed magpies alter their behavior and life history to consume more meat, start breeding almost 2 weeks earlier, and transfer at least part of the subsidy to their offspring[415].

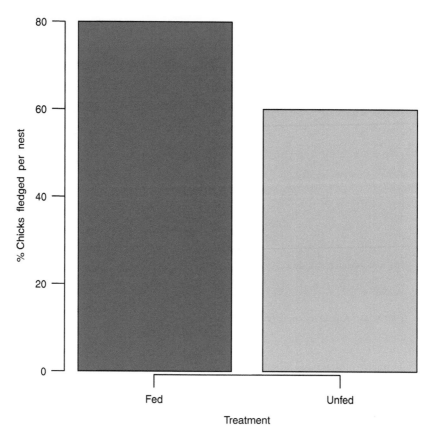

Figure 4.53 Effects of winter feeding on fledging success of blue tits in the next season (after Robb *et al.*, 2008).

The endangered San Joaquin kit fox *Vulpes macrotis mutica* has established a population in Bakersfield, California[400], that has lower year-to-year variability and higher population density than non-urban populations. Whereas rural foxes eat mostly kangaroo rats, urban foxes have branched out to consume ground squirrels, pocket gophers, birds, and some trash, with no evidence of negative effects on survival or reproduction. In fact, as in Bristol before the advent of mange (Section 4.4), the main cause of death for the urban population is motor vehicles.

Food derived from human discards and intentional feeding tends to be aggregated into large concentrations[130]. Locating this concentrated food often favors the social trait of foraging in groups[291] (Figure 4.54). Groups have more eyes to spot the food, after which the bounty can be shared and effectively defended. The resulting increased density of animals around food clumps further changes the social environment. Raccoons living near human-supplied food have unusually high population densities, leading to changes in behavior that include communal feeding and smaller home ranges[459], along with a greater potential for disease transmission (Section 4.4).

Figure 4.54 Social urban corvids, such as these carrion crows, have learned to capitalize on urban garbage.

Pollutants

Pollutants are the outputs of the urban metabolism, with their effects being largely unavoidable physiological responses. Ozone, the reactive compound O_3 created by reactions involving nitrogen and sunlight (Section 3.3), creates detrimental effects, particularly on plants. It enters leaves through the stomata, and causes extensive oxidative damage that harms plants more than all other forms of air pollution combined. High levels of ozone can lower crop yields by over 50%. Because the complex series of atmospheric chemical reactions that create ozone take substantial time (Section 3.3), prevailing winds can export the majority of urban-generated ozone to downwind non-urban areas, leading to reduced growth in non-urban plants compared with urban conspecifics[224] (Figure 4.55).

In contrast, increased atmospheric carbon dioxide serves as a nutrient that improves urban plant growth. Along with increased temperature and an extended growing season, this produces greater growth in urban ragweed *Ambrosia artemisiifolia* shortly after establishment[627]. Through a feedback with the environment, this rapid growth reverses when the buildup of leaf litter decreases the germination and survival of these annual plants[628] (Figure 4.56).

We have seen how habitat fragmentation disproportionately eliminates animals at higher trophic levels, such as parasitoids and predators. These same organisms are also highly susceptible to pesticides, which are designed to create unavoidable physiological damage to target pests. Spraying for the "Med fly", the Mediterranean fruit fly *Ceratitis*

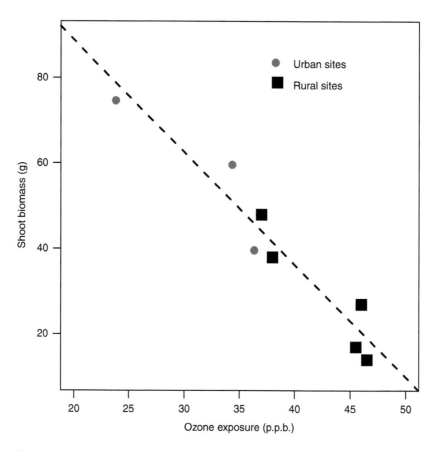

Figure 4.55 Urban ozone exposure levels (in parts per billion) versus shoot biomass in cottonwood trees in and near New York City (after Gregg *et al.*, 2003).

capitata, killed enough non-target parasitoid insects to induce outbreaks of a normally rare gall midge in California, outbreaks sufficiently severe to defoliate host plants[139]. The different physiology of predatory and herbivorous insects means that use of pesticides can increase the urban populations of mites and scales by reducing populations of their natural enemies[470].

The effect of polychlorinated biphenyls (PCBs) on the red fox *Vulpes vulpes* provides a rare demonstration of the physiological effects of urban toxic pollution on an urban mammal. In the vicinity of Zürich, Switzerland, male foxes maintain high levels of these pollutants throughout their lives, and foxes with higher PCB levels experience higher mortality. Females apparently pass these compounds on to their offspring in milk, and show reduced pollutant burdens and negative effects as they age[129].

Effects of urban ecosystem processes
The urban heat island
The urban heat island brings slightly warmer high temperatures and substantially warmer low temperatures, leading to increased heat stress and decreased cold stress.

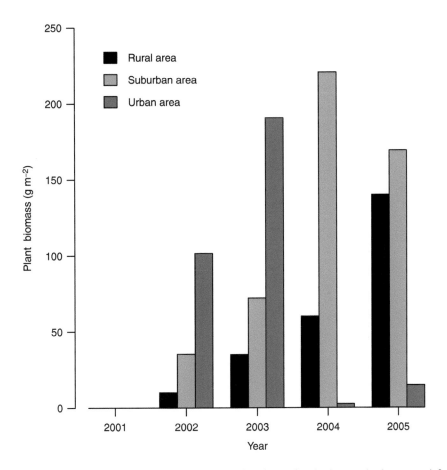

Figure 4.56 Biomass growth of ragweed populations in rural, suburban, and urban areas (after Ziska *et al.*, 2007).

For plants in many cities, this translates into a substantially longer growing season[625] (Figure 4.57), but at the cost of supporting populations of herbivores that begin growing and eating earlier (Section 4.3). In tropical cities, however, plants do not extend their growing season[206], perhaps because *phenology* is controlled more by humidity than by temperature[153]. The northerly city of Fairbanks, Alaska, also does not show earlier budburst, but for quite different reasons, hypothesized to be a reduction in the winter chilling that plants need to trigger germination in the spring[206]. Separating the physiological effects of temperature from other correlated changes, such as increases in carbon dioxide or ozone, can be challenging.

The urban heat island can create significant stresses. Many urban plants exhibit a morphological change, harder leaves, to better resist heat and drought[307]. Trees growing near pavement simultaneously face higher temperatures and reduced water availability, and respond behaviorally to this stress with a shorter period of active transpiration each day[612]. In Phoenix, the oleander *Nerium oleander*, a widely cultivated small tree, grows

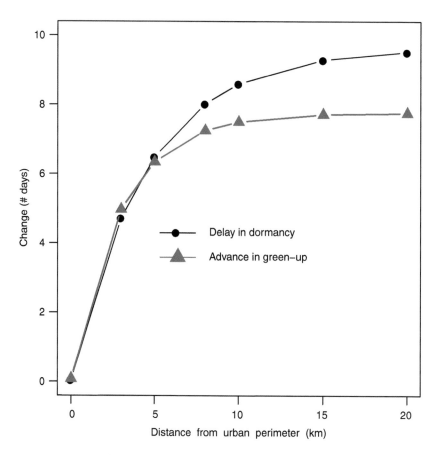

Figure 4.57 Change in the green-up and dormancy dates (in days) as a function of the distance from the urban periphery (after Zhang *et al.*, 2004).

faster in warmer plots near asphalt in the fall and winter, and more quickly in cooler vegetated mesiscapes in the spring and summer[391].

For animals, the urban heat island can open up new habitats and new opportunities. Melbourne, Australia, has increased temperature and rainfall, with more standing and piped-in water. This altered climate has allowed a nomadic bat species, the gray-headed flying fox *Pteropus poliocephalus*, to populate the city. In fact, the only recently established populations of this species have been in the city[426].

Although most birds are physiologically tolerant of moderate temperature variation as adults[525], the combination of milder winters, longer summers, and more food than in surrounding non-urban habitats has promoted decreased migratory behavior in urban populations of the European blackbird, the European robin *Erithacus rubecula*, and the dark-eyed junco[430]. Those birds that choose to winter in the city have greater overwinter survivorship, and gain a fitness advantage by beginning reproduction before migratory birds return[429]. Urban Florida scrub-jays *Aphelocoma coerulescens* start breeding about 3 weeks earlier than non-urban jays[172].

Figure 4.58 Street lights, here in Dublin, can act as ecological traps for insects and modify the urban lights and dark cycles.

In the European blackbird, the change in migratory behavior differs between the sexes. Urban males, but not females, migrate less than non-urban birds[430]. For males, the risks of not migrating might be outweighed by the benefits of being the first to set up territories. The larger males may also out-compete females for winter resources at urban sites, further decreasing the advantage to females of not migrating. Dark-eyed juncos on the campus of the University of California at San Diego capitalize on the warm urban climate by reducing migration and laying two clutches of eggs per year rather than just one. Because competition for mates and territories is often strongest among males just returning from their winter habitat, reduced migration might in turn be responsible for a behavioral change, a decrease in how aggressively these males respond to the songs of potential intruders[399].

Light

The energy that humans pump into urban ecosystems is converted into a range of forms including heat, light, and noise. Urban light can transform natural activity cycles (Figure 4.58). In non-urban ecosystems, for example, the phases of the moon play a major role in determining nocturnal behavior of rodents; many small rodents are more active on darker nights with a new moon than when the full moon makes them more visible to predators[334]. In fact, these rodents are nocturnal largely to avoid predators. Diurnal humans engineer the urban environment to extend daylight through artificial lighting. Some urban animals, such as predators, use the light to extend their foraging activity and switch from diurnal to more nocturnal behavior[130]. In contrast, some rodents switch from being nocturnal to diurnal in urban ecosystems, in response perhaps to increased light and predation at night or human food provisioning during the day[381].

Due to artificial lighting, urban birds start singing earlier in the day than non-urban conspecifics. Urban crows roost at well-lit sites, possibly to avoid owl predation[337]. In the European starling, urban birds gather in large groups in the evening and form large nocturnal roosts, but non-urban conspecifics do not[130].

The sight of moths and other insects fluttering around human lighting is well known. This is a highly maladaptive behavior, and is associated with worldwide declines of nocturnal insects. For their predators such as birds and bats, however, lights provide ideal feeding sites. Magpies in Budapest have found that caddisflies mistake the polarized light reflecting from glass buildings for water and regularly forage near buildings at sunrise and sunset[486]. These intelligent corvids are thus exploiting an ecological trap for their less behaviorally flexible insect prey.

Noise

The peaceful wilderness and the noisy city are nearly clichés. Animals that use sounds to communicate must change their behavior by changing the time, volume, or pitch of their vocalizations. In Australia, noisy miners respond more loudly to dogs in roosts close to

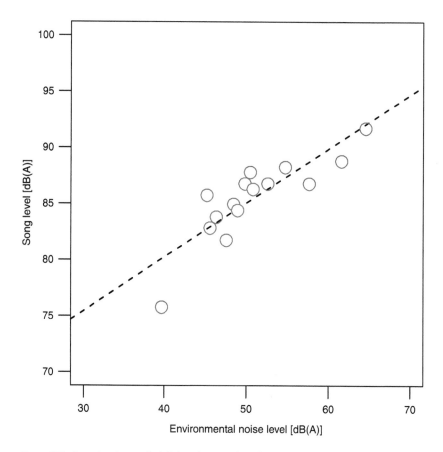

Figure 4.59 Song loudness of nightingales as a function of the level of ambient noise (after Brumm, 2004).

large roads, presumably to be heard above the ambient sound[343]. Nightingales *Luscinia megarhynchos* sing louder in locations with high levels of traffic noise, increasing volume from 77 to 91 Db, a more than five-fold increase in sound pressure[60] (Figure 4.59). As further evidence of the flexibility of this behavior, the urban birds sing less loudly on weekends.

Urban European robins sing more at night than their rural counterparts. Although locations with excessive noise during the day are highly correlated with those having higher light intensity at night, daytime noise better predicts this nocturnal singing behavior[190].

Much urban noise is of low frequency. Great tits sing at higher frequencies in urban sites[535], presumably to be heard above the background rumble. Males sing fewer low-pitched notes and replace many of their typical 2–4 note songs with a combination of brief one-note songs or longer songs with five or more high-pitched notes[534]. Similar song changes occurs in house finches *Carpodacus mexicanus* and song sparrows *Melospiza melodia* in North America[616] (Figure 4.60).

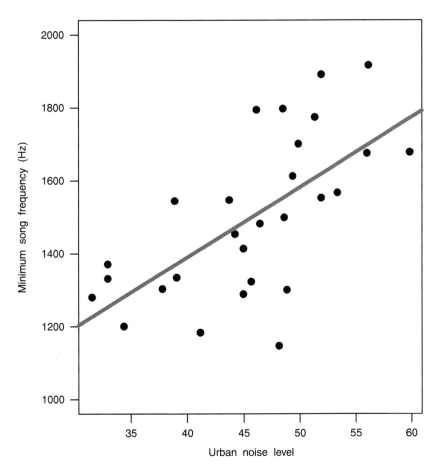

Figure 4.60 Minimum song frequency of song sparrows as a function of low-frequency urban noise (after Wood and Yezerinac, 2006).

European blackbirds in Vienna sing shorter songs with fewer elements and with loudest motifs at a higher frequency than birds in the nearby Vienna Woods[397]. There is little direct evidence, however, that this is an adaptive behavioral response. As an alternative explanation, stress can have similar effects on songs, and urban birds may experience sufficient stresses such as that due to high population density, to induce the changes directly.

Some birds learn by imitating songs they hear, and the notes that young birds cannot hear in the urban din may be thereby lost from their song repertoire. Birds' calls are typically simpler vocalizations used for alarm and other social communication. The calls of the silvereye *Zosterops lateralis* in Australia show a similar pattern of higher pitch in the low frequency range in many distant cities. Calls are not typically learned, creating a mystery as to how these changes could have occurred so quickly[453].

Effects of ecological interactions

Urbanization is associated with decreased predation when large body size, sensitivity to pesticides, or other stresses filter large predators from urban environments (Section 4.3). When prey face lower predation, their populations will be regulated more strongly by resources, leading to more intense competition. Concentrated resources place a further premium on efficiently collecting those resources and excluding competitors. This emphasis on competition favors a whole suite of behavioral traits, including increased aggression and decreased timidity.

The *giving-up density* provides a method to quantify the relative importance individuals place on predation and competition. To make this measurement, animals forage for a limited amount of food in environments that are either protected from or exposed

Dangerous site: Many seeds are left uneaten

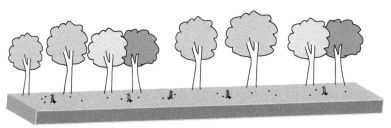

Safe site: Few seeds left uneaten

Figure 4.61 The giving-up density: the expected behavior of species that are sensitive to predators.

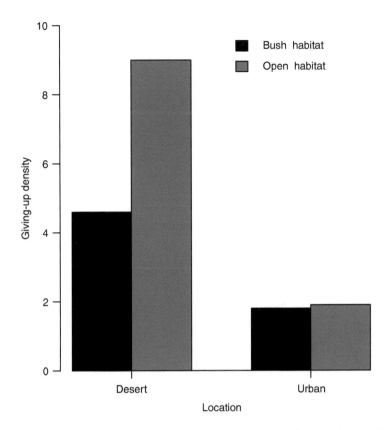

Figure 4.62 Giving-up densities of urban and desert birds (after Shochat, 2004).

to predators. If the animals fear predators, they will give up searching sooner in the presence of predators and leave more food behind, producing a high giving-up density. If they fear predators less and have adjusted to intense competition, they will continue searching even when food becomes hard to find, producing a low giving-up density[58] (Figure 4.61).

Birds in parks near Phoenix stop foraging from seed trays more quickly in potentially dangerous open habitat than in safer bush habitat. Birds in the city, in contrast, not only collect more seeds, but are indifferent to the perceived danger of the habitat[525] (Figure 4.62). The species with the lowest giving-up densities also differ between urban and non-urban settings, being small species in the desert and larger species in the city. Efficient large species, such as the mourning dove *Zenaida macroura*, have a behavioral trait, the low giving-up density, that gives an advantage in exploitation competition, and a morphological trait, large size, that gives an advantage in interference competition. In combination, these traits could lead to high abundance and domination of the urban habitat[524].

Along an urban to non-urban gradient in northern Virginia, gray squirrels *Sciurus carolinensis* have much lower giving up densities in urban areas than in non-urban areas (Figure 4.63a). Urban squirrels may be more desperate for food, less fearful of

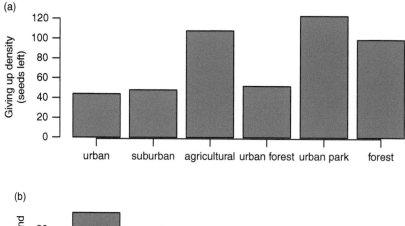

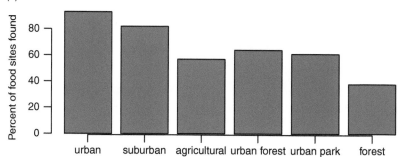

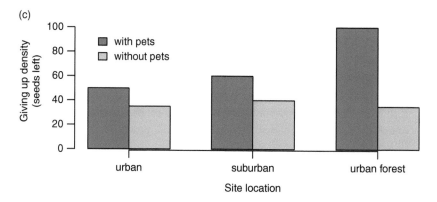

Figure 4.63 (a) Giving-up densities of squirrels, (b) the fraction of food sites that squirrels locate in a set of environments in northern Virginia, and (c) the giving-up density in response to pets in three contrasting environments (after Bowers and Breland, 1996).

predators, or, as seems to be the case in this system, both[50]. Squirrels are often abundant in urban parks[425], and urban squirrels locate a larger percentage of seed trays in the urban areas than non-urban squirrels. Squirrels in areas with pets show much higher giving-up densities, suggesting that pet predation remains a real threat (Figure 4.63c).

The amount of time spent looking for predators, the vigilance, provides another insight into how animals perceive the balance between predation and competition.

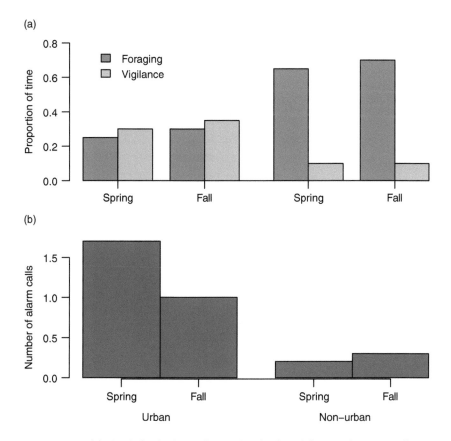

Figure 4.64 Prairie dog behavior in rural and urban habitats (after Ramirez and Keller, 2010).

If predation is typically low in urban environments while competition is high, animals should spend less time being vigilant and more time foraging. Adult urban fox squirrels *Sciurus niger* follow this prediction, even when exposed to calls from red-tailed hawks or coyotes[363]. Juvenile urban squirrels show the same level of anti-predator vigilance as non-urban squirrels, suggesting that adult urban squirrels have become habituated to urban disturbances.

Black-tailed prairie dogs *Cynomys ludovicianus* respond very differently to urbanization than fox squirrels. Urban prairie dogs spend more time being vigilant and give more warning calls in both spring and fall[469] (Figure 4.64). This apparently maladaptive behavior could result from a failure of prairie dogs to learn to recognize as harmless the most common urban disturbances, and is particularly surprising given the higher human hunting danger they face in rural locations.

Birds respond to disturbances by flying away. Like prairie dogs, urban birds face more interruptions from passing humans and cars, and flying from every perceived threat can be energetically draining. The *flight initiation distance* describes how closely humans can approach before birds fly, and we would predict that urban birds would respond to constant interruptions by having smaller flight initiation distances.

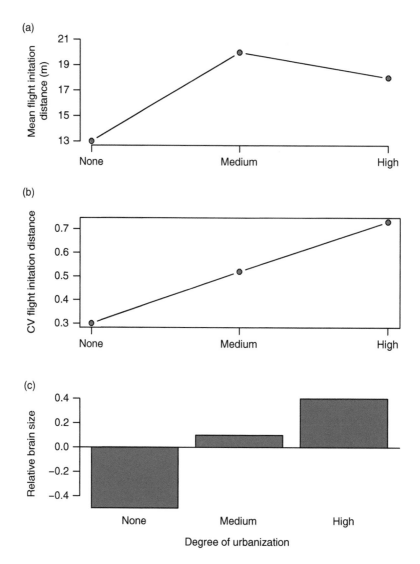

Figure 4.65 (a) The average flight initiation distance, (b) the coefficient of variation (CV) of flight initiation distance, and (c) relative brain size for bird species with different degrees of urbanization (after Carrete and Tella, 2011).

Urban birds generally follow this prediction, and the difference between urban and non-urban bird flight distances increases with the number of generations since the birds established a population in the urban environment, indicating a continual process of adaptation[387].

In the relatively young Argentine city of Bahia Blanca, the single best predictor of urban success was the *coefficient of variation* of the flight initiation distance. The coefficient of variation is a measure of variability within a species, meaning that species that harbor extensive variability in this behavior are most associated with urban areas[80] (Figure 4.65). Individual birds maintain a particular behavior, meaning

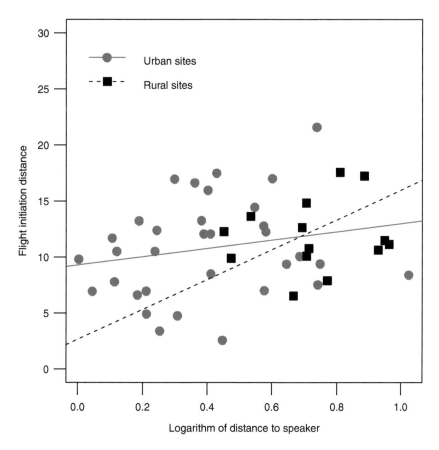

Figure 4.66 Relationship between the flight initiation distance and the closeness of approach to a speaker in song sparrows from towns and from rural areas (after Scales *et al.*, 2011).

that successful species are generalists through intraspecific variation rather than individual adjustment. Across species, this variability correlates strongly with relative brain size, fitting the generalization that the behavioral flexibility derived from greater cognitive capacity allows species to better cope with the novel stresses of the urban environment[356].

Reduced flight initiation distance is often associated with changes in aggressive behavior. Urban European blackbirds *Turdus merula* are more aggressive than forest conspecifics and mob simulated predators as a group while forest conspecifics often retreat[350]. Even in towns with as few as 1000 people, song sparrows show this same combination of boldness towards people and aggression[507]. Birds in towns have smaller flight initiation distances and more closely approach a speaker playing back songs of conspecifics (Figure 4.66).

High population density and the ability to ignore constant interruptions combine into an urban behavior syndrome of increased aggression toward conspecifics and less fear of predators. Urban gray squirrels near Washington DC and Baltimore, much like urban birds, are more aggressive toward conspecifics and show shorter escape distances

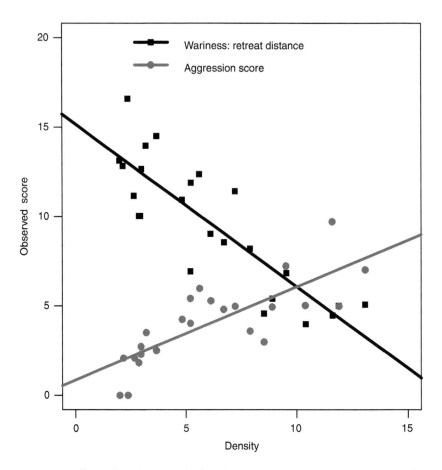

Figure 4.67 Effects of density on squirrel wariness and aggression (after Parker and Nilon, 2008).

from predators and other threats [425] (Figure 4.67). Like so many other generalizations in urban ecology, the exceptions provide additional insight into causes. We have seen that urban dark-eyed juncos exhibit lower intraspecific aggression, perhaps because the effects of habitat and climate modification outweigh those of disturbance and resources.

Case studies of interacting processes

Habitat modification, increased resource inputs, outputs in the form of pollution, high population density, and the other effects of urbanization work together to create a set of urban trait syndromes, like the combination of increased boldness and aggression seen in urban birds and squirrels. We examine syndromes that result from chronic stress and changes in body size, and then return to the well-studied house sparrow and European blackbird to look at how their traits interact and develop over time.

Chronic stress

A proper stress response is necessary for any organism to react appropriately to predators or other dangers. Vertebrates release glucocorticoid steroid hormones to facilitate a short-term adaptive response to stressful conditions that focus attention and memory. Over the long term, high levels of glucocorticoid steroid hormones can damage reproductive, immune, and brain functions. To avoid these costs, urban organisms, faced with frequent and novel interruptions, should exhibit a less extreme stress response than their non-urban counterparts. Urban European blackbirds at least partially support this prediction. Although their baseline glucocorticoid levels are no different from non-urban birds, urban birds increase their levels much less than non-urban birds in stressful situations, at least during the winter and spring months[431].

The complexity of these stress responses are only beginning to be explored. In European blackbirds, the stress response differs between seasons. In other species, the stress response differs between the sexes. Male and female white-crowned sparrows *Zonotrichia leucophrys* in paired urban and non-urban sites in California and Washington show different stress responses. Urban males have higher corticosteroid baseline levels than non-urban males, while females do not differ[42]. In the urban environment, however, female corticosteroid levels are negatively correlated with reproductive success. Those individuals better able to cope with the urban environment by maintaining a lower stress level might channel energy into reproduction more efficiently.

Urban tree lizards *Urosaurus ornatus* show decreased baseline and stress-induced glucocorticoids relative to non-urban conspecifics. Urban individuals also show higher immunocompetence, based on higher counts of cells important in fighting infection, than non-urban conspecifics[184]. Whether this higher immunocompetence is caused by a lower stress response or by other factors, such as greater immune challenges or improved energy reserves, remains to be shown.

Body size
Urban birds in northern latitudes typically have smaller body size than their rural conspecifics[87]. Several factors could explain this morphological trait.

1. Small size could be adaptive in urban environments for avoiding predators, particularly cats,
2. Small, poor quality birds might be able to survive and reproduce only in urban areas due to food subsidization,
3. Urban birds might be "living on credit" by maintaining lower fat reserves because food is highly predictable[523],
4. Urban diets could be high-quantity yet low-quality producing unhealthy nestlings and smaller adults.

As evidence for the last hypothesis, the urban-exploiting European starling produces fewer and smaller offspring in urban than non-urban nests due in part to lower quality food[379] (Figure 4.68).

For migratory birds such as the Acadian flycatcher *Empidonax virescens*, small individuals might be restricted to urban habitats. Urban habitats could be less preferred than non-urban habitats, especially if non-migratory urban bird species have already settled in the best urban sites. Large dominant flycatchers could choose superior non-urban sites leaving the inferior urban sites to small subordinate birds[488]. Even if the habitat

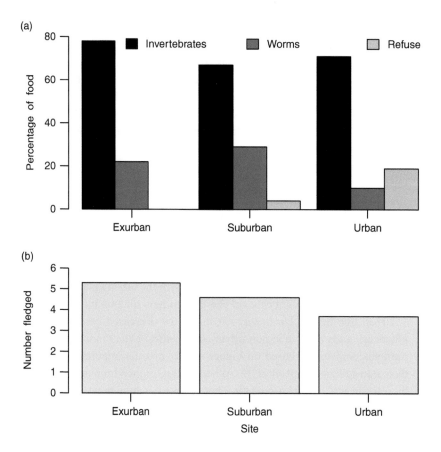

Figure 4.68 (a) Feeding rates and (b) fledging success of starlings in exurban, suburban, and urban sites (after Mennechez *et al.*, 2006).

were sufficiently favorable, these urban populations of weaker birds would likely be sinks that contribute little to the persistence of the species.

Like birds, some urban carabid beetles are smaller than non-urban beetles, but probably for different reasons[275,404]. These beetles consume organic biomass, particularly decaying plant material, which is often less available in urban sites. The resulting high levels of competition could restrict urban beetle body size. As evidence that food does play an important role in these detritivores, predaceous species of ground beetles do not show this body size pattern, and exhibit lower levels of competition[582]. Perhaps more importantly, small beetle species have relatively large wings while large species are usually wingless. Consistent with the importance of dispersal, small beetles[354] or large-winged species dominate some urban areas[499].

The house sparrow revisited

House sparrows (Figure 4.69) are among the most widespread urban exploiters, but their populations are declining throughout Europe, with the spread of the sparrowhawk

Figure 4.69 The house sparrow, a case study in the challenges of urban life.

one likely cause (Section 4.3). Sparrows captured in urban sites are exceeded in mass, length, and body condition by those captured in non-urban areas[331]. These differences persist even when birds are kept in aviaries under identical conditions.

Urban house sparrows are faced with the dual challenge of intense competition and high predation[38]. Even if they could grow large with low-quality food, urban house sparrows might avoid becoming too heavy because high weight increases the probability of being captured by cats or hawks. Slow growth of urban house sparrows may also result from having smaller home ranges in patchy urban habitats. In Ghent, Belgium, urban patches have few places to hide from sparrowhawks, which are quite active in the area[587]. The lack of hiding places forces birds to be more vigilant and feed less efficiently and for shorter times.

House sparrow population declines in urban areas could thus be due to an interaction between bottom-up and top-down effects (Section 4.3). In winter when food is less abundant, low weight increases the risk of starvation, while high weight increases the risk of predation. As evidence of the difficult choices these birds must make, urban house sparrows do not increase their giving-up density at greater distances from shelter, while the closely related and much less urbanized Spanish sparrow *Passer hispaniolensis* does[578]. The urban birds may suffer such strong competition that they have no choice but to forage in the face of danger.

Figure 4.70 The European blackbird.

The process of adaptation

Although physiological and behavioral changes generally occur more quickly than genetic evolution (Section 4.6), they too can take many generations. Some of the species that today are thoroughly urban took quite a long time to achieve that status. The European blackbird, a woodland species, colonized a few cities in Western Europe around 1820 (Figure 4.70). This habitat expansion was triggered by the winter urban heat island, the spread of bird feeding, the decrease in urban hunting, and changes in landscaping[156]. In the ensuing two centuries, these birds have colonized many different cities, and these colonizations seem to be multiple habitat switches rather than spread of the urbanized birds from one city to another[155]. Blackbirds remain absent to this day in some cities in eastern Europe. The closely related song thrush *Turdus philomelos* has currently urbanized only a few cities, and the fieldfare *Turdus pilaris* only began singing in the city of Warsaw in 1975. Amazingly, the rock pigeon colonized cities in Turkmenistan and Uzbekistan as late as the 1980s[156].

Slow spread results in part from the time it takes for animals to learn new behaviors and transmit them to a new generation. In New Guinea, black kites *Milvus migrans* learned to feed on road-killed toads in urban areas only after some decades of delay, and Goldie's lorikeets *Psitteuteles goldiei* began to feed on seeds available in towns after a similar delay[126]. White-tailed deer *Odocoileus virginianus* have become common in the moist cities of the eastern United States, and black-tailed jackrabbits *Lepus californicus* are beginning to invade Phoenix and could eventually become common[161]. Specialist insect herbivores only slowly colonize non-native plants due to the need for complex behavioral and physiological response to plant chemistry[561]. It can take centuries to

Table 4.3 Typical traits of successful and unsuccessful urban birds[86,154,345,388]

Successful	Less successful
Exotic	Native
Generalist	Specialist
Large brain size/flexible behavior	Smaller brain size
Widely distributed	Narrowly distributed
Omnivore/use of plant foods	Insectivore
Tree-nester	Ground or shrub-nester
Sedentary	Migratory
Bold	Fearful
High fecundity	Lower fecundity

assemble this insect fauna, with non-native plants accumulating only about 2% of the species richness of native insects after 100 years.

Conclusions

Urban plants and animals share a range of similarities that distinguish them from non-urban conspecifics, including changes in nesting and social behavior, daily or seasonal cycles, and aggression[291,350]. Although there are many exceptions, urban birds often have a particular syndrome of traits (Table 4.3).

The rock pigeon provides a case study in the traits that lead to urban success[278]. These relatively large and heavy birds tend to remain close to the site where they hatched and maintain genetic traits from years of domestication that reduce their fear of humans. They have high fecundity and can produce as many as 12 young per year. Populations do not explode because only about 1 out of 10 juveniles survives to reproduce, but remain relatively stable because 9 out of 10 adults survives to have a chance to breed in the next year. Pigeons subsist on human-provided foods (and incidentally add to the nitrogen cycle by converting these foods into 11.5 kg of droppings per year). These birds thus maintain their high biomass (Figure 4.7) through a combination of physiology, behavior, and life history that converts urban resources into offspring that can quickly increase the population size when resources become abundant.

With their rapidly changing array of diverse habitats, urban areas favor species that can cope with a variety of conditions, whether through tolerance, flexibility, or intraspecific variation. These favored traits, including the ability to use novel habitats and thrive at high densities, are similar to those that predict successful biological invaders, which helps explain why urban areas are so susceptible to invasion.

Whether urban birds and other animals are "street-smart" and able to more rapidly learn to cope with novel stimuli remains uncertain. A general overview of Israeli birds found no evidence for this trend[291], while a comparison of urban adapters and urban avoiders in 12 cities in France and Switzerland found that urban birds do have larger brains, even within bird families[356]. Two families with consistently large brains, the corvidae (crows, jays, magpies, and ravens) and the paridae (chickadees and tits), are also among the most consistently urban.

Figure 4.71 Urban birds show less fear of humans and sometimes act aggressively (drawing by C. L. Adler).

Morphological, physiological, behavioral, and social changes are among the most unexpected of unintended consequences of urbanization. Whether humans shape the environment for their own convenience, such as by lighting streets at night, or as a byproduct of the transportation network, such as the noise created by traffic, plants and animals that share the environment must find ways to cope. That birds respond to nocturnal light by establishing huge nocturnal roost sites or to low frequency noise by singing modified songs was definitely not part of the urban design plan.

Even intentional urban changes, such as the feeding of birds and elimination of large predators, filter down to produce unintended effects on behavior. Who would think that the stereotype of the "tough" urban youth carries over to the songbirds inhabiting a garden? But concentration of food, removal of predators, and constant interruption by humans compel birds to become less timid and more aggressive (Figure 4.71).

The slow spread of European blackbirds, the development of new behaviors, and the decline of stalwart urban exploiters such as house sparrows and European starlings show that urban ecosystems continue to change. Flexible behavior and physiology might allow many new species to colonize urban areas even while familiar species disappear. We can have little doubt that urban species will continue to surprise, provoke, and sometimes disappoint us.

Humans too are challenged by the many changes and stresses of the urban environment, ranging from light, noise, heat, and pollution to high population density and conflict over resources. The physical and psychological responses of humans, thought of as our health, can parallel those of other urban animals (Section 5.1). Understanding the traits of urban animals might well be a step toward understanding ourselves.

4.6   Urban evolution

The traits of urban organisms result from three processes: (1) sorting of those that can survive, (2) adjustment of traits in response to the environment, and (3) genetic *evolution* of traits that promote survival and reproduction (Section 4.5). Evolution requires the most stringent set of conditions and is the most difficult of these processes to identify and study. Finding that urban and non-urban populations differ does not demonstrate evolution, because differences could be due to sorting of individuals, phenotypic plasticity, or learning.

Although evolution takes many generations, examples of urban evolution have been documented even with the relatively brief existence of urban environments. Pinpointing the causes of phenotypic differences between urban and non-urban populations and identifying cases of genetic evolution is a key challenge for urban ecology. This section introduces the principles of evolution and then the best-studied cases of evolution in response to urban habitats, resources, ecosystem processes, and ecological interactions.

Principles of evolution in urban environments

Evolution requires that different genetic variants of a species have different *fitness* (levels of reproduction), and that those differences are *heritable* (can be passed from parent to offspring). Favorable genetic variants, with high fitness, increase in frequency in the population, eventually becoming common or even *fixed* and carried by all the individuals in a population. The speed with which a favorable variant comes to dominate a population depends on the strength of *natural selection*, the difference in its fitness from that of other types. Even a relatively small difference, such as 10% higher fitness, propel that type to dominate the population in 10 to 20 generations (Figure 4.72).

Fitness depends on an interaction between the organism and its environment. A trait that is favored in one environment, perhaps a pale color to blend in with snow, might be detrimental in another, such as one where snow was absent. In this case, visually oriented predators provide the selective force. In this example and in many real situations, the strongest selection depends on other organisms. Many of the strongest interactions occur with conspecifics, such as competition for resources, territories, and mates. Biologists often distinguish *sexual selection* from natural selection, wherein organisms evolve to attract mates with conspicuous colors or songs, or to defeat members of their own sex with specialized tools for fighting.

Fitness also depends on interactions of different traits within an individual. Almost any genetic change results in multiple effects on phenotype. For example, the genetic changes leading to the evolution of a large brain create developmental changes that affect other parts of the body. Furthermore, every change in phenotype has multiple effects on success. These possibly conflicting pressures create tradeoffs. Changing color to avoid predation might also change energy balance or attractiveness to mates. We have seen that reducing predator avoidance behavior through reduced fear can be correlated with increased intraspecific aggression.

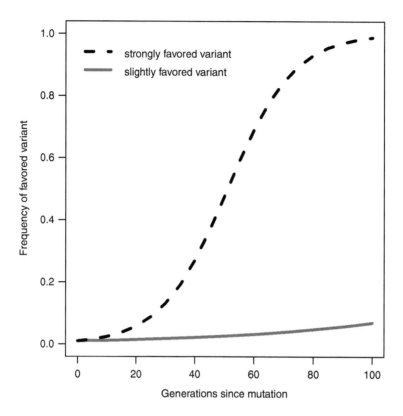

Figure 4.72 The spread of a favorable genetic variant through a population.

Even a highly favorable allele of a gene, one that modifies both the bearer and its off-spring to do well in an urban environment, may fail to spread for four main reasons [153] (Figure 4.73).

1. Very small populations, or those that were founded by only a few individuals, may lack this variant entirely, and it may take a long time to arise by mutation. Small remnant populations and new populations just colonizing a new habitat may thus lack the genetic variation that evolution requires to work.

2. Urban environments may form small islands of habitat in a much larger non-urban matrix. For species that persist in both habitats and move freely between them, the most urban fit type may fail to evolve because it is swamped by *gene flow* from the surrounding habitat where its traits may not be adaptive.

3. A favorable new trait might carry with it other less favorable traits, through tradeoffs, that reduce its chances of entering or spreading in a population.

4. Genetic evolution can be circumvented by phenotypic plasticity. If individuals can adjust their traits to cope with a novel urban challenge, a genetic mutation that plays the same role may be redundant and provide little or no additional benefit.

Nonetheless, cases of human-driven evolution have been observed. One well-established case involves the soapberry bug *Leptocoris tagalicus* of Australia. These

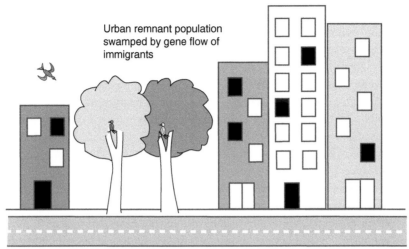

Urban remnant population swamped by gene flow of immigrants

Small population lacking genetic variation

Figure 4.73 Factors that can preclude adaptive evolution in an urban environment.

insects feed on seeds hidden within fruits, and their mouthparts are tuned to the size of their preferred food, the fruit of the woolly rambutan *Alectryon tomentosus*. When the invasive balloon vine *Cardiospermum grandiflorumtosus*, with a larger fruit capsule, spread throughout eastern Australia, the mouthparts of these bugs evolved to be longer[82]. The soapberry bugs *Jadera haematoloma* of the southeastern United States have evolved smaller mouthparts where their preferred native hosts have been replaced by horticultural species with smaller fruits[81].

Humans have been termed "the world's greatest evolutionary force" for three main reasons[424].

1. Many organisms evolve resistance to human control attempts, such as bacteria to antibiotics, plants to herbicides, and insects to insecticides.
2. Invasive species spread by humans not only induce evolutionary responses by natives, as in the soapberry bugs, but themselves often evolve rapidly in their new habitats.
3. Heavily harvested species, such as fish, evolve changes in size or reproductive behavior that help them avoid the new technologically advanced predator they face.

Although these forces occur throughout the world, many center around urban areas, the focus of the vast human enterprises of health care, food collection, and movement of materials and species.

Evolution in urban environments

Studies of urban evolution begin with showing that urban populations have the necessary genetic diversity in the face of small population size and gene flow. We have met the urban-adapted white-footed mouse *Peromyscus leucopus* as an agent of the spread of Lyme disease, particularly in suburbs (Section 4.4). However, even in the densely built environment of New York City, 20% of habitat is wooded, and these mice inhabit small, isolated forest fragments where they achieve extremely high population density. Population densities can be high for many reasons: resource inputs, reduced winter severity caused by the urban heat island, lowered predation, and perhaps the inability to disperse through inhospitable and dangerous intervening habitats when populations build up. Large population sizes have apparently buffered these populations from the loss of genetic diversity, and isolation has created substantial genetic differences among them[393]. These populations thus have the potential to evolve in the face of novel urban stresses.

Similar evolutionary potential exists in three species of dragonfly found in the Tokyo metropolitan area. Patches in urban areas have similar genetic diversity to those in non-urban areas, and are more genetically differentiated from each other[506]. The smooth yellow violet *Viola pubescens* shows little loss of genetic diversity in urban environments around Cincinnati, Ohio[110]. Highly mobile pollinators have prevented substantial differentiation among populations, and might provide enough gene flow to impede urban evolution. However, populations of the common dandelion in urban areas exhibit less genetic diversity, and those populations facing severe pollution stress have the least[297]. In this case, populations facing the potentially strong selection force created by pollutants might be slow to evolve due to low genetic variability.

Even when these genetic preconditions are met, identifying cases of genetic evolution in urban environments requires careful experimentation to distinguish evolution from other responses. The critical experiment is usually to raise organisms in a common environment to eliminate the effects of physiological or behavioral adjustment.

Effects of urban habitat modification

Urban habitats involve both new materials and alterations of existing materials. The classic case of urban evolution involves *industrial melanism* in the peppered moth *Biston betularia*. These moths rest on tree trunks during the day, and those that are camouflaged to blend in are better able to avoid predation. When trees were covered with soot during the industrial revolution, moths evolved a dark or melanistic form[301]. With a reduction in the use of coal, trees returned to their original light color, as did the moths[104] (Figure 4.74).

The habitat fragmentation characteristic of urban environments not only alters the genetic variation required for evolution, but also creates its own selection pressures. An environment segregated into small patches of suitable habitat separated by harsh uninhabitable areas can favor reduced dispersal, because most individuals that leave one patch will land in unsuitable surrounding matrix. In the sidewalks of Montpelier, France, the small flowering plant *Crepis sancta* grows in tiny patches of soil surrounding trees, while outside the city the plants grow in large unfragmented areas[133]. When plants from these two contrasting habitats are grown together in a common greenhouse, plants from the urban area produce fewer seeds with a fluffy pappus that allows them to float through the air (Figure 4.75). Seeds without a pappus tend to fall close to the parent plant[92]. Urban plants are thus less likely to disperse than non-urban plants, and growth

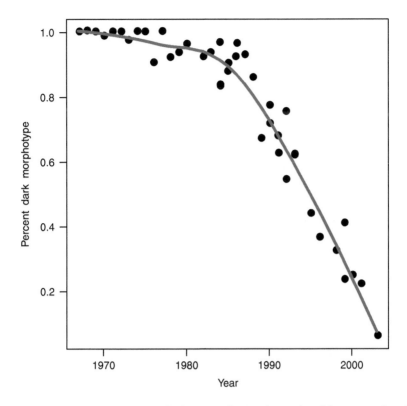

Figure 4.74 The decline in genetically determined dark morphs of the peppered moth in England (after Cook, 2003).

in a common greenhouse indicates that the changes are indeed an evolutionary response to the danger of dispersing in the urban area.

Effects of urban resource inputs

As in plants, evolution of reduced movement occurs in urban birds that give up migration[430] (Section 4.5). Unlike plants that reduce movement to avoid the inhospitable matrix, birds reduce movement to capitalize on additional food resources and milder winters. The lower migrational tendency of urban than non-urban European blackbirds persisted when birds were raised in a common environment, suggesting genetic change, although the birds could have received some physiological signal from a parent while still in the egg[430]. Other behavioral effects such as lower stress response and greater tameness also persist in urban birds raised in common rearing conditions, again indicating at least some genetic component to the response[431].

The blackcap *Sylvia atricapilla*, instead of evolving reduced migration, has evolved a whole new migration route. Wintering blackcaps in Britain come from continental Europe, rather than being summer breeders that remained. This new westerly migration tendency, replacing the usual southwesterly migration to the warmer areas in the western Mediterranean, is inherited by offspring[31]. This winter site is made possible primarily

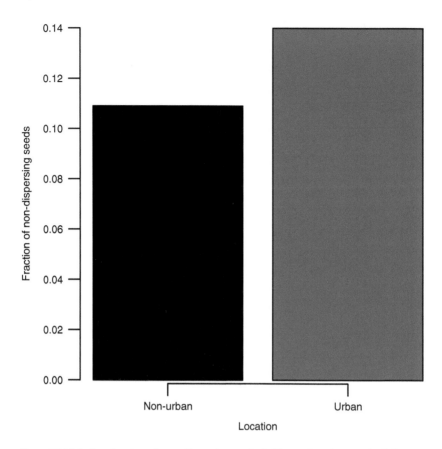

Figure 4.75 Median fraction of non-dispersing seeds (with a reduced pappus) of *Crepis sancta* from various urban and non-urban populations (after Cheptou *et al.*, 2008).

by increased winter food availability in urban areas, but has yet to spread to continental Europe where wintering birds remain unsuccessful[386].

The breeding populations of these blackcaps are potentially segregated by the timing of their return to their European breeding grounds from the different wintering grounds. Birds coming from the north arrive earlier, and mate before birds from the southern wintering ground arrive[23]. This process has already led to substantial genetic divergence within the population, including distinct wing and beak shapes and colors[489]. Only time will tell whether urbanization is in the process of creating a new species.

The food that urban humans provide, in addition to being available at a different time, can have quite different properties from non-urban foods. The sunflower seeds humans provide to house finches in and around Phoenix are much larger and harder to crack than the grass and cactus seeds found in the surrounding desert. Urban finches show increased beak size and correlated increases in bite force[11] (Figure 4.76). Although these birds are easily able to fly between the different habitats, populations show significant genetic differences, creating the appropriate conditions for evolution to proceed. Showing that differences are due to genetic rather than

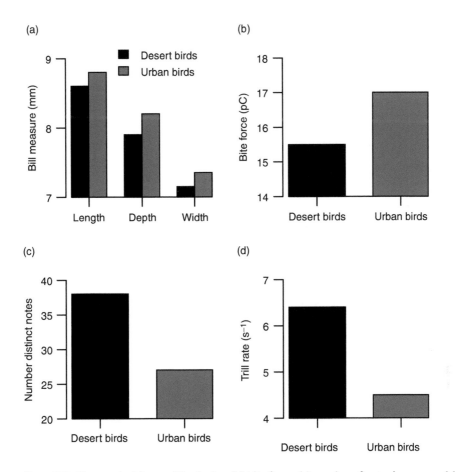

Figure 4.76 Changes in (a) overall beak size, (b) bite force, (c) number of notes in song, and (d) trill rate in urban house finches (after Badyaev *et al.*, 2008).

phenotypic plasticity is facilitated by an understanding of development. The bone morphogenetic proteins involved in beak growth are more active in the urban populations even early in life, indicating that larger beaks are not due solely to experience with larger seeds.

Birds use their beaks for more than cracking seeds. Urban house finches sing simpler songs with slower trills, perhaps because of the difficulty in rapidly moving a larger beak. What effects these changes have on the ability of male finches to attract mates remains unknown. Other studies of bird song show changes in response to urban noise (Section 4.5), although distinguishing evolution from behavioral adjustment in these rapidly learning species remains difficult[434]. If changes in song affect the selection of mates, then such changes could induce a rapid evolutionary response. Female birds may prefer songs similar to those they heard their fathers sing near the nest where they hatched. If they prefer to mate with males that sing similar "urban" songs, gene flow between urban and non-urban populations will decline and allow further genetic differentiation[489].

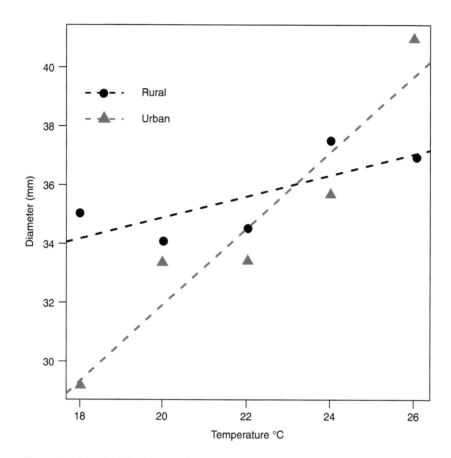

Figure 4.77 Growth of the fungus *Chrysosporium pannorum* at different temperatures (after McLean *et al.*, 2005).

Effects of urban ecosystem processes

Effects of urban noise and heat on urban physiology and behavior are widespread. Whether these urban challenges lead to evolutionary responses, is, as always, much harder to establish. The southern brown tree frog *Litoria ewingii* calls at higher frequencies in urban areas, presumably in order to be heard above low frequency urban noise[427]. Although female frogs generally prefer low pitched calls that indicate a large male, the audibility of higher pitched calls may outweigh their reduced attractiveness. Unlike birds, frogs do not learn their songs, and this change in song may result from recent genetic changes.

Although the urban heat island is one of the most widespread changes of the urban ecosystem, few evolutionary responses have been shown. Urban plants have extended growing seasons in response to climate warming (Figure 4.57), as do plants throughout the world[97]. To date, few studies have demonstrated that such changes are genetic[181]. The urban heat island increases heat stress, and some urban soil-dwelling fungi show an increased ability to tolerate high temperatures, apparently due to genetic evolution[375] (Figure 4.77). Some of these heat-tolerant fungus species grow more slowly at low temperatures, indicating a possible tradeoff that could restrict them from growing in colder non-urban areas.

Effects of urban ecological interactions

Although ecological interactions provide some of the strongest natural selection, they are quite difficult to study experimentally. In the population of dark-eyed juncos that have colonized the urbanized campus of the University of California at San Diego, we have seen that nesting preferences have changed (Section 4.3). Individuals that nest above the ground suffer much lower predation, and thus have higher fitness. However, evolution of this new trait seems to be impeded by the low correlation between mothers and daughters. This trait may not be sufficiently heritable to evolve.

In this same population, however, the amount of white on the tail, which acts as a signal of aggression and courtship by males, has been reduced[621]. This difference persists when birds are reared by hand, indicating that the trait is probably genetic, although it is possible that some signal comes from the mother. The apparently rapid evolution of this change could result from factors altering the importance of social competition. The urban habitat allows a longer breeding season, which gives males more opportunities to breed with the same female, and may favor investing energy in parental care rather than in competing for mates[460]. The relative importance of social signaling might be reduced by the low density of this population, which cannot use much of the extensively built habitat, or high visibility in a more open habitat that reduces the need for long-distance signaling to mates or competitors.

Conclusions

Evolutionary changes of urban organisms are among the most unexpected of unintended consequences. Bird feeding, intended to attract birds, alters the shape of their beaks. Planting trees near sidewalks alters the movement of the seeds of the small flowering plants that cluster around them in isolated patches of soil. The urban heat island favors changes in the way that organisms move and tolerate heat.

The idea of an ecological trap summarizes some of the challenges of coping with a new environment[509]. If urban areas are utterly unsuitable, a species simply goes locally extinct and is unable to evolve, even if it has the potential to do so. If urban areas are appealing but largely unsuitable, urban populations persist as a sink, where the population remains afloat due only to immigration from some outside source population. To evolve, these populations face an uphill fight against small population size and gene flow.

However, the expanding area of urban habitats, their increasing age, the extreme challenges they create, and the constant input of new species make evolution more and more likely to overcome these barriers. Changes in urban populations that have only begun may well become amplified during the next few decades, and distinct new varieties and even species may join urban biogeochemistry and urban communities as unexpected ecological products of the city.

4.7   Questions and readings

Discussion questions

For Section 4.1

1. How do changes in climate, water, and nutrients affect the biodiversity of urban ecosystems?

2. Sketch one chain of effects starting with habitat modification and ending with altered biodiversity.

3. Sketch another such chain starting with increased inputs.

4. Why are urban ecosystems sometimes more diverse than the surrounding area? Is this true where you live? Which types of organism are you thinking of?

5. Which areas near you have high and low diversity? Why do you think this is? Would your answer change if you increased or decreased the scale of the areas you were considering?

6. Is biodiversity important to consider in cities? Why? And should non-native species be considered equally with native ones? Why?

7. Did you consider the effects of urbanization on biodiversity in and out of the city when developing your ecological footprint? Why do you think you should or should not?

For Section 4.2

1. What aspects of urbanization increase the likelihood of invasive species becoming established, and what aspects decrease the likelihood?

2. According to Question 1, are all urban areas equally likely to facilitate the establishment of invasive species? Why, or why not?

3. How do the ecological effects of invasive species on the environment differ between urban and non-urban ecosystems? Design an experiment to support your answer to this question.

4. Why are urban environments possible ecological traps? Would you expect native or exotic species to be more likely to be stuck in an ecological trap?

5. Should non-native species be considered equally with native ones when valuing biodiversity? Why?

6. Are there non-native species that you would particularly like to see removed from your own area, or others you would like to maintain? What are your reasons, and how might you go about achieving these goals?

7. Read a paper on the biology of cancer[242] and use it to compare and contrast the stages of cancer progression with the steps of invasion as exemplified by the rule of 10.

For Section 4.3

1. Place the effects of urbanization onto Figure 4.31 at the beginning of this chapter. How many effects can work in contradictory ways?

2. How does urbanization affect competition for resources and predation? Why might this answer differ when considering native versus non-native species, and when considering different parts of the urban habitat?

3. What large animals live in your city, and what do you think controls their population growth? Would those animals live in the area if it were not urbanized, and if so, would the population regulation mechanisms still be the same?

4. With so much imported energy and nutrients, why is there a paucity of predators in urban ecosystems? What predators live in your city, are they native to the area, and how do they persist?

5. Develop a hypothesis for the interesting observation that urban birds in the northern and southern hemispheres make use of characteristically different competitive strategies. How would you test such a hypothesis?

6. Would you expect urban ecosystems to have more, less, or the same proportion of mutualisms as in their surrounding non-urban ecosystems? Why?

For Section 4.4

1. Choose one disease in this section and build a diagram like Figure 4.47 to show specifically how urbanization alters disease prevalence and its effects.

2. Including concepts from Chapter 3 and Chapter 4, how might urbanization affect direct and indirect disease transmission differently?

3. Are urban habitats more susceptible to epidemic or endemic disease dynamics? Why?

4. How does urbanization affect disease transmission across species? Are these effects always visible within the urban environment itself?

5. Explain the opposite trends for bobcats and foxes in Figure 4.45. What types of similar relationships might exist in your area?

6. Considering species interactions from Section 4.3, how might disease affect competition and predation in urban environments?

For Section 4.5

1. What are some of the behavioral changes humans make to live in cities? How do these changes affect the physical environment and other species living there?

2. Sketch chains of effects starting with habitat modification and ending with alteration of at least two of the five types of traits. Do the same for increased inputs.

3. Why do urban habitats often favor generalists? What would it mean to be an urban specialist? Do any such species exist?

4. How do urban animals deal with stress differently than their non-urban counterparts? Do you think that this is also true for humans?

5. In what ways are the responses of urban animals and plants similar and different? How do the characteristics of urban plants line up with those of urban birds in Table 4.3?

6. Summarize the stresses faced by urban house sparrows, and describe a set of measurements and experiments to understand which are most important in creating small body size or declining populations.

7. Describe one case where urban changes lead to trait changes and then to changes in species interactions, and another where changes in species interactions lead to trait changes. Do these chains of cause and effect seem predictable? Why or why not?

8. We have seen cases where urban predation is lower and others where it is higher than non-urban predation. Can you find a pattern for these differences?

9. Design an experiment to determine whether lower giving-up densities in urban versus non-urban habitats are due to reduced fear of predation or increased competition.

For Section 4.6

1. What factors reduce the chances of evolving traits favorable to an urban environment? How have these challenges been overcome in the cases of urban evolution?

2. Why are humans such a strong evolutionary force? Does (or did) this force affect humans? Why or why not?

3. Why is it difficult to distinguish between evolutionary change and morphological, physiological, or behavioral change in urban environments? How would you design an experiment to make such a distinction?

4. Make a list describing all of the adaptive traits you can think of for three particular organisms to thrive in an urban environment. Would those traits be most likely to arise as preadaptations, phenotypic plasticity, or genetic evolution?

Exercises

For Section 4.1

1. Simpson's diversity index provides a way to quantify diversity in comparison with species richness. It is the reciprocal of the probability that two individuals chosen at random come from the same species.

   (a) Suppose first that there are just two species, and that they are equally common. What is the probability that two individuals chosen come from the same species? The reciprocal of this is the Simpson diversity index, which should match the species richness.

   (b) Suppose again that there are two species, but that 80% of individuals come from one species and only 20% from the other. What is the probability that two consecutive individuals come from the first species? Add this to the probability that two consecutive individuals come from the second species to find the total probability. What is Simpson's diversity index and why is it smaller than the species richness?

(c) Now suppose that the two species take up fractions p and $1-p$ of the population, where $0 < p < 1$. Find and graph Simpson's diversity index as a function of p.

(d) With n species that take up fractions $p_1, p_2, \ldots, p_n$ of the population, Simpson's diversity index D takes on the value

$$D = \frac{1}{p_1^2 + p_2^2 + \ldots + p_n^2}.$$

Explain this formula. When does $D = n$?

(e) Test this formula on the example in the book, where $n = 5$, $p_1 = 0.96$, and $p_2, p_3, p_4,$ and p_5 are all equal to 0.01. Do you think D gives a useful summary of this community?

2. Consider the following data on the presence (1) or absence (0) of 10 species in 8 different patches.

Patch	Species									
	A	B	C	D	E	F	G	H	I	J
1	0	1	1	1	0	0	0	1	0	1
2	0	0	1	1	0	0	1	1	1	1
3	0	0	0	1	1	0	0	1	1	0
4	1	1	1	1	0	0	1	1	1	1
5	1	0	0	0	0	1	1	1	1	0
6	1	0	1	1	1	0	0	1	1	1
7	0	0	1	1	0	1	0	1	1	1
8	1	0	1	1	0	1	1	1	1	1

(a) What is the species richness of each patch?

(b) How often is each species seen?

(c) You can graph a species accumulation curve by finding the number of species in patch 1, then in patches 1 and 2, then in patches 1, 2, and 3, and so forth. How many patches are required to find the full set of species?

(d) How does the curve look if you included patches in the reverse order (starting with patch 8, then patches 8 and 7, then patches 8, 7, and 6)? Are you worried that it is different?

3. The theory of island biogeography describes the equilibrium number of species on an island or in a park as a function of the rates of colonization and extinction.

(a) Suppose that species arrive at rate 2.0/yr and each species present goes extinct with probability 0.1 in a given year. How many species are present when the average number that go extinct (the number of species times the probability of extinction) is equal to the number arriving?

(b) Suppose that the probability of extinction is a function of the park area A, in hectares, according to the formula $\frac{1.0}{1.0+A}$. How large is the park in (a)? How many species would we expect to find in a park of area A if the rate of colonization is 2.0 species/yr? When is this less than 1 species?

(c) Now suppose that rate of colonization depends on the distance x, in kilometers, of the park from a forest surrounding the city according to the formula $\frac{10.0}{4.0+0.5x}$. How isolated is the park in (a)? How many species would we expect to find in the park at distance x if the probability of extinction is 0.1 for each species? When is this less than 1 species?

(d) Now put the two effects together and come up with a formula for the number of species as a function of both A and x. Does it match Figure 4.6?

For Section 4.2

The first two problems are based on the following data[280]. NA refers to North America.

	Fish	Mammals	Birds
Native to both NA and Europe	11	20	104
Native only to Europe	220	207	361
Introduced to NA	14	13	40
Established in NA	9	11	12
Invasive in NA	5	8	8
Native only to NA	713	342	419
Introduced to Europe	35	9	28
Established in Europe	19	7	7
Invasive in Europe	12	5	2

1. We can use these values to compute the Simpson and Jaccard similarity indices for the two continents before and after human intervention.

   (a) Compute the Simpson and Jaccard similarity indices for fish, mammals, and birds before humans by using the values for native species only.

   (b) Compute the Simpson and Jaccard similarity indices after humans by finding the number of shared species (add those native to both to the number successfully established in either direction).

   (c) For which group of species are these values most changed by humans? Do you think they are highly homogenized?

2. We can use the values in Exercise 4.2.1 to test the rule of 10.

   (a) Find the fraction of introduced species that become established.

   (b) Find the fraction of established species that become invasive.

   (c) How do your results compare with the rule of 10? Why do you think the percentages are so much higher?

   (d) Is there a consistent difference between species that move from Europe to North America and vice versa? Are European species really more successful at becoming invasive?

   (e) Find the fraction of all native species that are introduced. Does this value differ in the two directions?

For Section 4.3

1. Although the underlying mathematics are a bit tricky, we can graphically study the differences and interactions between bottom-up and top-down control.

    (a) Graph how resources and a population of consumers might change over time if the resource supply rate were increased. If this is pure bottom-up control, the consumers should eventually increase enough to reduce the resources to their original level.
    (b) Graph how resources, a population of consumers, and a population of predators might change over time in the situation from (a). With pure bottom-up control, only the predator population will end up larger.
    (c) Graph the same situation with top-down control.
    (d) Graph the same situation with an interaction between bottom-up and top-down control as described in the text, where resources can be used by the consumers to protect against predators.

2. Herbivore population density D, in numbers of mammals per square kilometer, follows approximately

$$D = 50W^{-0.75}$$

(Exercises for Section 2.3, Question 2). It requires about 10 000 kg of prey to maintain 90 kg of predators[78].

    (a) How many prey of mass 100.0 g would survive in a patch of 0.5 km²?
    (b) What mass of predators could they support?
    (c) How large a park would be needed to support a small population of 12 foxes, each of which weighs 5.0 kg?
    (d) How would your answer change if the prey weighed 1.0 kg?

3. We can estimate directly how many birds are killed by cats and try to assess their effect on bird reproductive success. Suppose there are approximately twice as many birds as people (as in Sheffield, England[189]), that there are about 0.25 times as many cats as people, and that cats kill approximately 12 birds annually[584].

    (a) What fraction of birds would be killed according to these estimates? Does this seem strange?
    (b) Suppose that cats only kill fledgling birds, and that the average bird fledges 4 offspring per year. What fraction of fledglings would be killed by cats? Do you think that cats could drive the birds to extinction?
    (c) How would this differ if 10% of the birds killed by cats were adults, and the rest fledglings?

For Section 4.4

1. Epidemiologists, scientists who study the spread of disease, often focus on the *basic reproduction number* R_0, which is the number of new infections created by the first infected individual. If this value is greater than 1, the disease will spread because

each infected individual creates more than enough new infections to replace itself after recovery.

(a) For directly transmitted diseases, the value of R_0 is found by multiplying the rate at which individuals are infected by the duration of infection. Suppose raccoons are infected with a parasite that persists in each individual for an average of 10 days. How many raccoons would need to be infected per day for the disease to spread?

(b) The infection rate is proportional to the contact rate, the rate at which individuals encounter each other. Suppose each individual is contacted with probability 0.01 each day, and a contact leads to an infection half of the time. How large would the population have to be for the disease to spread?

(c) How much would this value change if urban raccoons had a larger food supply and were less susceptible to infection, being infected only 20% of the time after contact with an infected raccoon?

2. For a disease that is transmitted by a vector, such as Lyme disease that is transmitted by ticks, visits to hosts that do not carry the disease are "wasted" and can reduce the spread of the disease. This is the mechanism underlying the dilution effect. Suppose that ticks only transmit successfully if they visit two competent hosts (those that can carry the disease) consecutively.

(a) Assume that 50% of hosts are competent. Compute the probability that two competent hosts are visited in a row. How much lower is transmission than if all hosts are?

(b) Assume that a fraction p of hosts are competent. How does the probability of transmission depend on p? How does this affect the value of R_0, as defined in the previous problem?

(c) The dilution effect is related to the probability of successful transmission of pollen by pollinators. Suppose that pollen only works if the pollinator visits two plants of the same species consecutively. What fraction of pollen is transmitted successfully if 80% of plants come from one species and 20% from another? Does this remind you of Simpson's diversity index? How might planting highly diverse gardens affect pollination of native plants?

3. Suppose a disease infects individuals in a population that is growing at 10% per year. In particular, before the disease, 80% of individuals survive until the next year, and 30% successfully produce one offspring.

(a) What happens if the disease decreases the probability of adult survival by 10%?

(b) What happens if the disease decreases the probability of successful reproduction by 10%?

(c) What would happen if the disease killed only males?

For Section 4.5

1. Nightingales sing louder with ambient noise, following roughly the equation $L = A/3 + 65$ where A is ambient noise in decibels (dB) and L is nightingale song loudness[60].

   (a) What is the expected loudness of a nightingale's song with 40 dB of ambient noise? How about with 70 dB?
   (b) Suppose an increase of 10 dB requires the nightingale to use 10% more energy to sing. How much more energy would a nightingale use in a loud place?
   (c) Ten times as much power is required to create a sound 10 dB louder. How much more power does a nightingale need to produce in the loud environment?
   (d) The pressure is the square root of the power. How much more pressure does the nightingale need to generate in the loud environment?

2. The giving-up density describes the food density when an organism gives up on foraging at a particular site.

   (a) Suppose that a feeding tray in a park starts with 100 seeds, and that the time to find a seed is $300.0/S$ seconds where S is the current number of seeds. How long will it take to find the first seed?
   (b) Suppose that a bird stops searching when it takes 10 seconds to find a seed. How many seeds does it leave behind?
   (c) With a predator present, the bird stops searching when it takes 25 seconds to find a seed. How many seeds would be left in the tray?
   (d) How much earlier does it leave the tray when the predator is present?
   (e) Suppose each seed furnishes 0.5 kcal. How much energy is the bird sacrificing by leaving earlier?
   (f) What is the average rate of energy collection during the extra time the bird stays without a predator? Can you use this value to quantify the bird's fear of the predator?

3. People in the United States provide wild birds with about 450 million kg of bird seed per year. Suppose the average bird needs 10 kcal per day to survive, and that bird seed averages 3.0 kcal/g.

   (a) How many calories do people provide per day?
   (b) How many people could this support?
   (c) How many birds could this support?
   (d) How many birds is this per person? If about 20% of people feed birds, how many is each supporting?

4. Suppose that temperature changes linearly from a minimum daily average of 0.0°C on January 1 to a maximum of 25.0°C on July 1 and then declines linearly after that.

   (a) Graph the average daily temperature over the course of a year (your graph should look like a triangle).

(b) Suppose plants grow when the temperature is above 15.0°C. When will they start and stop growing? How long is the growing season?

(c) Suppose the urban heat island increases the average daily temperature by 3.0°C every day. How much would this extend the growing season?

(d) Suppose the urban heat island increases the average daily temperature by 5.0°C in January and by 1.0°C in July (but that the graph still looks like a triangle). Does this change the growing season by more or less than the constant urban heat island? Why?

For Section 4.6

1. Suppose annual plants with a new trait in an urban environment produce an average of 1.1 offspring per year, while those with the original trait produce an average of 1.0 offspring per year.

(a) If there are 10 of the new type and 1000 of the original type to begin with, what will their populations be after 10 years?

(b) What is the fraction of the new type to begin with? What is it after 10 years?

(c) How long would it take for the new type to make up 90% of the population?

(d) How would these values change if the new type produced only 1.01 offspring per year on average?

(e) This population would continue to grow without bound. What do you think would change as the new type became more common? How might you include this in the model?

(f) How would you include gene flow, in the form of immigration of the original type, into this model?

2. Human pressures lead to changes in the life history of organisms, with potentially huge consequences for fitness.

(a) Fish harvesting can favor fish that reproduce earlier even if they produce fewer offspring. Suppose that a fish that reproduces at age 3 years produces 20 eggs that will survive to adulthood, while one that reproduces at age 2 years produces only 5. If fish die after reproducing, which population will grow faster? One way to do this is to figure out which population would be larger after 6 years, which is two generations for those that reproduce every 3 years, and three generations for those that reproduce every 2 years.

(b) Suppose half of the fish are harvested between ages 2 and 3 years. Which age of reproduction is now favored? What other effects do you think this would have on the population?

(c) Compare this scenario to the effects of giving up migration. What information would you need to compute whether birds that spend the winter in cities will do better than those that continue to migrate?

Further Reading

For Section 4.1

- Angold, P., Sadler, J., Hill, M., *et al.* Biodiversity in urban habitat patches. *The Science of the Total Environment*, **360** (2006), 196–204.

- Blair, R. B. Land use and avian species diversity along an urban gradient. *Ecological Applications*, **6** (1996), 506–519.

- Chace, J. F. and Walsh, J. J. Urban effects on native avifauna: a review. *Landscape and Urban Planning*, **74** (2006), 46–69.

- Crooks, K. and Soulé, M. Mesopredator release and avifaunal extinctions in a fragmented system. *Nature*, **400** (1999), 563–566.

- Drayton, B. and Primack, R. B. Plant species lost in an isolated conservation area in Metropolitan Boston from 1894 to 1993. *Conservation Biology*, **10** (1996), 30–39.

- Faeth, S., Bang, C., and Saari, S. Urban biodiversity: patterns and mechanisms. *Annals of the New York Academy of Sciences*, **1223** (2011), 69–81.

- Gaston, K. Biodiversity and extinction: species and people. *Progress in Physical Geography*, **29** (2005), 239–247.

- Guirado, M., Pino, J., and Roda, F. Understorey plant species richness and composition in metropolitan forest archipelagos: effects of forest size, adjacent land use and distance to the edge. *Global Ecology and Biogeography*, **15** (2006), 50–62.

- Hope, D., Gries, C., Zhu, W. X., *et al.* Socioeconomics drive urban plant diversity. *Proceedings of the National Academy of Sciences*, **100** (2003), 8788–8792.

- Marzluff, J. M. Island biogeography for an urbanizing world: how extinction and colonization may determine biological diversity in human-dominated landscapes. *Urban Ecology*, **8** (2008), 355–371.

- McKinney, M. Effects of urbanization on species richness: a review of plants and animals. *Urban Ecosystems*, **11** (2008), 161–176.

- Shochat, E., Warren, P. S., Faeth, S. H., *et al.* From patterns to emerging processes in mechanistic urban ecology. *Trends in Ecology & Evolution*, **21** (2006), 186–191.

- Tratalos, J., Fuller, R. A., Evans, K. L., *et al.* Bird densities are associated with household densities. *Global Change Biology*, **13** (2007), 1685–1695.

For Section 4.2

- La Sorte, F. A. and McKinney, M. L. Compositional similarity and the distribution of geographical range size for assemblages of native and non-native species in urban floras. *Diversity and Distributions*, **12** (2006), 679–686.

- Loram, A., Thompson, K., Warren, P. H., and Gaston, K. J. Urban domestic gardens (XII): The richness and composition of the flora in five UK cities. *Journal of Vegetation Science*, **19** (2008), 321–330.

- McKinney, M. L. Urbanization as a major cause of biotic homogenization. *Biological Conservation*, **127** (2006), 247–260.

- Plowes, R., Dunn, J., and Gilbert, L. The urban fire ant paradox: native fire ants persist in an urban refuge while invasive fire ants dominate natural habitats. *Biological Invasions*, **9** (2007), 825–836.
- von der Lippe, M. and Kowarik, I. Do cities export biodiversity? Traffic as dispersal vector across urban–rural gradients. *Diversity and Distributions*, **14** (2008), 18–25.

For Section 4.3

- Dreistadt, S. H., Dahlsten, D. L., and Frankie, G. W. Urban forests and insect ecology. *Bioscience*, **40** (1990), 192–198.
- Faeth, S. H., Warren, P. S., Shochat, E., and Marussich, W. A. Trophic dynamics in urban communities. *Bioscience*, **55** (2005), 399–407.
- Heneghan, L., Steffen, J., and Fagen, K. Interactions of an introduced shrub and introduced earthworms in an Illinois urban woodland: impact on leaf litter decomposition. *Pedobiologia*, **50** (2007), 543–551.
- Holway, D. and Suarez, A. Homogenization of ant communities in mediterranean California: the effects of urbanization and invasion. *Biological Conservation*, **127** (2006), 319–326.
- Raupp, M. J., Shrewsbury, P. M., and Herms, D. A. Ecology of herbivorous arthropods in urban landscapes. *Annual Review of Entomology*, **55** (2010), 19–38.
- Rodewald, A., Kearns, L., and Shustack, D. Anthropogenic resource subsidies decouple predator–prey relationships. *Ecological Applications*, **21** (2010), 936–943.
- Sims, V., Evans, K., Newson, S., Tratalos, J., and Gaston, K. Avian assemblage structure and domestic cat densities in urban environments. *Diversity and Distributions*, **14** (2008), 387–399.
- van Heezik, Y., Smyth, A., Adams, A., and Gordon, J. Do domestic cats impose an unsustainable harvest on urban bird populations? *Biological Conservation*, **143** (2010), 121–130.

For Section 4.4

- Boal, C. W. and Mannan, R. W. Comparative breeding ecology of Cooper's hawks in urban and exurban areas of southeastern Arizona. *Journal of Wildlife Management*, **63** (1999), 77–84.
- Bradley, C. A. and Altizer, S. Urbanization and the ecology of wildlife diseases. *Trends in Ecology & Evolution*, **22** (2007), 95–102.
- Deplazes, P., Hegglin, D., Gloor, S., and Romig, T. Wilderness in the city: the urbanization of *Echinococcus multilocularis*. *Trends in Parasitology*, **20** (2004), 77–84.
- Soulsbury, C. D., Iossa, G., Baker, P. J., The impact of sarcoptic mange *Sarcoptes scabiei* on the British fox *Vulpes vulpes* population. *Mammal Review*, **37** (2007), 278–296.

For Section 4.5

- Bókony, V., Kulcsár, A., and Liker, A. Does urbanization select for weak competitors in house sparrows? *Oikos*, **119** (2010), 437–444.
- Buczkowski, G. Extreme life history plasticity and the evolution of invasive characteristics in a native ant. *Biological Invasions*, **12** (2010), 1–7.
- Carrete, M. and Tella, J. L. Inter-individual variability in fear of humans and relative brain size of the species are related to urban invasion in birds. *PLoS ONE*, **6** (2011), e18859.
- Ditchkoff, S. S., Saalfeld, S. T., and Gibson, C. J. Animal behavior in urban ecosystems: modifications due to human-induced stress. *Urban Ecosystems*, **9** (2006), 5–12.
- Evans, K. L., Gaston, K. J., Frantz, A. C., *et al.* Independent colonization of multiple urban centres by a formerly forest specialist bird species. *Proceedings of the Royal Society B: Biological Sciences*, **276** (2009), 2403.
- Kark, S., Iwaniuk, A., Schalimtzek, A., and Banker, E. Living in the city: can anyone become an 'urban exploiter'? *Journal of Biogeography*, **34** (2007), 638–651.
- Knapp, S., Kühn, I., Wittig, R., *et al.* Urbanization causes shifts in species' trait state frequencies. *Preslia*, **80** (2008), 375–388.
- Maklakov, A., Immler, S., Gonzalez-Voyer, A., Rönn, J., and Kolm, N. Brains and the city: big-brained passerine birds succeed in urban environments. *Biology Letters*, **7** (2011), 730–732.
- Nemeth, E. and Brumm, H. Blackbirds sing higher-pitched songs in cities: adaptation to habitat acoustics or side-effect of urbanization? *Animal Behaviour*, **78** (2009), 637–641.
- Partecke, J., Schwabl, I., and Gwinner, E. Stress and the city: urbanization and its effects on the stress physiology in European blackbirds. *Ecology*, **87** (2006), 1945–1952.
- Shochat, E. Credit or debit? Resource input changes population dynamics of city-slicker birds. *Oikos*, **106** (2004), 622–626.
- Ziska, L. H., George, K., and Frenz, D. A. Establishment and persistence of common ragweed *Ambrosia artemisiifolia* (L.) in disturbed soil as a function of an urban–rural macro-environment. *Global Change Biology*, **13** (2007), 266–274.

For Section 4.6

- Badyaev, A., Young, R., Oh, K., and Addison, C. Evolution on a local scale: developmental, functional, and genetic bases of divergence in bill form and associated changes in song structure between adjacent habitats. *Evolution*, **62** (2008), 1951–1964.
- Cheptou, P., Carrue, O., Rouifed, S., and Cantarel, A. Rapid evolution of seed dispersal in an urban environment in the weed *Crepis sancta*. *Proceedings of the National Academy of Sciences*, **105** (2008), 3796–3799.
- Cook, L. The rise and fall of the carbonaria form of the peppered moth. *The Quarterly Review of Biology*, **78** (2003), 399–417.

- Munshi-South, J. and Kharchenko, K. Rapid, pervasive genetic differentiation of urban white-footed mouse (*Peromyscus leucopus*) populations in New York City. *Molecular Ecology*, **19** (2010), 4242–4254.
- Palumbi, S. R., Humans as the world's greatest evolutionary force. *Science*, **293** (2001), 1786–1790.
- Rolshausen, G., Segelbacher, G., Hobson, K., and Schaefer, H. Contemporary evolution of reproductive isolation and phenotypic divergence in sympatry along a migratory divide. *Current Biology*, **19** (2009), 2097–2101.
- Yeh, P. Rapid evolution of a sexually selected trait following population establishment in a novel habitat. *Evolution*, **58** (2004), 166–174.

Labs

A. Using the species counts from earlier labs, or developing new ones from your sampling sites, compute species richness and biodiversity measures for each sampling site. Plot the data and the mean values along the urban–rural gradient, and examine graphs of how biodiversity depends on other local habitat information such as temperature, soil type, and disturbance for each site. For each site, record the values of homes for sale. Is there a relationship between real estate value and habitat characteristics or species richness?

B. Using the species data from **A**, determine how many species are native, and investigate possible relationships between habitat characteristics and native species, including distance from the urban core. Compare the biodiversity values with the native species values at each site.

C. At the same sampling sites as above, pick a common deciduous species and record the date when leaves develop, and when they fall. Compare these dates between urban and non-urban sites.

D. At the sampling sites used in **A**, place a known quantity of bird seed within a 1 × 1 m square. Record the maximum number of birds feeding simultaneously within each square, the giving-up density of food for each site with a simulated predator nearby (e.g., a cat), and the minimum distance you can reach by walking toward the box before all of the birds stop foraging and leave the square. Compare these data for urban and non-urban sites.

E. Look back through the principles and factors introduced in Section 1.4. Give examples of how each has been changed in the urban environment. Make a concept map or diagram showing how these changes are interrelated.

5   Implications of urban ecology

Cities probably arose when people clustered together for protection and for food. These clusters, however, began to change human needs almost as soon as they came into existence. New forms of government, society, and transportation developed, and with them the beginnings of the infrastructure that defines modern urban areas. Human population regulation no longer fit the ecological top-down or bottom-up models, but resulted from complex social, political, and economic forces rather than local availability of food or other resources.

This book has explored how this transformation of human ecology changes the functioning of the ecosystem and the structure of the ecological communities that coexist with people in the built environment. Those changes are profound, reaching from the way that molecules move and are processed to the way that populations interact and organisms evolve, with most being unintended consequences of human activities designed for other purposes and goals.

This chapter outlines some of the implications of these unintended consequences from the human perspective. First, human residents of urban areas, much like the other organisms that live there, experience new stresses. The first section focuses on the health effects of urban living on humans that often parallel the effects on other animals. These health effects are part of a much larger range of effects on humans that play a considerable role in determining the quality of life within cities, including access to cultural and social resources, aesthetics, safety, and equality. Every urban planning decision carries with it implications for both the urban ecosystem and its human residents, which are often associated with quite different value systems. Most of these issues lie outside the scope of this book, but ecological principles cast new light upon them. Section 5.2 examines policy decisions from the scientific perspective. How does the science of urban ecology affect or illuminate the consequences of policy choices? And how do policy choices affect our ability to conduct the science? The book concludes with a glimpse into the ecological future through the increasingly well-focused lens of urban ecology.

5.1   Human health and disease

A classic study of recovery in hospitals separated patients recovering from gall bladder surgery into two groups, one with windows overlooking a courtyard with trees and the other looking onto a brick wall. Patients with the view of trees recovered more quickly, complained less, and used substantially less pain-killer medication than those with a view of a wall[581]. Although the majority of people now live in cities and spend much of their time with views of walls, the human mind and body still seem to crave the greener world in which they evolved. Many of the ways that people have historically interacted with nature, by moving through, observing, and interacting with other living beings remain part of the life of urban residents through walking, playing with pets, gardening, and nature study[290].

Until recently, the unhealthy effects of cities resulted primarily from infectious diseases. Controlling the scourges of plagues and pandemics, driven by high urban population density and unclean air and water, had to await the nineteenth century[416]. Hospitals also concentrated infectious diseases. Because urban areas had more hospitals, infant mortality rates were higher in urban than in rural Germany until the 1870s. Only thereafter, with the advent of improved hygiene, did urban infant mortality drop[192]. The urban planning of the late nineteenth century derived from the growing understanding that infectious diseases could be controlled by cleaning drinking water, removing sewage, and eliminating breeding habitat for mosquitoes that carried such remarkably widespread diseases as malaria and yellow fever[443]. Public hygiene improvements often spread inward from the suburbs, creating the still existing view that cities are less healthy than their less densely populated surroundings. These public health improvements had a greater effect on human life expectancy than did antibiotics or other later medical breakthroughs.

Few cities had self-sustaining populations during the era of infectious disease, and thus acted as human ecological sinks[75]. But people moved into cities, as they still do, for reasons that include "push factors" that drive people away from rural areas, such as disasters and poverty, as well as "pull factors" that attract people to the city, particularly economic and cultural opportunities[219]. Migration, rather than internal growth, has led to the explosive growth of megacities such as Mexico City and Shanghai in recent years. When a growing population of immigrants overwhelms existing public health infrastructure, sections of these cities can return to the era of insufficient sanitation and disease outbreaks.

With the exception of a few extremely poor areas, access to health care tends to maintain current urban mortality at low levels[219]. Although comparisons are difficult, recent statistics in Scotland find the lowest life expectancy in urban areas for both males and females, and the highest life expectancy in remote rural areas[209]. These differences are relatively small, being a matter of two or three years for people well into their seventies.

The principles of urban human health

We have studied the three broad ways that organisms respond to an environment: sorting, phenotypic adjustment, and genetic evolution (Section 4.5). Humans have the same potential responses, but supplemented and transformed by our status as ecosystem engineers (Section 1.1) and our ability to transform the environment itself. These changes, as their intended consequences, make previously unsuitable environments, such as deserts, fully habitable. That some of these transformations have unintended negative effects on human health can hardly be surprising.

Migration and movement complicate the analysis of plant and animal traits in urban environments, and similarly make it difficult to establish the health effects of urban life. Some people thrive in cities while others cannot tolerate them, and sufficient social and economic freedom allows people to sort themselves into their favored environment. Life expectancy in cities could be lower not because of the direct effects of urban life, but instead because people who move to cities, or choose to remain in them, are less healthy than those who remain in or move to the countryside[590]. More subtle effects, such as psychological problems or autoimmune disease, are deeply entangled with the personal choices people make of how and where to live in cities.

Negative human health effects can be thought of as physiological or psychological responses to a new environment. Obesity is the body's response to an imbalance between food intake and energy used. Asthma is an unwanted physiological response to allergens and pollutants. Adaptive responses, such as the ability to sleep through noise or to adjust one's schedule to altered light levels, also play a role in determining which people thrive in cities but have yet to be carefully studied.

Although many health problems people face in cities, including obesity and asthma, have a strong genetic component, there is little evidence that humans have evolved specific responses to urban challenges. However, the alleles for resistance to tuberculosis, a disease most common in high density populations, has higher frequency in places with a longer history of urbanization[17]. Humans and human societies change rapidly through *cultural evolution*, the spread of ideas and technology, that can solve problems much faster than genetic evolution. Some alleles have been proposed to confer some resistance to smallpox[196], but in the current world this aspect of their phenotype has become irrelevant thanks to the cultural innovations that allowed the eradication of this disease.

Human health in cities

The health effects of urban living depend on the closely linked social and physical environments[598]. Humans face the same panoply of challenges as do other animals, challenges that drive physiological, behavioral, and evolutionary responses to novel habitats, resource availability, ecosystem processes, and ecological interactions. The greatest differences between urban humans and other animals lie in their interactions with other species, particularly the nearly complete elimination of competition and predation and the current reduction in infectious disease.

Effects of urban habitat modification

Urbanization induces reduced movement in animals, of both escape distances and the propensity to migrate (Section 4.5). The urban infrastructure, with its emphasis on the automobile, tends to do the same to humans[186]. In most American cities, over 90% of trips are now taken while seated in a car. This trend has accelerated recently. While 70% of today's parents walked to school, only 22% of their children do[7]. These patterns of behavior differ within the city. The inconvenience of driving and parking in cities can lead residents of the inner city to walk more than their suburban counterparts[59].

Urban sprawl in the United States is associated with fewer minutes walked and higher measures of obesity[158]. Although the health effects are difficult to determine, obesity in Chinese cities increased from 1.5% to 12.6% from 1989 to 1997, but obesity decreased in rural areas over the same time period. Obesity levels in urban and non-urban areas in the United States, however, do not differ significantly[7], although the percentage of green in neighborhoods may correlate with prevalence of obesity in children[332].

The appearance and working order of the physical environment affect both human psychology and behavior. A decaying built environment can cause depression[192]. Day-to-day annoyances such as non-functioning kitchen equipment, breakdowns of heating, and peeling paint, in addition to dangers such as deteriorating buildings and fires, act as risk factors for depression[193].

Urban green spaces come in many types, ranging from parks and tree-lined streets to cemeteries and recreational areas (Section 1.2). Urban greenery can improve health and well-being and aspects of behavior and cognition, along with extending social networks,

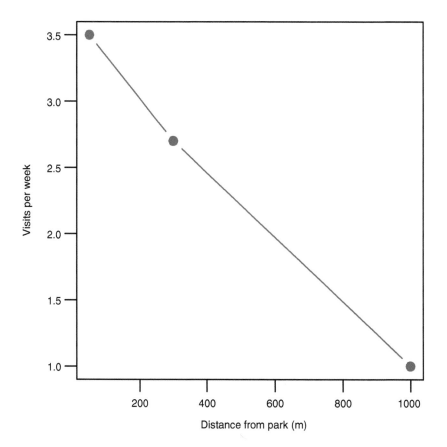

Figure 5.1 Frequency of visits to green space as a function of distance (after Barton and Pretty, 2010).

although it is difficult to correct for the potential bias that healthier people choose to live near green areas[580]. Five year survival of seniors in Tokyo was higher in those with access to green space[560]. The frequency with which people visit green areas declines strongly with how far they live from those areas[19] (Figure 5.1). In Sheffield, England, the average distance to public green space is 400 m, with 36.5% living within 300 m[239].

A deteriorating, dangerous, or unpleasant outdoor environment with little access to green open space not only results in poor mental well-being[235], but also tends to further reduce physical activity. Such environments are typically inhabited by people with low socio-economic status. These neighborhoods also tend to have high population density, which has the converse effect of increasing the proportion of people who walk to work and use public transportation[45]. Although the causes are difficult to ascertain, the increase in mortality associated with lower income was found to be significantly less steep among people with higher access to green space[383] (Figure 5.2). This large study

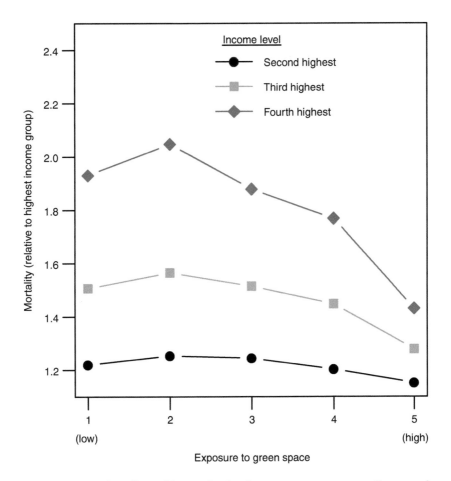

Figure 5.2 Interacting effects of income level and access to green space on all-causes of mortality, relative to the highest income group (after Mitchell and Popham, 2008).

of people throughout England could not control for the selection bias mentioned above or for other unmeasured factors.

For animals, the urban physical environment brings a constant stream of disturbances that they must learn to filter or ignore in order to be able to feed and reproduce successfully (Section 4.5). Humans must do the same, or risk suffering from mental fatigue, the collective cost of paying attention to the demands of urban life that range from driving, talking, and planning[290]. Visiting or even viewing nature might give the mind a rest, leading to improved mental health and reduced stress. Animals and caves, for example, are intrinsically fascinating to people, and help restore the mind by attracting involuntary attention. People reported more reflection and sense of identity from spending time in places with higher plant species richness, and more of a sense of continuity with the past with higher bird species richness[188], although broader health effects have not been established. Paradoxically, the sense of well-being can be lower with high plant species richness, and few people could actually identify 12 common urban species[113] (Figure 5.3).

In a controlled study in a Chicago housing development, women living in apartment buildings surrounded by vegetation showed less aggression toward both their partners and their children than those surrounded by pavement[315] (Figure 5.4). As a clue to the mechanism, the effects of green views are explained largely by improved scores on a memory test, indicating that aggression might be caused by attentional fatigue.

People's reaction to densely vegetated parks in urban areas can be polarizing. Some people are attracted by the natural habitats, while others fear that vegetation might

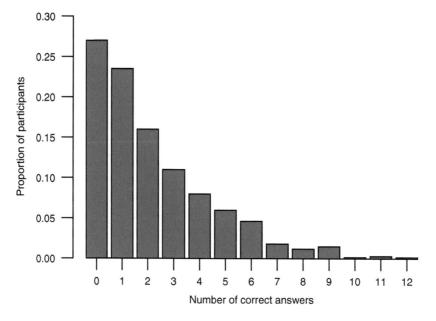

Figure 5.3 Fraction of people with each number of correct answers in identifying by common or scientific name 12 relatively common urban species including four birds, four butterflies, and four plants (after Dallimer *et al.*, 2012).

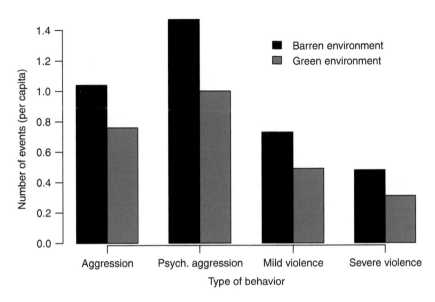

Figure 5.4 Effects of having a view of greenery on the number of incidents of aggression towards a partner over the past year (after Kuo and Sullivan, 2001).

conceal criminals[570]. More dispersed vegetation, as on the grounds of an apartment complex, can encourage groups of people to spend more time outside without fear of crime, in addition to reducing stress. At a different Chicago housing development, crime rates, including both property and violent crimes, were lower in buildings surrounded by more vegetation[316].

Effects of urban resource inputs

Urban residents in developed countries have access to essentially unlimited food from around the globe (Section 3.4). But the nature of that food depends on the type of city and neighborhood within that city. Areas with low socio-economic status have a higher ratio of fast food establishments to supermarkets, promoting the consumption of a diet high in fatty and salty processed foods but low in fresh foods[45]. Having a store that sells fresh fruit and vegetables in the neighborhood does predict the consumption of a more balanced diet[390]. Obesity results at least in part from the consumption of high-calorie foods, and is exacerbated by reduced activity levels[7]. As noted above, however, obesity is hardly an urban condition.

Effects of urban ecosystem processes

Changes in climate, particularly the urban heat island, can create substantial heat stress that leads to deaths particularly among the urban elderly and poor[192]. Heat waves are the single largest source of weather-related mortality in the United States[46], and the frequency of heat stroke rises quickly at higher temperatures[522]. Heat can exacerbate air pollution, and facilitate the range expansion of animal hosts and mosquito vectors of novel infectious diseases[436].

Air pollutants such as ozone, carbon monoxide, nitrogen oxides, and particulates are concentrated in urban areas (Section 3.4). The resulting health effects depend on the pollutant, the extent of exposure, and the sensitivity of the person exposed[186]. Ozone-related mortality increases in cities as a function of higher ozone levels in the previous week[27]. Exercising with fine and ultra-fine particulates amplifies their effects and may increase the probability of heart attacks and arrhythmias in the hours and days following exposure[518]. Children, with their immature immune systems, relatively large lung area, and habit of playing outside, face the challenge of asthma rather than the heart problems found in older people[71].

Urban asthma rates can be double those in non-urban areas, and result from a variety of causes characteristic of urban environments, air pollution high among them. Two natural experiments give some idea of its importance. During the Olympics in Atlanta, traffic temporarily dropped by 22% and ozone by 28%, leading to comparably large drops in asthma patient admissions[185]. In Utah, a strike at a large steel plant led to a 50% reduction in asthma patient admissions, with a strong correlation with particulate levels[450]. Increased exposure to pollutants, through proximity to roads with diesel vehicles or playing outdoor sports in highly polluted areas, accentuates the risk of asthma, as do allergens from cockroaches, dust mites, mice, and rats[71].

Urban residents face pollutants from water and land in addition to air. Historically, unclean water provided the major conduit for deadly pathogens such as cholera, but even today rapidly growing clusters of cities in China have substantial amounts of water that is not of drinkable quality due to the influx of untreated industrial and domestic waste-water[516]. Solid waste in dumps can be an economic resource, but a highly dangerous one that can also contribute to water pollution and mosquito breeding[389].

Water pollution can interact with infectious disease through behavior of insect vectors such as mosquitoes. The main vector of West Nile virus in the southeastern United States, *Culex quinquefasciatus*, preferentially lays eggs in nutrient-enriched waters that can result when sewage overflows into streams after heavy rains[91]. Untreated sewage that leaves an urban area can, after a complex chain of events involving mosquito behavior and the infection and movement of birds, come back in the form of increased human cases of a potentially dangerous infectious disease.

Cities are brightly lit and noisy. Until the advent of electricity, nights were dark, and even indoor lighting through candles and lanterns was limited. Electric light differs in intensity, spectrum, and timing from natural sunlight, and now provides much of the light to which humans are exposed both during the day and night. Although it is difficult to determine the causes, older people in Tokyo with sunlight in their residence do have a higher probability of surviving for 5 years[560]. Changes in the timing and type of light can disrupt the circadian clock that controls daily behaviors and may induce endocrine system dysfunction, leading to depression, reproductive anomalies, and even increased breast cancer rates due to altered melatonin levels[553]. Urban noise can cause higher stress, and noise from neighbors was among the factors most clearly identified with poor mental well-being[235].

Effects of ecological interactions

Although humans face little competition, except from the insects, mollusks, and mammals that consume produce from urban gardens, a few types of predation have increased recently. Coyotes have become both more common and more acclimated to human presence in urban areas, such as in California, leading to increased attacks, primarily on pets, but occasionally on children, with similar risks from mountain lions and alligators.

Infectious diseases, historically the most important ecological interaction for humans in cities, may be again increasing due to changes in development patterns and the encroachment of densely settled urban areas into their non-urban surroundings. These dispersed patterns of settlement bring humans and their pets into increased contact with wildlife. Although one might imagine that rural areas act as key points of contact between humans and wildlife or domesticated animals, more new infectious diseases emerge in areas of high human population density[288].

The evolution of antibiotic resistance provides another important source of new infectious diseases, often concentrated in urban hospitals (Section 4.6). Nonetheless, the majority of emerging diseases in humans continue to derive from other animals. The majority of these in turn come from wildlife, with a smaller proportion from agricultural species[288] (Figure 5.5), with each of these sources becoming more important in areas of high population density. Once again, urban areas boast high biodiversity, although in this case not the type of biodiversity many urban dwellers value.

The deadly Hendra virus is carried by flying foxes, including the gray-headed flying fox that has become an urban resident in Australia (Section 4.5). Some of these urban bats have given up migration, live at high density, and can drop virus on lands used by horses who then can transmit the virus to humans[449]. These factors might interact to create spill-over events. High density bat populations might be temporarily isolated from virus due to lack of migration and lose resistance. When the virus is reintroduced, the urban bats can suffer an epidemic, which has little effect on their health, but greatly increases the prevalence and the chance for transmission to horses and eventually humans.

In Colorado, people in the urban fringe encounter plague-infested prairie dogs *Cynomys ludovicianus*, which can only be relocated at great danger and expense[117]. The helminth worm *Echinococcus multilocularis* (Section 4.4) can cause human alveolar echinococcosis. Because this pathogen transfers readily between foxes and dogs, human risk is highest at the rural–urban contact zone, where people and dogs most frequently contact foxes or their droppings[124]. The bacterial infection ehrlichiosis, a tick-borne disease carried mainly by deer, has had outbreaks in several golf-oriented retirement communities that are surrounded by wildlife reserves[550]. In an unusual interaction with human behavior, poor golfers who report high golf scores are most likely to contract the infection, probably due to their need to retrieve balls from vegetated areas.

In the urban core itself, and in the highly built and managed suburbs, people often have little contact with animals or soil. The high prevalence of certain disorders of the immune system, like atopic dermatitis and multiple sclerosis, have been correlated with

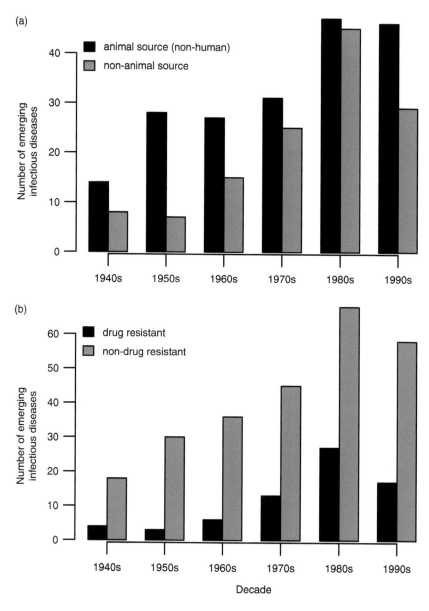

Figure 5.5 Percentage of emerging diseases comparing (a) animal and non-animal sources and (b) drug resistant and non-drug resistant sources (after Jones *et al.*, 2008).

too little exposure to soil and common pathogens. The *hygiene hypothesis* proposes that people need contact with soil and its resident population of micro-organisms in order to properly train the immune system not to attack the body itself[597] (Figure 5.6). Children on farms have lower rates of asthma, as do children exposed to more indoor bacteria, perhaps through modulating the immune system or when innocuous bacteria provide protection from harmful bacteria[143]. In Finland, *atopy* rates are lower in people

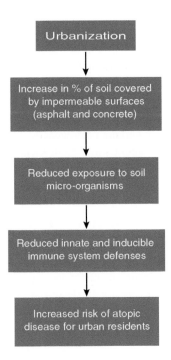

Figure 5.6 Possible chain of effects leading from urban habitat change to increased risk of atopic disease (after von Hertzen and Haahtela, 2006).

with more vegetation within 3.0 km of their homes[244]. More specifically, low diversity of flowering plants and of a particular group of bacteria on the skin, the gammaproteobacteria, predict more atopy. As evidence of the mechanism, gammaproteobacteria are ecologically associated with flowering plants and immunologically associated with specific mechanisms of immune regulation.

Humans are social animals, yet for many people, cities provide an excess of social interaction. Crowding can cause stress[152] and creates the conditions for many secondary effects. Prevalence of gonorrhea, a sexually transmitted pathogen, can be twice as high in urban areas[327]. Levels of violent crime are similarly elevated in urban areas. In addition to the direct effects of violence, exposure to violence in the home can play as large a role as exposure to antigens in promoting asthma, perhaps due to the effects of chronic stress on the immune system[71].

Excessive crowding, and perhaps more importantly, a social environment that fails to make sense to urban residents, create the conditions for pathologies ranging from mental illness to violence. Several studies, although not all, have found higher rates of mental illness in urban than in non-urban areas. Both mild and severe psychosis are more common in the urban areas of northern Europe, but not in the United States or the United Kingdom[585]. Growing up in a more urbanized environment can be associated with schizophrenia, and moving to an urban environment later in life can increase the risk of this mental illness[442].

One clue to the mechanism behind these problems is that minorities and unmarried singles are particularly susceptible when the groups they belong to are relatively rare in a given neighborhood[311]. Finding oneself out of place among strangers with whom one has little in common constitutes the *social isolation* that can lead to mental illness. Violence also tends to be higher in cities with more income inequality[186].

The broader concept of *social disorganization*, characterized by residential instability, family disruption, and ethnic heterogeneity, can lead to violence[422]. Whether and how other urban animals might suffer from social isolation and disorganization remains to be seen.

Conclusions

The litany of ill effects of the urban environment on human health is long: HIV and other sexually transmitted diseases, drugs and alcohol, infant mortality, lead poisoning, asthma, failure to immunize, tuberculosis, pneumonia, suicide, and malnutrition[327]. Yet for most people, cities are not the death-traps they were during the era of rampant infectious disease.

Huge disparities in lifespan can exist within blocks of each other. The primary causes are neither the infectious diseases of the past, nor the drugs and violence that justly receive substantial attention, but instead more complex health conditions that result from the full range of urban environmental, aesthetic, and social challenges: asthma, cardiovascular disease, diabetes, and kidney disease[173]. Modern technology, when backed with enough financial resources, insulates many but not all urban residents from the detrimental health effects of deteriorating ecosystem services[328].

The physiological challenges of urban life, which in many ways resemble those faced by other urban animals, interact with the social challenges of high population density to create a distinctively urban set of health conditions. In animals, being subordinate often creates chronic stress. People in close proximity can experience the strongest sense of *relative deprivation*, exposure to others with far greater economic well-being than themselves. Relative deprivation can lead to more chronic stress than absolute deprivation, where all people find themselves in roughly the same situation[173].

Yet William Wordsworth, the English poet famous as a prophet of nature, could stand upon Westminster Bridge, in the heart of London, during the early morning of September 3, 1802, and be inspired to write a sonnet praising the beauty of London that begins

> Earth has not anything to show more fair:
> Dull would he be of soul who could pass by
> A sight so touching in its majesty.

Residents of the famous cities of the world, of Paris, New York, San Francisco, and Buenos Aires, can all testify to their stunning beauty coexisting alongside what can be the harshest ugliness. This strange and sharp juxtaposition provides the surface image of the many conjunctions that characterize the urban ecosystem: abundance and deprivation, simplicity and complexity, diversity and uniformity. We are only beginning to learn how the human mind and body respond to these contrasts, and how cities can be designed to enhance health.

5.2   Ecological principles and urban policy

Every action humans take in planning or using a city creates a chain of intended and unintended consequences. Whether specific policies effectively achieve their intended goals is the central challenge for urban planners. Will a new road reduce traffic congestion? Will a new stadium bring economic development to a declining neighborhood? In addition to the challenge of achieving intended goals, a wide range of unintended and often unexpected consequences haunt urban planners. A new road might spur new housing development and in fact increase traffic, or it might isolate a formerly vibrant neighborhood. A new stadium might support only seasonal industries and end up exporting wealth into other areas.

Because of the unique features of every city and every neighborhood, using past experience and computer models to anticipate unintended consequences remains as much an art as a science for urban planners. Furthermore, many urban consequences result less from planning than from unplanned human behavior. People choose where to live and where to leave, and where to drive, work, and play. Families decide whether to feed birds, and what to plant in their lawns and gardens. Although these choices generally follow predictable trends, unforeseen actions can have significant political, social, and ecological consequences.

This book has described and evaluated some of the unintended consequences of urban policy and human behavior for ecosystems, plants, and animals. The science of urban ecology remains in its infancy, and the complex changes created by human decisions remain difficult to predict[112]. This section provides examples, without attempting to be comprehensive, of how urban policy decisions affect ecosystem and community processes, and concludes with a discussion of the challenges and opportunities for ecological research in the urban environment.

Policies affecting urban habitats and ecosystems

Humans dominate the resource flows in and out of urban systems, and even subtle changes in building materials or planning can ripple through the whole urban ecosystem. The interconnection among the flows of water, energy, and resources mean that policies enacted to control one problem may indirectly solve, or worsen, other problems. The following examples illustrate how ecological principles help make sense of the unintended consequences of urban policy.

Urban habitats
Urban areas are defined by the quantity of built habitat, but evaluated as places to live as much for the green and blue open spaces that maintain urban ecosystem processes, support urban biodiversity, and enhance human health and well-being. Policy issues

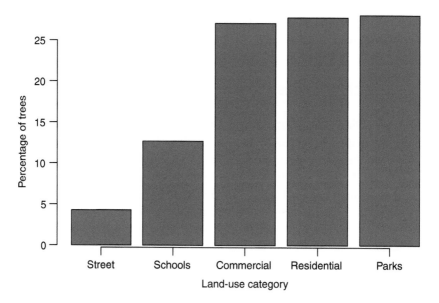

Figure 5.7 Percentage of trees by land-use category in Milwaukee, USA (after Heynen *et al.*, 2005).

range from protecting open space from development, managing that open space for human and ecological purposes, and restoring abandoned sites. Although some of the functions and benefits of urban green space have been established, effective ways to balance the planning and design challenges of ecology, politics, and economics remain, perhaps necessarily, a case-by-case problem[276].

Even evaluating the costs and benefits of the choice and management of urban trees is complex[433]. The varied ownership of the sites where trees live complicates all decision-making[255] (Figure 5.7). Attempting to balance the costs and benefits of urban trees requires accounting for many potentially conflicting effects[377] (Table 5.1). These elements depend on the size and the climate of the city, and the ratio of estimated benefits to costs varies greatly even among cities in the western United States[377] (Figure 5.8).

Policies must address the distribution of green space with respect to socio-economic status. Trees in Milwaukee are concentrated in areas with higher income and fewer Hispanics[255]. In Los Angeles, the park bond measure Proposition K attempted with mixed success to increase access to parks for all city residents[614]. However,

Table 5.1 Some of the costs and benefits of urban trees

Benefits	Costs
Aesthetic	Administration and inspection
Air quality improvement	Production of VOCs and allergens
Stormwater control	Irrigation
Temperature amelioration	Pruning, planting, and removal
Carbon dioxide sequestration	Infrastructure damage and liability

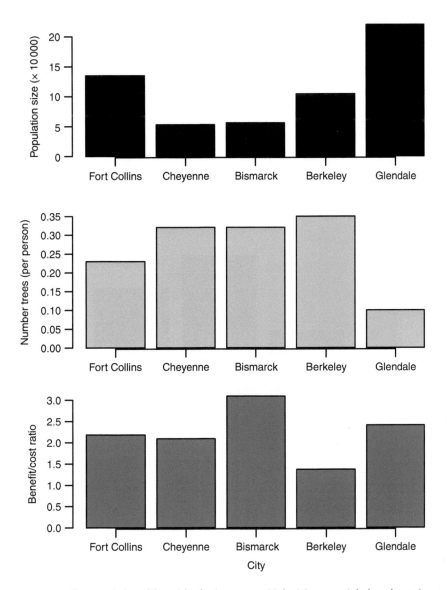

Figure 5.8 Characteristics of five cities in the western United States and their estimated costs and benefits of trees (after McPherson *et al.*, 2005).

neighborhoods with many children received fewer bond dollars per child while neighborhoods with better park access received more bonds. Population characteristics and access to parks still differ greatly, with non-white groups having higher density, more children, and many fewer park acres per person (Figure 5.9). Because people who do not visit green spaces as children are less likely to do so as adults, this inequity might have lifelong consequences[565]. In a surprising twist, fewer white residents of Los Angeles live close to parks, due to the sprawl created by low density wealthy neighborhoods along but not directly abutting the Santa Monica mountains[614].

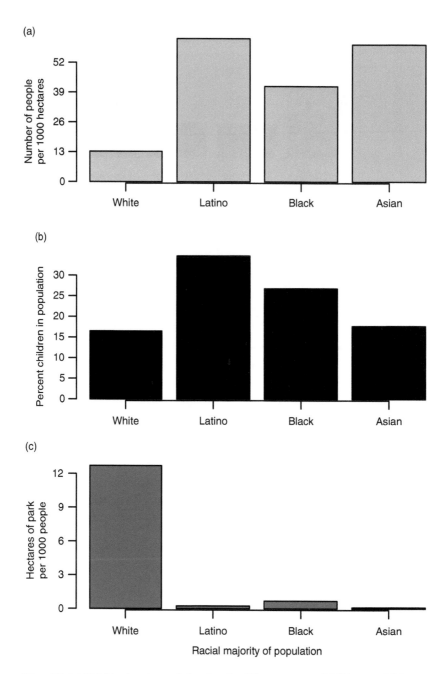

Figure 5.9 (a) Neighborhood population density, (b) percentage of children, and (c) access to parks in neighborhoods with different majority populations in Los Angeles (after Wolch *et al.*, 2005).

Although many parks preserve habitats that have been relatively unaffected by human modification, others are created through habitat restoration. The United Kingdom has a large urban regeneration program in Birmingham[132]. Eastside is an industrial area that currently has many abandoned sites, with planners looking to use this area to extend the downtown for learning, leisure, and heritage. Current habitats include abandoned buildings colonized by some birds and bats, and derelict open spaces of several types, along with managed parks dominated by grasslands and introduced woody plants. The abandoned sites often have higher plant and insect diversity than managed sites. To preserve this, planners have proposed such novel ideas as "brown" roofs to replace diverse brownfields as they are redeveloped, and reduction of mowing and management on more traditional green spaces.

The urban water cycle

Urban areas, with their large areas of impermeable surface, speed the movement of water, especially during and after storms. Rapid runoff reduces infiltration into the soil, carries accumulated nutrients and pollutants, and can overwhelm water export and cleaning capacity.

Ecologically based urban water policy takes four main directions.

- **Slowing the movement of water** requires decreasing impermeable surface area and increasing vegetation. Zoning plans can create more green space, through smaller housing lots connected by narrower roads and shorter driveways, or can explicitly include wetlands or ponds to retain the highest flows[30]. For example, King Farm, a transit-oriented development in suburban Maryland, uses higher housing density to decrease impermeable surface area and preserve sensitive riparian and wetland areas[30].

- **Removing pollutants within the urban environment** prevents downstream effects by capitalizing on the ability of vegetation, particularly forests and wetlands, to filter and denitrify water[407]. Direct intervention, such as more frequent and effective street cleaning, can remove pollutants before storms wash them downstream.

- **Improving treatment capacity** requires separating wastewater and stormwater sewer systems. Although standard in newer cities, many older cities can have their treatment systems overwhelmed when the runoff from large storms enters the combined system[168].

- **Reducing water usage** requires both more appropriate use of water to irrigate lawns and gardens[131] and more efficient use in homes and manufacturing.

Slowing peak flows can also improve stream health[44]. Biological integrity improves in streams surrounded by more vegetated riparian habitat and less impermeable surface area. The health of urban streams in Melbourne, Australia, was poor when the percentage of impermeable surface exceeded 10%, and policies that increase vegetation without reducing this percentage have little effect[601]. In and around Puget Sound, although the area of impermeable surface predicts low stream biodiversity, the number of road crossings provides an even better predictor. Crossings may concentrate disturbance,

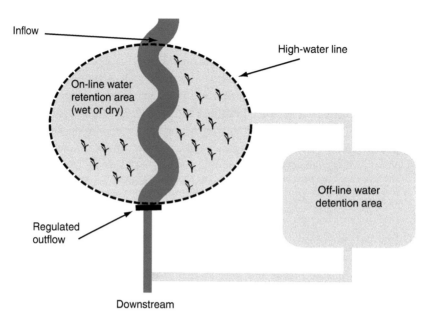

Inflow

High-water line

On-line water
retention area
(wet or dry)

Off-line water
detention area

Regulated
outflow

Downstream

Figure 5.10 The two kinds of retention pond.

pollutants, and sediments directly above and along the waterway[4], and provide an opportunity to develop new building approaches.

Flood control combines elements that accelerate water flow with methods for temporarily storing peak flows, often with *retention ponds*. Retention ponds come in two types: *on-line* or *off-line* (Figure 5.10). Although designed with the same purpose, these types have different hydrological and ecological consequences.

- **On-line** ponds impound river flow either continuously or during flooding episodes. These impoundments tend to increase water temperature and sediment deposition, can impede fish migration up or downstream, facilitate algal blooms, and may serve as points for introduction of non-native species.
- **Off-line** ponds fill during flooding episodes, then either gradually release water back into the stream system as water levels decline (detention), or allow water to gradually seep below the surface or evaporate (retention). Because they collect water only when needed, off-line ponds tend to produce fewer unintended consequences, but can warm water and support non-native species.

Urban climate
The urban heat island creates health challenges for humans, physiological stress on animals and plants, and enhances production of urban ozone. In a positive feedback, a 1°C temperature rise increases energy demand for cooling in the summer by as much as 2–4%[1]. Because paved surfaces again play the key role, many policies seek to alter or reduce pavement.

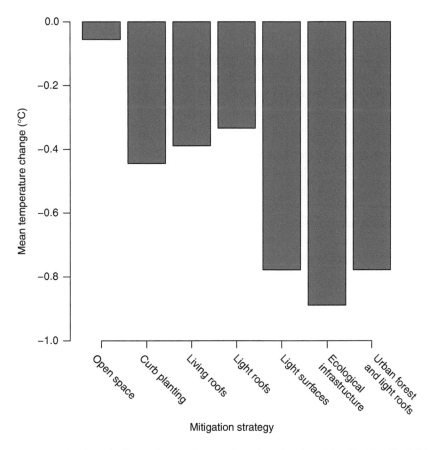

Figure 5.11 Projected effects of strategies to reduce the urban heat island in New York City (after Rosenzweig *et al.*, 2006). Ecological infrastructure includes urban forests and living roofs.

Nighttime minimum temperatures in densely urbanized New York City exceed non-urban temperatures by as much as 4.0°C[207]. Strategies to mitigate this effect include increasing vegetated area through urban forestry, increasing use of green roofs, and altering the heat absorbing properties of pavement with lighter colored materials. Trees can reduce temperatures through increased evapotranspiration and the resulting latent heat flux, but the cooling effects of turfgrass are localized to the area directly over the grass without cooling even adjacent walls[249].

Depending on location, different heat control methods have the potential to substantially reduce temperature, although even in combination far from enough to eliminate the urban heat island entirely (Figure 5.11). Building with light-colored materials may have the most potential due to the huge areas affected, especially in heavily built areas[612]. Curbside planting of trees may create additional benefits such as cleaning the air and reducing energy demand via shading[493], but, as we have seen, create their own set of challenges and tradeoffs (Table 5.1).

Urban nutrient dynamics

Each nutrient, whether carbon, nitrogen, or phosphorus, has different sources and effects on the ecosystem. To illustrate thinking about urban nutrient policy, this section focuses on nitrogen, the nutrient with the most complex biological cycle and one of the greatest degrees of human amplification[595].

Policies to reduce nitrogen flow parallel those designed for urban water: slowing inputs, controlling outputs, and enhancing recycling[30].

- **Reducing nitrogen imports** involves each anthropogenic source, particularly fertilizer, sewage, and fossil fuel emissions. Homeowners and other lawn managers can be educated to use less fertilizer. Encouraging public transit or walking can reduce emissions. Pollution control laws in the United States do not currently regulate vehicular emissions of ammonia, a substantial source of urban nitrogen and a potential target of future control.
- **Better wastewater treatment** ranges from adding levels of potentially expensive treatment to the ancient tradition of recycling human waste as agricultural fertilizer. For many large cities, however, agricultural fields are too few or too distant, and transporting large amounts of partially treated waste may pose disease risks.
- **Improved retention and denitrification** parallels approaches to reduce stormwater runoff through local collection, bioretention, and wetland and riparian zone restoration. However, a wetland's capacity to denitrify and absorb ammonium and nitrate can be overwhelmed by excessive nitrogen loading or when urbanization creates aerobic conditions. In these cases, wetlands can release undesirable forms of nitrogen such as volatile ammonia in addition to inert N_2 (Section 3.3). *Daylighting*, which brings previously buried streams back to the surface, can reduce channelization, slow water flow, and allow more area and time for denitrification in riparian zones[72]. Denitrification also releases nitrogen oxide into the atmosphere, which plays a role in the creation of ozone and acts as a potent greenhouse gas. In the face of a large problem like removal of excess nitrogen, no single solution is likely to suffice.

Urban soils, trees, and lawns have the potential to sequester substantial amounts of carbon dioxide. However, the energy used to mow, irrigate, and create fertilizer for these habitats may release enough carbon dioxide to balance sequestration, and to exceed it with heavy fertilizer use[572]. In addition, nitrous oxide releases alone may have sufficient global warming potential to exceed the carbon sequestration effects of lawns.

Urban pollution

Urban ecosystems, through the density of construction and the rates of water, material, and energy flows, are among the most intense ecosystems on Earth. The consequences stretch from amplifying natural processes of water, climate, and nutrients, to the addition of novel chemicals in the form of pollution. Controlling pollution involves reducing rates of material use or movement, capturing pollutants at their sources, or increasing recycling of polluted materials. Achieving these goals can be done either directly

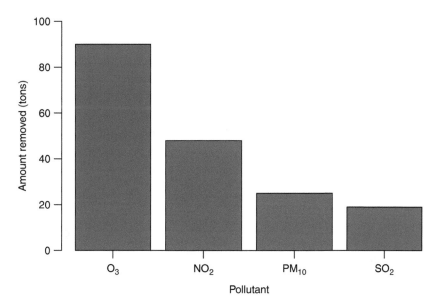

Figure 5.12 The components of pollution removed by 20 hectares of green roofs (after Yang *et al.*, 2008). The percentage of the total atmospheric pollution removed, however, is small.

through regulation, or through *cap and trade* systems that set an upper limit and allow individual producers to effectively pay for the right to pollute up to that limit. Such programs have been effective in reducing the sulfur dioxide implicated in acid rain[396] (Section 3.3).

Landfills for solid waste can be rethought not as places to dump unwanted outputs, but as places for recycling. In addition, landfills can perform other services. For example, rather than using large amounts of energy to treat waste byproducts, landfills can be put to alternative use to produce methane that replaces some of that imported energy.

Vegetation plays a key role in slowing the movement of water and capturing nitrogen as well as many other nutrients. Plants also capture pollutants. For example, 20 hectares of green roofs in Chicago, a dense metropolis with little open space for vegetation, removed 1675 kg of air pollutants in a single year (Figure 5.12). The roofs are most effective during the spring and summer growth season, including the hot and often polluted month of June[620], but still remove only a small fraction of the total pollution load (Figure 3.40). Lower particulate loads observed in some recreational areas[283] are due to a combination of removal by vegetation, fewer sources such as vehicles, or altered air movement.

Policies affecting population and community ecology

The majority of animals and plants that inhabit the urban environment attract little or no attention from humans. Most policies thus focus on the noticeable minority, either preserving desirable species or eliminating undesirable ones. These policies often produce indirect effects on less conspicuous species. How policies alter the more subtle functioning of individual organisms through their physiology, behavior, interactions, and evolution has only begun to receive attention from policy-makers[284].

Urban biodiversity

Habitat is the key to biodiversity. Habitable space in urban areas can be preserved, managed, or connected to promote target species. Gardens and yards can be managed to promote biodiversity, and particularly native biodiversity.

Biodiversity near homes can be actively encouraged through creation of habitats for specific target organisms. For example, native species of birds near Tucson, Arizona, prefer homes where gardens are planted with native vegetation[267]. In the moister climate of England, several methods for increasing biodiversity in yards have been tested, with varying degrees of success[204].

1. Creating artificial nests for solitary bees and wasps succeeded in recruiting more species.
2. Artificial nests specifically for bumblebees failed to attract these large and appealing bees.
3. The extensive labor required to create small ponds succeeded in enhancing biodiversity only if the desired organisms, such as frogs, can immigrate through the intervening matrix of habitat. The insects quickest to colonize these ponds, however, included the generally undesirable larvae of mosquitoes.
4. Allowing dead wood to accumulate might provide habitat for a variety of fungi, but few species appeared during the 2 years of the experiment.
5. Nettles such as *Urtica dioica* failed to attract butterflies.

Golf courses stand out among urban managed habitats for the large area they cover and their range of management plans[99]. An 18-hole course averages 54 hectares in area, of which approximately half is unplayable and thus potentially available to species other than grass and golfers. In comparison with nearby green areas, golf courses have higher species richness in a majority of cases, but primarily when the nearby habitat is itself highly disturbed (Figure 5.13). Even though golf courses often have high species richness, they cannot fully compensate for the effects of management because they generally lack urban avoiders that require undisturbed habitat.

Golf courses are just one part of the urban habitat mosaic, the diverse mixture of habitats that characterizes cities. The theory of island biogeography (Section 4.1) describes how habitat isolation and habitat size shape biodiversity. For a given quantity of habitat, its spatial distribution matters, with many widely distributed small patches being less effective in supporting a population than a small number of large closely spaced patches[112]. Corridors create connections of sufficiently conducive habitat to enable and encourage dispersal between these patches (Section 4.1). We have seen how Eastern long-necked turtles use suburban culverts as unintentionally designed corridors between patches of suitable habitat[474] (Section 4.5). In contrast, culverts were a significant barrier to upstream movements of caddisflies in Christchurch, New Zealand[36].

Highways act as dangerous barriers for many species. Near Los Angeles, underpasses and drainage culverts are used by coyotes, deer, raccoons, bobcats, rodents, and humans

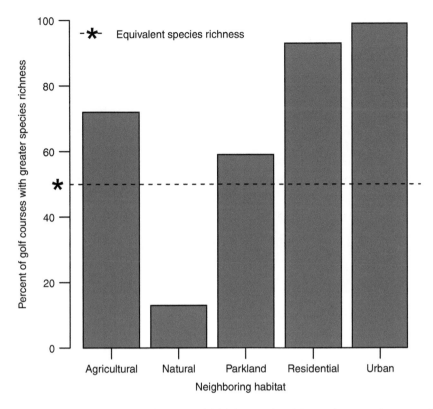

Figure 5.13 Percentage of golf courses with higher species richness than a nearby comparison habitat (after Colding and Folke, 2008).

as ways to cross[401]. The surrounding habitat plays a significant role in their use, with bobcats avoiding passages surrounded by development, and raccoons and coyotes favoring those surrounded by buildings.

For highly mobile species such as carabid beetles and butterflies, corridors are much less important than the quality of the habitat patches themselves[8]. Such corridors as abandoned railways, riverside greenways, and trails function more as additional habitat than as connections between other patches, but are often of relatively low quality[136]. Narrower, more heavily managed urban greenways surrounded by pavement or earth can have low species richness and abundance, particularly of sensitive forest species[360].

Green roofs create small patches of habitat, often distant from one another (Figure 5.14). Nonetheless, after 8 years, green roofs in London accumulated a variety of grassland plants and up to 54 species of invertebrates[223]. Establishing roofs with a thick layer of soil and gravel creates the drainage plants need to survive droughts, and contributes to a high diversity of beetles and spiders on roofs in Basel, Switzerland[56].

Invasive species

Some local governments regulate the import of potentially invasive plants, but most invasive species arrive both unregulated and uninvited. It is rarely possible to eliminate

Figure 5.14 Green roofs in Monte Carlo.

undesirable species. However, in small areas such as parks, intense and consistent methods of direct eradication can be effective. One-time and repeated removal of exotic plants in the forest understory of an urban park in Raleigh, North Carolina, reduced exotic species numbers compared with a control treatment of no removal[591]. In the longer term, native species richness failed to recover because the abundance of exotic seeds, both in the soil seed bank and falling from the sky, enabled non-native species to bounce back quickly after one-time removal. Only long-term studies can establish whether continual removal of exotic adult plants would allow native species to recover, or whether additional and more active restoration methods are necessary.

In more managed sites, such as lawns, homeowners have a choice of whether to use native or non-native plants, but must overcome the concern that native lawns will be browner and more subject to infestation by weeds. Bermudagrass *Cynodon dactylon* is classified as an invasive and noxious weed in some regions, but is popular as a lawn grass because it can tolerate trampling and may repel weeds[531]. However, in comparison with the native buffalograss *Bouteloua dactyloides* or mixtures of native plants, weed populations were higher in the bermudagrass monoculture.

Interactions and diseases

With studies of urban species richness only beginning, and still tending to focus on one or a few species[198], our understanding of how policies can alter species interactions remains limited. Many restoration projects focus on plants that are relatively easy to acquire and introduce into desired locations. In the coastal sage scrub of California, restoration has succeeded in rebuilding a vegetation community like that of nearby non-urban sites. However, even after many years, arthropods in the area have not recovered, with fewer native scavengers and predators. Although most of the exotic plants have been removed, exotic arthropods, such as the Argentine ant and the European earwig, have remained abundant and continue to alter the structure of the community[336].

Urban environments concentrate animals and bring them in close contact with humans and pets that can be both sources and targets of disease. Human encroachment shrinks wildlife habitat and increases wildlife density and contact rates with humans and pets[116], such as plague-infested prairie dogs, creating the policy dilemma of either controlling rapidly spreading human communities or relocating prairie dogs at great danger and expense[117] (Section 4.4).

Conversely, pet diseases can spill over to endanger wild animals either in, near, or far downstream of urban areas. The toxoplasmosis that plays a role in slowing growth of sea otter populations in California (Section 4.4) is likely spread by cat feces that have been deposited outside or discarded via flushable or compostable kitty litter. For cat owners, this creates a conflict between different goals. Compostable litter reduces waste disposal needs and the cat's ecological footprint, but might promote the spread of disease[102].

Traits of urban organisms

Urban ecological policy rarely has the luxury of addressing issues more subtle than the presence and survival of desirable animals[284]. The extremely popular activity of bird feeding, in combination with climate change, has contributed to changes in migratory behavior (Section 4.5). These factors have sufficiently reduced gene flow between migratory and non-migratory populations of the blackcap to initiate the first steps of speciation[489] (Section 4.6). Should people adjust their own behavior, and wait to fill feeders until the migratory birds have left for the winter, and thus provide supplements only for winter residents? Some ornithological organizations used to recommend waiting to fill feeders until the migrants had left so as not to induce them to remain in what were thought to be unsuitable conditions, but these organizations usually no longer do so.

Many birds seem able to adjust quickly to urban winters. In other cases, the novelty of urban environments can exceed a species' ability to adjust appropriately, potentially creating an ecological trap. For example, pierid butterflies lay eggs on the invasive garlic mustard plant, although it cannot support maturation of larvae. One proposed policy creates refuges for native species that are sufficiently protected to maintain the population, but sufficiently novel to allow adaptation to the new environment[509].

The physiological challenges that urban environments pose for human beings, in the forms of physical and psychological health, have been the subject of much debate and study. Urban planning initially began to slow the spread of infectious diseases (Section 5.1). Today's planners face the task of addressing new health problems faced by urban residents, such as autoimmune disease, obesity, and mental illness. These complex issues lie well beyond the scope of this book, but the challenges of testing whether improvements can be attributed to a specific policy, evaluating positive and negative effects, and observing unintended consequences closely parallel those of evaluating other urban ecological policies[569].

Science in the urban environment

Ecologists have long sought to work in undisturbed ecosystems, due not only to the insights they provide into the long-term dynamics of communities, but also to the logistic convenience of working in field sites with established ownership and protocols for doing research. Urban areas, in contrast, necessarily involve a complex mosaic of land use and habitat types, and thus a complex mix of ownership and access that scientists must navigate. Many of the results examined in this book come from *observational* or *uncontrolled studies*, where scientists capitalize on existing variation. Approaches include[558]

- use of urban-rural gradients,
- studying biodiversity within patches using the framework of island biogeography,
- studying the dynamics of patches themselves, including ecological succession and the dynamics of matrix habitats,
- comparing the responses of natives and exotics,
- studies of ecosystem function such as nutrient cycling.

Although observational studies provide the foundation for any new science, they cannot control for other variables, or correlated effects, in the way that controlled experiments can.

Scientific experiments are designed to ask specific questions under controlled conditions with enough samples and measurements to establish cause and effect (Figure 5.15). Controlled experiments at a small scale are possible (such as the study of ragweed[628] in Section 4.5), but larger scale studies remain difficult and uncommon.

Urban planners also experiment with different approaches to achieve their goals, but can almost never achieve the level of control or replication that scientists seek.

Weaknesses	Approach	Strengths
Correlative, little control of confounding variables	Urban-rural gradients	Non-manipulative, easy to find
Poor control	Social interventions	Comprehensive
Limited to fine-scale processes	Fine-scale experiments	Rigorous and inconspicuous
Correlative, little control of confounding variables	Temporal analysis	Non-manipulative, easy to find
Difficult to implement, collaboration and funding	Designed experiments	Rigorous, replicated, and educational value

Figure 5.15 Comparison of different approaches to urban ecological experiments (after Felson and Pickett, 2005).

Both scientists and planners must work around financial and logistic constraints, and both must be increasingly prepared to broaden their view to include the whole range of effects of humans on ecosystems. The final challenge of urban policy is then to find ways to acquire the information needed to better understand urban ecology, the chains of unintended consequences, and the implications of decision-making. The interaction between science and planning creates what has been characterized as a "wicked problem," one that is hard to formulate and where the study itself necessarily changes the subject of study[200].

Unlike natural areas, where experimental manipulation acts as a form of unfamiliar human disturbance, urban environments are constantly being manipulated and disturbed at all scales, from the individual yard to entire watersheds. Cooperating with these existing uncontrolled "experiments" provides an opportunity for more *designed experiments* that incorporate scientific principles of control and interpretation into design plans that are already under way. In some cases, direct comparisons can be made between controlled pairs of communities, such as ones set up in Jordan Cove in Waterford, Connecticut[164]. The control community follows ordinary design principles, with widely spaced lots, storm sewers, and wide streets paved with impermeable materials and bordered by curbs to channel water. The experimental community has low impact development with more concentrated housing, gardens to absorb stormwater, and narrower streets with porous surfaces and no curbs. These designs allow absorption of some rainwater, while the rest runs off onto grassy areas along roadsides.

Following up with a concerted monitoring program is the next crucial step[83]. Although many cities have developed daylighting programs, few have collected the data needed to evaluate the ecological, economic, and health benefits of these changes[63]. In Jordan Cove, subsequent measurements have shown that water movement has indeed been slowed and peak flows reduced[266] (Figure 5.16). The building process itself provides a form of control, as the amount of impermeable area increases over time. In the control development, runoff, nitrogen, and phosphorus outputs all increased quickly during building, with no such increases observed in the low impact development[128].

Involvement of a wide range of people in the community, from planners and developers to residents, is essential to create effective scientific studies in urban areas. In some cases, people can even be involved in the collection of data[558]. Bird-feeding is a worldwide experiment and a worldwide research opportunity[287]. Project FeederWatch, run by the Cornell Laboratory of Ornithology, involves *citizen scientists* who collect data on the birds they see, which can be integrated into maps of distribution and behavior of birds that incorporate far more data than an individual researcher or ordinary research team could hope to collect. Of course, the quality of data collected by many people with different levels of experience and motivation can differ greatly, creating another set of challenges that few scientists are trained to handle.

Conclusions

Disturbed natural areas often encourage us to envision restoring nature to a pre-human state, although all that can be realistically achieved might be managing the extent of human effects. Urban ecological policy faces no such internal contradiction. Planners

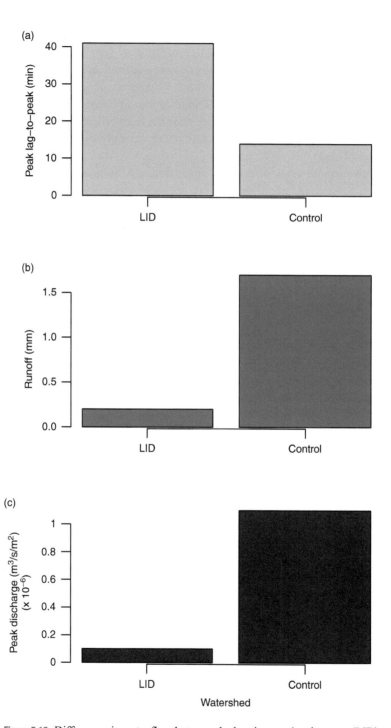

Figure 5.16 Differences in water flow between the low impact development (LID) and control development at Jordan Cove (after Hood *et al.*, 2007), showing (a) the delay between a rainfall event and the peak in runoff, (b) the total runoff after a rainfall event, and (c) the maximum rate of water flow after a rainfall event.

must confront the decision of what people want the urban environment to be, and how humans interface with the other living beings who share it. The human species faces the challenge of balancing its needs with those of other organisms, and seeking solutions that ideally benefit both.

Natural areas in urban environments remain in several forms, as relicts that have escaped development, managed sites such as parks and golf courses, and spontaneous resurgences in abandoned and unmanaged corners of the landscape[623]. How people perceive these different habitats affects how they treat them. Some might see land awaiting development, while others see patches of wilderness in the city that provide ecological, psychological, and economic benefits that should be protected. The most successful urban policies might take a cue from natural systems where different habitats abut, and emphasize that different uses, such as recreation, education, and shopping, should not be segregated, no more than people of different ages, social classes, and ethnic groups[5]. Cross-connections between people and purposes can create a more vibrant city for people and other urban organisms, particularly when green spaces integrate with buildings and architecture[540].

Can urban policies decrease the urban ecological footprint? In 1979, the city of Portland, Oregon, established an urban growth boundary. Little development was permitted outside the boundary, with denser and mixed-use development encouraged within, the approach referred to among urban policy scholars as urban intensification or the *compact cities* movement. To decrease vehicular traffic, the city developed a light rail system and nonmotorized transport rights-of-way. Such a policy, coupled with low impact development, green roofs, and other approaches to slow the urban metabolism, may halt the resource use and footprint expansion associated with urban sprawl. But did it work? As always, confounding factors make it difficult to evaluate. The density of dwellings within the boundary did indeed increase, as did pedestrian access and connectivity among different elements[541]. The effects on ecological processes and the economic decisions that drive them, however, have yet to be fully evaluated.

This section provides only a few examples of how ecological thinking can inform policy-making. Vast expertise has been applied to balance the ecological, economic, and human functions of cities. The more voices involved in making decisions, including those of scientists familiar with the complex chains of unintended consequences that characterize urban ecology, the better that planning will be.

5.3   Cities and the future

During the twentieth century, humans became vastly more effective in marshaling energy and resources for their own needs. Simultaneously, people and their needs became concentrated in cities. The early twenty-first century has marked a milestone in human history, with the majority of people occupying urban areas for the first time. These trends have created the conditions for the themes of this book.

- The built environment consists of a wide range of *modified habitats.*
- Concentration of energy and resource-demanding humans in urban areas requires enormous *inputs* and *outputs* of materials and nutrients.

- Habitat modification and increased inputs and outputs create chains of *intended and unintended consequences* for the urban ecosystem and the plants and animals that occupy them.

What will Earth be like in 2100? The specific implications of these themes in today's cities provide the best guess we have. The cities of today have

- elevated temperatures and altered rainfall patterns,
- accelerated water movement,
- increased levels of carbon dioxide, nitrogen, and other nutrients,
- land fragmented into diverse human-altered habitats,
- numerous extralimital native and exotic species,
- changed community structure and simplified trophic interactions,
- characteristic sets of traits of surviving urban organisms, and
- species and individuals rapidly adapting to novel circumstances.

These effects already reach well beyond the urban boundary and draw the entire Earth into the ecological orbit of cities. As this influence continues to spread over the next century, much of the planet will be warmer, nutrient-enriched, directly modified by humans, and biologically and functionally homogenized.

Loss of species is among the most prominent of today's ecological concerns. The following factors have been identified as those most likely to affect global biodiversity over the next century[501]:

- land-use change,
- climate change,
- nitrogen deposition,
- biotic exchange,
- increased carbon dioxide.

These effects are precisely those focused in urban habitats. Urban environments again provide a window into the future of our planet and which species will succeed in a changing world.

Urban growth will surely continue for at least some decades. Growing cities will require more land area, and the physical extent of cities will also continue to increase. Humans and human institutions will continue to adapt to this still relatively new environment. Plants and animals, increasingly unable to avoid urban challenges, will either disappear, physiologically adapt, or evolve. Cities will drive a nearly unprecedented burst of biological change, ranging from extinction to speciation.

For their human residents, cities of the future may well be more heterogeneous than they are today. The differences between wealthy and impoverished areas might be accentuated, along with consequent local environmental differences in the urban heat island, biodiversity, and disease spread. How these local effects will develop and scale up to entire cities plays a huge and unknown role in the future of cities.

Although natural scientists and early ecologists predicted urban ecology would be a vital part of global ecology, the ecological processes operating in cities have been largely overlooked until recently[624]. Scientific study of the urban ecosystem has exploded recently, and indeed grown more rapidly than urban areas themselves. Long-term studies initiated in the 1990s will acquire the perspective of decades of change. Ecological theory and thinking will be extended to make sense of new observations and results. New conceptual frameworks that include human behavior and institutions within the broader interdisciplinary science, the "ecology of cities," will become established new fields[226,445]. Ideally, policy will be integrated with scientific data, and scientific data will be collected in concert with policy decisions.

Whether new technologies will change the course of current ecological trends, such as climate change, nutrient loading, and biodiversity loss, is impossible to predict. Methods for efficiently absorbing or sequestering carbon dioxide, new energy sources, new materials, and genetic engineering could transform some ecological processes. The rise of the internet and modern communications has encouraged people to live in a virtual world, communicating over long distances apparently free from the limitations of nature. But even as technology continues to advance, the food that we eat, the air we breathe, and the power for our machines will still come from the physical world.

Virtual reality notwithstanding, the perception that the human enterprise faces limits set by ecological systems will become more widespread. This consciousness, we hope, will be complemented by increased awareness of the urban ecosystem that confronts people when they go outdoors. The changes in that ecosystem and the way that we interact with it may require us to rethink who we are, the way that we live, and what nature itself is.

How cities and our perception of cities develop and change will determine which metaphor will be most powerful in shaping our view (Chapter 2).

- Efficient and livable cities could be increasingly seen as *superorganisms*, with parts working together for a common set of goals.
- Integration of ecosystem processes within an urban area might make cities seem more like *ecological communities*, persisting via links between different processes and organisms.
- Separation of urban needs from the areas that support them could make cities seem ever more like *parasites* that must accept or ignore the damage they cause in order to survive.
- Uncontrollable urban growth and development could make cities seem like *cancers*, deadly outgrowths of the human need to reproduce, consume, and innovate.
- That cities face an ever-changing set of problems that can be diagnosed and treated, allows us to think of them as *patients*.

The metaphor we choose, whether one of these or some other, is not an inevitable consequence of urban development. Instead, the metaphor will frame how cities are imagined and play a key if often unconscious role in shaping urban policy.

In 2100, a seed from a tree will germinate in the heart of one of the world's great cities, dropped perhaps by a tree that itself germinated nearby in the very different world of a century earlier. Water will awaken it. Nitrogen will fertilize it. Light and carbon dioxide will give it energy. Insects and pathogens will attack it. The novel world of new materials, exotic species, altered atmosphere, and passing people and vehicles will stress and disturb it. Understanding how that tree and the community of plants and animals that surround it will respond to these factors emerges directly from our understanding of urban ecology today. If indeed the principles of ecology apply in urban areas and continue to apply in the future, the developing science sketched in this book will be the foundation for making sense of the new environments being created today and the future of the entire planet.

5.4   Questions and readings

Discussion questions

For Section 5.1

1. How are the physiological effects of urbanization the same, and how are they different, for humans compared to other animals that inhabit cities? How do humans compensate differently from other animals?

2. If humans feel better looking at trees rather than bricks, why are there so many more views of bricks than trees in urban environments? Do all aspects of the built environment trigger such a negative response?

3. How do sociological and ecological factors play a role in your answer to Question 2? Overall, are the links between sociological and ecological factors in urban habitats qualitatively and/or quantitatively different than non-urban habitats? Why?

4. What are the health costs and benefits of outdoor exercise in cities? How could you evaluate different types of exercise?

5. Historically, why did urban areas have such a high incidence of disease and mortality? What factors in cities changed this trend? In what way are urban areas again becoming hotspots for disease?

For Section 5.2

1. Much of this book has been about intended versus unintended consequences relating to the process of converting ecosystems to urban ecosystems. Make a list of 12 things unique to urban ecosystems. For each item, what was its intended purpose, and name at least one unintended effect.

2. What aspects of a city draw non-urban humans to immigrate, and what aspects of a city lead them to emigrate? What roles do sociological and ecological factors play in each case?

3. Considering your answer to Question 2, how could urban planning be modified to make cities more hospitable? Come up with 10 specific policies (including material from throughout the book) that would be consistent with your thinking. How would these ideas make cities more hospitable, and would they be more hospitable for other organisms as well as humans? For each idea, write down one possible unintended consequence.

4. What difficulties do urban planners and policy-makers experience that are not as problematic in less urbanized ecosystems? Are there any advantages to planning and policy in urbanized areas? Think of your answers to both of these questions in local versus global terms. Are there any inconsistencies?

5. Why have ecologists historically been interested in studying undisturbed habitats? How, and why, is this changing? What kinds of ecological studies would be most useful for urban planning? Based on the examples in this book, are these the kinds of studies that are being done?

6. What difficulties exist in integrating urban ecological studies with urban planning? How can these difficulties be overcome?

For Section 5.3

1. What aspects of urban ecology are of the greatest concern over the next decade? What related issues must be included to address this issue? Although these links are common throughout ecological studies, why are they often most unavoidable in urban ecology?

2. How would your answers to Question 1 differ for concerns over the next century instead of decade?

3. Historically, why has ecology been considered a non-urban field of study? Should ecologists switch their efforts to study solely highly disturbed and urban sites? Is there any value in seeking out and studying relatively pristine sites?

4. How would an ecological focus on the urban environment change people's perspectives regarding where they live, what organisms also live there, where their food and energy come from, and where it goes? What effects would this have locally, and globally?

5. The answers to Question 4 were no doubt positive, but now, how could you begin to effect this change in perspective? For example, does awareness alone lead to change in human behavior?

6. What do you think cities and planet Earth will look like in 100 years? Are the global ecological concerns regarding climate change and loss of biodiversity overblown, inevitable, or destined to be overcome by human ingenuity?

7. If a time-traveling ecologist arrived from 100 years in the future, what is the first scientific question you would ask her?

Exercises

For Section 5.1

1. Until relatively recently, cities were population sinks for humans, and were supported by immigration.

   (a) Suppose a population of people increases by 5% per year by reproduction but decreases by 10% due to mortality from infectious disease. How quickly would it decline? How many years would it take for a population of 1.0×10^6 to be reduced by half?

(b) Under these same circumstances, suppose that 2000 people per year immigrate into the city from nearby rural areas. What would happen to the population of a city that starts with 1.0×10^6 people? Would it grow or decline? What about a city with with 1.0×10^5 people?

(c) If public health programs reduced the mortality probability to 5%, what would happen to the population of this city?

(d) If public health programs reduced the mortality probability to 2%, the city would grow even without immigration. How much difference would immigration make if the city started with 1.0×10^5 people?

2. Both the number and specific locations of parks determines how far people must travel to get to them. For simplicity, suppose that a city is laid out on a perfect grid, with streets 0.1 km apart and parks placed as shown. The rest of the area is filled with housing.

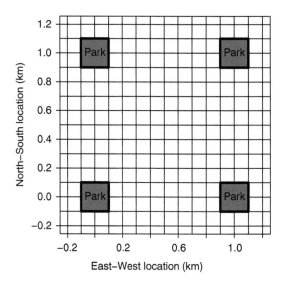

(a) What is the maximum distance a person lives from a park?

(b) What fraction of people would live within 300 m of a park?

(c) According to the data in Figure 5.1, how often would the average person visit a park?

(d) The parks shown take up four city blocks. What would be the effect on distances if there were four times as many parks of just one city block each? How would you best position them? How would you evaluate whether this was a better approach?

3. In Osaka, Japan, the number of heat stroke patients H requiring an ambulance is determined by the daily maximum air temperature T approximately according to[522]:

$$H = \begin{cases} 0 & \text{if} \quad T < 30 \\ T - 30 & \text{if} \quad T > 30 \end{cases}$$

Assume that the fraction of days with maximum temperature in the following ranges is

Temperature range (°C)	Fraction of days
26–28	0.08
28–30	0.05
30–32	0.02
32–34	0.01
34–36	0.005
36–38	0.002
38–40	0.001
> 40	0.0005

(a) How many heat stroke patients would you expect to get in a year of 365 days? What assumptions did you have to make?
(b) How much would this increase if the temperature moved up by 2°C? Did you have to make any additional assumptions?
(c) How much would this increase if the temperature moved up by 4°C?

For Section 5.2

1. The values for the costs and benefits of urban trees in five cities in the western United States are[377]:

Statistic	Fort Collins	Cheyenne	Bismarck	Berkeley	Glendale
Population	135 000	53 011	56 234	104 000	220 000
Area (sq mi)	49.4	22.9	27.5	18.1	59.0
Street trees	16 409	8 907	17 821	30 779	13 184
Park trees	14 534	8 103	0	5 706	8 297
Benefits	2 170 799	688 029	979 094	3 247 545	665 856
Costs	997 638	327 897	316 640	2 372 000	276 436

Costs and benefits are given in dollars.

(a) Convert the units from square miles to hectares.
(b) Find the number of people and trees per hectare in each city.
(c) How does the cost and benefits per tree differ among the cities? How about costs and benefits per person?
(d) Look at the original paper to examine the components of the costs and benefits. Do any stand out?

2. Consider the layout of parks in Section 5.1, Exercise 2.

   (a) Where would you add corridors to connect them? How long are your corridors?

   (b) For different widths of corridors, how much area would they take up? How does this area compare with the area of the parks themselves?

   (c) How would your corridors change the distance that people live from public green space?

   (d) What problems would this corridor placement create?

3. Suppose that housing density averages 20 houses per hectare.

   (a) If the city were on a grid like that in Section 5.1, Exercise 2, how would you lay out houses, parks, and roads to minimize the amount of impermeable surface? How wide are your roads? How large are your yards?

   (b) Look at the road designs for Jordan Cove[266]. Would these help in reducing the impermeable surface area? Is it possible to get below the 10% figure above which water movement changes significantly?[528]

Further Reading

For Section 5.1

- Byrd, R. S. and Joad, J. P. Urban asthma. *Current Opinion in Pulmonary Medicine*, **12** (2006), 68–74.
- Evans, G. W. The built environment and mental health. *Journal of Urban Health*, **80** (2003), 536–555.
- Fleischman, A. R. and Barondess, J. A. Urban health: a look out our windows. *Academic Medicine*, **79** (2004), 1130–1132.
- Frumkin, H. F. Urban sprawl and public health. *Public Health Reports*, **120** (2002), 201–217.
- Galea, S. and Vlahov, D. Urban health: evidence, challenges, and directions. *Annual Review of Public Health*, **26** (2005), 341–365.
- Godfrey, R. and Julien, M. Urbanisation and health. *Clinical Medicine*, **5** (2005), 137–141.
- Guite, H. F., Clark, C., and Ackrill, G. The impact of the physical and urban environment on mental well-being. *Public Health*, **120** (2006), 1117–1126.
- Kaplan, S. The restorative benefits of nature: toward an integrative framework. *Journal of Environmental Psychology*, **15** (1995), 169–182.
- Liu, G. C., Wilson, J. S., Qi, R., and Ying, J. Green neighborhoods, food retail and childhood overweight: differences by population density. *American Journal of Health Promotion*, **21** (2007), 317–325.
- Mitchell, R. and Popham, F. Effect of exposure to natural environment on health inequalities: an observational population study. *Lancet*, **372** (2008), 1655–1660.
- Peen, J. and Dekker, J. Is urbanicity an environmental risk-factor for psychiatric disorders? *Lancet*, **363** (2004), 2012–2013.

- Tzoulas, K., Korpela, K., Venn, S., *et al.* Promoting ecosystem and human health in urban areas using Green Infrastructure: a literature review. *Landscape and Urban Planning*, **81** (2007), 167–178.

For Section 5.2

- Akbari, H., Pomerantz, M., and Taha, H. Cool surfaces and shade trees to reduce energy use and improve air quality in urban areas. *Solar Energy*, **70** (2001), 295–310.
- Alberti, M., Booth, D., Hill, K., *et al.* The impact of urban patterns on aquatic ecosystems: an empirical analysis in Puget lowland sub-basins. *Landscape and Urban Planning*, **80** (2007), 345–361.
- Bernhardt, E., Band, L., Walsh, C., and Berke, P. Understanding, managing, and minimizing urban impacts on surface water nitrogen loading. *Annals of the New York Academy of Sciences*, **1134** (2008), 61–96.
- Donovan, R., Sadler, J., and Bryson, J. Urban biodiversity and sustainable development. *Engineering Sustainability*, **158** (2005), 105–114.
- Felson, A. and Pickett, S. Designed experiments: new approaches to studying urban ecosystems. *Frontiers in Ecology and the Environment*, **3** (2005), 549–556.
- Jones, D. and Reynolds, S. J. Feeding birds in our towns and cities: a global research opportunity. *Journal of Avian Biology*, **39** (2008), 265–271.
- Mason, J., Moorman, C., Hess, G., and Sinclair, K. Designing suburban greenways to provide habitat for forest-breeding birds. *Landscape and Urban Planning*, **80** (2007), 153–164.
- McPherson, G., Simpson, J. R., Peper, P. J., Maco, S. E., and Xiao, Q. Municipal forest benefits and costs in five US cities. *Journal of Forestry*, **103** (2005), 411–416.
- Rosenzweig, C., Solecki, W. D., Parshall, L., *et al.* Mitigating New York City's heat island: integrating stakeholder perspectives and scientific evaluation. *Bulletin of the American Meteorological Society*, **90** (2009), 1297–1312.
- Wolch, J., Wilson, J. P., and Fehrenbach, J. Parks and park funding in Los Angeles: an equity-mapping analysis. *Urban Geography*, **26** (2005), 4–35.
- Yang, J., Yu, Q., and Gong, P. Quantifying air pollution removal by green roofs in Chicago. *Atmospheric Environment*, **42** (2008), 7266–7273.

For Section 5.3

- Grimm, N. B., Faeth, S. H., Golubiewski, N. E., *et al.* Global change and the ecology of cities. *Science*, **319** (2008), 756–761.
- Pickett, S. T. A., Cadenasso, M. L., Grove, J. M., *et al.* Beyond urban legends: an emerging framework of urban ecology, as illustrated by the Baltimore ecosystem study. *Bioscience*, **58** (2008), 139–150.
- Sala, O. E., Chapin III, F., Armesto, J., A., *et al.* Global biodiversity scenarios for the year 2100. *Science*, **287** (2000), 1770–1774.

Labs

A. In the city where you live or a nearby city, develop a sampling protocol to record the number of trees planted along streets, at schools, on commercial properties, on residential properties, and in parks. How do these values compare with those of Milwaukee, Wisconsin (Figure 5.7)? Use these data to estimate the number of trees per person in this city. How does this value compare with other cities of similar and different sizes (Figure 5.8)? Who makes planning decisions about trees in your city, and what criteria are used?

B. Using Google Earth, develop a sampling protocol to determine the amount of park or green space within 1 km^2 samples. Find the average price of homes for sale in each sample, and determine if there is a correlation between property value and the number of parks in your city.

C. Find a water retention site in your city, and sample water from upstream and downstream of it. Compare characteristics such as temperature, oxygen levels, nutrient levels, toxins, or other contaminants, and organisms present in your samples. Record the plant abundance and diversity near the retention site and compare it with an urban park and a non-urban green space. Is the retention pond creating ecological services or disservices besides modification of water flow?

Glossary

Abiotic: the non-living components of an ecosystem, such as solar radiation, water, and nutrients.

Abundance: the number of members of a species present in an ecosystem. Relative abundance is the proportion of that species.

Adaptation: the evolutionary process by which a species becomes better suited to the environment via natural selection.

Adaptive: an appropriate response to the environment that improves the fitness of an organism.

Aerosol: the suspension of small solid or liquid particles in a gas, such as water, pollen, or smoke.

Albedo: the percentage of radiation, such as solar energy, that an object reflects. Albedo ranges from 0 (a black surface that absorbs 100% of the radiation it receives) to 1 (a white surface that reflects 100% of the radiation it receives).

Anaerobic: without oxygen, such as an environment where oxygen is not present, or an organism that lives without oxygen.

Annual plants: plants that germinate, grow, flower, produce seeds, and die in a single season.

Aquatic habitat: an ecosystem within a body of water.

Aquifer: an underground layer of permeable rock or sand from which groundwater can be extracted.

Archaeophyte: a non-native plant species that was introduced to a region long ago, generally before 1500 A.D.

Atopy: condition of being susceptible to allergic reactions including skin rashes, hay fever, and asthma.

Autotroph: an organism that can fix organic carbon from inorganic compounds using light or chemical energy.

Behavioral ecology: the study of the relationship between an organism's actions and its ability to persist in its environment.

Biodiversity: the number or variability of species present in a habitat or ecosystem.

Biodiversity land: component of some ecological footprint measures to represent land needed to maintain native biodiversity.

Biogeochemical cycles: biological, geological, and chemical process by which substances or elements move among the biotic and physical reservoirs on Earth.

Biological invasion: the introduction, establishment, and subsequent ecological effects of a non-native organism that becomes common, usually to the detriment of native species.

Biomass: the amount, or mass, of living organisms within a habitat or ecosystem at any time.

Biotic environment: the living things that share and shape a habitat.

Biotic homogenization: the process by which the types of living organisms in different regions become similar via the introduction and establishment of non-native species.

Biotic resistance: the capacity of an ecosystem to deter invasion by non-native species.

Bottom-up control: the regulation of population by competition for resources.

Brood parasite: animals, often birds, that use other individuals of their own or different species to raise their offspring.

Brownfield: abandoned industrial or commercial site.

Building-barrier effect: process by which the vertical structure of the built environment reduces or redirects synoptic wind and weather patterns.

Built environment: human-made surroundings or infrastructure.

Cap and trade: economic incentive to control pollution by setting a total emission limit and allowing sale and resale of discharge permits.

Carbohydrate: an organic compound comprised of the elements carbon, oxygen, and hydrogen, such as sugars and cellulose, that store energy and form structures.

Central place foraging: a behavior where an organism returns to a particular place, such as a nest, to consume, store, or distribute food it collects.

Circulation cell: movement of air in a cyclic pattern due to thermal energy, in which warm air rises and is replaced with cooler air. The rising air cools, spreads out, descends, and replaces the cool air, completing the cycle.

Citizen science: large-scale collection of data or dissemination of information via a public network of volunteers.

Climate: summary of a region's temperature, humidity, atmospheric pressure, wind, and precipitation over a long time period.

Coarse-grained: description of a system using relatively few large components giving broad information with little detail, or a system comprised of relatively few different components.

Coefficient of variation: a measure of variability equal to the ratio of the standard deviation to the mean.

Coevolution: the change or adaptation of one species in response to changes in another.

Coexistence: the situation whereby two species occupy the same area.

Community: a set of interacting populations of several species.

Community assembly: the process by which species come to coexist in a common area.

Community ecology: the study of distributions, abundances, demographies, and interactions among populations occupying the same geographical area.

Compact city: urban design concept focusing on high residential density, efficient public transport, mixed land use, low per-capita energy consumption, and social interaction among inhabitants.

Competition: contest among individuals or groups for a limiting resource.

Competitive exclusion: the principle that two species that share the same resources and needs cannot coexist indefinitely.

Conspecific: two or more organisms or populations that belong to the same species.

Convection: the movement of molecules within liquids or gases, often including diffusion and advection, responsible for large-scale transfer of heat and materials.

Corridor: habitat allowing the movement of individuals between populations that have been separated, usually by human activity.

Cultural evolution: the description of how societies develop over time, often as a result of changes to the social environment.

Decomposer: organisms, usually bacteria and fungi, that use dead or decaying organic material as a food source.

Denitrification: the reduction of nitrates (NO_3) to nitrogen gas (N_2) via bacteria respiration. This part of the nitrogen cycle returns nitrogen to the atmosphere, and generally occurs in anaerobic environments such as soils or wetlands.

Density–diversity paradox: situation where heavily built areas have low diversity of species, but high overall population density due to a small number of highly successful species.

Designed experiment: an information-gathering exercise in which a treatment is applied to some objects, but not others (controls), to investigate the effects of the treatment.

Detritivore: organisms, such as earthworms, that feeds on dead organic matter.

Dilution effect: process by which high species diversity reduces the impact of a particular species interaction, usually the prevalence of a disease.

Dimethyl sulfide: organic compound containing sulfur, $(CH_3)_2S$, emitted by marine algae, bacteria in sewage systems, and some wetlands.

Direct transmission: passage of a disease from an infected to a susceptible host via physical contact.

Dispersal: movement of an organism from one region to another.

Disturbance: temporary change in environmental conditions that has a large impact on an ecosystem, by altering or even removing the local community.

Dormancy: period of an organism's life when growth, development, and activity are temporarily reduced to survive or conserve energy, usually during times of unfavorable environmental conditions.

Early successional: species that quickly colonize an area after a disturbance, generally characterized by high dispersal and fast growth.

Ecological footprint: a measure of humans' demands on the Earth's ecosystems in terms of how much land and sea would be required to produce the resources consumed and to process the waste produced.

Ecological succession: the changes in structure and composition of a community after a disturbance.

Ecological trap: situation when organisms misinterpret environmental cues and settle in an attractive but low-quality habitat.

Ecology in cities: the study of species' distributions, abundances, and interactions with their biological and physical surroundings in an urban environment.

Ecology of cities: extension of ecology in cities to include the study of the sociological, economical, and political factors that shape the environment.

Ecosystem disservices: the financial, health, and other costs created by natural elements within urban environments.

Ecosystem ecology: study of the flows of energy, water, nutrients, and other materials and their interactions with the organisms living in a particular area.

Ecosystem engineer: an organism that substantially modifies its habitat.

Ecosystem services: the benefits provided to humans through naturally occurring processes such as water cleaning, waste decomposition, and carbon dioxide sequestration.

Ectotherm: organism that controls body temperature via environmental sources.

Endemic disease: a disease that is maintained within a population over a long period of time.

Endemic species: a species found only in a particular region.

Endotherm: organism that controls body temperature via internal metabolic processes.

Energy: the ability of a physical system to do work on another physical system.

Energy land: component of the ecological footprint quantifying the land required to produce energy or receive carbon dioxide.

Energy pyramid: the graphical representation of the flow of energy from the sun to primary producers, consumers, and eventually detritivores.

Epidemic: an outbreak of an infectious disease in a community above typical background levels.

Equilibrium: the state of a system when opposing forces are in balance, characterized by little or no net change.

Estivation: state of animal dormancy in which inactivity and lowered metabolic rate help protect the individual during times of high heat stress and potential water loss.

Eutrophication: an increase in the plant and algal biomass of a body of water due to the addition of nutrients such as nitrates or phosphates.

Evaporation: the vaporization of a liquid, which in the case of water requires substantial energy and plays a key role in the global water cycle.

Evapotranspiration: liquid water lost from the Earth's surface to the atmosphere due to both evaporation and plant transpiration.

Evolution: scientific framework explaining the modification and diversification of life through changes from parents to offspring.

Evolutionary ecology: the study of the adaptation of a species to its biotic and abiotic environment.

Evolutionary theory: description of the change of the genetic and physical properties of a species due to natural selection, mutation, migration, and genetic drift.

Exotic species: species living outside its native distribution range.

Exploitation competition: contest for a limiting resource, such as when consumption of the resource by one competitor makes it unavailable to the other competitors.

Extinction debt: the number of species in an area that will disappear in the future as a result of current events due to a time delay between an event like habitat destruction and the complete loss of the species.

Extralimital native: non-native species that originates from the same continent.

Exurban: a low-density residential area that lies beyond the suburbs, from which people commute to work in an urban center.

Fecundity: the actual or potential reproduction of an organism or species.

Fine-grained: description of a system using many small components giving detailed information on a focused area, or a system comprised of many different components.

Fitness: the success of an organism in survival and reproduction, and thus in passing on its genes to the next generation.

Fixed genetic variant: a genetic trait shared by all members of a population.

Flight initiation distance: the distance at which birds fly from a perceived threat.

Foraging theory: study of feeding behaviors of organisms with respect to their physical and biotic environments, often comparing gains (food acquired) with costs (such as energy spent or risk of predation).

Fragmentation: the breaking of habitats into separated and often small patches.

Functional homogenization: creation of similar ecosystem properties, such as rates of nutrient use and movement, through alteration of the habitat or species composition.

Gene flow: the transfer of alleles of genes from one population to another.

Generalist: a species that can use a variety of different resources or live in a variety of environmental conditions.

Gigaton: measure of mass equal to 10^9 metric tons, or one teragram.

Giving-up density: the amount of food that an animal leaves in a patch.

Greywater: water outputs from household use, excluding sewage, that can be reused for irrigation.

Guild: a group of species that make use of the same resources, often in a similar manner.

Habitat fragmentation: the creation of discontinuities in an organism's preferred environment.

Heat capacity: measure of the heat storage capacity of a substance, defined as how much heat energy is required to raise its temperature.

Herbivory: consumption of plants by animals.

Heritable: a trait that can be passed from parent to offspring by genetic factors.

Heterotroph: an organism that uses organic carbon for growth, but cannot itself fix the carbon from inorganic compounds and must acquire it by consuming autotrophs or other heterotrophs.

Homogenization: the process of reducing biotic differences between habitats.

Host: an organism that harbors another organism and provides it with resources such as food or shelter.

Humidity: the amount of water vapor in the air.

Hydrological cycle: description of the movement of water among solid, liquid, and gas phases, on, above, and below the Earth's surface. Also called the water cycle.

Hydrological drought: reduction of water levels in lakes, aquifers, soils, or other locations.

Hydrology: study of the movement, distribution, and quality of water.

Hygiene hypothesis: the idea that a lack of childhood exposure to pathogens, parasites, and symbiotic microorganisms increases susceptibility to allergic diseases by not promoting normal immune system development.

Hypoxic: reduced oxygen availability.

Impermeable surfaces: surfaces that do not allow fluids to pass through (sometimes called impervious surfaces).

Indirect transmission: the passing of an infectious disease from one host to another via a third party, such as another organism, contaminated water, or a surface.

Industrial melanism: increase in the amount of dark pigmentation in organisms in response to anthropogenic pollution.

Infiltration: the process by which surface water enters the ground.

Insolation: the measure of solar radiation energy received by an area during a specified period of time, such as kilowatt-hours per square meter per day.

Interference competition: direct contest for a limiting resource in which competitors interact with each other through fighting or other forms of conflict.

Intermediate disturbance hypothesis: concept that local biodiversity is highest when ecological disturbances occur with moderate frequency, thus allowing the coexistence of early and late-successional species.

Intermediate productivity hypothesis: concept that local biodiversity is highest when productivity is neither too low nor too high.

Invasive species: organisms not native to an area that have negative effects on native species and ecosystems.

Jaccard index: statistic for similarity of the species present in two areas, equal to the number of species found in both habitats divided by the sum of the number of species in both habitats and in either habitat.

Joule: a unit of energy equal to the work done to produce one watt of power for one second.

Keystone species: a species that has a disproportionately large effect on the local environment relative to its abundance in that environment.

Land subsidence: downward shifting of the surface due to removal of groundwater, minerals, or petrochemicals.

Late successional: species that can establish and persist in habitats long after disturbance. These species are typically slow growing, shade tolerant, and strong competitors.

Latent heat loss: the energy expended, or temperature lost to the environment, as a liquid changes phase to gas. Also called evaporative cooling.

Life history: series of changes an organism experiences between conception and death, including its schedule of reproduction and lifespan.

Limiting nutrient: a resource that controls the growth of an organism or population due to low availability.

Long-wave radiation: the energy leaving the Earth's surface as low-energy infrared radiation.

Made land: urban soil composed partly of construction materials and urban waste.

Maladaptive: an inappropriate or inadequate response to the environment.

Matrix sensitive: description of an urban-adapted species that depends on contiguous suitable habitat and does poorly on other habitats.

Mesic: habitat type characterized by a moderate, well-balanced supply of water.

Mesopredator: medium-sized predator that occupies a middle trophic level.

Microclimate: climate associated with a small region that contrasts with the surrounding area.

Mineralization: process in the soil by which organic matter decomposes and is oxidized, making the chemical compounds accessible to plants.

Morphology: the form and structure of an organism, including its size and shape.

Mutualism: interaction which benefits two organisms or species.

Mycorrhizal fungi: symbiotic, often mutualistic, interaction between a fungus and the roots of a plant in which the fungus colonizes the host plant's roots. The plant generally receives water and mineral nutrients, while the fungus receives carbohydrates.

Natural enemy: a predator, herbivore, parasite, or parasitoid that attacks or destroys another organism.

Natural selection: process describing how individuals that are well-suited to their environment have more offspring than individuals that are not.

Naturalized species: species non-native to a region that establishes and persists but does not create the harmful effects of invasive species.

Neophyte: a plant species recently introduced to an area, generally after 1500 A.D.

Nitrate: a negatively charged ion consisting of one nitrogen and three oxygen atoms.

Nitrification: process in which soil bacteria oxidize ammonia into nitrate, which can then be assimilated by plants.

Nitrogen fixation: process of converting atmospheric nitrogen into ammonia.

Nitrogen-fixing bacteria: bacteria that use the enzyme nitrogenase to convert atmospheric nitrogen to ammonia.

Non-equilibrium community: ecological community in which new species are continually arriving while others become extinct and where species interactions are always changing.

Non-point source pollution: unwanted or detrimental substances that cannot be traced back to a single location.

Nutrient: chemical or other substance from the environment needed by an organism to survive and grow.

Observational study: an investigation where inferences are drawn about the effects of a treatment or process without the investigator controlling where, how, or to whom the treatment is applied.

Organic compound: any molecule or combination of molecules that contain the element carbon.

Organism: any contiguous, living system, such as a plant, animal, or bacterium.

Parasitoid: an animal, usually an insect, that develops within or attached to a host animal, ending with the host being sterilized, killed, or consumed.

Particulates: small pieces of solid matter suspended in a gas or liquid medium. As a pollutant, these are called particulate matter with size designated in microns; for example, PM_{10} refers to particles of size less than 10 μm.

Patch: a relatively small, discrete section of habitat, often providing a limiting resource.

Pathogen: an infectious agent that causes disease in its host.

Perennial plants: plants that survive multiple years and survive winters or dry periods as roots or woody above-ground structures.

Persistence: ability of a species to remain in a particular habitat.

pH: a measure of concentration of hydronium ions, with low values indicating an acidic solution and high values a basic solution.

Phenology: the timing of the life cycles of plants and animals, especially in response to the seasons.

Phenotype: organism's observable traits, resulting from a combination of genetic and environmental factors.

Phenotypic plasticity: ability of an organism to adjust its phenotype in response to changes in the environment.

Photosynthesis: the process of converting atmospheric carbon dioxide into organic compounds using light as the source of energy.

Phylogenetic diversity: a measure of biodiversity in a region that includes the degree of relatedness among species, computed as the sum of the evolutionary distances among those species.

Physical environment: surrounding conditions, excluding living things, of an organism.

Physiological ecology: study of how organisms function in a given environment.

Point-source pollution: unwanted or detrimental substances that can be traced back to a single location.

Pollution: unwanted contaminant introduced to an area that is detrimental to the physical and/or biological environment.

Population density: the number of members of a species per unit area.

Population ecology: study of the population size of a particular species and how it interacts with the physical and biological environments.

Population regulation: process that limits a population's growth, such as a top-down or bottom-up mechanism.

Positive feedback: mechanism by which the output of a process is reapplied to the input, increasing the rate or magnitude of the system's behavior.

Power: rate at which work is performed or energy is used, typically measured in watts.

Preadapted: a preexisting trait of an organism that proves adaptive in an environment different from that in which it evolved.

Predation: biological interaction in which one organism, the predator, kills and feeds on another, its prey.

Prevalence: the fraction of individuals in a particular state, often applied to describe the fraction of hosts infected by a disease.

Primary productivity: the rate at which organic compounds are produced by photosynthesis in a given location or region.

Prion: infectious protein in a misfolded form, affecting the structure of the brain or other neural tissue.

Pseudo-tropical bubble: description of how the urban environment mimics the temperature and reduced seasonality of the tropics due to anthropogenic processes.

Rank abundance curve: visual representation of a habitat's species richness in which each species' relative abundance on the vertical axis is plotted against its abundance rank on the horizontal axis.

Redfield ratio: molecular ratio of carbon, nitrogen, and phosphorus (106:16:1), originally developed by Alfred Redfield for marine plankton.

Reflected radiation: radiation that changes direction at the interface between two media, often the atmosphere and a reflective surface, so that the wave of radiation returns into the medium from which it came.

Relative deprivation: experience of discontent for lacking access to something that others can access.

Relative humidity: the amount of water vapor in the air as a percentage of the total that the air could hold.

Reservoir host: species that can harbor a pathogen indefinitely with little or no ill effects. Also known as a natural reservoir.

Respiration: process by which nutrients are converted into usable energy, with carbon dioxide as the major output.

Retention pond: an artificial lake for collecting stormwater runoff to prevent downstream flooding and recharge groundwater supply.

Riparian habitat: zone of interface between land and water characterized by plants that require a steady supply of water.

Rule of 10: description of the probability that an introduced species becomes invasive, stating that roughly one of 10 species makes the transition from introduction to naturalization, or the transition from naturalization to invasion.

Scale: the size, duration, or magnitude characterizing a phenomenon or process.

Seed bank: pool of dormant seeds within the soil.

Sensible heat transfer: energy exchange in which the only effect is a change in temperature, such as through movement of fluids.

Sequestration: process of removing and storing something in a reservoir, such as carbon in forests or soils.

Sexual selection: differences in fitness resulting from competition for mates in a sexually reproducing species, either through traits attractive to the opposite sex or effective in defeating rivals of the same sex.

Short-wave radiation: energy received by an ecosystem in the form of high-energy photons from the sun.

Simpson's similarity index: statistic for similarity of the species present in two areas, equal to the number of species found in both habitats divided by the sum of that number and the number of species unique to the habitat with the fewest unique species.

Sink: ecosystem or habitat in which a population can only be maintained by immigration of new individuals from a source population.

Sky view factor: fraction of the sky visible from a given point, ranging from 0 when the sky is completely blocked by buildings, to 1 when the sky is completely visible.

Social disorganization: theory directly linking sociological pathologies such as crime rates with the breakdown of family or social structure.

Social isolation: lack of interaction with family, friends, and neighbors with common interests.

Solar input: energy received by an ecosystem as short-wave radiation from the sun.

Source: ecosystem or habitat where population size can increase and extra individuals emigrate to other areas.

Spatial scale: the size, length, area, or distance characterizing a phenomenon or process.

Specialist: a species that makes use of a narrow range of environmental conditions or resources.

Species accumulation curve: graphical representation of the number of species found as a function of the number of sites surveyed.

Species area curve: graphical representation of the number of species found as a function of the area surveyed.

Species richness: number of different species in a given area.

Species sorting: concept that only certain species can become established and persist in a particular habitat due to their traits.

Spillover host: species infected with a pathogen but which typically cannot transmit the pathogen.

Soil compaction: process by which air is displaced from between soil particles, such as by pressure from heavy machinery.

Stomata: pores on plant leaves that can be opened to allow entry of carbon dioxide or closed to prevent water loss.

Stream daylighting: the process of returning waterways that had been piped underground to the surface.

Substrate: the type of surface on which organisms live.

Succession: process by which the species in a community change after a disturbance that removes most organisms from the habitat.

Superorganism: collection of agents or organisms that act in concert for the survival of all.

Surface energy budget: accounting mechanism quantifying incoming and outgoing energy and energy use in a particular region.

Synanthropic: non-domesticated plants and animals that live near and benefit from close associations with humans and their effects.

Synoptic: observations from a broad view or large spatial scale. In meteorology, this scale is thousands of kilometers and refers to large weather patterns.

Synurbanized: species that have traits needed to succeed in urban environments.

Temporal scale: the duration or time characterizing a phenomenon or process.

Teragram: 10^{12} grams, equal to one megaton.

Terrestrial: situated or taking place on land rather than in water.

Thermal conductivity: a measure of how quickly heat moves through or out of a substance.

Topography: the physical features of a land surface.

Top-down control: regulation of a population by predation, herbivory, or other forms of consumption.

Toxin: poisonous substance, generally produced by living cells or organisms.

Transmission: the passing of an infectious disease from one organism to another.

Transpiration: vaporization of liquid water by plants.

Trophic structure: description of the structure of a community in terms of what resources and other organisms particular species consume.

Troposphere: lowest portion of the Earth's atmosphere, from the surface to approximately 20 km in altitude.

Uncontrolled study: experiment in which a treatment is performed on a group of subjects and their responses are recorded without being compared to a control group that did not receive the treatment.

Unicolonial: social structure, primarily in ants, in which members of one nest or colony can move without restriction into other nests or colonies from a wide geographical area.

Urban CO$_2$ dome: combination of anthropogenic and biogenic factors leading to high carbon dioxide concentrations in urban centers.

Urban adapter: a species that tolerates humans and anthropogenic factors, but does not rely on them for persistence in urban habitats.

Urban avoider: a species that is poorly adapted to humans and anthropogenic factors and persists in non-urban habitats.

Urban boundary layer: portion of the atmosphere above and mixing with the urban canopy.

Urban canopy layer: portion of the atmosphere in urban areas, from the surface to the tops of buildings and the urban boundary layer, where pollution and particulates remain trapped.

Urban canyon: built environment in which vertical structures create physical properties similar to natural canyons.

Urban dust dome: phenomenon where air circulates by leaving and re-entering an urban area, each time accumulating particulate matter and pollution.

Urban exploiter: a species that takes advantage of, and generally relies on, the ecological effects of urbanization.

Urban heat island: phenomenon in which urban areas are warmer than surrounding non-urban environments, particularly during the night and winter.

Urban metabolism: quantification of the flow of nutrients, energy, and materials into, through, and out of an urban ecosystem.

Urban sprawl: growth and spread of a city, leading to automobile-dependent development of suburbs that remain economically and culturally linked to the urban core.

Urban–rural gradient: description of the changes from urban to rural ecological conditions as one moves away from the urban core.

Vector: agent that carries and transmits an infectious agent or pathogen.

Virulence: degree of pathogenicity of a species of parasite indicated by its effect on mortality or health of hosts.

Waste habitat: portion of land or water near human settlement where refuse is discarded.

Water cycle: description of the movement of water among solid, liquid, and gas phases, on, above, and below the Earth's surface.

Water table: level below which the ground is saturated with water and above which it is not.

Water vapor pressure: the pressure created by water vapor alone as a component of the atmosphere; a measure of absolute humidity.

Watt: unit of power describing the rate of energy conversion to work, equal to one joule per second.

Weather: local or short-term climatic conditions including temperature, humidity, atmospheric pressure, wind, and precipitation.

Wetlands: area of land in which the soil is saturated with water and vegetation is dominated by water-loving plants.

Xeric: habitat characterized by a small amount of moisture, with generally less than 25 cm of precipitation annually.

References

[1] H. Akbari, M. Pomerantz, and H. Taha. Cool surfaces and shade trees to reduce energy use and improve air quality in urban areas. *Solar Energy*, **70** (2001), 295–310.

[2] M. Alberti. Urban patterns and environmental performance: what do we know? *Journal of Planning Education and Research*, **19** (1999), 151–163.

[3] M. Alberti. The effects of urban patterns on ecosystem function. *International Regional Science Review*, **28** (2005), 168–192.

[4] M. Alberti, D. Booth, K. Hill, *et al.* The impact of urban patterns on aquatic ecosystems: an empirical analysis in Puget lowland sub-basins. *Landscape and Urban Planning*, **80** (2007), 345–361.

[5] C. Alexander. A city is not a tree. *Architectural Forum*, **122** (1965), 58–62.

[6] L. Allen, F. Lindberg, and C. S. B. Grimmond. Global to city scale urban anthropogenic heat flux: model and variability. *International Journal of Climatology*, **31** (2011), 1990–2005.

[7] P. M. Anderson and K. E. Butcher. Childhood obesity: trends and potential causes. *The Future of Children*, **16** (2006), 19–45.

[8] P. G. Angold, J. P. Sadler, M. O. Hill, *et al.* Biodiversity in urban habitat patches. *The Science of the Total Environment*, **360** (2006), 196–204.

[9] A. J. Arnfield. Two decades of urban climate research: a review of turbulence, exchanges of energy and water, and the urban heat island. *International Journal of Climatology*, **23** (2003), 1–26.

[10] C. L. Arnold Jr and C. J. Gibbons. Impervious surface coverage: the emergence of a key environmental indicator. *Journal of the American Planning Association*, **62** (1996), 243–258.

[11] A. V. Badyaev, R. L. Young, K. P. Oh, and C. Addison. Evolution on a local scale: developmental, functional, and genetic bases of divergence in bill form and associated changes in song structure between adjacent habitats. *Evolution*, **62** (2008), 1951–1964.

[12] L. A. Baker. Can urban P conservation help to prevent the brown devolution? *Chemosphere*, **84** (2011), 779–784.

[13] L. A. Baker, A. J. Brazel, N. Selover, *et al.* Urbanization and warming of Phoenix (Arizona, USA): impacts, feedbacks and mitigation. *Urban Ecosystems*, **6** (2002), 183–203.

[14] L. A. Baker, D. Hope, Y. Xu, J. Edmonds, and L. Lauver. Nitrogen balance for the Central Arizona–Phoenix (CAP) ecosystem. *Ecosystems*, **4** (2001), 582–602.

[15] R. V. Barbehenn, Z. Chen, D. N. Karowe, and A. Spickard. C_3 grasses have higher nutritional quality than C_4 grasses under ambient and elevated atmospheric CO_2. *Global Change Biology*, **10** (2004), 1565–1575.

[16] O. Barbosa, J. A. Tratalos, P. R. Armsworth, *et al.* Who benefits from access to green space? A case study from Sheffield, UK. *Landscape and Urban Planning*, **83** (2007), 187–195.

[17] I. Barnes, A. Duda, O. G. Pybus, and M. G. Thomas. Ancient urbanization predicts genetic resistance to tuberculosis. *Evolution*, **65** (2011), 842–848.

[18] A. D. Barnosky, P. L. Koch, R. S. Feranec, S. L. Wing, and A. B. Shabel. Assessing the causes of late Pleistocene extinctions on the continents. *Science*, **306** (2004), 70–75.

[19] J. Barton and J. Pretty. Urban ecology and human health and wellbeing. In K. J. Gaston, ed., *Urban Ecology*. (Cambridge: Cambridge University Press, 2010), pp. 202–229.

[20] R. R. Bates and D. Kennedy. *Air Pollution, The Automobile, and Public Health.* (Washington DC: National Academy Press, 1988).

[21] N. H. Batjes. Total carbon and nitrogen in the soils of the world. *European Journal of Soil Science*, **47** (1996), 151–163.

[22] M. E. Bauer, B. C. Loffelholz, and B. Wilson. Estimating and mapping impervious surface area by regression analysis of landsat imagery. In Q. Weng, ed., *Remote Sensing of Impervious Surfaces.* (London: Taylor & Francis Group, 2008), pp. 3–19.

[23] S. Bearhop, W. Fiedler, R. W. Furness, *et al.* Assortative mating as a mechanism for rapid evolution of a migratory divide. *Science*, **310** (2005), 502–504.

[24] A. P. Beckerman, M. Boots, and K. J. Gaston. Urban bird declines and the fear of cats. *Animal Conservation*, **10** (2007), 320–325.

[25] K. P. Beckett, P. H. Freer-Smith, and G. Taylor. Urban woodlands: their role in reducing the effects of particulate pollution. *Environmental Pollution*, **99** (1998), 347–360.

[26] C. P. Bell, S. W. Baker, N. G. Parkes, M. D. L. Brooke, and D. E. Chamberlain. The role of the Eurasian sparrowhawk (*Accipiter nisus*) in the decline of the house sparrow (*Passer domesticus*) in Britain. *The Auk*, **127** (2010), 411–420.

[27] M. L. Bell, A. McDermott, S. L. Zeger, J. M. Samet, and F. Dominici. Ozone and short-term mortality in 95 US urban communities, 1987–2000. *Journal of the American Medical Assocation*, **292** (2004), 2372–2378.

[28] T. L. Bell, D. Rosenfeld, K. M. Kim, and M. Hahnenberger. Midweek increase in US summer rain and storm heights suggests air pollution invigorates rainstorms. *Journal of Geophysical Research*, **113** (2008), DO2209.

[29] S. Benvenuti. Weed dynamics in the Mediterranean urban ecosystem: ecology, biodiversity and management. *Weed Research*, **44** (2004), 341–354.

[30] E. S. Bernhardt, L. E. Band, C. J. Walsh, and P. E. Berke. Understanding, managing, and minimizing urban impacts on surface water nitrogen loading. *Annals of the New York Academy of Sciences*, **1134** (2008), 61–96.

[31] P. Berthold, A. J. Helbig, G. Mohr, and U. Querner. Rapid microevolution of migratory behaviour in a wild bird species. *Nature*, **360** (1992), 668–670.

[32] Best Foot Forward and Institute of Wastes Management. *City Limits: A Resource Flow and Ecological Footprint Analysis of Greater London.* (London: Best Foot Forward, 2002).

[33] L. Bettencourt, J. Lobo, D. Helbing, C. Kühnert, and G. B. West. Growth, innovation, scaling, and the pace of life in cities. *Proceedings of the National Academy of Sciences*, **104** (2007), 7301–7306.

[34] R. B. Blair. Land use and avian species diversity along an urban gradient. *Ecological Applications*, **6** (1996), 506–519.

[35] R. B. Blair. Birds and butterflies along urban gradients in two ecoregions of the United States: is urbanization creating a homogeneous fauna? In J. L. Lockwood and

M. L. McKinney, eds, *Biotic Homogenization*. (Dordrecht, the Netherlands: Kluwer Academic, 2001), pp. 33–56.

[36] T. J. Blakely, J. S. Harding, A. R. Mcintosh, and M. J. Winterbourn. Barriers to the recovery of aquatic insect communities in urban streams. *Freshwater Biology*, **51** (2006), 1634–1645.

[37] C. W. Boal and R. W. Mannan. Comparative breeding ecology of Cooper's hawks in urban and exurban areas of southeastern Arizona. *Journal of Wildlife Management*, **63** (1999), 77–84.

[38] V. Bókony, A. Kulcsár, and A. Liker. Does urbanization select for weak competitors in house sparrows? *Oikos*, **119** (2010), 437–444.

[39] D. T. Bolger, A. C. Alberts, and M. E. Soule. Occurrence patterns of bird species in habitat fragments: sampling, extinction, and nested species subsets. *The American Naturalist*, **295** (1991), 155–166.

[40] D. T. Bolger, A. V. Suarez, K. R. Crooks, S. A. Morrison, and T. J. Case. Arthropods in urban habitat fragments in Southern California: area, age, and edge effects. *Ecological Applications*, **10** (2000), 1230–1248.

[41] P. Bolund and S. Hunhammar. Ecosystem services in urban areas. *Ecological Economics*, **29** (1999), 293–301.

[42] F. Bonier, P. R. Martin, K. S. Sheldon, J. P. Jensen, S. L. Foltz, and J. C. Wingfield. Sex-specific consequences of life in the city. *Behavioral Ecology*, **18** (2007), 121–129.

[43] F. Bonier, P. R. Martin, and J. C. Wingfield. Urban birds have broader environmental tolerance. *Biology Letters*, **3** (2007), 670–673.

[44] D. B. Booth, J. R. Karr, S. Schauman, *et al.* Reviving urban streams: land use, hydrology, biology and human behavior. *Journal of the American Water Research Association*, **40** (2004), 1351–1364.

[45] K. M. Booth, M. M. Pinkston, and W. S. C. Poston. Obesity and the built environment. *Journal of the American Dietetic Association*, **105S** (2005), 110–117.

[46] K. A. Borden and S. L. Cutter. Spatial patterns of natural hazards mortality in the United States. *International Journal of Health Geographics*, **7** (2008), 64.

[47] R. Bornstein and Q. Lin. Urban heat islands and summertime convective thunderstorms in Atlanta: three case studies. *Atmospheric Environment*, **34** (2000), 507–516.

[48] P. Bousquet, P. Ciais, J. B. Miller, *et al.* Contribution of anthropogenic and natural sources to atmospheric methane variability. *Nature*, **443** (2006), 439–443.

[49] T. W. Boutton, G. N. Cameron, and B. N. Smith. Insect herbivory on C_3 and C_4 grasses. *Oecologia*, **36** (1978), 21–32.

[50] M. A. Bowers and B. Breland. Foraging of gray squirrels on an urban–rural gradient: use of the GUD to assess anthropogenic impact. *Ecological Applications*, **6** (1996), 1135–1142.

[51] C. A. Bradley and S. Altizer. Urbanization and the ecology of wildlife diseases. *Trends in Ecology & Evolution*, **22** (2007), 95–102.

[52] C. A. Bradley, S. E. J. Gibbs, and S. Altizer. Urban land use predicts West Nile Virus exposure in songbirds. *Ecological Applications*, **18** (2008), 1083–1092.

[53] N. C. Brady and R. R. Weil. *The Nature and Property of Soils*. (Upper Saddle River, NJ: Prentice Hall, 1996).

[54] A. Brazel, N. Selover, R. Vose, and G. Heisler. The tale of two climates: Baltimore and Phoenix urban LTER sites. *Climate Research*, **15** (2000), 123–135.

[55] S. W. Brazel and R. C. Balling Jr. Temporal analysis of long-term atmospheric moisture levels in Phoenix, Arizona. *Journal of Applied Meteorology*, **25** (1986), 112–117.

[56] S. Brenneisen. Space for urban wildlife: designing green roofs as habitats in Switzerland. *Urban Habitats*, **4** (2006), 27–33.

[57] W. H. Brock. *The Norton History of Chemistry*. (New York: Norton Press, 1992).

[58] J. S. Brown. Patch use as an indicator of habitat preference, predation risk, and competition. *Behavioral Ecology and Sociobiology*, **22** (1988), 37–47.

[59] R. C. Brownson, T. K. Boehmer, and D. A. Luke. Declining rates of physical activity in the United States: what are the contributors? *Annual Review of Public Health*, **26** (2005), 421–443.

[60] H. Brumm. The impact of environmental noise on song amplitude in a territorial bird. *Journal of Animal Ecology*, **73** (2004), 434–440.

[61] P. H. Brunner. Reshaping urban metabolism. *Journal of Industrial Ecology*, **11**(2) (2007), 11–13.

[62] S. Brunzel, S. F. Fischer, J. Schneider, J. Jetzkowitz, and R. Brandl. Neo- and archaeo-phytes respond more strongly than natives to socio-economic mobility and disturbance patterns along an urban–rural gradient. *Journal of Biogeography*, **36** (2009), 835–844.

[63] T. Buchholz and T. Younos. Urban stream daylighting: case study evaluations. *Virginia Water Resources Research Center*, Special Report SR35-2007 (2007).

[64] G. Buczkowski. Extreme life history plasticity and the evolution of invasive characteristics in a native ant. *Biological Invasions*, **12** (2010), 3343–3349.

[65] F. Bulleri and M. G. Chapman. The introduction of coastal infrastructure as a driver of change in marine environments. *Journal of Applied Ecology*, **47** (2010), 26–35.

[66] Y. Bulut, S. Toy, M. A. Irmak, H. Yilmaz, and S. Yilmaz. Urban–rural climatic differences over a 2-year period in the City of Erzurum, Turkey. *Atmósfera*, **21** (2008), 121–133.

[67] K. T. Burghardt, D. W. Tallamy, and G. W. Shriver. Impact of native plants on bird and butterfly biodiversity in suburban landscapes. *Conservation Biology*, **23** (2009), 219–224.

[68] D. E. Burhans and F. R. Thompson III. Songbird abundance and parasitism differ between urban and rural shrublands. *Ecological Applications*, **16** (2006), 394–405.

[69] D. E. Burhans and F. R. Thompson III. Habitat patch size and nesting success of Yellow-breasted Chats. *The Wilson Bulletin*, **111** (1999), 210–215.

[70] A. Buyantuyev and J. Wu. Urban heat islands and landscape heterogeneity: linking spatiotemporal variations in surface temperatures to land-cover and socioeconomic patterns. *Landscape Ecology*, **25** (2010), 17–33.

[71] R. S. Byrd and J. P. Joad. Urban asthma. *Current Opinion in Pulmonary Medicine*, **12** (2006), 68–74.

[72] M. L. Cadenasso, S. T. Pickett, P. M. Groffman, *et al.* Exchanges across land-water-scape boundaries in urban systems. *Annals of the New York Academy of Sciences*, **1134** (2008), 213–232.

[73] M. L. Cadenasso and S. T. A. Pickett. Urban principles for ecological landscape design and maintenance: scientific fundamentals. *Cities and the Environment*, **1** (2008), Article 4.

[74] M. L. Cain, W. D. Bowman, and S. D. Hacker. *Ecology*. (Sunderland, MA: Sinauer Associates, Inc., 2008).

[75] J. Cairns. *Matters of Life and Death: Perspectives on Public Health, Molecular Biology, Cancer, and the Prospects for the Human Race*. (Princeton, NJ: Princeton University Press, 1998).

[76] D. E. Canfield, E. Kristensen, and B. Thamdrup. The phosphorus cycle. *Advances in Marine Biology*, **48** (2005), 419–440.

[77] D. G. Capone and A. N. Knapp. A marine nitrogen cycle fix? *Nature*, **445** (2007), 159–160.

[78] C. Carbone and J. L. Gittleman. A common rule for the scaling of carnivore density. *Science*, **295** (2002), 2273–2276.

[79] A. Carlsson-Kanyama, M. P. Ekström, and H. Shanahan. Food and life cycle energy inputs: consequences of diet and ways to increase efficiency. *Ecological Economics*, **44** (2003), 293–307.

[80] M. Carrete and J. L. Tella. Inter-individual variability in fear of humans and relative brain size of the species are related to urban invasion in birds. *PLoS ONE*, **6** (2011), e18859.

[81] S. P. Carroll and C. Boyd. Host race radiation in the soapberry bug: natural history with the history. *Evolution*, **46** (1992), 1052–1069.

[82] S. P. Carroll, J. E. Loye, H. Dingle, *et al.* And the beak shall inherit: evolution in response to invasion. *Ecology Letters*, **8** (2005), 944–951.

[83] T. Carter, C. R. Jackson, J. Maerz, *et al.* Beyond the urban gradient: barriers and opportunities for timely studies of urbanization effects on aquatic ecosystems. *Journal of the North American Benthological Society*, **28** (2009), 1038–1050.

[84] C. P. Catterall, D. Lunney, and S. Burgin. Birds, garden plants and suburban bushlots: where good intentions meet unexpected outcomes. In D. Lunney and S. Bergen, eds, *Urban Wildlife: More Than Meets the Eye.* (Sydney, Australia: Royal Zoological Society of New Southwales, 2001), pp. 21–31.

[85] S. Caula, P. Marty, and J. L. Martin. Seasonal variation in species composition of an urban bird community in Mediterranean France. *Landscape and Urban Planning*, **87** (2008), 1–9.

[86] J. F. Chace and J. J. Walsh. Urban effects on native avifauna: a review. *Landscape and Urban Planning*, **74** (2006), 46–69.

[87] D. E. Chamberlain, A. R. Cannon, M. P. Toms, *et al.* Avian productivity in urban landscapes: a review and meta-analysis. *Ibis*, **151** (2009), 1–18.

[88] N. Chambers, C. Simmons, and M. Wackernagel. *Sharing Nature's Interest: Ecological Footprints as an Indicator of Sustainability.* (London: Earthscan Publications, 2000).

[89] S. A. Changnon. Inadvertent weather modification in urban areas: lessons for global climate change. *Bulletin of the American Meteorological Society*, **73** (1992), 619–627.

[90] F. S. Chapin III, B. H. Walker, R. J. Hobbs, *et al.* Biotic control over the functioning ecosystem. *Science*, **277** (1997), 500–504.

[91] L. F. Chaves, C. L. Keogh, G. M. Vazquez-Prokopec, and U. D. Kitron. Combined sewage overflow enhances oviposition of *Culex quinquefasciatus* (Diptera: Culicidae) in urban areas. *Journal of Medical Entomology*, **46** (2009), 220–226.

[92] P. O. Cheptou, O. Carrue, S. Rouifed, and A. Cantarel. Rapid evolution of seed dispersal in an urban environment in the weed *Crepis sancta*. *Proceedings of the National Academy of Sciences*, **105** (2008), 3796–3799.

[93] J. C. Chow, J. G. Watson, D. H. Lowenthal, and R. J. Countess. Sources and chemistry of PM_{10} aerosol in Santa Barbara County, CA. *Atmospheric Environment*, **30** (1996), 1489–1499.

[94] F. J. Christie and D. F. Hochuli. Elevated levels of herbivory in urban landscapes: are declines in tree health more than an edge effect? *Ecology and Society*, **10** (2005), 10.

[95] G. Churkina, D. G. Brown, and G. Keoleian. Carbon stored in human settlements: the conterminous United States. *Global Change Biology*, **16** (2010), 135–143.

[96] K. M. Clarke, B. L. Fisher, and G. LeBuhn. The influence of urban park characteristics on ant (Hymenoptera, Formicidae) communities. *Urban Ecosystems*, **11** (2008), 317–334.

[97] E. E. Cleland, I. Chuine, A. Menzel, H. A. Mooney, and M. D. Schwartz. Shifting plant phenology in response to global change. *Trends in Ecology & Evolution*, **22** (2007), 357–365.

[98] W. S. Cleveland, T. E. Graedel, B. Kleiner, and J. L. Warner. Sunday and workday variations in photochemical air pollutants in New Jersey and New York. *Science*, **186** (1974), 1037–1038.

[99] J. Colding and C. Folke. The role of golf courses in biodiversity conservation and ecosystem management. *Ecosystems*, **12** (2008), 191–206.

[100] C. G. Collier. The impact of urban areas on weather. *Quarterly Journal of the Royal Meteorological Society*, **132** (2006), 1–25.

[101] J. P. Collins, A. Kinzig, N. B. Grimm, *et al.* A new urban ecology. *American Scientist*, **88** (2000), 416–425.

[102] P. A. Conrad, M. A. Miller, C. Kreuder, *et al.* Transmission of *Toxoplasma*: clues from the study of sea otters as sentinels of *Toxoplasma gondii* flow into the marine environment. *International Journal for Parasitology*, **35** (2005), 1155–1168.

[103] L. M. Cook. The rise and fall of the carbonaria form of the peppered moth. *The Quarterly Review of Biology*, **78** (2003), 399–417.

[104] L. M. Cook and J. R. G. Turner. Decline of melanism in two British moths: spatial, temporal and inter-specific variation. *Heredity*, **101** (2008), 483–489.

[105] M. T. Cooke. The spread of the European starling in North America (to 1928). *US Department of Agriculture*, **40** (1928), 1–9.

[106] R. Costanza, R. d'Arge, R. de Groot, *et al.* The value of the world's ecosystem services and natural capital. *Nature*, **387** (1997), 253–260.

[107] K. R. Crooks. Relative sensitivities of mammalian carnivores to habitat fragmentation. *Conservation Biology*, **16** (2002), 488–502.

[108] K. R. Crooks and M. E. Soulé. Mesopredator release and avifaunal extinctions in a fragmented system. *Nature*, **400** (1999), 563–566.

[109] P. J. Crutzen. New directions: the growing urban heat and pollution "island" effect: impact on chemistry and climate. *Atmospheric Environment*, **38** (2004), 3539–3540.

[110] T. M. Culley, S. J. Sbita, and A. Wick. Population genetic effects of urban habitat fragmentation in the perennial herb *Viola pubescens* (Violaceae) using ISSR markers. *Annals of Botany*, **100** (2007), 91–100.

[111] M. A. Cunningham, E. Snyder, D. Yonkin, M. Ross, and T. Elsen. Accumulation of deicing salts in soils in an urban environment. *Urban Ecosystems*, **11** (2008), 17–31.

[112] V. H. Dale, S. Brown, R. A. Haeuber, *et al.* Ecological principles and guidelines for managing the use of land. *Ecological Applications*, **10** (2000), 639–670.

[113] M. Dallimer, K. N. Irvine, A. M. J. Skinner, *et al.* Biodiversity and the feel-good factor: understanding associations between self-reported human well-being and species richness. *BioScience*, **62** (2012), 47–55.

[114] J. Damuth. Population density and body size in mammals. *Nature*, **290** (1981), 699–700.

[115] G. D. Daniels and J. B. Kirkpatrick. Comparing the characteristics of front and back domestic gardens in Hobart, Tasmania, Australia. *Landscape and Urban Planning*, **78** (2006), 344–352.

[116] P. Daszak, A. A. Cunningham, and A. D. Hyatt. Emerging infectious diseases of wildlife: threats to biodiversity and human health. *Science*, **287** (2000), 443–449.

[117] P. Daszak, A. A. Cunningman, and A. D. Hyatt. Anthropogenic environmental change and the emergence of infectious diseases in wildlife. *Acta Tropica*, **78** (2001), 103–116.

[118] N. Dauphine and R. J. Cooper. Pick one: outdoor cats or conservation. *Wildlife Professional*, Spring (2011), 50–56.

[119] G. F. M. Dawe. Street trees and the urban environment. In I. Douglas, D. Goode, M. C. Houck, and R. Wang, eds. *The Routledge Handbook of Urban Ecology*, (London: Routledge, 2011), pp. 424–449.

[120] M. D. Dearing and L. Dizney. Ecology of hantavirus in a changing world. *Annals of the New York Academy of Sciences*, **1195** (2010), 99–112.

[121] E. H. Decker, S. Elliott, F. A. Smith, D. R. Blake, and F. S. Rowland. Energy and material flow through the urban ecosystem. *Annual Reviews in Energy and the Environment*, **25** (2000), 685–740.

[122] K. L. Denman, G. Brasseur, A. Chidthaisong, *et al.* Coupling between changes in the climate system and biogeochemistry. In S. Solomon, D. Qin, M. Manning, *et al.*, eds, *Climate Change 2007: The Physical Science Basis. Contribution of Working Group I to the Fourth Assessment Report of the Intergovernmental Panel on Climate Change.* (Cambridge: Cambridge University Press, 2007), pp. 500–537.

[123] C. Denys and H. Schmidt. Insect communities on experimental mugwort (*Artemisia vulgaris* L.) plots along an urban gradient. *Oecologia*, **113** (1998), 269–277.

[124] P. Deplazes, D. Hegglin, S. Gloor, and T. Romig. Wilderness in the city: the urbanization of *Echinococcus multilocularis*. *Trends in Parasitology*, **20** (2004), 77–84.

[125] V. Devictor, R. Julliard, D. Couvet, A. Lee, and F. Jiguet. Functional homogenization effect of urbanization on bird communities. *Conservation Biology*, **21** (2007), 741–751.

[126] J. M. Diamond. Rapid evolution of urban birds. *Nature*, **324** (1986), 107–108.

[127] J. E. Diem and D. P. Brown. Anthropogenic impacts on summer precipitation in Central Arizona, USA. *The Professional Geographer*, **55** (2003), 343–355.

[128] M. E. Dietz and J. C. Clausen. Stormwater runoff and export changes with development in a traditional and low impact subdivision. *Journal of Environmental Management*, **87** (2008), 560–566.

[129] R. Dip, D. Hegglin, P. Deplazes, *et al.* Age- and sex-dependent distribution of persistent organochlorine pollutants in urban foxes. *Environmental Health Perspectives*, **111** (2003), 1608–1612.

[130] S. S. Ditchkoff, S. T. Saalfeld, and C. J. Gibson. Animal behavior in urban ecosystems: modifications due to human-induced stress. *Urban Ecosystems*, **9** (2006), 5–12.

[131] E. Domene, D. Saurí, and M. Parés. Urbanization and sustainable resource use: the case of garden watering in the metropolitan region of Barcelona. *Urban Geography*, **26** (2005), 520–535.

[132] R. Donovan, J. Sadler, and J. Bryson. Urban biodiversity and sustainable development. *Engineering Sustainability*, **158** (2005), 105–114.

[133] A. Dornier, V. Pons, and P. O. Cheptou. Colonization and extinction dynamics of an annual plant metapopulation in an urban environment. *Oikos*, **120** (2011), 1240–1246.

[134] I. Douglas. Suburban mosaic of houses, roads, gardens and mature trees. In I. Douglas, D. Goode, M. C. Houck, and R. Wang, eds, *The Routledge Handbook of Urban Ecology*. (New York: Routledge, 2011), pp. 264–273.

[135] I. Douglas. Urban hydrology. In I. Douglas, D. Goode, M. C. Houck, and R. Wang, eds, *The Routledge Handbook of Urban Ecology*. (New York: Routledge, 2011), pp. 148–158.

[136] I. Douglas and J. Sadler. Urban wildlife corridors: conduits for movement or linear habitat? In I. Douglas, D. Goode, M. C. Houck, and R. Wang, eds, *The Routledge Handbook of Urban Ecology*. (New York: Routledge, 2011), pp. 274–288.

[137] J. W. Dover and B. Rowlingson. The western jewel butterfly (*Hypochrysops halyaetus*): factors affecting adult butterfly distribution within native Banksia bushland in an urban setting. *Biological Conservation*, **122** (2005), 599–609.

[138] B. Drayton and R. B. Primack. Plant species lost in an isolated conservation area in Metropolitan Boston from 1894 to 1993. *Conservation Biology*, **10** (1996), 30–39.

[139] S. H. Dreistadt, D. L. Dahlsten, and G. W. Frankie. Urban forests and insect ecology. *Bioscience*, **40** (1990), 192–198.

[140] C. T. Driscoll, G. B. Lawrence, A. J. Bulger, *et al.* Acidic deposition in the northeastern United States: sources and inputs, ecosystem effects, and management strategies. *BioScience*, **51** (2001), 180–198.

[141] R. P. Duncan, S. E. Clemants, R. T. Corlett, Plant traits and extinction in urban areas: a meta-analysis of 11 cities. *Global Ecology and Biogeography*, **20** (2011), 509–519.

[142] W. R. Effland and R. V. Pouyat. The genesis, classification, and mapping of soils in urban areas. *Urban Ecosystems*, **1** (1997), 217–228.

[143] M. J. Ege, M. Mayer, A. C. Normand, *et al.* Exposure to environmental microorganisms and childhood asthma. *New England Journal of Medicine*, **364** (2011), 701–709.

[144] J. G. Ehrenfeld. Exotic invasive species in urban wetlands: environmental correlates and implications for wetland management. *Journal of Applied Ecology*, **45** (2008), 1160–1169.

[145] F. Eigenbrod, S. J. Hecnar, and L. Fahrig. Quantifying the road effect zone: threshold effects of a motorway on anuran populations in Ontario, Canada. *Ecology and Society*, **14** (2009), 24–41.

[146] G. W. Elmes. Ant colonies and environmental disturbance. *Symposium of the Zoological Society of London*, **63** (1991), 15–32.

[147] C. S. Elton. *Animal Ecology*. (London: Sidgwick & Jackson, Ltd., 1927).

[148] C. D. Elvidge, C. Milesi, J. B. Dietz, U. S. constructed area approaches size of Ohio. *Eos*, **85** (2004), 233–240.

[149] J. T. Emlen. An urban bird community in Tucson, Arizona: derivation, structure, regulation. *The Condor*, **76** (1974), 184–197.

[150] J. Emsley. *The Elements*, 3rd edition. (Oxford: Clarendon Press, 1998).

[151] W. A. Estes and R. W. Mannan. Feeding behavior of Cooper's hawks at urban and rural nests in southeastern Arizona. *The Condor*, **105** (2003), 107–116.

[152] G. W. Evans. The built environment and mental health. *Journal of Urban Health*, **80** (2003), 536–555.

[153] K. L. Evans. Individual species and urbanisation. In K. J. Gaston, ed., *Urban Ecology*. (Cambridge: Cambridge University Press, 2010), pp. 53–87.

[154] K. L. Evans, D. E. Chamberlain, B. J. Hatchwell, R. D. Gregory, and K. J. Gaston. What makes an urban bird? *Global Change Biology*, **17** (2011), 32–44.

[155] K. L. Evans, K. J. Gaston, A. C. Frantz, *et al.* Independent colonization of multiple urban centres by a formerly forest specialist bird species. *Proceedings of the Royal Society B: Biological Sciences*, **276** (2009), 2403–2410.

[156] K. L. Evans, B. J. Hatchwell, M. Parnell, and K. J. Gaston. A conceptual framework for the colonisation of urban areas: the blackbird *Turdus merula* as a case study. *Biological Reviews*, **85** (2010), 643–667.

[157] R. Ewing, R. Pendall, and D. Chen. Measuring sprawl and its transportation impacts. *Journal of the Transportation Research Board*, **1831** (2003), 175–183.

[158] R. Ewing, T. Schmid, R. Killingsworth, A. Zlot, and S. Raudenbush. Relationship between urban sprawl and physical activity, obesity, and morbidity. In E. Shulenberger, W. Endlicher, M. Alberti, *et al.*, eds, *Urban Ecology: An International Perspective on the Interaction between Humans and Nature.* (Berlin: Springer Verlag, 2008), 567–582.

[159] J. Færge, J. Magid, and F. W. T. Penning de Vries. Urban nutrient balance for Bangkok. *Ecological Modelling*, **139** (2001), 63–74.

[160] S. H. Faeth, C. Bang, and S. Saari. Urban biodiversity: patterns and mechanisms. *Annals of the New York Academy of Sciences*, **1223** (2011), 69–81.

[161] S. H. Faeth, P. S. Warren, E. Shochat, and W. A. Marussich. Trophic dynamics in urban communities. *Bioscience*, **55** (2005), 399–407.

[162] D. P. Faith. Conservation evaluation and phylogenetic diversity. *Biological Conservation*, **61** (1992), 1–10.

[163] M. L. Farnsworth, L. L. Wolfe, N. T. Hobbs, *et al.* Human land use influences chronic wasting disease prevalence in mule deer. *Ecological Applications*, **15** (2005), 119–126.

[164] A. J. Felson and S. T. A. Pickett. Designed experiments: new approaches to studying urban ecosystems. *Frontiers in Ecology and the Environment*, **3** (2005), 549–556.

[165] B. Felzer, D. Kicklighter, J. Melillo, *et al.* Effects of ozone on net primary production and carbon sequestration in the conterminous United States using a biogeochemistry model. *Tellus*, **56** (2004), 230–248.

[166] E. Fernández-Juricic. Avifaunal use of wooded streets in an urban landscape. *Conservation Biology*, **14** (2000), 513–521.

[167] E. D. Fetridge, J. S. Ascher, and G. A. Langellotto. The bee fauna of residential gardens in a suburb of New York City (Hymenoptera: Apoidea). *Annals of the Entomological Society of America*, **101** (2008), 1067–1077.

[168] E. J. Finnemore and W. G. Lynard. Management and control technology for urban stormwater pollution. *Journal of the Water Pollution Control Federation*, **54** (1982), 1099–1111.

[169] M. Fischer-Kowalski. Society's metabolism. The intellectual history of materials flow analysis, part I, 1860–1970. *Journal of Industrial Ecology*, **2** (1998), 61–78.

[170] M. Fischer-Kowalski and W. Hüttler. Society's metabolism. The intellectual history of materials flow analysis, part II, 1970–1998. *Journal of Industrial Ecology*, **2** (1999), 107–136.

[171] C. Fissore, L. A. Baker, S. E. Hobbie, *et al.* Carbon, nitrogen, and phosphorus fluxes in household ecosystems in the Minneapolis-Saint Paul, Minnesota, urban region. *Ecological Applications*, **21** (2011), 619–639.

[172] A. L. Fleischer Jr, R. Bowman, and G. E. Woolfenden. Variation in foraging behavior, diet, and time of breeding of Florida scrub-jays in suburban and wildland habitats. *The Condor*, **105** (2003), 515–527.

[173] A. R. Fleischman and J. A. Barondess. Urban health: a look out our windows. *Acade Medicine*, **79** (2004), 1130–1132.

[174] C. Folke, A. Jansson, J. Larsson, and R. Costanza. Ecosystem appropriation by cities. *Ambio*, **26** (1997), 167–172.

[175] P. Forster, V. Ramaswamy, P. Artaxo, *et al.* Changes in atmospheric constituents and in radiative forcing. In S. Solomon, D. Qin, M. Manning, *et al.*, eds, *Climate Change 2007: The Physical Science Basis. Contribution of Working Group I to the Fourth Assessment Report of the Intergovernmental Panel on Climate Change.* (Cambridge: Cambridge University Press, 2007), 747–845.

[176] P. M. de F. Forster and S. Solomon. Observations of "weekend effect" in diurnal temperature range. *Proceedings of the National Academy of Sciences*, **100** (2003), 11225–11230.

[177] K. Fortuniak, K. Kłysik, and J. Wibig. Urban–rural contrasts of meteorological parameters in Łódź. *Theoretical and Applied Climatology*, **84** (2006), 91–101.

[178] C. D. Francis, C. P. Ortega, and A. Cruz. Noise pollution changes avian communities and species interactions. *Current Biology*, **19** (2009), 1415–1419.

[179] R. A. Francis. Positioning urban rivers within urban ecology. *Urban Ecosystems*, **15** (2012), 285–291.

[180] C. Frankenberg, J. F. Meirink, M. Van Weele, U. Platt, and T. Wagner. Assessing methane emissions from global space-borne observations. *Science*, **308** (2005), 1010–1014.

[181] S. J. Franks, S. Sim, and A. E. Weis. Rapid evolution of flowering time by an annual plant in response to a climate fluctuation. *Proceedings of the National Academy of Sciences*, **104** (2007), 1278–1282.

[182] M. E. Frederickson, M. J. Greene, and D. M. Gordon. "Devil's gardens" bedevilled by ants. *Nature*, **437** (2005), 495–496.

[183] C. Freeman, A. Maurice, S. Hughes, B. Reynolds, and J. A. Hudson. Nitrous oxide emissions and the use of wetlands for water quality amelioration. *Environmental Science & Technology*, **31** (1997), 2438–2440.

[184] S. S. French, H. B. Fokidis, and M. C. Moore. Variation in stress and innate immunity in the tree lizard (*Urosaurus ornatus*) across an urban–rural gradient. *Journal of Comparative Physiology B: Biochemical, Systemic, and Environmental Physiology*, **178** (2008), 997–1005.

[185] M. S. Friedman, K. E. Powell, L. Hutwagner, L. R. M. Graham, and W. G. Teague. Impact of changes in transportation and commuting behaviors during the 1996 Summer Olympic Games in Atlanta on air quality and childhood asthma. *Journal of the American Medical Assocation*, **285** (2001), 897–905.

[186] H. Frumkin. Urban sprawl and public health. *Public Health Reports*, **117** (2002), 201–217.

[187] R. Fuge and M. J. Andrews. Fluorine in the UK environment. *Environmental Geochemistry and Health*, **10** (1988), 96–104.

[188] R. A. Fuller, K. N. Irvine, P. Devine-Wright, P. H. Warren, and K. J. Gaston. Psychological benefits of greenspace increase with biodiversity. *Biology Letters*, **3** (2007), 390–394.

[189] R. A. Fuller, J. Tratalos, and K. J. Gaston. How many birds are there in a city of half a million people? *Diversity and Distributions*, **15** (2009), 328–337.

[190] R. A. Fuller, P. H. Warren, and K. J. Gaston. Daytime noise predicts nocturnal singing in urban robins. *Biology Letters*, **3** (2007), 368–370.

[191] S. R. Gaffin, C. Rosenzweig, R. Khanbilvardi, *et al.* Variations in New York City's urban heat island strength over time and space. *Theoretical and Applied Climatology*, **94** (2008), 1–11.

[192] S. Galea and D. Vlahov. Urban health: evidence, challenges, and directions. *Annual Review of Public Health*, **26** (2005), 341–365.

[193] S. Galea, J. Ahern, S. Rudenstine, Z. Wallace, and D. Vlahov. Urban built environment and depression: a multilevel analysis. *Journal of Epidemiology and Community Health*, **59** (2005), 822–827.

[194] J. N. Galloway. Anthropogenic mobilization of sulfur and nitrogen. *Annual Review of Energy and the Environment*, **21** (1996), 261–292.

[195] J. N. Galloway, W. H. Schlesinger, H. Levy, A. Michaels, and J. L. Schnoor. Nitrogen fixation: anthropogenic enhancement–environmental response. *Global Biogeochemical Cycles*, **9** (1995), 235–235.

[196] A. P. Galvani and M. Slatkin. Evaluating plague and smallpox as historical selective pressures for the ccr5-δ32 hiv-resistance allele. *Proceedings of the National Academy of Sciences*, **100** (2003), 15276–15279.

[197] P. I. Garaffa, J. Filloy, and M. I. Bellocq. Bird community responses along urban-rural gradients: does the size of the urbanized area matter? *Landscape and Urban Planning*, **90** (2009), 33–41.

[198] J. Garden, C. McAlpine, A. Peterson, D. Jones, and H. Possingham. Review of the ecology of Australian urban fauna: a focus on spatially explicit processes. *Austral Ecology*, **31** (2006), 126–148.

[199] K. J. Gaston. Biodiversity and extinction: species and people. *Progress in Physical Geography*, **29** (2005), 239–247.

[200] K. J. Gaston. Urban ecology. In K. J. Gaston, ed., *Urban Ecology*. (Cambridge: Cambridge University Press, 2010), pp. 1–9.

[201] K. J. Gaston. Urbanisation. In K. J. Gaston, ed., *Urban Ecology*. (Cambridge: Cambridge University Press, 2010), pp. 10–34.

[202] K. J. Gaston and K. L. Evans. Birds and people in Europe. *Proceedings of the Royal Society B: Biological Sciences*, **271** (2004), 1649–1655.

[203] K. J. Gaston, Z. G. Davies and J. L. Edmondson. Urban environments and ecosystem functions. In K. J. Gaston, ed., *Urban Ecology*. (Cambridge: Cambridge University Press, 2010), 35–52.

[204] K. J. Gaston, R. M. Smith, K. Thompson, and P. H. Warren. Urban domestic gardens (II): Experimental tests of methods for increasing biodiversity. *Biodiversity and Conservation*, **14** (2005), 395–413.

[205] E. Gaublomme, F. Hendrickx, H. Dhuyvetter, and K. Desender. The effects of forest patch size and matrix type on changes in carabid beetle assemblages in an urbanized landscape. *Biological Conservation*, **141** (2008), 2585–2596.

[206] R. Gazal, M. A. White, R. Gillies, *et al.* GLOBE students, teachers, and scientists demonstrate variable differences between urban and rural leaf phenology. *Global Change Biology*, **14** (2008), 1568–1580.

[207] S. D. Gedzelman, S. Austin, R. Cermak, *et al.* Mesoscale aspects of the urban heat island around New York City. *Theoretical and Applied Climatology*, **75** (2003), 29–42.

[208] R. J. Geider and J. Roche. The role of iron in phytoplankton photosynthesis, and the potential for iron-limitation of primary productivity in the sea. *Photosynthesis Research*, **39** (1994), 275–301.

[209] General Register Office. *Life Expectancy in Special Areas (Urban/Rural Deprivation and Community Health Partnership) within Scotland, 2005–2007.* (Edinburgh, Scotland: National Statistics, 2009).

[210] H. W. Georgii. The effects of air pollution on urban climates. *Bulletin of the World Health Organization*, **40** (1969), 624–635.

[211] J. C. Gering and R. B. Blair. Predation on artificial bird nests along an urban gradient: predatory risk or relaxation in urban environments? *Ecography*, **22** (1999), 532–541.

[212] H. Gibb and D. F. Hochuli. Habitat fragmentation in an urban environment: large and small fragments support different arthropod assemblages. *Biological Conservation*, **106** (2002), 91–100.

[213] J. N. Gibbs. Intercontinental epidemiology of Dutch elm disease. *Annual Review of Phytopathology*, **16** (1978), 287–307.

[214] O. L. Gilbert. *The Ecology of Urban Habitats*. (New York: Chapman and Hall, 1989).

[215] S. E. Gilman, M. C. Urban, J. Tewksbury, G. W. Gilchrist, and R. D. Holt. A framework for community interactions under climate change. *Trends in Ecology & Evolution*, **25** (2010), 325–331.

[216] A. Givati and D. Rosenfeld. Quantifying precipitation suppression due to air pollution. *Journal of Applied Meteorology*, **43** (2004), 1038–1056.

[217] D. S. Glazier. Temporal variability of abundance and the distribution of species. *Oikos*, **47** (1986), 309–314.

[218] M. A. Goddard, A. J. Dougill, and T. G. Benton. Scaling up from gardens: biodiversity conservation in urban environments. *Trends in Ecology & Evolution*, **20** (2009), 610–616.

[219] R. Godfrey and M. Julien. Urbanisation and health. *Clinical Medicine*, **5** (2005), 137–141.

[220] M. E. Gompper and A. N. Wright. Altered prevalence of raccoon roundworm (*Baylisascaris procyonis*) owing to manipulated contact rates of hosts. *Journal of Zoology*, **266** (2005), 215–219.

[221] G. A. Gonzalez. Urban sprawl, global warming and the limits of ecological modernisation. *Environmental Politics*, **14** (2005), 344–362.

[222] D. M. Gordon. *Ants at Work: How an Insect Society is Organized*. (New York: Free Press, 1999).

[223] G. Grant. Extensive green roofs in london. *Urban Habitats*, **4** (2006), 51–65.

[224] J. W. Gregg, C. G. Jones, and T. E. Dawson. Urbanization effects on tree growth in the vicinity of New York City. *Nature*, **424** (2003), 183–187.

[225] J. W. Gregg, C. G. Jones, and T. E. Dawson. Physiological and developmental effects of O_3 on cottonwood growth in urban and rural sites. *Ecological Applications*, **16** (2006), 2368–2381.

[226] N. B. Grimm, S. H. Faeth, N. E. Golubiewski, *et al.* Global change and the ecology of cities. *Science*, **319** (2008), 756–761.

[227] C. S. B. Grimmond, T. S. King, F. D. Cropley, C. Nowak, and D. J. Souch. Local-scale fluxes of carbon dioxide in urban environments: methodological challenges and results from Chicago. *Environmental Pollution*, **116** (2002), S243–S254.

[228] C. S. B. Grimmond and T. R. Oke. Heat storage in urban areas: local-scale observations and evaluation of a simple model. *Journal of Applied Meteorology*, **38** (1999), 922–940.

[229] C. S. B. Grimmond, T. R. Oke, and D. G. Steyn. Urban water balance 1. A model for daily totals. *Water Resources Research*, **22** (1986), 1397–1403.

[230] P. M. Groffman, D. J. Bain, L. E. Band, *et al.* Down by the riverside: urban riparian ecology. *Frontiers in Ecology and the Environment*, **1** (2003), 315–321.

[231] P. M. Groffman, N. J. Boulware, W. C. Zipperer, *et al.* Soil nitrogen cycle processes in urban riparian zones. *Environmental Science & Technology*, **36** (2002), 4547–4552.

[232] P. M. Groffman and M. K. Crawford. Denitrification potential in urban riparian zones. *Journal of Environmental Quality*, **32** (2003), 1144–1149.

[233] P. M. Groffman, N. L. Law, K. T. Belt, L. E. Band, and G. T. Fisher. Nitrogen fluxes and retention in urban watershed ecosystems. *Ecosystems*, **7** (2004), 393–403.

[234] M. Guirado, J. Pino, and F. Roda. Understorey plant species richness and composition in metropolitan forest archipelagos: effects of forest size, adjacent land use and distance to the edge. *Global Ecology and Biogeography*, **15** (2006), 50–62.

[235] H. F. Guite, C. Clark, and G. Ackrill. The impact of the physical and urban environment on mental well-being. *Public Health*, **120** (2006), 1117–1126.

[236] Y. Guo. Hydrologic design of urban flood control detention ponds. *Journal of Hydrologic Engineering*, **6** (2001), 472–479.

[237] K. R. Gurney, D. L. Mendoza, Y. Zhou, *et al.* High resolution fossil fuel combustion CO2 emission fluxes for the United States. *Environmental Science & Technology*, **43** (2009), 5535–5541.

[238] A. K. Hahs, M. J. McDonnell, M. A. McCarthy, *et al.* A global synthesis of plant extinction rates in urban areas. *Ecology Letters*, **12** (2009), 1165–1173.

[239] J. Hale J. Sadler, A. Bates, and P. James. Bringing cities alive: the importance of urban green spaces for people and biodiversity. In K. J. Gaston, ed., *Urban Ecology*. (Cambridge: Cambridge University Press, 2010), 230–260.

[240] R. O. Hall Jr., J. L. Tank, D. J. Sobota, *et al.* Nitrate removal in stream ecosystems measured by 15N addition experiments: total uptake. *Limnology and Oceanography*, **54** (2009), 653–665.

[241] A. J. Hamer and M. J. McDonnell. Amphibian ecology and conservation in the urbanising world: a review. *Biological Conservation*, **141** (2008), 2432–2449.

[242] D. Hanahan and R. A. Weinberg. The hallmarks of cancer. *Cell*, **100** (2000), 57–70.

[243] L. M. Hanks and R. F. Denno. Natural enemies and plant water relations influence the distribution of an armored scale insect. *Ecology*, **74** (1993), 1081–1091.

[244] I. Hanski, L. von Hertzen, N. Fyhrquist, *et al.* Environmental biodiversity, human microbiota, and allergy are interrelated. *Proceedings of the National Academy of Sciences*, **109** (2012), 8334–8339.

[245] I. N. Harman and S. E. Belcher. The surface energy balance and boundary layer over urban street canyons. *Quarterly Journal of the Royal Meteorological Society*, **132** (2006), 2749–2768.

[246] M. D. Harrison, P. M. Groffman, P. M. Mayer, S. S. Kaushal, and T. A. Newcomer. Denitrification in alluvial wetlands in an urban landscape. *Journal of Environmental Quality*, **40** (2011), 634–646.

[247] D. A. Hartz, A. J. Brazel, and G. M. Heisler. A case study in resort climatology of Phoenix, Arizona, USA. *International Journal of Biometeorology*, **51** (2006), 73–83.

[248] B. A. Hawkins, R. Field, H. V. Cornell, *et al.* Energy, water, and broad-scale geographic patterns of species richness. *Ecology*, **84** (2003), 3105–3117.

[249] J. L. Heilman and R. W. Gesch. Effects of turfgrass evaporation on external temperatures of buildings. *Theoretical and Applied Climatology*, **43** (1991), 185–194.

[250] A. J. Helden and S. R. Leather. Biodiversity on urban roundabouts: Hemiptera, management and the species–area relationship. *Basic and Applied Ecology*, **5** (2004), 367–377.

[251] L. Heneghan, J. Steffen, and K. Fagen. Interactions of an introduced shrub and introduced earthworms in an Illinois urban woodland: impact on leaf litter decomposition. *Pedobiologia*, **50** (2007), 543–551.

[252] E. I. Hennig and J. Ghazoul. Plant–pollinator interactions within the urban environment. *Perspectives in Plant Ecology, Evolution and Systematics*, **13** (2011), 137–150.

[253] W. Hern. Urban malignancy: similarity in the fractal dimensions of urban morphology and malignant neoplasms. *International Journal of Anthropology*, **23** (2008), 1–19.

[254] B. E. Heterick, J. Casella, and J. D. Majer. Influence of Argentine and coastal brown ant (Hymenoptera: Formicidae) invasions on ant communities in Perth gardens, Western Australia. *Urban Ecosystems*, **4** (2000), 277–292.

[255] N. Heynen, H. A. Perkins, and P. Roy. The political ecology of uneven urban green space. *Urban Affairs Review*, **42** (2006), 3–25.

[256] S. J. Hinners, C. Kearns, and C. A. Wessman. Roles of scale, matrix and native habitat in supporting a diverse suburban pollinator assemblage. *Ecological Applications*, in press, **22** (2012) 1923–1935.

[257] D. J. Hodkinson and K. Thompson. Plant dispersal: the role of man. *Journal of Applied Ecology*, **34** (1997), 1484–1496.

[258] B. D. Hoffmann and C. L. Parr. An invasion revisited: the African big-headed ant (*Pheidole megacephala*) in northern Australia. *Biological Invasions*, **10** (2008), 1171–1181.

[259] D. M. Hogan and M. R. Walbridge. Urbanization and nutrient retention in freshwater riparian wetlands. *Ecological Applications*, **17** (2007), 1142–1155.

[260] E. Holden and I. T. Norland. Three challenges for the compact city as a sustainable urban form: household consumption of energy and transport in eight residential areas in the greater Oslo region. *Urban Studies*, **42** (2005), 2145–2166.

[261] B. Hölldobler and E. O. Wilson. *The Ants*. (New York: Belknap, 1990).

[262] B. Hölldobler and E. O. Wilson. *The Superorganism: The Beauty, Elegance, and Strangeness of Insect Societies*. (New York: W. W. Norton & Co., 2008).

[263] D. Y. Hollinger, S. V. Ollinger, A. D. Richardson, *et al.* Albedo estimates for land surface models and support for a new paradigm based on foliage nitrogen concentration. *Global Change Biology*, **16** (2010), 696–710.

[264] D. A. Holway. Effect of Argentine ant invasions on ground-dwelling arthropods in northern California riparian woodlands. *Oecologia*, **116** (1998), 252–258.

[265] D. A. Holway and A. V. Suarez. Homogenization of ant communities in mediterranean California: the effects of urbanization and invasion. *Biological Conservation*, **127** (2006), 319–326.

[266] M. J. Hood, J. C. Clausen, and G. S. Warner. Comparison of stormwater lag times for low impact and traditional residential development. *Journal of the American Water Resources Association*, **43** (2007), 1036–1046.

[267] D. Hope, C. Gries, W. X. Zhu, *et al.* Socioeconomics drive urban plant diversity. *Proceedings of the National Academy of Sciences*, **100** (2003), 8788–8792.

[268] R. W. Howarth, E. W. Boyer, W. J. Pabich, and J. N. Galloway. Nitrogen use in the United States from 1961–2000 and potential future trends. *Ambio*, **31** (2002), 88–96.

[269] P. E. Hulme. Herbivory, plant regeneration, and species coexistence. *Journal of Ecology*, **84** (1996), 609–615.

[270] P. E. Hulme, S. Bacher, M. Kenis, *et al.* Grasping at the routes of biological invasions: a framework for integrating pathways into policy. *Journal of Applied Ecology*, **45** (2008), 403–414.

[271] T. Ichinose, K. Shimodozono, and K. Hanaki. Impact of anthropogenic heat on urban climate in Tokyo. *Atmospheric Environment*, **33** (1999), 3897–3909.

[272] C. D. Idso, S. B. Idso, and R. C. Balling. An intensive two-week study of an urban CO_2 dome in Phoenix, Arizona, USA. *Atmospheric Environment*, **35** (2001), 995–1000.

[273] H. Ikeda. Testing the intermediate disturbance hypothesis on species diversity in herbaceous plant communities along a human trampling gradient using a 4-year experiment in an old-field. *Ecological Research*, **18** (2003), 185–197.

[274] M. L. Imhoff, L. Bounoua, R. DeFries, *et al.* The consequences of urban land transformation on net primary productivity in the United States. *Remote Sensing of Environment*, **89** (2004), 434–443.

[275] M. Ishitani, D. J. Kotze, and J. Niemela. Changes in carabid beetle assemblages across an urban–rural gradient in Japan. *Ecography*, **26** (2003), 481–489.

[276] P. James, K. Tzoulas, M. D. Adams, *et al.* Towards an integrated understanding of green space in the European built environment. *Urban Forestry & Urban Greening*, **8** (2009), 65–75.

[277] C. Jansson, J. Ekman, and A. von Brömssen. Winter mortality and food supply in tits *Parus* spp. *Oikos*, **37** (1981), 313–322.

[278] P. J. Jarvis. Feral animals in the urban environment. In I. Douglas, D. Goode, M. C. Houck, and R. Wang, eds, *The Routledge Handbook of Urban Ecology*. (New York: Routledge, 2011), pp. 361–370.

[279] G. D. Jenerette, S. L. Harlan, A. Brazel, *et al.* Regional relationships between surface temperature, vegetation, and human settlement in a rapidly urbanizing ecosystem. *Landscape Ecology*, **22** (2007), 353–365.

[280] J. M. Jeschke and D. L. Strayer. Invasion success of vertebrates in Europe and North America. *Proceedings of the National Academy of Sciences*, **102** (2005), 7198–7202.

[281] D. A. Jessup and M. A. Miller. The trickle-down effect: how toxoplasmosis from cats can kill sea otters. *Wildlife Professional*, Spring (2011), 62–64.

[282] C. Y. Jim. Urban woodlands as distinctive and threatened nature-in-city patches. In I. Douglas, D. Goode, M. C. Houck, and R. Wang, eds, *The Routledge Handbook of Urban Ecology*. (New York: Routledge, 2011), pp. 323–337

[283] C. Y. Jim and W. Y. Chen. Assessing the ecosystem service of air pollutant removal by urban trees in Guangzhou (China). *Journal of Environmental Management*, **88** (2008), 665–676.

[284] J. Jokimäki, M. L. Kaisanlahti-Jokimäki, J. Suhonen, *et al.* Merging wildlife community ecology with animal behavioral ecology for a better urban landscape planning. *Landscape and Urban Planning*, **100** (2011), 383–385.

[285] A. Jones. An environmental assessment of food supply chains: a case study on dessert apples. *Environmental Management*, **30** (2002), 560–576.

[286] C. G. Jones, J. H. Lawton, and M. Shachak. Organisms as ecosystem engineers. *Oikos*, **69** (1994), 373–386.

[287] D. N. Jones and S. J. Reynolds. Feeding birds in our towns and cities: a global research opportunity. *Journal of Avian Biology*, **39** (2008), 265–271.

[288] K. E. Jones, N. G. Patel, M. A. Levy, *et al.* Global trends in emerging infectious diseases. *Nature*, **451** (2008), 990–993.

[289] E. Kalnay and M. Cai. Impact of urbanization and land-use change on climate. *Nature*, **423** (2003), 528–531.

[290] S. Kaplan. The restorative benefits of nature: toward an integrative framework. *Journal of Environmental Psychology*, **15** (1995), 169–182.

[291] S. Kark, A. Iwaniuk, A. Schalimtzek, and E. Banker. Living in the city: can anyone become an "urban exploiter"? *Journal of Biogeography*, **34** (2007), 638–651.

[292] S. S. Kaushal, P. M. Groffman, L. E. Band, *et al.* Interaction between urbanization and climate variability amplifies watershed nitrate export in Maryland. *Environmental Science & Technology*, **42** (2008), 5872–5878.

[293] S. S. Kaushal, P. M. Groffman, G. E. Likens, *et al.* Increased salinization of fresh water in the northeastern United States. *Proceedings of the National Academy of Sciences of the United States of America*, **102** (2005), 13517–13520.

[294] J. P. Kaye, I. C. Burke, A. R. Mosier, and J. Pablo Guerschman. Methane and nitrous oxide fluxes from urban soils to the atmosphere. *Ecological Applications*, **14** (2004), 975–981.

[295] J. P. Kaye, P. M. Groffman, N. B. Grimm, L. A. Baker, and R. V. Pouyat. A distinct urban biogeochemistry? *Trends in Ecology & Evolution*, **21** (2006), 192–199.

[296] J. P. Kaye, R. L. McCulley, and I. C. Burke. Carbon fluxes, nitrogen cycling, and soil microbial communities in adjacent urban, native and agricultural ecosystems. *Global Change Biology*, **11** (2005), 575–587.

[297] B. Keane, M. H. Collier, and S. H. Rogstad. Pollution and genetic structure of North American populations of the common dandelion (*Taraxacum officinale*). *Environmental Monitoring and Assessment*, **105** (2005), 341–357.

[298] W. W. Kellogg, R. D. Cadle, E. R. Allen, A. L. Lazrus, and E. A. Martell. The sulfur cycle. *Science*, **175** (1972), 587–596.

[299] C. Kennedy, J. Cuddihy, and J. Engel-Yan. The changing metabolism of cities. *Journal of Industrial Ecology*, **11** (2007), 43–59.

[300] M. E. Kentula, S. E. Gwin, and S. M. Pierson. Tracking changes in wetlands with urbanization: sixteen years of experience in Portland, Oregon, USA. *Wetlands*, **24** (2004), 734–743.

[301] H. B. D. Kettlewell. The phenomenon of industrial melanism in Lepidoptera. *Annual Review of Entomology*, **6** (1961), 245–262.

[302] A. P. Kinzig, P. Warren, C. Martin, D. Hope, and M. Katti. The effects of human socioeconomic status and cultural characteristics on urban patterns of biodiversity. *Ecology and Society*, **10** (2005), 23.

[303] R. Kjelgren and T. Montague. Urban tree transpiration over turf and asphalt surfaces. *Atmospheric Environment*, **32** (1998), 35–41.

[304] S. Knapp, I. Kühn, V. Mosbrugger, and S. Klotz. Do protected areas in urban and rural landscapes differ in species diversity? *Biodiversity and Conservation*, **17** (2008), 1595–1612.

[305] S. Knapp, I. Kühn, O. Schweiger, and S. Klotz. Challenging urban species diversity: contrasting phylogenetic patterns across plant functional groups in Germany. *Ecology Letters*, **11** (2008), 1054–1064.

[306] S. Knapp, I. Kühn, J. Stolle, and S. Klotz. Changes in the functional composition of a Central European urban flora over three centuries. *Perspectives in Plant Ecology, Evolution and Systematics*, **12** (2010), 235–244.

[307] S. Knapp, I. Kühn, R. Wittig, *et al.* Urbanization causes shifts in species' trait state frequencies. *Preslia*, **80** (2008), 375–388.

[308] R. Knowles. Denitrification. *Microbiology and Molecular Biology Reviews*, **46** (1982), 43–70.

[309] B. Koerner and J. Klopatek. Anthropogenic and natural CO_2 emission sources in an arid urban environment. *Environmental Pollution*, **116** (2002), 45–51.

[310] I. Kowarik. On the role of alien species in urban flora and vegetation. In P. Pysek, K. Prach, M. Rejmanek, and P. M. Wade, eds, *Plant Invasions: General Aspects and Special Problems*. (Amsterdam: SPB Academic, 1995), pp. 85–103.

[311] L. Krabbendam and J. van Os. Schizophrenia and urbanicity: a major environmental influence – conditional on genetic risk. *Schizophrenia Bulletin*, **31** (2005), 795–799.

[312] S. Kübler, S. Kupko, and U. Zeller. The kestrel (*Falco tinnunculus* L.) in Berlin: investigation of breeding biology and feeding ecology. *Journal of Ornithology*, **146** (2005), 271–278.

[313] I. Kuhn, R. Brandl, and S. Klotz. The flora of German cities is naturally species rich. *Evolutionary Ecology Research*, **6** (2004), 749–764.

[314] I. Kuhn and S. Klotz. Urbanization and homogenization: comparing the floras of urban and rural areas in Germany. *Biological Conservation*, **127** (2006), 292–300.

[315] F. E. Kuo and W. C. Sullivan. Aggression and violence in the inner city. *Environment and Behavior*, **33** (2001), 543–571.

[316] F. E. Kuo and W. C. Sullivan. Environment and crime in the inner city. *Environment and Behavior*, **33** (2001), 343–367.

[317] W. Kuttler and A. Strassburger. Air quality measurements in urban green areas – a case study. *Atmospheric Environment*, **33** (1999), 4101–4108.

[318] P. W. Lambdon, P. Pyšek, C. Basnou, *et al.* Alien flora of Europe: species diversity, temporal trends, geographical patterns and research needs. *Preslia*, **80** (2008), 101–149.

[319] H. E. Landsberg. *The Urban Climate*. (Waltham, MA: Academic Press, 1981).

[320] D. A. Lashof and D. R. Ahuja. Relative contributions of greenhouse gas emissions to global warming. *Nature*, **344** (1990), 529–531.

[321] N. Law, L. Band, and M. Grove. Nitrogen input from residential lawn care practices in suburban watersheds in Baltimore County, MD. *Journal of Environmental Planning and Management*, **47** (2004), 737–755.

[322] D. O. Lee. The influence of atmospheric stability and the urban heat island on urban-rural wind speed differences. *Atmospheric Environment*, **13** (1979), 1175–1180.

[323] P. F. Lee, T. S. Ding, F. H. Hsu, and S. Geng. Breeding bird species richness in Taiwan: distribution on gradients of elevation, primary productivity and urbanization. *Journal of Biogeography*, **31** (2004), 307–314.

[324] E. A. Leger and M. L. Forister. Colonization, abundance, and geographic range size of gravestone lichens. *Basic and Applied Ecology*, **10** (2009), 279–287.

[325] M. Lenzen and G. M. Peters. How city dwellers affect their resource hinterland. *Journal of Industrial Ecology*, **14** (2009), 73–90.

[326] S. A. Levin. Community equilibria and stability, and an extension of the competitive exclusion principle. *The American Naturalist*, **104** (1970), 413–423.

[327] L. C. Leviton, E. Snell, and M. McGinnis. Urban issues in health promotion strategies. *American Journal of Public Health*, **90** (2000), 863–866.

[328] K. Levy, G. Daily, and S. S. Myers. Human health as an ecosystem service: a conceptual framework. In J. C. Ingram, F. Declerek, and C. Rumbaitis del Rio, eds, *Integrating Ecology and Poverty Reduction: Ecological Dimensions*. (Berlin: Springer, 2012), 231–251.

[329] L. Lewan and C. Simmons. The uses of ecological footprint and biocapacity analysis as sustainability indicators for sub-national geographical areas: a recommended way forward. *European Common Indicators Project* (2001), pp. 1–49.

[330] G. E. Likens, C. T. Driscoll, and D. C. Buso. Long-term effects of acid rain: response and recovery of a forest ecosystem. *Science*, **272** (1996), 244–246.

[331] A. Liker, Z. Papp, V. Bokony, and A. Z. Lendvai. Lean birds in the city: body size and condition of house sparrows along the urbanization gradient. *Journal of Animal Ecology*, **77** (2008), 789–795.

[332] G. C. Liu, J. S. Wilson, R. Qi, and J. Ying. Green neighborhoods, food retail and childhood overweight: differences by population density. *American Journal of Health Promotion*, **21** (2007), 317–325.

[333] J. Liu, G. C. Daily, P. R. Ehrlich, and G. W. Luck. Effects of household dynamics on resource consumption and biodiversity. *Nature*, **421** (2003), 530–533.

[334] R. B. Lockard and D. H. Owings. Moon-related surface activity of bannertail (*Dipodomys spectabilis*) and Fresno (*D. nitratoides*) kangaroo rats. *Animal Behaviour*, **22** (1974), 262–273.

[335] K. LoGiudice, R. S. Ostfeld, K. A. Schmidt, and F. Keesing. The ecology of infectious disease: effects of host diversity and community composition on Lyme disease risk. *Proceedings of the National Academy of Sciences*, **100** (2003), 567–571.

[336] T. Longcore. Terrestrial arthropods as indicators of ecological restoration success in coastal sage scrub (California, USA). *Restoration Ecology*, **11** (2003), 397–409.

[337] T. Longcore and C. Rich. Ecological light pollution. *Frontiers in Ecology and the Environment*, **2** (2004), 191–198.

[338] A. Loram, K. Thompson, P. H. Warren, and K. J. Gaston. Urban domestic gardens (XII): the richness and composition of the flora in five UK cities. *Journal of Vegetation Science*, **19** (2008), 321–330.

[339] K. Lorenz and R. Lal. Biogeochemical C and N cycles in urban soils. *Environment International*, **35** (2009), 1–8.

[340] S. R. Loss, M. O. Ruiz, and J. D. Brawn. Relationships between avian diversity, neighborhood age, income, and environmental characteristics of an urban landscape. *Biological Conservation*, **142** (2009), 2578–2585.

[341] G. M. Lovett, M. M. Traynor, and R. V. Pouyat. Atmospheric deposition to oak forests along an urban-rural gradient. *Environmental Science & Technology*, **34** (2000), 4294–4300.

[342] D. Lowry, C. W. Holmes, N. D. Rata, P. O'Brien, and E. G. Nisbet. London methane emissions: use of diurnal changes in concentration and $\delta^{13}C$ to identify urban sources and verify inventories. *Journal of Geophysical Research*, **106** (2001), 7427–7448.

[343] H. Lowry, A. Lill, and B. B. M. Wong. How noisy does a noisy miner have to be? Amplitude adjustments of alarm calls in an avian urban "adapter". *PLoS ONE*, **7** (2012), e29960.

[344] G. W. Luck. A review of the relationships between human population density and biodiversity. *Biological Reviews*, **82** (2007), 607–645.

[345] G. W. Luck and L. T. Smallbone. Species diversity and urbanisation: patterns, drivers and implications. In K. J. Gaston, ed., *Urban Ecology*. (Cambridge: Cambridge University Press, 2010), 88–119.

[346] M. A. Luck, G. D. Jenerette, J. Wu, and N. B. Grimm. The urban funnel model and the spatially heterogeneous ecological footprint. *Ecosystems*, **4** (2001), 782–796.

[347] J. Lundholm. Urban cliffs. In I. Douglas, D. Goode, M. C. Houck, and R. Wang, eds, *The Routledge Handbook of Urban Ecology*. (London: Routledge, 2011), 252–263.

[348] J. T. Lundholm. How novel are urban ecosystems? *Trends in Ecology & Evolution*, **21** (2006), 659–660.

[349] J. T. Lundholm and A. Marlin. Habitat origins and microhabitat preferences of urban plant species. *Urban Ecosystems*, **9** (2006), 139–159.

[350] M. Luniak and R. Mulsow. Ecological parameters in urbanization of the European blackbird. In L. Tomialojc and F. R. Gehlbach, eds, *Avian Population Responses to Man-made Environments*. (Ottawa, Canada: University of Ottawa Press, 1988), 1787–1793.

[351] W. P. MacKay. A comparison of the energy budgets of three species of *Pogonomyrmex* harvester ants (Hymenoptera: Formicidea). *Oecologia*, **66** (1985), 484–494.

[352] J. A. MacMahon, J. F. Mull, and T. O. Crist. Harvester ants (*Pogonomyrmex* spp.): their community and ecosystem influences. *Annual Review of Ecology and Systematics*, **31** (2000), 265–291.

[353] S. B. Magle, P. Reyes, J. Zhu, and K. R. Crooks. Extirpation, colonization, and habitat dynamics of a keystone species along an urban gradient. *Biological Conservation*, **143** (2010), 2146–2155.

[354] T. Magura, B. Tóthmérész, and T. Molnár. Changes in carabid beetle assemblages along an urbanisation gradient in the city of Debrecen, Hungary. *Landscape Ecology*, **19** (2004), 747–759.

[355] R. E. Major, G. Gowing, and C. E. Kendal. Nest predation in Australian urban environments and the role of the pied currawong, *Strepera graculina*. *Austral Ecology*, **21** (1996), 399–409.

[356] A. A. Maklakov, S. Immler, A. Gonzalez-Voyer, J. Rönn, and N. Kolm. Brains and the city: big-brained passerine birds succeed in urban environments. *Biology Letters*, **7** (2011), 730–732.

[357] G. Manley. On the frequency of snowfall in metropolitan England. *Quarterly Journal of the Royal Meteorological Society*, **84** (1958), 70–72.

[358] P. J. Marcotullio. Urban soils. In I. Douglas, D. Goode, M. C. Houck, and R. Wang, eds, *The Routledge Handbook of Urban Ecology*. (London: Routledge, 2011), pp. 164–186.

[359] J. M. Marzluff. Island biogeography for an urbanizing world: how extinction and colonization may determine biological diversity in human-dominated landscapes. *Urban Ecology*, **8** (2008), 355–371.

[360] J. Mason, C. Moorman, G. Hess, and K. Sinclair. Designing suburban greenways to provide habitat for forest-breeding birds. *Landscape and Urban Planning*, **80** (2007), 153–164.

[361] P. A. Matson, W. J. Parton, A. G. Power, and M. J. Swift. Agricultural intensification and ecosystem properties. *Science*, **277** (1997), 504–509.

[362] K. C. Matteson, J. S. Ascher, and G. A. Langellotto. Bee richness and abundance in New York city urban gardens. *Annals of the Entomological Society of America*, **101** (2008), 140–150.

[363] R. A. Mccleery. Changes in fox squirrel anti-predator behaviors across the urban–rural gradient. *Landscape Ecology*, **24** (2009), 483–493.

[364] M. J. McDonnell and A. K. Hahs. The use of gradient analysis studies in advancing our understanding of the ecology of urbanizing landscapes: current status and future directions. *Landscape Ecology*, **23** (2008), 1143–1155.

[365] M. J. McDonnell and S. T. A. Pickett. Ecosystem structure and function along urban-rural gradients: an unexploited opportunity for ecology. *Ecology*, **71** (1990), 1232–1237.

[366] M. J. McDonnell, S. T. A. Pickett, P. Groffman, *et al.* Ecosystem processes along an urban-to-rural gradient. *Urban Ecosystems*, **1** (1997), 21–36.

[367] N. E. McIntyre. Ecology of urban arthropods: a review and call to action. *Annals of the Entomological Society of America*, **93** (2000), 825–835.

[368] N. E. McIntyre and M. E. Hostetler. Effects of land use on pollinators (Hymenoptera: Apoidea) communities in a desert metropolis. *Basic and Applied Ecology*, **2** (2001), 209–218.

[369] N. E. McIntyre and M. E. Hostetler. Effects of urban land use on pollinator (Hymenoptera: Apoidea) communities in a desert metropolis. *Basic and Applied Ecology*, **2** (2001), 209–218.

[370] M. L. McKinney. Urbanization, biodiversity, and conservation. *Bioscience*, **52** (2002), 883–890.

[371] M. L. McKinney. Urbanization as a major cause of biotic homogenization. *Biological Conservation*, **127** (2006), 247–260.

[372] M. L. McKinney. Effects of urbanization on species richness: a review of plants and animals. *Urban Ecosystems*, **11** (2008), 161–176.

[373] M. L. McKinney. Urban futures. In K. J. Gaston, ed., *Urban Ecology*. (Cambridge: Cambridge University Press, 2010), 287–308.

[374] M. L. McKinney and F. A. La Sorte. Invasiveness and homogenization: synergism of wide dispersal and high local abundance. *Global Ecology and Biogeography*, **16** (2007), 394–400.

[375] M. A. McLean, M. J. Angilletta, and K. S. Williams. If you can't stand the heat, stay out of the city: thermal reaction norms of chitinolytic fungi in an urban heat island. *Journal of Thermal Biology*, **30** (2005), 384–391.

[376] P. McManus and G. Haughton. Planning with ecological footprints: a sympathetic critique of theory and practice. *Environment and Urbanization*, **18** (2006), 113–127.

[377] G. McPherson, J. R. Simpson, P. J. Peper, S. E. Maco, and Q. Xiao. Municipal forest benefits and costs in five US cities. *Journal of Forestry*, **103** (2005), 411–416.

[378] S. B. Menke, W. Booth, R. R. Dunn, *et al.* Is it easy to be urban? Convergent success in urban habitats among lineages of a widespread native ant. *PLoS ONE*, **5** (2010), e9194.

[379] G. Mennechez and P. Clergeau. Effect of urbanisation on habitat generalists: starlings not so flexible? *Acta Oecologica*, **30** (2006), 182–191.

[380] C. D. Meurk. Recombinant ecology of urban areas: characterisation, context and creativity. In I. Douglas, D. Goode, M. C. Houck, and R. Wang, eds, *The Routledge Handbook of Urban Ecology*. (London: Routledge, 2011), 198–220.

[381] J. Meyer, N. Klemann, and S. Halle. Diurnal activity patterns of coypu in an urban habitat. *Acta Theriologica*, **50** (2005), 207–211.

[382] C. Milesi, S. W. Running, C. D. Elvidge, *et al.* Mapping and modeling the biogeochemical cycling of turf grasses in the United States. *Environmental Management*, **36** (2005), 426–438.

[383] R. Mitchell and F. Popham. Effect of exposure to natural environment on health inequalities: an observational population study. *Lancet*, **372** (2008), 1655–1660.

[384] V. G. Mitchell, T. A. McMahon, and R. G. Mein. Components of the total water balance of an urban catchment. *Environmental Management*, **32** (2003), 735–746.

[385] S. F. Moffatt, S. M. McLachlan, and N. C. Kenkel. Impacts of land use on riparian forest along an urban–rural gradient in southern Manitoba. *Plant Ecology*, **174** (2004), 119–135.

[386] K. Mokwa. Wintering range of the blackcap (*Sylvia atricapilla*) in Europe: stabilized or changing? *The Ring*, **31** (2009), 45–58.

[387] A. P. Møller. Flight distance of urban birds, predation, and selection for urban life. *Behavioral Ecology and Sociobiology*, **63** (2008), 63–75.

[388] A. P. Møller. Successful city dwellers: a comparative study of the ecological characteristics of urban birds in the western palearctic. *Oecologia*, **159** (2009), 849–858.

[389] M. Moore, P. Gould, and B. S. Keary. Global urbanization and impact on health. *International Journal of Hygiene and Environmental Health*, **206** (2003), 269–278.

[390] K. Morland, S. Wing, and A. D. Roux. The contextual effect of the local food environment on residents' diets: the atherosclerosis risk in communities study. *American Journal of Public Health*, **92** (2002), 1761–1767.

[391] E. C. Mueller and T. A. Day. The effect of urban ground cover on microclimate, growth and leaf gas exchange of oleander in Phoenix, Arizona. *International Journal of Biometeorology*, **49** (2005), 244–255.

[392] D. B. Müller, T. Wang, B. Duval, and T. E. Graedel. Exploring the engine of anthropogenic iron cycles. *Proceedings of the National Academy of Sciences*, **103** (2006), 16111–16116.

[393] J. Munshi-South and K. Kharchenko. Rapid, pervasive genetic differentiation of urban white-footed mouse (*Peromyscus leucopus*) populations in New York City. *Molecular Ecology*, **19** (2010), 4242–4254.

[394] S. Naeem, L. J. Thompson, S. P. Lawler, J. H. Lawton, and R. M. Woodfin. Declining bio-diversity can alter the performance of ecosystems. *Nature*, **368** (1994), 734–737.

[395] R. J. Naiman. Animal influences on ecosystem dynamics. *BioScience*, **38** (1988), 750–752.

[396] S. Napolitano, J. Schreifels, G. Stevens, *et al.* The US acid rain program: key insights from the design, operation, and assessment of a cap-and-trade program. *The Electricity Journal*, **20** (2007), 47–58.

[397] E. Nemeth and H. Brumm. Blackbirds sing higher-pitched songs in cities: adaptation to habitat acoustics or side-effect of urbanization? *Animal Behaviour*, **78** (2009), 637–641.

[398] C. Nevison. A reexamination of the impact of anthropogenically fixed nitrogen on atmospheric N_2O and the stratospheric O_3 layer. *Journal of Geophysical Research*, **102** (1997), 25519–25536.

[399] M. M. Newman, P. J. Yeh, and T. D. Price. Reduced territorial responses in dark-eyed juncos following population establishment in a climatically mild environment. *Animal Behaviour*, **71** (2006), 893–899.

[400] S. D. Newsome, K. Ralls, C. V. H. Job, M. L. Fogel, and B. L. Cypher. Stable isotopes evaluate exploitation of anthropogenic foods by the endangered San Joaquin kit fox (*Vulpes macrotis mutica*). *Journal of Mammalogy*, **91** (2010), 1313–1321.

[401] S. J. Ng, J. W. Dole, R. M. Sauvajot, S. P. D. Riley, and T. J. Valone. Use of highway under-crossings by wildlife in southern California. *Biological Conservation*, **115** (2004), 499–507.

[402] N. S. Ngo and D. E. Pataki. The energy and mass balance of Los Angeles County. *Urban Ecosystems*, **11** (2008), 121–139.

[403] J. Niemela. Is there a need for urban ecology? *Urban Ecosystems*, **3** (1999), 57–65.

[404] J. Niemela, D. J. Kotze, S. Venn, *et al.* Carabid beetle assemblages (Coleoptera, Carabidae) across urban–rural gradients: an international comparison. *Landscape Ecology*, **17** (2002), 387–401.

[405] C. H. Nilon, C. N. Long, and W. C. Zipperer. Effects of wildland development on forest bird communities. *Landscape and Urban Planning*, **32** (1995), 81–92.

[406] D. J. Nowak, D. E. Crane, and J. C. Stevens. Air pollution removal by urban trees and shrubs in the United States. *Urban Forestry & Urban Greening*, **4** (2006), 115–123.

[407] D. J. Nowak and J. T. Walton. Projected urban growth (2000–2050) and its estimated impact on the US forest resource. *Journal of Forestry*, **103** (2005), 383–389.

[408] E. P. Odum. *Ecology, 2nd edn.* (Boston, MA: Holt, Rinehart, and Winston, 1975).

[409] E. P. Odum. *Ecology: a Bridge Between Science and Society.* (Sunderland, MA: Sinauer, 1997).

[410] T. R. Oke. The energetic basis of the urban heat island. *Quarterly Journal of the Royal Meteorological Society*, **108** (1982), 1–24.

[411] T. R. Oke. *Boundary Layer Climates, 2nd edn.* (New York: Routledge, 1987).

[412] T. R. Oke. Urban heat islands. In I. Douglas, D. Goode, M. C. Houck, and R. Wang, eds, *The Routledge Handbook of Urban Ecology.* (New York: Routledge, 2011), pp. 120–131.

[413] T. R. Oke, R. A. Spronken-Smith, E. Jauregui, and C. S. B. Grimmond. The energy balance of central Mexico City during the dry season. *Atmospheric Environment*, **33** (1999), 3919–3930.

[414] J. D. Olden. Biotic homogenization: a new research agenda for conservation biogeography. *Journal of Biogeography*, **33** (2006), 2027–2039.

[415] R. O'Leary and D. N. Jones. The use of supplementary foods by Australian magpies *Gymnorhina tibicen*: implications for wildlife feeding in suburban environments. *Austral Ecology*, **31** (2006), 208–216.

[416] A. R. Omram. The epidemiologic transition: a theory of the epidemiology of population change. *Bulletin of the World Health Organization*, **79** (2001), 161–170.

[417] A. S. Oneal and J. T. Rotenberry. Riparian plant composition in an urbanizing landscape in southern California, USA. *Landscape Ecology*, **23** (2008), 553–567.

[418] M. Oprea, P. Mendes, T. B. Vieira, and A. D. Ditchfield. Do wooded streets provide connectivity for bats in an urban landscape? *Biodiversity and Conservation*, **18** (2009), 2361–2371.

[419] G. H. Orians and J. H. Heerwagen. Evolved responses to landscapes. In J. H. Barkow, L. Cosmides, and J. Tooby, eds, *The Adapted Mind: Evolutionary Psychology and the Generation of Culture*. (Oxford: Oxford University Press, 1992), 555–579.

[420] A. Ortega-Guerrero, J. A. Cherry, and D. L. Rudolph. Large-scale aquitard consolidation near Mexico City. *Ground Water*, **31** (1993), 708–718.

[421] C. P. Osborne and D. J. Beerling. Nature's green revolution: the remarkable evolutionary rise of C_4 plants. *Philosophical Transactions of the Royal Society B*, **361** (2006), 173–194.

[422] D. W. Osgood and J. M. Chambers. Social disorganization outside the metropolis: an analysis of rural youth violence. *Criminology*, **38** (2000), 81–116.

[423] L. K. Page, S. D. Gehrt, and N. P. Robinson. Land-use effects on prevalence of raccoon roundworm (*Baylisascaris procyonis*). *Journal of Wildlife Diseases*, **44** (2008), 594–599.

[424] S. R. Palumbi. Humans as the world's greatest evolutionary force. *Science*, **293** (2001), 1786–1790.

[425] T. S. Parker and C. H. Nilon. Gray squirrel density, habitat suitability, and behavior in urban parks. *Urban Ecosystems*, **11** (2008), 243–255.

[426] K. M. Parris and D. L. Hazell. Biotic effects of climate change in urban environments: the case of the grey-headed flying-fox (*Pteropus poliocephalus*) in Melbourne, Australia. *Biological Conservation*, **124** (2005), 267–276.

[427] K. M. Parris, M. Velik-Lord, and J. M. A. North. Frogs call at a higher pitch in traffic noise. *Ecology and Society*, **14** (2009), 25.

[428] H. Parsons, R. E. Major, and K. French. Species interactions and habitat associations of birds inhabiting urban areas of Sydney, Australia. *Austral Ecology*, **31** (2006), 217–227.

[429] J. Partecke and E. Gwinner. Underlying physiological control of reproduction in urban and forest-dwelling European blackbirds *Turdus merula*. *Journal of Avian Biology*, **36** (2005), 295–305.

[430] J. Partecke and E. Gwinner. Increased sedentariness in European blackbirds following urbanization: a consequence of local adaptation? *Ecology*, **88** (2007), 882–90.

[431] J. Partecke, I. Schwabl, and E. Gwinner. Stress and the city: urbanization and its effects on the stress physiology in European blackbirds. *Ecology*, **87** (2006), 1945–1952.

[432] D. E. Pataki, D. R. Bowling, and J. R. Ehleringer. Seasonal cycle of carbon dioxide and its isotopic composition in an urban atmosphere: anthropogenic and biogenic effects. *Journal of Geophysical Research*, **108** (2003), 4735.

[433] D. E. Pataki, M. M. Carreiro, J. Cherrier, *et al.* Coupling biogeochemical cycles in urban environments: ecosystem services, green solutions, and misconceptions. *Frontiers in Ecology and the Environment,* **9** (2011), 27–36.

[434] G. L. Patricelli and J. L. Blickley. Avian communication in urban noise: causes and consequences of vocal adjustment. *The Auk,* **123** (2006), 639–649.

[435] M. A. Patten and D. T. Bolger. Variation in top-down control of avian reproductive success across a fragmentation gradient. *Oikos,* **101** (2003), 479–488.

[436] J. A. Patz and S. H. Olson. Climate change and health: global to local influences on disease risk. *Annals of Tropical Medicine and Parasitology,* **100** (2006), 535–549.

[437] S. Pauleit and F. Duhme. Assessing the environmental performance of land cover types for urban planning. *Landscape and Urban Planning,* **52** (2000), 1–20.

[438] M. Pautasso and M. L. McKinney. The botanist effect revisited: plant species richness, county area, and human population size in the United States. *Conservation Biology,* **21** (2007), 1333–1340.

[439] M. A. Pavao-Zuckerman and L. B. Byrne. Scratching the surface and digging deeper: exploring ecological theories in urban soils. *Urban Ecosystems,* **12** (2009), 9–20.

[440] M. A. Pavao-Zuckerman and D. C. Coleman. Decomposition of chestnut oak (*Quercus prinus*) leaves and nitrogen mineralization in an urban environment. *Biology and Fertility of Soils,* **41** (2005), 343–349.

[441] M. Pećarević, J. Danoff-Burg, and R. R. Dunn. Biodiversity on Broadway: enigmatic diversity of the societies of ants (Formicidae) on the streets of New York City. *PLoS ONE,* **5** (2010), e13222.

[442] J. Peen and J. Dekker. Is urbanicity an environmental risk-factor for psychiatric disorders? *Lancet,* **363** (2004), 2012–2013.

[443] W. C. Perdue, L. O. Gostin, and L. A. Stone. Public health and the built environment: historical, empirical, and theoretical foundations for an expanded role. *Journal of Law Medicine & Ethics,* **31** (2003), 557–566.

[444] S. T. A. Pickett, M. L. Cadenasso, J. M. Grove, *et al.* Urban ecological systems: linking terrestrial ecological, physical, and socioeconomic components of metropolitan areas. *Annual Review of Ecology and Systematics,* **32** (2001), 127–157.

[445] S. T. A. Pickett, M. L. Cadenasso, J. M. Grove, *et al.* Beyond urban legends: an emerging framework of urban ecology, as illustrated by the Baltimore ecosystem study. *Bioscience,* **58** (2008), 139–150.

[446] M. Piringer, C. S. B. Grimmond, S. M. Joffre, *et al.* Investigating the surface energy balance in urban areas – recent advances and future needs. *Water, Air, & Soil Pollution,* **2** (2002), 1–16.

[447] C. E. R. Pitcairn, I. D. Leith, L. J. Sheppard, *et al.* The relationship between nitrogen deposition, species composition and foliar nitrogen concentrations in woodland flora in the vicinity of livestock farms. *Environmental Pollution,* **102** (1998), 41–48.

[448] R. M. Plowes, J. G. Dunn, and L. E. Gilbert. The urban fire ant paradox: native fire ants persist in an urban refuge while invasive fire ants dominate natural habitats. *Biological Invasions,* **9** (2007), 825–836.

[449] R. K. Plowright, P. Foley, H. E. Field, *et al.* Urban habituation, ecological connectivity and epidemic dampening: the emergence of hendra virus from flying foxes (*Pteropus* spp.). *Proceedings of the Royal Society B: Biological Sciences,* **278** (2011), 3703–3712.

[450] C. A. Pope 3rd. Respiratory disease associated with community air pollution and a steel mill, Utah Valley. *American Journal of Public Health,* **79** (1989), 623–628.

[451] W. M. Post, T. H. Peng, W. R. Emanuel, *et al.* The global carbon cycle. *American Scientist*, **78** (1990), 310–326.

[452] S. L. Postel. Entering an era of water scarcity: the challenges ahead. *Ecological Applications*, **10** (2000), 941–948.

[453] D. A. Potvin, K. M. Parris, and R. A. Mulder. Geographically pervasive effects of urban noise on frequency and syllable rate of songs and calls in silvereyes (*Zosterops lateralis*). *Proceedings of the Royal Society B: Biological Sciences*, **278** (2011), 2464–2469.

[454] F. H. Pough. Acid precipitation and embryonic mortality of spotted salamanders, *Ambystoma maculatum*. *Science*, **192** (1976), 68–70.

[455] R. V. Pouyat and M. J. McDonnell. Heavy metal accumulations in forest soils along an urban–rural gradient in southeastern New York, USA. *Water, Air, & Soil Pollution*, **57** (1991), 797–807.

[456] R. V. Pouyat, M. J. McDonnell, and S. T. A. Pickett. Litter decomposition and nitrogen mineralization in oak stands along an urban–rural land use gradient. *Urban Ecosystems*, **1** (1997), 117–131.

[457] R. V. Pouyat, I. D. Russell-Anelli, J. Neerchal, *et al.* Soil chemical and physical properties that differentiate urban land-use and cover types. *Soil Science Society of America Journal*, **71** (2007), 1010–1019.

[458] R. V. Pouyat, I. D. Yesilonis, and N. E. Golubiewski. A comparison of soil organic carbon stocks between residential turf grass and native soil. *Urban Ecosystems*, **12** (2009), 45–62.

[459] S. Prange, S. D. Gehrt, and E. P. Wiggers. Influences of anthropogenic resources on raccoon (*Procyon lotor*) movements and spatial distribution. *Journal of Mammalogy*, **85** (2004), 483–490.

[460] T. D. Price, P. J. Yeh, and B. Harr. Phenotypic plasticity and the evolution of a socially selected trait following colonization of a novel environment. *The American Naturalist*, **172S** (2008), 49–62.

[461] P. Pysek, Z. Chocholouskova, A. Pysek, *et al.* Trends in species diversity and composition of urban vegetation over three decades. *Journal of Vegetation Science*, **15** (2004), 781–788.

[462] Y. F. Qian and F. Ronald. Assessing soil carbon sequestration in turfgrass systems using long-term soil testing data. *Agronomy Journal*, **94** (2002), 930–935.

[463] N. N. Rabalais, R. E. Turner, and W. J. Wiseman Jr. Gulf of Mexico Hypoxia, a.k.a. "The Dead Zone". *Annual Review of Ecology and Systematics*, **33** (2002), 235–263.

[464] S. M. Raciti, P. M. Groffman, and T. J. Fahey. Nitrogen retention in urban lawns and forests. *Ecological Applications*, **18** (2008), 1615–1626.

[465] S. M. Raciti, L. Hutyra, P. Rao, and A. C. Finzi. Inconsistent definitions of "urban" result in different conclusions about the size of urban carbon and nitrogen stocks. *Ecological Applications*, (2012), in press.

[466] D. M. Ramakrishna and T. Viraraghavan. Environmental impact of chemical deicers: a review. *Water, Air, & Soil Pollution*, **166** (2005), 49–63.

[467] C. E. Ramalho and R. J. Hobbs. Time for a change: dynamic urban ecology. *Trends in Ecology & Evolution*, **27** (2011), 179–188.

[468] V. Ramanathan, P. J. Crutzen, J. T. Keihl, and D. Rosenfeld. Aerosols, climate, and the hydrological cycle. *Science*, **294** (2001), 2119–2124.

[469] J. E. Ramirez and G. S. Keller. Effects of landscape on behavior of black-tailed prairie dogs (*Cynomys ludovicianus*) in rural and urban habitats. *The Southwestern Naturalist*, **55** (2010), 167–171.

[470] M. J. Raupp, P. M. Shrewsbury, and D. A. Herms. Ecology of herbivorous arthropods in urban landscapes. *Annual Review of Entomology*, **55** (2010), 19–38.

[471] D. Rayfield, J. W. S. Longhurst, A. F. R. Watson, *et al.* A methodology for estimation of vehicle emissions in an urban environment: an example from Greater Manchester. *The Environmentalist*, **18** (1998), 175–182.

[472] J. A. Reale and R. B. Blair. Nesting success and life-history attributes of bird communities along an urbanization gradient. *Urban Habitats*, **3** (2005), 1–24.

[473] A. C. Redfield. On the proportions of organic derivatives in sea water and their relation to the composition of plankton. In R. J. Daniel, ed., *James Johnstone Memorial Volume.* (Liverpool, UK: University Press of Liverpool, 1934), 177–192.

[474] M. Rees, J. H. Roe, and A. Georges. Life in the suburbs: behavior and survival of a freshwater turtle in response to drought and urbanization. *Biological Conservation*, **142** (2009), 3172–3181.

[475] W. Rees and M. Wackernagel. Urban ecological footprints: why cities cannot be sustainable? And why they are a key to sustainability. *Environmental Impact Assessment Review*, **16** (1996), 223–248.

[476] W. E. Rees. Patch disturbance, ecofootprints, and biological integrity: revisiting the limits to growth (or why industrial society is inherently unsustainable). In D. Pimentel, L. Westra, and R. F. Noss, eds, *Ecological Integrity: Integrating Environment, Conservation, and Health.* (Washington DC: Island Press, 2000), pp. 139–156.

[477] W. E. Rees. Understanding urban ecosystems: an ecological economics perspective. In A. Berkowitz, C. H. Nilon, and K. S. Hollweg, eds, *Understanding Urban Ecosystems.* (Berlin: Springer-Verlag, 2003), pp. 115–136.

[478] W. K. Reisen, R. M. Takahashi, B. D. Carroll, and R. Quiring. Delinquent mortgages, neglected swimming pools, and West Nile virus, California. *Emerging Infectious Diseases*, **14** (2008), 1747–1749.

[479] M. Richter and U. Weiland. *Applied Urban Ecology: A Global Framework.* (Wiley Online Library, 2011).

[480] S. P. D. Riley, G. T. Busteed, L. B. Kats, *et al.* Effects of urbanization on the distribution and abundance of amphibians and invasive species in southern California streams. *Conservation Biology*, **19** (2005), 1894–1907.

[481] S. P. D. Riley, J. Foley, and B. Chomel. Exposure to feline and canine pathogens in bobcats and gray foxes in urban and rural zones of a National Park in California. *Journal of Wildlife Diseases*, **40** (2004), 11–22.

[482] F. Rindi. Diversity, distribution and ecology of green algae and cyanobacteria in urban habitats. In J. Seckbach, ed., *Algae and Cyanobacteria in Extreme Environments.* (Berlin: Springer, 2007), pp. 619–638.

[483] S. M. Robaa. Urban-suburban/rural differences over Greater Cairo, Egypt. *Atmosfera*, **16** (2003), 157–172.

[484] G. N. Robb, R. A. McDonald, D. E. Chamberlain, and S. Bearhop. Food for thought: supplementary feeding as a driver of ecological change in avian populations. *Frontiers in Ecology and the Environment*, **6** (2008), 476–484.

[485] G. N. Robb, R. A. McDonald, D. E. Chamberlain, *et al.* Winter feeding of birds increases productivity in the subsequent breeding season. *Biology Letters*, **4** (2008), 220–223.

[486] B. Robertson, G. Y. Kriska, V. Horváth, and G. Horváth. Glass buildings as bird feeders: urban birds exploit insects trapped by polarized light pollution. *Acta Zoologica Academiae Scientiarum Hungaricae*, **56** (2010), 283–293.

[487] A. D. Rodewald, L. Kearns, and D. Shustack. Anthropogenic resource subsidies decouple predator–prey relationships. *Ecological Applications*, **21** (2010), 936–943.

[488] A. D. Rodewald and D. P. Shustack. Urban flight: understanding individual and population–level responses of Nearctic–Neotropical migratory birds to urbanization. *Journal of Animal Ecology*, **77** (2008), 83–91.

[489] G. Rolshausen, G. Segelbacher, K. A. Hobson, and H. M. Schaefer. Contemporary evolution of reproductive isolation and phenotypic divergence in sympatry along a migratory divide. *Current Biology*, **19** (2009), 2097–2101.

[490] L. S. Rose, J. A. Stallins, and M. L. Bentley. Concurrent cloud-to-ground lightning and precipitation enhancement in the Atlanta, Georgia (United States), urban region. *Earth Interactions*, **12** (2008), 1–30.

[491] D. Rosenfeld. Suppression of rain and snow by urban and industrial air pollution. *Science*, **287** (2000), 1793–1796.

[492] R. N. Rosenfield, S. J. Taft, W. E. Stout, *et al.* Low prevalence of *Trichomonas gallinae* in urban and migratory Cooper's hawks in northcentral North America. *The Wilson Journal of Ornithology*, **121** (2009), 641–644.

[493] C. Rosenzweig, W. D. Solecki, L. Parshall, *et al.* Mitigating New York City's heat island: integrating stakeholder perspectives and scientific evaluation. *Bulletin of the American Meteorological Society*, **90** (2009), 1297–1312.

[494] T. Rosswall. The internal nitrogen cycle between microorganisms, vegetation and soil. *Ecological Bulletins*, **22** (1976), 157–167.

[495] M. Roth. Review of urban climate research in (sub)tropical regions. *International Journal of Climatology*, **27** (2007), 1859–1873.

[496] D. L. Royer, R. A. Berner, I. P. Montañez, N. J. Tabor, and D. J. Beerling. CO_2 as a primary driver of Phanerozoic climate. *GSA Today*, **14** (2004), 4–10.

[497] M. K. Rust and D. A. Reierson. Use of extreme temperatures in urban insect pest management. In G. J. Hallman and D. L. Denlinger, eds, *Temperature Sensitivity in Insects and Application in Integrated Pest Management*. (Boulder, CO: Westview Press, 1998), pp. 179–200.

[498] T. B. Ryder, R. Reitsma, B. Evans, and P. P. Marra. Quantifying avian nest survival along an urbanization gradient using citizen-and scientist generated data. *Ecological Applications*, **20** (2010), 419–426.

[499] J. P. Sadler, E. C. Small, H. Fiszpan, M. G. Telfer, and J. Niemela. Investigating environmental variation and landscape characteristics of an urban–rural gradient using woodland carabid assemblages. *Journal of Biogeography*, **33** (2006), 1126–1138.

[500] R. F. Sage and R. K. Monson. *C_4 Plant Biology*. (New York: Academic Press, 1999).

[501] O. E. Sala, F. S. Chapin III, J. J. Armesto, *et al.* Global biodiversity scenarios for the year 2100. *Science*, **287** (2000), 1770–1774.

[502] M. J. Samways and N. S. Steytler. Dragonfly (Odonata) distribution patterns in urban and forest landscapes, and recommendations for riparian management. *Biological Conservation*, **78** (1996), 279–288.

[503] D. Sands. Conserving the Richmond birdwing butterfly over two decades: where to next? *Ecological Management & Restoration*, **9** (2008), 4–16.

[504] J. L. Sarmiento and N. Gruber. Sinks for anthropogenic carbon. *Physics Today*, **55** (2002), 30–36.

[505] J. D. Sartor, G. B. Boyd, and F. J. Agardy. Water pollution aspects of street surface contaminants. *Journal of the Water Pollution Control Federation*, **46** (1974), 458–467.

[506] M. Sato, Y. Kohmatsu, M. Yuma, and Y. Tsubaki. Population genetic differentiation in three sympatric damselfly species in a highly fragmented urban landscape (Zygoptera: Coenagrionidae). *Odonatologica*, **37** (2008), 131–144.

[507] J. Scales, J. Hyman, and M. Hughes. Behavioral syndromes break down in urban song sparrow populations. *Ethology*, **117** (2011), 1–9.

[508] D. W. Schindler, M. A. Turner, and R. H. Hesslein. Acidification and alkalinization of lakes by experimental addition of nitrogen compounds. *Biogeochemistry*, **1** (1985), 117–133.

[509] M. A. Schlaepfer, P. W. Sherman, B. Blossey, and M. C. Runge. Introduced species as evolutionary traps. *Ecology Letters*, **8** (2005), 241–246.

[510] M. D. Schlesinger, P. N. Manley, and M. Holyoak. Distinguishing stressors acting on land bird communities in an urbanizing environment. *Ecology*, **89** (2008), 2302–2314.

[511] M. Schmidt. Global climate change: the wrong parameter. In *Proceedings of Rio 9, World Energy and Climate Event*, (2009), pp. 167–176.

[512] D. M. Schultz, S. Mikkonen, A. Laaksonen, and M. Richman. Weekly precipitation cycles: lack of evidence from the United States surface stations. *Geophysical Research Letters*, **34** (2007), L22815.

[513] M. C. Scott. Winners and losers among stream fishes in relation to land use legacies and urban development in the southeastern US. *Biological Conservation*, **127** (2006), 301–309.

[514] S. Seitzinger, J. A. Harrison, J. K. Bohlke, A. F. Bouwman, R. Lowrance, B. Peterson, C. Tobias, and G. Drecht. Denitrification across landscapes and waterscapes: a synthesis. *Ecological Applications*, **16** (2006), 2064–2090.

[515] P. Shahmohamadi, C. A. Ai, K. N. A. Maulud, N. M. Tawil, and N. A. G. Abdullah. The impact of anthropogenic heat on formation of urban heat island and energy consumption balance. *Urban Studies Research*, (2011), Article ID 497524.

[516] M. Shao, X. Tang, Y. Zhang, and W. Li. City clusters in China: air and surface water pollution. *Frontiers in Ecology and the Environment*, **4** (2006), 353–361.

[517] A. M. Shapiro. The California urban butterfly fauna is dependent on alien plants. *Diversity and Distributions*, **8** (2002), 31–40.

[518] J. E. Sharman, J. R. Cockcroft, and J. S. Coombes. Cardiovascular implications of exposure to traffic air pollution during exercise. *QJM*, **97** (2004), 637–643.

[519] J. M. Shepherd. A review of current investigations of urban-induced rainfall and recommendations for the future. *Earth Interactions*, **9** (2005), 1–27.

[520] J. M. Shepherd and S. J. Burian. Detection of urban-induced rainfall anomalies in a major coastal city. *Earth Interactions*, **7** (2003), 1–17.

[521] J. M. Shepherd, J. A. Stallins, M. L. Jin, and T. L. Mote. Urban effects on precipitation and associated convective processes. In I. Douglas, D. Goode, M. C. Houck, and R. Wang, eds, *The Routledge Handbook of Urban Ecology*. (New York: Routledge, 2011), pp. 132–147.

[522] Y. Shimoda. Adaptation measures for climate change and the urban heat island in Japan's built environment. *Building Research & Information*, **31** (2003), 222–230.

[523] E. Shochat. Credit or debit? Resource input changes population dynamics of city-slicker birds. *Oikos*, **106** (2004), 622–626.

[524] E. Shochat, S. B. Lerman, J. M. Anderies, *et al.* Invasion, competition, and biodiversity loss in urban ecosystems. *Bioscience*, **60** (2010), 199–208.

[525] E. Shochat, S. B. Lerman, M. Katti, and D. B. Lewis. Linking optimal foraging behavior to bird community structure in an urban-desert landscape: field experiments with artificial food patches. *The American Naturalist*, **164** (2004), 232–243.

[526] E. Shochat, W. L. Stefanov, M. E. A. Whitehouse, and S. H. Faeth. Urbanization and spider diversity: influences of human modification of habitat structure and productivity. *Ecological Applications*, **14** (2004), 268–280.

[527] E. Shochat, P. S. Warren, S. H. Faeth, N. E. McIntyre, and D. Hope. From patterns to emerging processes in mechanistic urban ecology. *Trends in Ecology & Evolution*, **21** (2006), 186–191.

[528] W. D. Shuster, J. Bonta, H. Thurston, E. Warnemuende, and D. R. Smith. Impacts of impervious surface on watershed hydrology: a review. *Urban Water Journal*, **2** (2005), 263–275.

[529] A. Shwartz, S. Shirley, and S. Kark. How do habitat variability and management regime shape the spatial heterogeneity of birds within a large Mediterranean urban park? *Landscape and Urban Planning*, **84** (2008), 219–229.

[530] J. Silvertown, P. Poulton, E. Johnston, *et al.* The Park Grass Experiment 1856–2006: its contribution to ecology. *Journal of Ecology*, **94** (2006), 801–814.

[531] M. Simmons, M. Bertelsen, S. Windhager, and H. Zafian. The performance of native and non-native turfgrass monocultures and native turfgrass polycultures: an ecological approach to sustainable lawns. *Ecological Engineering*, **37** (2011), 1095–1103.

[532] L. Simon. Heavy metals, sodium and sulphur in roadside topsoils and in the indicator plant chicory (*Cichorium intybus* L.). *Acta Agronomica Hungarica*, **49** (2001), 1–13.

[533] V. Sims, K. L. Evans, S. E. Newson, J. A. Tratalos, and K. J. Gaston. Avian assemblage structure and domestic cat densities in urban environments. *Diversity and Distributions*, **14** (2008), 387–399.

[534] H. Slabbekoorn and A. den Boer-Visser. Cities change the songs of birds. *Current Biology*, **16** (2006), 2326–2331.

[535] H. Slabbekoorn and M. Peet. Birds sing at a higher pitch in urban noise. *Nature*, **424** (2003), 267.

[536] V. Smil. Energy in the twentieth century: resources, conversions, costs, uses, and consequences. *Annual Reviews in Energy and the Environment*, **25** (2000), 21–51.

[537] V. Smil. Phosphorus in the environment: natural flows and human interferences. *Annual Review of Energy and the Environment*, **25** (2000), 53–88.

[538] B. E. Smith. Structure: nitrogenase reveals its inner secrets. *Science*, **297** (2002), 1654–1655.

[539] B. R. Smith. Re-thinking wastewater landscapes: combining innovative strategies to address tomorrow's urban wastewater treatment challenges. *Water Science and Technology*, **60** (2009), 1465–1473.

[540] R. Snep and P. Opdam. Integrating nature values in urban planning and design. In K. J. Gaston, ed., *Urban Ecology*. (Cambridge: Cambridge University Press, 2010), pp. 261–286.

[541] Y. Song and G. J. Knaap. Is Portland winning the war on sprawl? *Journal of the American Planning Association*, **70** (2004), 210–225.

[542] F. A. La Sorte and F. R. Thompson III. Poleward shifts in winter ranges of North American birds. *Ecology*, **88** (2007), 1803–1812.

[543] F. A. La Sorte and M. L. McKinney. Compositional similarity and the distribution of geographical range size for assemblages of native and non-native species in urban floras. *Diversity and Distributions*, **12** (2006), 679–686.

[544] F. A. La Sorte, M. L. McKinney, and P. Pysek. Compositional similarity among urban floras within and across continents: biogeographical consequences of human-mediated biotic interchange. *Global Change Biology*, **13** (2007), 913–921.

[545] M. E. Soulé, D. T. Bolger, A. C. Alberts, *et al.* Reconstructed dynamics of rapid extinctions of chaparral-requiring birds in urban habitat islands. *Conservation Biology*, **2** (1988), 75–92.

[546] C. D. Soulsbury, G. Iossa, P. J. Baker, *et al.* The impact of sarcoptic mange *Sarcoptes scabiei* on the British fox *Vulpes vulpes* population. *Mammal Review*, **37** (2007), 278–296.

[547] S. Spatari, M. Bertram, K. Fuse, T. E. Graedel, and E. Shelov. The contemporary European zinc cycle: 1-year stocks and flows. *Resources, Conservation and Recycling*, **39** (2003), 137–160.

[548] M. R. Speight, R. S. Hails, M. Gilbert, and A. Foggo. Horse chestnut scale (*Pulvinaria regalis*)(Homoptera: Coccidae) and urban host tree environment. *Ecology*, **79** (1998), 1503–1513.

[549] J. A. Stallins and L. S. Rose. Urban lightning: current research, methods, and the geographical perspective. *Geography Compass*, **2** (2008), 620–639.

[550] S. M. Standaert, J. E. Dawson, W. Schaffner, *et al.* Ehrlichiosis in a golf-oriented retirement community. *The New England Journal of Medicine*, **333** (1995), 420–425.

[551] W. L. Stefanov, L. Prashad, C. Eisinger, A. Brazel, and S. L. Harlan. Investigation of human modifications of landscape and climate in the Phoenix Arizona metropolitan area using MASTER data. *The International Archives of the Photogrammetry, Remote Sensing, and Spatial Information Sciences*, **35** (2004),1339–1347.

[552] D. A. Steinberg, R. V. Pouyat, R. W. Parmelee, and P. M. Groffman. Earthworm abundance and nitrogen mineralization rates along an urban–rural land use gradient. *Soil Biology and Biochemistry*, **29** (1997), 427–430.

[553] R. G. Stevens and M. S. Rea. Light in the built environment: potential role of circadian disruption in endocrine disruption and breast cancer. *Cancer Causes and Control*, **12** (2001), 279–287.

[554] G. H. Stewart, M. E. Ignatieva, C. D. Meurk, and R. D. Earl. The re-emergence of indigenous forest in an urban environment, Christchurch, New Zealand. *Urban Forestry & Urban Greening*, **2** (2004), 149–158.

[555] B. Strauss and R. Biedermann. Urban brownfields as temporary habitats: driving forces for the diversity of phytophagous insects. *Ecography*, **29** (2006), 928–940.

[556] G. Suzan and G. Ceballos. The role of feral mammals on wildlife infectious disease prevalence in two nature reserves within Mexico City limits. *Journal of Zoo and Wildlife Medicine*, **36** (2005), 479–484.

[557] C. M. Swan, B. Healey, and D. C. Richardson. The role of native riparian tree species in decomposition of invasive tree of heaven (*Ailanthus altissima*) leaf litter in an urban stream. *Ecoscience*, **15** (2008), 27–35.

[558] K. Szlavecz, P. Warren, and S. Pickett. Biodiversity on the urban landscape. In R. P. Cincotta and L. J. Gorenfio, eds, *Human Population*. (Berlin: Springer, 2011), 75–101.

[559] C. J. Tait, C. B. Daniels, and R. S. Hill. Changes in species assemblages within the Adelaide metropolitan area, Australia, 1836–2002. *Ecological Applications*, **15** (2005), 346–359.

[560] T. Takano, K. Nakamura, and M. Watanabe. Urban residential environments and senior citizens' longevity in megacity areas: the importance of walkable green spaces. *Journal of Epidemiology and Community Health*, **56** (2002), 913–918.

[561] D. W. Tallamy. *Bringing Nature Home: How Native Plants Sustain Wildlife in Our Gardens*. (London: Timber Press, 2007).

[562] P. Tans. Trends in atmospheric carbon dioxide. *National Oceanic and Atmospheric Administration Earth System Research Laboratory*, Volume **6**, (2009).

[563] P. H. Templer and T. M. McCann. Effects of the hemlock woolly adelgid on nitrogen losses from urban and rural northern forest ecosystems. *Ecosystems*, **13** (2010), 1–12.

[564] W. H. Terjung and S. S. Louie. Solar radiation and urban heat islands. *Annals of the Association of American Geographers*, **63** (1973), 181–207.

[565] C. W. Thompson, P. Aspinall, and A. Montarzino. The childhood factor: adult visits to green places and the significance of childhood experience. *Environment and Behavior*, **40** (2008), 111–143.

[566] K. Thompson, K. C. Austin, R. M. Smith, *et al.* Urban domestic gardens (I): putting small-scale diversity in context. *Biodiversity and Conservation*, **14** (2003), 71–78.

[567] K. Thompson, J. G. Hodgson, R. M. Smith, P. H. Warren, and K. J. Gaston. Urban domestic gardens (III): composition and diversity of lawn floras. *Journal of Vegetation Science*, **15** (2004), 373–378.

[568] K. Thompson and A. Jones. Human population density and prediction of local plant extinction in Britain. *Conservation Biology*, **13** (1999), 185–189.

[569] H. Thomson, R. Atkinson, M. Petticrew, and A. Kearns. Do urban regeneration programmes improve public health and reduce health inequalities? A synthesis of the evidence from UK policy and practice (1980–2004). *Journal of Epidemiology & Community Health*, **60** (2006), 108–115.

[570] J. H. Tilt. Urban nature and human physical health. In I. Douglas, D. Goode, M. C. Houck, and R. Wang, eds. *The Routledge Handbook of Urban Ecology.* (London: Routledge, 2011), pp. 394–407.

[571] G. H. Tomlinson. Acidic deposition, nutrient leaching and forest growth. *Biogeochemistry*, **65** (2003), 51–81.

[572] A. Townsend-Small and C. I. Czimczik. Carbon sequestration and greenhouse gas emissions in urban turf. *Geophysical Research Letters*, **37** (2010), L02707.

[573] H. Tran, D. Uchihama, S. Ochi, and Y. Yasuoka. Assessment with satellite data of the urban heat island effects in Asian mega cities. *International Journal of Applied Earth Observations and Geoinformation*, **8** (2006), 34–48.

[574] J. Tratalos, R. A. Fuller, K. L. Evans, *et al.* Bird densities are associated with household densities. *Global Change Biology*, **13** (2007), 1685–1695.

[575] J. Tratalos, R. A. Fuller, P. H. Warren, R. G. Davies, and K. J. Gaston. Urban form, biodiversity potential and ecosystem services. *Landscape and Urban Planning*, **83** (2007), 308–317.

[576] L. K. Trocha, J. Oleksyn, E. Turzanska, M. Rudawska, and P. B. Reich. Living on the edge: ecology of an incipient *Betula* – fungal community growing on brick walls. *Trees: Structure and Function*, **21** (2007), 239–247.

[577] K. Trusilova and G. Churkina. The response of the terrestrial biosphere to urbanization: land cover conversion, climate, and urban pollution. *Biogeosciences Discussions*, **5** (2008), 2445–2470.

[578] I. Tsurim, Z. Abramsky, and B. P. Kotler. Foraging behavior of urban birds: are human commensals less sensitive to predation risk than their nonurban counterparts? *The Condor*, **110** (2008), 772–776.

[579] T. Tyrrell. The relative influences of nitrogen and phosphorus on oceanic primary production. *Nature*, **400** (1999), 525–531.

[580] K. Tzoulas, K. Korpela, S. Venn, *et al.* Promoting ecosystem and human health in urban areas using Green Infrastructure: a literature review. *Landscape and Urban Planning*, **81** (2007), 167–178.

[581] R. S. Ulrich. View through a window may influence recovery from surgery. *Science*, **224** (1984), 420–421.

[582] W. Ulrich, K. Komosinski, and M. Zalewski. Body size and biomass distributions of carrion visiting beetles: do cities host smaller species? *Ecological Research*, **23** (2008), 241–248.

[583] S. van der Veken, K. Verheyen, and M. Hermy. Plant species loss in an urban area (Turnhout, Belgium) from 1880 to 1999 and its environmental determinants. *Flora*, **199** (2004), 516–523.

[584] Y. van Heezik, A. Smyth, A. Adams, and J. Gordon. Do domestic cats impose an unsustainable harvest on urban bird populations? *Biological Conservation*, **143** (2010), 121–130.

[585] J. van Os, M. Hanssen, R. V. Bijl, and W. Vollebergh. Prevalence of psychotic disorder and community level of psychotic symptoms: an urban-rural comparison. *Archives of General Psychiatry*, **58** (2001), 663–668.

[586] F. Vandevenne, E. Struyf, W. Clymans, and P. Meire. Agricultural silica harvest: have humans created a new loop in the global silica cycle? *Frontiers in Ecology and the Environment*, **10** (2012), 243–248.

[587] C. Vangestel, B. P. Braeckman, H. Matheve, and L. Lens. Constraints on home range behaviour affect nutritional condition in urban house sparrows (*Passer domesticus*). *Biological Journal of the Linnean Society*, **101** (2010), 41–50.

[588] J. Venetoulis and J. Talberth. Refining the ecological footprint. *Environment, Development and Sustainability*, **10** (2008), 441–469.

[589] B. V. Venkatarama Reddy and K. S. Jagadish. Embodied energy of common and alternative building materials and technologies. *Energy & Buildings*, **35** (2003), 129–137.

[590] R. A. Verheij. Explaining urban-rural variations in health: a review of interactions between individual and environment. *Social Science & Medicine*, **42** (1996), 923–935.

[591] R. L. Vidra, T. H. Shear, and J. M. Stucky. Effects of vegetation removal on native understory recovery in an exotic-rich urban forest. *Journal of the Torrey Botanical Society*, **134** (2007), 410–419.

[592] A. A. Vinogradova, E. I. Fedorova, I. B. Belikov, *et al.* Temporal variations in carbon dioxide and methane concentrations under urban conditions. *Izvestiya Atmospheric and Oceanic Physics*, **43** (2007), 599–611.

[593] P. M. Vitousek, J. D. Aber, R. W. Howarth, *et al.* Human alteration of the global nitrogen cycle: sources and consequences. *Ecological Applications*, **7** (1997), 737–750.

[594] P. M. Vitousek and R. W. Howarth. Nitrogen limitation on land and in the sea: how can it occur? *Biogeochemistry*, **13** (1991), 87–115.

[595] P. M. Vitousek, H. A. Mooney, J. Lubchenco, and J. M. Melillio. Human domination of the earth's ecosystems. *Science*, **277** (1997), 494–499.

[596] M. von der Lippe and I. Kowarik. Do cities export biodiversity? Traffic as dispersal vector across urban–rural gradients. *Diversity and Distributions*, **14** (2008), 18–25.

[597] L. von Hertzen and T. Haahtela. Disconnection of man and the soil: reason for the asthma and atopy epidemic? *Journal of Allergy and Clinical Immunology*, **117** (2006), 334–344.

[598] L. C. von Hertzen and T. Haahtela. Asthma and atopy: the price of affluence? *Allergy*, **59** (2004), 124–137.

[599] M. Wackernagel and W. Rees. *Our Ecological Footprint: Reducing Human Impact on the Earth*. (Gabriola Island, Canada: New Society Publishers, 1996).

[600] C. J. Walsh. Urban impacts on the ecology of receiving waters: a framework for assessment, conservation and restoration. *Hydrobiologia*, **431** (2000), 107–114.

[601] C. J. Walsh, T. D. Fletcher, and A. R. Ladson. Stream restoration in urban catchments through redesigning stormwater systems: looking to the catchment to save the stream. *Journal of the North American Benthological Society*, **24** (2005), 690–705.

[602] A. Wania, I. Kuhn, and S. Klotz. Plant richness patterns in agricultural and urban landscapes in Central Germany: spatial gradients of species richness. *Landscape and Urban Planning*, **75** (2006), 97–110.

[603] P. S. Ward. Ants. *Current Biology*, **16** (2006), 152–155.

[604] K. Warren-Rhodes and A. Koenig. Escalating trends in the urban metabolism of Hong Kong: 1971–1997. *Ambio*, **30** (2001), 429–438.

[605] Q. Weng, D. Lu, and B. Liang. Urban surface biophysical descriptors and land surface temperature variations. *Photogrammetric Engineering & Remote Sensing*, **72** (2006), 1275–1286.

[606] C. P. Wheater. *Urban Habitats.* (New York: Routledge, 1999).

[607] C. P. Wheater. Walls and paved surfaces: urban complexes with limited water and nutrients. In I. Douglas, D. Goode, M. C. Houck, and R. Wang, eds, *The Routledge Handbook of Urban Ecology.* (New York: Routledge, 2011), pp. 239–251.

[608] J. G. White, M. J. Antos, J. A. Fitzsimons, and G. C. Palmer. Non-uniform bird assemblages in urban environments: the influence of streetscape vegetation. *Landscape and Urban Planning*, **71** (2005), 123–135.

[609] M. C. Wichmann, M. J. Alexander, M. B. Soons, *et al.* Human-mediated dispersal of seeds over long distances. *Proceedings of the Royal Society B: Biological Sciences*, **276** (2009), 523–532.

[610] N. S. G. Williams, M. W. Schwartz, P. A. Vesk, *et al.* A conceptual framework for predicting the effects of urban environments on floras. *Journal of Ecology*, **97** (2009), 4–9.

[611] M. H. Williamson. *Biological Invasions.* (New York: Springer, 1996).

[612] W. G. Wilson. *Constructed Climates: A Primer on Urban Environments.* (Chicago, IL: University of Chicago Press, 2011).

[613] J. C. Witte, M. R. Schoeberl, A. R. Douglass, *et al.* Satellite observations of changes in air quality during the 2008 Beijing olympics and paralympics. *Geophysical Research Letters*, **36** (2009), L17803.

[614] J. Wolch, J. P. Wilson, and J. Fehrenbach. Parks and park funding in Los Angeles: an equity-mapping analysis. *Urban Geography*, **26** (2005), 4–35.

[615] B. E. Wolfe, V. L. Rodgers, K. A. Stinson, and A. Pringle. The invasive plant *Alliaria petiolata* (garlic mustard) inhibits ectomycorrhizal fungi in its introduced range. *Journal of Ecology*, **96** (2008), 777–783.

[616] W. E. Wood and S. M. Yezerinac. Song sparrow (*Melospiza melodia*) song varies with urban noise. *The Auk*, **123** (2006), 650–659.

[617] M. Woods, R. A. Mcdonald, and S. Harris. Predation of wildlife by domestic cats *Felis catus* in Great Britain. *Mammal Review*, **33** (2003), 174–188.

[618] E. Worrell, L. Price, N. Martin, C. Hendriks, and L. Meida. Carbon dioxide emissions from the global cement industry. *Annual Review of Energy and the Environment*, **29** (2001), 303–229.

[619] G. R. Wright, S. Jewczyk, J. Onrot, P. Tomlinson, and R. J. Shephard. Carbon monoxide in the urban atmosphere: hazards to the pedestrian and the street-worker. *Archives of Environmental Health*, **30** (1975), 123–129.

[620] J. Yang, Q. Yu, and P. Gong. Quantifying air pollution removal by green roofs in Chicago. *Atmospheric Environment*, **42** (2008), 7266–7273.

[621] P. J. Yeh. Rapid evolution of a sexually selected trait following population establishment in a novel habitat. *Evolution*, **58** (2004), 166–174.

[622] P. J. Yeh, M. E. Hauber, and T. D. Price. Alternative nesting behaviours following colonisation of a novel environment by a passerine bird. *Oikos*, **116** (2007), 1473–1480.

[623] V. Yli-Pelkonen and J. Niemela. Linking ecological and social systems in cities: urban planning in Finland as a case. *Biodiversity and Conservation*, **14** (2005), 1947–1967.

[624] R. F. Young. Interdisciplinary foundations of urban ecology. *Urban Ecosystems*, **12** (2009), 311–331.

[625] X. Zhang, M. A. Friedl, C. B. Schaaf, A. H. Strahler, and A. Schneider. The footprint of urban climates on vegetation phenology. *Geophysical Research Letters*, **31** (2004), L12209.

[626] X. G. Zhu, S. P. Long, and D. R. Ort. What is the maximum efficiency with which photosynthesis can convert solar energy into biomass? *Current Opinion in Biotechnology*, **19** (2008), 153–159.

[627] L. H. Ziska, J. A. Bunce, and E. W. Goins. Characterization of an urban–rural CO_2/temperature gradient and associated changes in initial plant productivity during secondary succession. *Oecologia*, **139** (2004), 454–458.

[628] L. H. Ziska, K. George, and D. A. Frenz. Establishment and persistence of common ragweed *Ambrosia artemisiifolia* (L.) in disturbed soil as a function of an urban–rural macroenvironment. *Global Change Biology*, **13** (2007), 266–274.

Index of organisms

Accipiter cooperii: Cooper's hawk (Section 4.3)
Accipiter nisus: Eurasian sparrowhawk (Section 4.3)
Acromyrmex: leaf-cutter ant (Section 2.4)
Ailanthus altissima: tree of heaven (Section 4.3)
Alectryon tomentosus:. woolly rambutan (Section 4.6)
Alliaria petiolata: garlic mustard (Section 4.3)
Ambrosia artemisiifolia: annual ragweed (Sections 4.5 and 5.2)
Angophora costata: smooth-barked apple (Section 4.3)
Aphelocoma californica: western scrub-jay (Section 4.3)
Aphelocoma coerulescens: Florida scrub-jay (Section 4.5)
Aristolochia elegans: Dutchman's pipe (Section 4.2)
Artemisia vulgaris: mugwort (Section 4.3)
Atta: leaf-cutter ant (Section 2.4)
Azteca: Azteca ant (Section 2.4)
Baylisascaris procyonis: raccoon roundworm (Section 4.4)
Biston betularia: peppered moth (Section 4.6)
Blatta orientalis: Oriental cockroach (Section 4.2)
Borrelia burgdorferi: Lyme disease (Section 4.4)
Bouteloua dactyloides: buffalograss (Section 5.2)
Bromus tectorum: cheatgrass (Section 1.1)
Bryum argenteum: silvergreen bryum moss (Section 1.3)
Buteo jamaicensis: red-tailed hawk (Section 4.3)
Canis latrans: coyote (Sections 4.1 and 4.3)
Canis lupis: gray wolf (Section 1.3)
Cardiospermum grandiflorumtosus: balloon vine (Section 4.6)
Carpodacus mexicanus: house finch (Sections 4.5 and 4.6)
Cecropia: Cecropia tree (Section 2.4)
Ceratitis capitata: Mediterranean fruit fly (Section 4.5)
Ceratocystis ulmi: Dutch elm disease (Section 4.4)
Chelodina longicollis: eastern long-necked turtle (Sections 4.5 and 5.2)
Columba livia: rock pigeon (Sections 1.3, 4.1, 4.2, 4.5)
Corvus corone: carrion crow (Section 4.1)
Crematogaster perthensis: crematogaster ant (Section 4.3)
Crepis sancta: hawksbeard (Section 4.6)

Subject index

Terms in bold refer to where the term is defined, many of which are described further in the glossary.